*the politics
of
progress*

the politics
of
progress

Raymond E. Wolfinger
University of California, Berkeley

Prentice-Hall, Inc., Englewood Cliffs, New Jersey

Library of Congress Cataloging in Publication Data

WOLFINGER, RAYMOND E
   The politics of progress.

   Includes bibliographical references.
   1. New Haven—Politics and government. 2. Lee,
Richard C. I. Title.
JS1195.2.W64   320.9'746'8   73–4206
ISBN 0–13–687079–1

Printed in the United States of America

10   9   8   7   6   5   4   3   2   1

Prentice-Hall International, Inc., *London*
Prentice-Hall of Australia, Pty. Ltd., *Sydney*
Prentice-Hall of Canada, Ltd., *Toronto*
Prentice-Hall of India Private Limited, *New Delhi*
Prentice-Hall of Japan, Inc., *Tokyo*

To Barbara Kaye Wolfinger

Everything is very simple in war, but the simplest thing is difficult. . . . Activity in war is movement in a resistant medium. Just as a man immersed in water is unable to perform with ease and regularity the most natural and simple movement, that of walking, so in war one cannot, with ordinary powers, keep even the line of mediocrity. . . .

Clausewitz

contents

vii

acknowledgments

This book originated in an extraordinary opportunity to observe New Haven politics at close quarters. I am grateful to Robert Dahl for that opportunity, as well as for his profound and enduring influence on my development as a political scientist. His intellectual power and clarity of expression continue to set an example for me, and his openness, directness, and warmth greatly encouraged me during our research on New Haven and afterward.

Richard C. Lee and Edward J. Logue made my study possible by letting me watch and participate in their activities and by submitting to my questioning in the breathing spaces of their busy days. Many other officials of the City of New Haven also went out of their way to be helpful. I am particularly indebted to Norris Andrews, L. Thomas Appleby, Harold Grabino, Charles I. Shannon, and H. Ralph Taylor for their patience and consideration in trying to initiate me into the mysteries of city planning and urban renewal, and to Heman A. Averill, Jan Puckett, Peter F. Villano, and Sheila Wellington for making my stay in city hall pleasant and enlightening. Hundreds of citizens and officials contributed to our research by their willingness to be interviewed or to respond to questionnaires. These informants are seldom named in this book, but I am no less grateful to them for their contributions of time and information.

Nelson Polsby and I first became colleagues working on this study. Ever since he has been generous and painstaking with information and advice. Charles E. Lindblom kindly subjected my ideas and writing style to a meticulous and invaluable scrutiny. My learned friend and collaborator, Fred Greenstein, has been advising, correcting, informing, and encouraging me for more than eight years.

I am fortunate also to have had help in data gathering or comments on previous manuscript drafts from William Flanigan, Lawrence M. Friedman, Alexander L. George, Harold Grabino, Herbert Kaufman, John Meyer, William K. Muir, Jr., Russell D. Murphy, Alan Rosenthal, Martin Shapiro, and Frank J. Sorauf. Ann Sale Barber, Adelle R. Rosenzweig, and Carolyn Davidson ably edited successive drafts of the manuscript. Anne L. Laskow, Susan Abrams, and Phyllis Dexter typed the final manuscript with skill and speed.

Financial support for my research in New Haven and for the subsequent analysis and writing came from the Ford Foundation, the Laura and Maurice Falk Foundation, the Social Science Research Council, the Center for Advanced Study in the Behavioral Sciences, and the Graduate Division of Stanford University.

Permission to include here material previously published elsewhere has been granted by the *American Political Science Review,* the *Public Opinion Quarterly,* the *Journal of Politics,* and Prentice-Hall, Inc. Passages from Robert A. Dahl's *Who Governs?* are quoted with the permission of the Yale University Press.

the politics
of
progress

1 *introduction*

This book has two major purposes. The first is to explain how important innovative policies were conceived and executed in New Haven. The second is to use findings about New Haven to test and revise prevailing theories about local politics.

The book includes several interrelated case studies of political events, centered in the late 1950s, with some episodes from the previous and subsequent decades. These accounts are concerned with "progress," by which I mean major changes in the social and physical aspects of urban life produced through governmental action. The focus of these narratives is New Haven's extraordinary urban renewal achievements, which, together with the closely associated antipoverty program, led one Cabinet officer in the Johnson administration to call the city "the greatest success story in the history of the world."[1]

Like war, politics is an arena in which even the simplest actions become difficult. This seems particularly true in the United States, where political organizations and processes are notoriously biased against innovation. Fragmentation of formal authority, weakness of instrumentalities to mobilize effective policy-making power, diffusion of accountability, and the consequent bafflement of popular control all protect the status quo and impede development of major new policies that require widespread coordination or protracted steadiness of purpose.

The accomplishments that made New Haven so conspicuous an example of extensive innovation resulted from the long mayoralty of Richard C. Lee, who was first elected in 1953 and retired at the end of 1969. The range and extent of policy innovations in New Haven reflect Lee's political skill and ambition to rise high in the world on a reputation as a mayor of spectacular achievements.

Analysis of political leadership requires attention to the environment that produces and constrains the leader and which he reacts to and manipulates. These case studies, therefore, are embedded in a description of the New Haven political scene. I have also discussed at length various interesting

1 This accolade by Secretary of Labor W. Willard Wirtz is quoted in Fred Powledge, "The Flight From City Hall," *Harper's Magazine* (November 1969), 76. For data on the size and character of New Haven's urban renewal and poverty programs, see Chapter 6.

aspects of local politics, although they often are not central to a study of the techniques and limitations of political leadership.

While the book's *structure* reflects my intention to explain fully the environment and techniques of political leadership in New Haven, the amount of *space* in each chapter devoted to my second purpose—theorizing about various aspects of local politics—reflects my ability to use the relevant New Haven material to test and develop theory. In some chapters attempts to revise prevailing theoretical notions outweigh descriptive material; in others the narrative far exceeds the analytical passages.

Part I deals with the context of politics in New Haven. Chapter 2 is a general description of the city's social and economic structure, its formal governmental institutions, and such miscellaneous background topics as the local press, the role of Yale University, and the question of how typical the city is. Chapter 3 analyzes the origins and consequences of the political role played by nationality group consciousness. Chapter 4 is concerned with machine politics. Chapters 3 and 4 use data from New Haven as a point of departure for extended reformulation of commonplace theoretical approaches.

Chapter 5 describes the postwar urban decline in America, the rationale of urban renewal, and its political dangers. The main theme is the specific kinds of difficulties impeding urban renewal efforts (and, by extension, other comprehensive innovation) in American cities. This material is included not only for its intrinsic value, but also to provide the criteria for a satisfactory analysis of innovation. Chapter 5 raises the questions that should be answered about the Lee administration's achievements.

An urban renewal project is likely to be expensive, lengthy, and potentially unpopular. Therefore the resources, calculations, and strategies of politicians undertaking an ambitious renewal program must be understood. Any project requires the consistent approval of the municipal legislature for personnel appointments, budgets, and endorsement of various formal stages in the procedure prescribed by the federal government. The policies of the various municipal line agencies and commissions that touch on urban renewal should be concerted. Urban renewal affects the vital interests of major community elements, many of which ordinarily are politically quiescent. It activates special publics, particularly business interests, that must be reassured, mobilized, or neutralized. Attaining all these goals requires control of political nominations, a campaign organization sufficient to insure policy independence, and ability to win both general political support and endorsement from the "urban renewal publics." Obviously, a renewal program of any magnitude provides an occasion for studying many important aspects of local politics. I have yielded readily to temptations to digress from descriptions of events in New Haven to more general discussions suggested by intersections between my data and the literature.

The rationale stated above guided the organization of Part II, which describes how Lee solved these various problems and thus developed the political foundation for massive urban renewal. Chapter 6 presents the explicit political background against which Lee attained the mayoralty, and then provides an overview of events during his administration. It describes his ambitions, his strategies, and how he won the electoral majorities that he considered a prerequisite as well as a consequence of his substantive achievements. Chapter 7 deals with the problems of policy coordination, the techniques by which formally fragmented public agencies were subjected to the mayor's central control. Chapter 8 describes Lee's successful efforts to gain the support of the urban renewal publics, in which businessmen were the most important element. It also discusses the general subject of business participation in local politics.

Parts I and II are an introduction to Part III, which describes in detail the beginnings of urban renewal in New Haven; the development of various techniques of organization, publicity, and administration; and the inception and early stages of the city's first two projects. One of these projects was not particularly noteworthy, but the second, the Church Street Project, made Lee's and New Haven's reputation. It was an ambitious, perilous, and eventually successful scheme to demolish and rebuild much of the city's central business district. Chapter 11 is a story of failure, not success. It describes the defeat of Lee's attempt to revise the city charter so as to institutionalize the level of coordination that he had achieved by informal means. It is an important illustration of the limits to his ability to innovate.

In the final chapter I examine the slim probabilities that the impressive talents displayed by Lee will be found in other American mayors. The book concludes with consideration of an alternative model to heroic mayoral leadership.

Sources of Data

I have drawn freely and extensively on the data gathered in the study of New Haven directed by Robert A. Dahl and reported in his *Who Governs?*[2] A full description of these data and the methods by which they were collected appears in Appendix B of *Who Governs?*

As Dahl's research assistant, I was a participant-observer in city hall for a year. From July 1957 through January 1958 I worked for Edward J. Logue, then in charge of all aspects of the city's urban renewal program and also the mayor's closest adviser. I performed some assignments for Logue, in both urban renewal and the 1957 mayoralty campaign. Much of the time, however, I watched and listened. I attended meetings, talked with Logue and members

[2] Robert A. Dahl, *Who Governs? Democracy and Power in an American City* (New Haven, Conn.: Yale University Press, 1961).

of his staff, read his files and daily correspondence, and intruded into as many conversations as possible. There were some things—not many, I believe —that my friends there would not tell me, and they often seemed to use an unduly high proportion of pronouns when I was present. (Or so I thought. A persistent faint worry about being excluded seems to be the fate of participant-observers.) But because they had agreed to my presence and could not then easily treat me as an outsider, because they sometimes forgot that I was not another staff member, because they were very proud of their program, and because they were genuinely interested in helping me understand what they were doing, the renewal and planning officials were fairly frank with me.

In February 1958 I moved next door to the mayor's office and spent the next five months watching Lee do his job. Whenever Lee was in his office I sat in a corner. Occasionally he would ask me to leave the room, ask a visitor to accompany him outside, or whisper. In general, I was least likely to be excluded if Lee was talking with a member of his administration. The latter, seeing me around and often not knowing what I was doing, came to accept me as part of the mayor's office. Here, as with Logue, I was usually regarded as an ally, not a neutral. (It is unlikely that I would have been accepted at city hall in the first place had I not been a Democrat.) I followed Lee around a good deal and usually went along when he spoke out of town during the day. I seldom lunched with him or accompanied him to private talks in offices outside city hall. I rarely saw him after he left his office each afternoon and thus missed his frequent visits to wakes and nighttime appearances at dinners and other meetings. Occasionally I did an odd job for the mayor, but mostly I just sat and listened. Lee's level of frankness varied amazingly. Discussing the same topic, he would range from moralism to realism in successive sentences. His explanation to me of a scene I had just witnessed could be based on either the Boy Scout Oath or *The Prince*—or, most disconcertingly, on both.

Thus I did not see everything that the mayor did and was largely excluded from some areas, notably his dealings with the party organization. But I did see and hear a good deal, and there were plenty of clues about the most restricted areas. Lee was busy and impatient; it is unlikely that he would have devoted much time to acting out deceptions for my benefit. Hence I can be fairly sure that I was seldom victimized by red herrings.

My city hall experience permitted me to organize and evaluate information acquired by other methods. The direct observation at city hall imparted a basic frame of reference to all the data. Being behind the scenes, I could be fairly sure that more accessible information was not just part of a facade behind which the city's rulers made policy.

After I left city hall in the summer of 1958 I talked with various people there from time to time for the next fifteen months, and I spent a week in

September 1960 catching up on recent developments and clearing up questions about the past.

The second important source of data for this book is 49 unstructured interviews with major political actors in New Haven conducted in 1957 and 1958 by Dahl and, usually, Nelson W. Polsby. These interviews were generally recorded verbatim. They range in length from 30 minutes to six hours, and average about 75 minutes. The interviewees included leaders of both parties, city officials in education and renewal, almost all the executive committee of the Citizens Action Commission, and a variety of other figures. Some informants were consistently evasive and homiletic. Others were extremely thoughtful, frank, and painstaking. Few could offer useful generalizations or answer questions about the causes of local political phenomena. The interviews were particularly valuable as a source of information about the attitudes and behavior of various elements in the community. All interviewees were told that their replies would not be attributed to them unless they gave permission. I interviewed about a dozen people myself from 1958 to 1960. In addition to these formal sessions I could "interview" my associates while on the job in city hall and did so incessantly, particularly after I had been there long enough to be accepted.

William H. Flanigan directed two sample surveys of registered voters. One, dealing with the 1958 charter revision campaign, is described in Chapter 11. The other, conducted in the summer of 1959 with a sample of 525 respondents chosen randomly from ward voting lists, was planned by Dahl and Flanigan. It covered a variety of politically relevant attitudes and behaviors. Mayor Lee commissioned a number of opinion surveys by Louis Harris and Associates, to which I refer on occasion. Voting records and demographic data were compiled for each of the city's 33 wards.

I kept a file of relevant newspaper clippings from the summer of 1957 through the fall of 1959. For more recent events I have used a variety of sources which are cited in the text. Various specialized sources of information are described throughout the book as they are used.

Before I went to work for them, I did not discuss with Lee or Logue the problem of disclosing what I learned in my year at city hall. Afterward, Dahl and I felt that because the mayor and his staff had made their activities so accessible, we could not betray their confidence by wholly unrestrained disclosure of what I had seen and heard. We decided to refrain from revealing any specific item of information, *obtained through my privileged access,* that would embarrass the Lee administration. This self-denial did not extend to interpretations, generalizations, or evaluations, nor to facts we learned from other sources, although I might have obtained the same information at city hall as well. This policy resulted in only a few deletions, which do not affect my description of important events nor seriously deplete the evidence available to support generalizations.

This book originated in a doctoral dissertation completed in 1961, a few months before *Who Governs?* was published by the Yale University Press. At that time, and for some nine years thereafter, everyone concerned assumed that the revised dissertation would also be published by Yale Press in the near future. In 1968 Chester Kerr, director of the Yale Press, offered me a contract and advance, which I declined pending completion of the revised manuscript.

I sent Lee a copy of my dissertation in 1961. He felt that it contained embarrassing material and asked that the dissertation be treated as confidential. He also wrote me that

> under no circumstances can this be published as long as I am in office. If you disagree with this, or if you are upset about it, I am very sorry, but this is simply the way it will have to be. If necessary, I'll go to the Director of the Yale Press, or, if necessary, to the Executive Committee of the Yale University Press Board or even to [President] Griswold. This book cannot appear while I am holding office.

I asked Lee to specify the material that he considered troublesome, but he did not do so.

I had no intention of acceding to Lee's demand that my dissertation be suppressed, but I had never planned to publish it without extensive revision and expansion of its theoretical aspects. In the early 1960s I wrote three articles on findings about New Haven politics,[3] but did not press for a showdown with Lee. At the time I was planning, and then doing, research which involved working on the staff of Senator Hubert Humphrey and acceptance by other national Democratic politicians, and I did not want to jeopardize these arrangements by open conflict with a well-known Democratic mayor. In 1965, having completed the participant-observation phase of my Washington research, I pressed Lee for his specific comments and we discussed the dissertation in detail. He asked me to delete several stories that he feared would cause him trouble and I agreed to do so where I had obtained the information directly from my city hall experience. He also made factual corrections unrelated to potentially embarrassing material. For the most part, however, our conversation consisted of his explanation and amplification of various points in the dissertation. Inevitably, we disagreed on some matters of interpretation.

---

3 "The Influence of Precinct Work on Voting Behavior," *Public Opinion Quarterly,* 27 (Fall 1963), 387–98; "The Development and Persistence of Ethnic Voting," *American Political Science Review,* 59 (December 1965), 896–908; and "Some Consequences of Ethnic Politics," in *The Electoral Process,* eds. M. Kent Jennings and L. Harmon Zeigler (Englewood Cliffs, N.J.: Prentice-Hall, Inc., 1966), pp. 42–54. Revisions of the last two articles constitute most of Chapter 3. The bulk of the first article appears in Chapter 11.

It should be clear from the foregoing that Lee has not been responsible for the length of time it has taken to complete the final manuscript of this book. The narrative material that comprised the dissertation has been revised and condensed. Except for Chapter 3, the theoretical component of this book was written in the late 1960s. The entire manuscript was then revised.

Disclaimers

A few years before our research on New Haven Floyd Hunter wrote *Community Power Structure*,[4] which quickly became a milestone in the history of political science and sociology. Hunter's use of reputations for power as valid and sufficient indices of the actual distribution of power, and his concern with the identity of Atlanta's "power structure," which was assumed to be small and harmonious, were duplicated in a host of other studies.[5] Like Hunter, these researchers tended to claim that tiny groups of businessmen dominated local politics.[6] While planning and doing our research, Polsby, Dahl, and I wrote criticisms of the assumptions, methods, evidence, and criteria of proof of these "elitists."[7] In our study of New Haven we were alert to the possibility that politics there was dominated by a cohesive business elite and thus kept this hypothesis in mind while gathering and analyzing our data.

We found that "only a small number of persons have much *direct* influence, in the sense that they successfully initiate or veto proposals for policies."[8] Political influence was, however, specialized by issues. Looking just at urban renewal, we might think the decision-making pattern an example of the elitist model of local politics: initiation of policy alternatives and participation in their development and implementation were in the hands of a very small number of people; the vast majority of voters did not share directly in making decisions. On the other hand, the most influential individuals in this process—those who initiated alternatives and prevailed in the

[4] Floyd Hunter, *Community Power Structure* (Chapel Hill: University of North Carolina Press, 1953).

[5] For a 240-item bibliography on "community power" see Willis D. Hawley and Frederick M. Wirt, eds., *The Search for Community Power* (Englewood Cliffs, N.J.: Prentice-Hall, Inc., 1968), pp. 367–79.

[6] John Walton, "Substance and Artifact: The Current Status of Research on Community Power Structure," *American Journal of Sociology,* 71 (January 1966), 430–38.

[7] Dahl, "A Critique of the Ruling Elite Model," *American Political Science Review,* 52 (June 1958), 563–69; Polsby, *Community Power and Political Theory* (New Haven, Conn.: Yale University Press, 1964); Raymond E. Wolfinger, "Reputation and Reality in the Study of 'Community Power,'" *American Sociological Review,* 25 (October 1960), 636–44.

[8] Dahl, *Who Governs?,* p. 163 (emphasis in the original).

onerous business of realizing their goals—were public officials. The most powerful of them all, the man responsible for putting urban renewal at the top of the local political agenda, was elected mayor every two years in hotly contested elections. Reelection was seldom out of his thoughts and his first priority was nurturance of his generally large electoral majorities, that is, of public opinion. In terms of the *number* of direct decision makers, then, New Haven's "power structure" was elitist. But with respect to the occupations of these men, the sources of their power, and the extent to which they were constrained by their anticipation of voters' responses, it was not.[9]

After publication of *Who Governs?*, devotees of the elitist school took a new tack: it was insufficient to study decision making, since the most significant aspects of a political system might be found in what is *not* discussed, in the "nondecision-making process."[10] In studying New Haven we had taken "no account of the fact that power may be, and often is, exercised by confining the scope of decision-making to relatively 'safe' issues."[11] The notion of "nondecision" is more complicated than it first appears. I have tried to unravel it elsewhere and will not repeat the attempt here.[12] To say that Lee did not do certain (undescribed) things because of anticipated adverse reactions is not by itself very enlightening, for what politicians anywhere are unconstrained by their assessments of what is politically risky? (For Lee the most adverse consequences would have been loss of votes in the next election. Oddly, this particular example of power manifested through anticipated reactions was explicitly rejected by the scholars who introduced the concept of "nondecisions."[13]) Issues that are not discussed and groups that could participate in politics if they chose to do so doubtless are interesting research topics, but concentration on them leaves untouched the subject of how public policies are made, by whom, and for what purposes. In the immediate context, insisting that we should have studied what Lee did not do slides past the fact that he did an extraordinary amount, and that explaining his very unusual level of accomplishment may be of some value.

---

9 I have argued elsewhere (see note 12), as have others, that the difficulties of achieving satisfactory and comprehensive ways of measuring political power suggest that it is not a very useful concept for empirical research. But there are circumstances where measurement problems do not appear to prevent adequate testing of some propositions. For example: (1) If a public decision is adopted over the determined opposition of A, this is evidence against the proposition that A is powerful. (2) If policies that were frustrated or not attempted previously are adopted when a new actor enters the arena and vigorously pursues those policies, this is evidence that the new actor is powerful. The second situation describes Lee's role in urban renewal politics in New Haven.

10 Peter Bachrach and Morton S. Baratz, "Two Faces of Power," *American Political Science Review*, 56 (December 1962), 949.

11 *Ibid.*, p. 948.

12 Raymond E. Wolfinger, "Nondecisions and the Study of Local Politics," *American Political Science Review*, 65 (December 1971), 1063–80.

13 *Ibid.*, pp. 1067–68.

This book is not intended or organized as a book about New Haven's "power structure." The central proposition from the community power literature is not confirmed by our data and the rest of that literature is not germane to our findings. Power is not a very useful or interesting general empirical concept in any event, and trying to analyze local politics in terms of a "power structure" imposes a number of sterile rigidities without substantial accompanying theoretical strength. While this book is not part of the "community power" genre, it does contain a good deal of evidence relevant to propositions that have been developed in that literature, and on occasion I will allude to these data and their implications.

The essential irrelevance of "community power" to this book may be further illuminated by brief discussion of another staple subject of controversy: "pluralism." Some of the stated or implicit definitions of "pluralist" follow, along with my position with respect to each.

1. A pluralist is someone who reports that political power is specialized, decentralized, and/or dependent on elections in some particular city or set of cities. I think that this is a fair characterization of New Haven, during both the highly active, enterprising Lee administration and the torpid regime of Lee's predecessor. Since pluralism in this sense is such an undiscriminating term, it is not very useful, even if one thinks that power is a worthwhile empirical concept.

2. A pluralist entertains no assumptions about the distribution of power in a city before studying it, and thus is likely to reject research techniques based on the "thesis that *some* group necessarily dominates a community."[14] Guilty, but the indictment is not too relevant to this book.

3. "Pluralists quite vigorously deny the permanency of power—or to put it differently, that power is structured in any way. Thus if superficial evidence suggests that no power exists in a particular community, pluralist presuppositions warrant the conclusion that any further examination might well turn out to be a waste of time."[15] I plead innocent. I found that power was indeed exerted in New Haven politics. Moreover, nothing in this book is intended to suggest that political resources and the willingness and ability to use them were equally distributed, that political officials did not behave disingenuously, or other such allegations often attributed to people called "pluralists."

4. Pluralists write favorable evaluations of American politics.[16] Again, I plead not guilty. Those passages in this book that evaluate particular political patterns are largely critical.

[14] Polsby, *Community Power and Political Theory,* p. 113 (emphasis in the original).

[15] Thomas J. Anton, "Power, Pluralism, and Local Politics," *Administrative Science Quarterly,* 7 (March 1963), 454.

[16] This seems to be what William Connolly has in mind in *The Bias of Pluralism* (New York: Atherton Press, 1968).

5. "Group or pluralist theory attempts to explain the formulation of public policy and the maintenance of public order in terms of the interplay among the contending group forces of society. . . . In the final analysis, policy will be a function of how many groups get involved, at what levels of frequency and intensity, with what effects for the relative pay-off capabilities of the different resources all the groups bring to the scene."[17] This book presents no single theory to explain public policy, but I interpret urban renewal policy in New Haven as a function of individual political ambition, not of interest group pressure.

This listing, by no means exhaustive, indicates that "pluralism" can refer to choice of research topics, to assumptions (or the lack of them) about what kinds of data will be found, to categories for analyzing data, to propositions about what has been found, and to evaluations of research findings. There is no particular reason why a "pluralist" of one type must subscribe to other varieties of "pluralism." Hardly any political scientist now admits to being a "pluralist" and the phrase seems to have become almost exclusively the property of scholars who employ it as a weapon of attack. Its use for this purpose has grown so indiscriminate that it should be retired from scholarly discourse on grounds of excessive ambiguity.

Furthermore, the pluralist–elitist dichotomy occupies a limited and dull segment of the subject matter of political science. Few interesting and controversial subjects seem to be subsumed under this rubric, and knowing whether a particular political scientist is considered a "pluralist" or an "elitist" does not help classify him with respect to such issues. For example, Dahl and I, both labeled "pluralists," have written opposite views on ethnic politics, while Michael Parenti, a certified antipluralist, has embraced my position on the subject.[18] Polsby was the first scholar to offer a political interpretation of Senator Joseph McCarthy's popularity, thus challenging the speculations of a collection of "pluralist" writers; his position was later developed by Michael P. Rogin, who said that the position taken by Polsby's targets was an error of "pluralism."[19] In other words, calling a political scientist a "pluralist" does not express a very clear message.

"Group theory," associated most conspicuously with the work of Arthur

17 Darryl Baskin, "American Pluralism: Theory, Practice, and Ideology," *Journal of Politics,* 32 (February 1970), 73, 76.

18 Dahl, *Who Governs?,* pp. 34–36; Parenti, "Ethnic Politics and the Persistence of Ethnic Identification," *American Political Science Review,* 61 (September 1967), 717–26; Wolfinger, "The Development and Persistence of Ethnic Voting," and "Some Consequences of Ethnic Politics."

19 Polsby, "Toward an Explanation of McCarthyism," in *Politics and Social Life,* eds. Polsby, Robert A. Dentler, and Paul A. Smith (Boston: Houghton Mifflin Company, 1963), pp. 809–24; Daniel Bell, ed., *The New American Right* (New York: Criterion Books, 1955); and Michael P. Rogin, *The Intellectuals and McCarthy* (Cambridge, Mass.: The M.I.T. Press, 1967).

F. Bentley, Earl Latham, and David B. Truman,[20] is an important influence in the study of American politics. (It is often attributed to "pluralists"; see definition 5, above.) If one explicates a theory from the work of these scholars, its propositions are, like those of the ruling elite literature, not very helpful in understanding policy formation in New Haven.[21] Bentley saw in the activities of interest groups a sufficient explanation of governmental decisions: "When the groups are adequately stated, everything is stated. When I say everything, I mean everything."[22] Latham and Truman, while not so categorical, also saw public policies as reflections of conflicts and treaties between private interests.[23] According to this school, political leaders "get their programme out of the groupings which they reflect."[24] Once one knows what groups support a particular regime, one knows what public policy is going to be.[25]

While there are important points of controversy between the group and elitist schools, the two share a belief that politicians are unimportant. To Bentley, the government is just a "registration clerk."[26] To the elitists, politicians are the lackeys of the establishment, whose dominance in social and economic circles is transferred to the political arena. This focus on the clients of government, to the exclusion of its officials, results in a tendency to analyze politics solely in terms of the private interests helped and hurt by governmental action, and thus to explain policies by pointing to the motivations and gratifications of constituent groups. Doubtless in many cities the mayor is content to preside over a series of accommodations between contending interests and imparts little direction to the course of public policy.[27]

[20] Bentley, *The Process of Government* (Cambridge, Mass.: Harvard University Press, 1967); Latham, *The Group Basis of Politics* (Ithaca, N.Y.: Cornell University Press, 1952); and Truman, *The Governmental Process* (New York: Alfred A. Knopf, Inc., 1955).

[21] These books, particularly Truman's, are far more than statements of a general theory of politics. Moreover, some writers have argued that in practice adherence to the "group theory" consists chiefly of "a realization that interest groups are 'very important' and that a lot of attention should be given them." See R. E. Dowling, "Pressure Group Theory: Its Methodological Range," *American Political Science Review,* 54 (December 1960), 951.

[22] Bentley, *The Process of Government,* pp. 208–9.

[23] Truman, *The Governmental Process,* p. 505; Latham, *The Group Basis of Politics,* p. 35.

[24] Bentley, *The Process of Government,* p. 405; see also pp. 197, 223; and Latham, *The Group Basis of Politics,* p. 38.

[25] Bentley, *The Process of Government,* p. 342. See also Murray S. Stedman, Jr., "A Group Interpretation of Politics," *Public Opinion Quarterly,* 17 (Summer 1953), 226

[26] Bentley, *The Process of Government,* p. 153.

[27] According to Edward C. Banfield, this is the role customarily played by Mayor Richard Daley of Chicago. See Banfield, *Political Influence* (New York: The Free Press, 1961), pp. 253, 270, 346.

In other cities municipal policy may well be nothing more than the wishes of a ruling elite. But in New Haven the mayor played the leading role in policy formation, activating and manipulating interest groups. More than anything else, urban renewal policy resulted from his ambitions, not those of private groups.

My vantage point at city hall and my emphasis on politicians' strategies rather than on private interests do not imply preconceptions about either the sources of political initiative in New Haven or the importance of public as opposed to private decisions in the lives of the city's residents. As to the first point, governmental decisions must be promulgated by public officials regardless of the actual locus of political power. If there is a hidden force (or an overt boss, for that matter) manipulating the politicians, its effects must still be registered at city hall, and thus a watch kept at the formal seat of government can lead one to the processes by which policy is made. On the second point, many decisions of great importance are made outside the political arena. Family, friends, lovers, neighbors, employers, employees, customers, ministers, and a host of others may be more significant forces in individual lives than political actors. In concentrating on government, I do not deny the importance of other kinds of activity, but only assert that the government's actions are worth studying.

For the most part I have not evaluated the impact of the policies whose inception and enactment I describe. Many of the general problems raised by what I call progress are the same regardless of the specific content of policy. Conservative, liberal, and radical politicians alike are balked by short tenure in office, fragmentation of real governmental power, transitory public attention, and so on. By the same token, conservative and liberal presidents chafe at an unruly Congress, disloyal bureaucrats, competing lobbyists, and an indifferent public. As readers of this book will see, describing how some of the policies of one administration in one city were developed is a formidable job. The task of assessing these policies is for a different book and another author.

I   *the context of politics in New Haven*

2 an introduction
to New Haven

New Haven resembles many cities in the northeastern United States: it is old, its economy is based largely on traditional manufacturing, its population has been slowly diminishing for a generation, and its residents are mostly working-class and lower-middle-class Catholics, Jews, and Negroes. Local political practices include heavy emphasis on ethnicity in voting decisions and campaign appeals, and political organization of the style that has been called "old fashioned" for the past 40 years. These features add up to a familiar archetype of American local politics.

The Economy

New Haven is on Long Island Sound, about a third of the way from New York to Boston. The city was one of the first centers of American industry and in the nineteenth century its residents contributed many important innovations to the world's technology. One of them, Eli Whitney, invented the cotton gin and then revolutionized manufacturing by developing the technique of mass-produced interchangeable parts. But by the beginning of the twentieth century New Haven's great era of industrial creativity and expansion had ended, and for at least 50 years the local economy has been relatively stable. Although manufacturing is still the most important economic activity, the city is also an important transportation and distribution center, for it lies astride the main rail and highway connections between New York and New England.

Perhaps because there were no major sources of water power nearby, New Haven never became an important textile manufacturing center and thus escaped the fate of many other New England cities whose principal industries moved closer to raw materials and cheap labor. Lacking any outstanding adjacent natural resources, local industry is devoted mainly to a variety of light products made by small and medium-sized firms. At the time of our research (1957–59), the biggest employer in town was the Winchester-Western Division of the Olin Corporation, with 5,200 employees. (This was the old Winchester Repeating Arms Company, a New Haven firm absorbed by a nationwide corporation.) Fifteen other manufacturers had

15

between 250 and 1,500 employees, and 85 more employed from 50 to 250 workers each.[1]

After Winchester the biggest employer was Yale University, with perhaps 3,000 full-time and part-time nonacademic employees and about 1,600 faculty members. The New York, New Haven and Hartford Railroad and the Southern New England Telephone Company each employed about 3,650 people.[2] The City of New Haven employed more than 3,000. No single firm or industry dominates the city's economy or controls a major part of its labor force. Most of the biggest employers are locally oriented in that they are locally owned, would find it difficult to move out of town, sell mainly to a local market, or have their welfare closely intertwined with that of the area, if not of the city itself.

Almost half the assets of the city's seven commercial banks were held by the First New Haven National Bank; 85 percent were held by three banks.[3] In addition to the commercial banks there were three savings banks and three savings and loan associations. In 1957 the 50 biggest property owning persons or organizations, comprising one-sixteenth of one percent of all taxpayers, owned almost one-third of all taxable property in the city. This group of 50 included 16 manufacturers, 9 retail or wholesale firms, 6 public utilities, 5 banks, and Yale;[4] the rest were estates, trusts, and individuals.

In 1920 New Haven's population was 162,537. It remained virtually stable for 20 years, then began declining at a progressively steeper rate, and by 1960 was 152,048.[5] The main reason for this trend is the scarcity of available open land within the city limits to accommodate the housing demands of an increasingly affluent population. Moreover, the form of local governmental organization in Connecticut prohibits urban expansion through annexation. As in most older cities, prosperity led the middle classes out to the suburbs, which had a 1960 population of 159,000, more than double the 1940 figure. Seventeen percent of the city's residents had incomes of less than $3,000, as did only 7 percent of the people living in the rest of its metropolitan area.

[1] Data on larger employers were obtained from each firm in the fall of 1959. Other employment information was supplied by the Manufacturers Association of New Haven County in 1957.

[2] The telephone company, whose central office is in New Haven, serves almost all of Connecticut and had a total of more than 11,000 employees. The railroad's headquarters and extensive yard facilities were in New Haven.

[3] Figures on bank assets are for December 31, 1959.

[4] This refers only to the university's holdings in taxable property, largely downtown real estate. Yale also has, of course, an enormous amount of tax-exempt property.

[5] The Census shows a population increase of 3,838 people from 1940 to 1950, but Yale students were counted for the first time in 1950. Comparable figures for each Census: 1940—160,605, excluding Yale students. 1950—164,443, including 8,519 Yale students; the net population was 155,924. 1960—152,048, including 7,793 Yale students; net population was 144,255. The city's total population shrank to 137,707 by 1970.

Compared to other American cities, New Haven has a smaller proportion of educated, white-collar, native-stock residents.[6] This does not merely reflect the great black influx of the past 20 years, for it was also the case in 1950, when only 6 percent of the city's population was black.[7] In 1960 the median schooling of all New Haven residents aged 25 or over was 10.1 years, compared to 11.0 years for all American cities in its population class (100,000 to 250,000). Forty-four percent of the population over the age of 24 had not completed even one year of high school, compared to 36 percent of the same age group in all American urban areas. Forty-two percent of the city's residents were born abroad or had at least one foreign-born parent, which is just double the foreign-stock proportion in all medium-sized cities. Forty-two percent of the labor force had white-collar jobs, compared to 45 percent in all comparable cities. Table 2-1 summarizes basic population data about New Haven, all American cities in its population category, and all northeastern cities of this size. As the table shows, New Haven's demographic characteristics are not unusual for cities in its region, which tend to be more plebeian than communities elsewhere in the country, except that it had somewhat more Negroes than the average northeastern city (15 percent as compared with 8 percent in 1960).

TABLE 2-1.   Demographic characteristics of New Haven and other cities of similar size—1960

	New Haven	All U.S. cities, population 100,000 to 250,000	All north-eastern[a] cities, population 100,000 to 250,000
Median family income in 1959	$5,864	$5,883	$5,917
Percent foreign stock[b]	42	21	38
Median school years[c]	10.1	11.0	10.1
Percent nonwhite	15	14	8
Percent of labor force in white-collar occupations	42	45	41

[a] The three Middle Atlantic states and New England.

[b] People born abroad or with at least one parent born abroad.

[c] For people 25 and older.

Source: 1960 Census. I am grateful to John Osgood Field and Kwan Lee for these tabulations.

[6] Sources of unattributed demographic data are the 1950 and 1960 Censuses.

[7] For a comparison of New Haven and all urban areas using 1950 Census data, see Robert A. Dahl, *Who Governs?* (New Haven, Conn.: Yale University Press, 1961), p. 329.

New Haven's physical plant was rather aged at the time of our study. The center of town conforms to the street pattern devised by the original settlers shortly after their arrival in 1638. Because most of the streets were laid out before the invention of the automobile, they are narrow and seldom run in a straight line for more than a few blocks. Many residential neighborhoods consist largely of rows of dreary two- and three-family houses. In 1950, 71 percent of all dwelling units had been built before 1920. In 1953, according to the New Haven Housing Authority, 23,000 people lived in "overcrowded, improperly heated, insanitary or structurally unsafe buildings."[8] Only 32 percent of all dwellings were owner-occupied, compared to 51 percent in all urban areas. Homeowners thus were likely to be relatively well-to-do. The median value of owner-occupied dwellings was $12,187 in 1950, compared to the national urban median of $8,380.

Ethnics and Elites

New Haven was founded by a band of Puritans. For the better part of two centuries it was ruled by a fairly small group of landowners, merchants, lawyers, and Congregational ministers. This patrician elite was simultaneously challenged by the lower orders and infiltrated by nouveau riche manufacturers in the first half of the nineteenth century. The decline of the old order in New Haven paralleled the national enfeeblement and demise of the Federalist party.

By the 1840s manufacturing was flourishing in New Haven. This boom was not the work of the old upper class, but of entrepreneurs with humbler origins and more evangelistic religions. The city's Anglo-Saxon Protestant homogeneity was broken in the same decade by substantial numbers of Irish immigrants, come to work on internal improvements and in the new factories. For forty years the Irish and a sprinkling of Germans—both Jews and Christians—were the only significant non-British immigrants. In the 1880s Italians, Poles, and Eastern European Jews began to settle in New Haven. Together with the Irish, they soon outnumbered the Yankees.[9] The 1910 Census revealed that fully two-thirds of the city's residents were first- or second-generation Americans. Fifty years later these categories still accounted

8 This quotation is from the 1953 Annual Report of the New Haven Housing Authority. Other housing data are from the 1950 Census, which I used for this purpose in preference to the 1960 Census because of extensive clearance and rehabilitation resulting from urban renewal projects in the late 1950s.

9 *Yankee* is used in its New England sense to refer to more or less old settlers of British stock. I will use the terms *ethnic group* and *nationality group* interchangeably to refer to people whose national origins set them apart from the Yankees. For the sake of brevity I will call people of Irish descent "Irish," Italo-Americans "Italians," and so on.

for 42 percent of the population, and an additional 15 percent were Negroes.[10]

More detailed information on the city's ethnic composition comes from our sample survey of 525 registered voters, conducted in the summer of 1959.[11] Thirty-one percent of the respondents were born in Italy or were in the second or third generation of Italian immigrants, and 11 percent were of similarly recent Irish origin.[12] All in all, 56 percent of the sample were Catholics and 15 percent were Jews; 9 percent were black.

Although Yankees have been a minority in New Haven for at least two generations and constituted less than 20 percent of the 1960 population, the city's leading businessmen were still mostly Protestants. This can be seen most easily by examining the ethnic composition of the 123 people who made up New Haven's economic elite at the time of our study. This group consists of anyone who was in one or more of the following categories in 1958:

1. President or chairman of the board of any bank or public utility, or any other firm which was among the city's top 50 taxpayers in any of the five preceding years

2. Any individual or group of individuals whose property was assessed at more than $250,000 during either of the past two years[13]

3. Any individual who was a director of three or more banks, corporations assessed at $250,000 or more, manufacturing firms employing more than 50 persons, retail firms employing more than 25 persons, or any combination thereof[14]

These criteria are concerned with control of economic resources *in New Haven,* not ownership of wealth.[15] Ownership of ten million dollars worth of General Motors stock would not put a New Haven resident on this list.

10 These two groups are not categorically mutually exclusive, of course, but because few of the city's Negroes come from the West Indies, it is safe to conclude that the foreign-stock population is white.

11 The summer survey sample, being drawn from voting lists, excluded all Yale undergraduates and most graduate students. It also underrepresented groups with large numbers of newcomers and big families, such as Negroes.

12 This figure undoubtedly underrepresents the number of Irish in New Haven, since 83 percent of all Irish immigrants came to the United States before 1900. See U.S. Bureau of the Census, *Statistical Abstract of the United States: 1955* (Washington, D.C.: U.S. Government Printing Office, 1955), p. 95.

13 In cases of joint tenancy or tenancy in common, each tenant was listed separately, except that where both husband and wife were listed in the tax records, only the husband was counted.

14 My associates in the New Haven study also used such lists, but included *all* bank directors. See Dahl, *Who Governs?,* Chap. 6; and Nelson W. Polsby, *Community Power and Political Theory* (New Haven, Conn.: Yale University Press, 1964), pp. 84–86. I did not do so because I saw no reason to think that bank directors were more influential in institutional policy making than the directors of other firms.

15 It is likely that influential attorneys are underrepresented on the list (doubtless they exercise control in some trusts and estates), as are some men whose business does

About a third of the economic elite lived in New Haven itself, half lived in the surrounding suburbs, and the remainder lived outside the metropolitan area. A fairly good indication of the ethnicity of the elite can be had from inspection of their names, supplemented by personal knowledge and information contributed by people familiar with the business community. A fifth of the elite were Jews, 4 percent more were Italians, and the rest were Anglo-Saxon. This is not a particularly surprising finding. What is far more interesting is the fact that while the great majority of these businessmen were not ethnics, *they were not old-family Yankees either; most of them were not even natives of New Haven.* Our interviews with many prominent local businessmen revealed that most of them—all but one or two of whom were of North European Protestant descent—were not born in New Haven and often had modest family backgrounds. It should be emphasized that they were not executives from national corporations transferred to New Haven to run absentee-owned branches.

Historical accounts suggest that this is not a new departure in New Haven, that ever since the industrial boom of the 1840s the resident patricians have not produced most of the city's business leadership.[16] One illustration of this phenomenon is a comparison of the business leaders with the city's social elite, which can also be defined with some degree of precision. While there was no current *Social Register* in New Haven, a fairly objective index of high social status can be found in the invitation list of the Cotillion, the area's prime social event, where young ladies made their formal debuts into society. For present purposes the social elite will consist of those persons invited to the 1958 or 1959 Cotillions.[17] (The two groups are almost identical.) The combined list amounts to 198 names, with each married couple counted as one name. It includes the names of many distinguished families whose members had been leading citizens in past generations. Aside from two Jews and two Italians, the social elite was wholly Yankee. These were not, however, the same people who ran the city's economy, for only seven members of the economic elite were invited to the Cotillion. A strict test of the overlap between the two groups would exclude from the economic elite all absentee owners and all Jews, as both of these groups, for different reasons, were ineligible for the Cotillion. This leaves an eligible group of 85, of which the seven invited to the Cotillion comprise just 8 percent. The social elite enjoy high incomes, to be sure, but they do not control New Haven's major economic resources.

---

not require ownership of large quantities of raw materials, machinery, real estate, sales facilities, or inventory. By the same token, the interests of such men are less likely to be affected by municipal governmental activities.

16 These and other unattributed historical remarks are based on *Who Governs?* and the sources cited there.

17 Dahl and Polsby included people on the 1951 Cotillion list.

Sooner or later, of course, successful business families are accepted in the highest social circles. This status is not quickly attained, however. Consider the following complaint from one Protestant businessman whose father, a Yale graduate, came to New Haven and started the nationally-known family firm more than fifty years ago:

> We noticed that we weren't readily accepted into the inner circle, you might say, the sanctorum of New Haven society the way those old multi-generation families were. We've only been here for forty years. We're newcomers. We're *nouveau riche.* We're trying to crash. I mean, the old society crowd looks upon us as trying to horn in on the Lawn Club, your Cotillions, your assemblies, places like that.

Many of the social elite, however, did not inherit their standing, but attained it after coming to New Haven. A third of the Cotillion list is comprised of Yale staff and faculty. As this indicates, many patricians consider the university connection superior to the world of modern business.

People who enjoy high social status as a result of their ancestors' acquisitive skills often disdain similar talents among their contemporaries. If for no other reason, this scorn for money making serves to protect their social prestige from being too readily matched by new generations of the rich. Family, life style, manners, accents, and education all can be more important indicators of acceptance to those who already have money. Status by ascription replaces status by achievement. This distinction is, of course, commonplace among sociologists, although the topic is by no means uncontroversial.[18] For present purposes, the interesting thing is that the importance of ascribed as opposed to achieved status seems to be a good deal greater in New Haven (and, one suspects, elsewhere in New England) than in much of the rest of the country.

This explains the absence of arriviste businessmen in the social elite, and also helps account for the corresponding scarcity of patricians in the economic elite. A prominent, old-family lawyer told Dahl and Polsby, "I think that there's a growing conviction among all [Yankees] that it's better to be in a profession now that the practices and tempo of business are not according to their taste." When asked how business had changed, he replied:

> Why, it has changed with the tax picture. The tax picture made for a regal type of living on the part of executives and an outlook on the money standards and the standards of business achievement which is utterly foreign to the Yankee.... My friend in the Shell Oil Company, my God almighty, he might

---

[18] Sociologists are in two camps on the question of whether American social classes can be delineated adequately by income alone, or whether status distinctions reflect a variety of factors. See the summary of the literature in Seymour Martin Lipset, "Social Class," in *International Encyclopedia of the Social Sciences,* 15, ed. David L. Sills (New York: The Macmillan Company, 1968), pp. 296–316.

just as well be a maharajah and he's only second-in-command in _____. My God, there's limousines meeting him everywhere and he flies here and there and everybody gets everything for him and everything's on the expense account. Well, that kind of thing is—well—we just haven't grown up with it, that's all— at least most of us haven't.

It did appear that there were more recognizable "old names" among the city's professionals—chiefly attorneys and at Yale—than in the business world. Banking also seemed to be somewhat more attractive to patricians than other forms of business. Directors of the city's banks were Protestants almost to a man.[19]

Patrician distaste for business is not the whole story, however, for members of the city's old families were scarce in almost *all* areas of economic and civic life. The Yankee lawyer quoted above said this about them:

I don't know what the hell they do, but they certainly don't seem to me to be pulling their weight. I never see them. I don't know where the hell they eat lunch. Some cases are just misfits. _____ _____'s boy just isn't equipped to go out in society. I think it's largely a case of a family's vitality just wearing out.

Every informant whom we asked about the patricians' withdrawal from active community participation (except social life) thought that the main reason was that "their blood has run thin." One middle-aged member of an old family summed up the lives of his childhood friends: "They've gone away or gone to seed."

Many sociologists who have studied community stratification systems treat income as the major source of status.[20] "Community power" specialists who report small, cohesive political ruling groups almost invariably assume a unitary socioeconomic elite.[21] New Haven's bifurcated elite suggests that

[19] There is one interesting exception to this generalization. A generation ago a group of Jewish businessmen, believing that the city's banks were giving their requests for credit less than fair consideration, founded their own bank. This institution, the General Bank and Trust Company, survived. At the time of our study it was the city's smallest bank, with assets of $3.5 million, compared to $159.4 million for the First New Haven National Bank. Many of its officers were leading figures in the Democratic party organization. Its president, William Horowitz, was treasurer of the New Haven Democratic Town Committee in the 1950s. His wife, Miriam, served two terms as city treasurer in the Lee administration. John Golden, the Irish Catholic leader of the Democratic organization during our study, was a member of the board of directors.

[20] August B. Hollingshead, a Yale sociologist and well-known specialist in social stratification, studied New Haven's class system shortly before we began our research. Although he recognized the Cotillion's importance, he failed to report the bifurcation of the city's elites. See August B. Hollingshead and Frederick C. Redlich, *Social Class and Mental Illness* (New York: John Wiley & Sons, Inc., 1958), pp. 69–84.

[21] See Polsby, *Community Power,* for references to this literature.

there is reason to be cautious about assumptions of unidimensional social stratification. More constructively, this finding provides further reason for thinking that New Haven is even more heterogeneous than one would expect on the basis of familiarity with its income and ethnic structure. Even in a city of 150,000 there are diverse sources of prestige and channels of communication among people with high levels of political resources. Considerations of how to achieve concerted political action must confront the problem of a community with multiple interaction systems. I will say more about New Haven's lack of a common communication network in later chapters.

The Formal Political Structure

New Haven has the mayor-council form of government, rather than a city commission or a council acting through a city manager. Thirty-nine percent of all American medium-sized cities and 75 percent of those in the Northeast use the mayor-council form. In every odd-numbered year the voters elected a mayor, two registrars of voters (one for each party), three constables, three selectmen, a town clerk, a registrar of vital statistics, a treasurer, a tax collector, a city clerk, a city sheriff, and 33 aldermen.

Municipal elections are partisan; the two major parties nominate candidates for each office who campaign as Republicans or Democrats and are so designated on the ballot. Two-fifths of all medium-sized cities and three-quarters of those in the Northeast use the partisan ballot. Independent and third-party candidates sometimes run for local office, but seldom receive many votes. In each municipal election the voter may vote for candidates for 15 offices. Since Connecticut uses the "party column" ballot form, the voter can more easily resolve all 15 choices by a straight party vote than would be the case with the "office block" ballot, which requires individual choices for each office. The state's voting machines were so designed that one could vote a straight ticket simply by pulling a party lever, while ticket splitting was a painstaking, complicated, and time-consuming procedure. To observers in the polling place, the length of time the voter spent in the booth revealed the strength of his devotion to the party ticket, particularly since a bell would ring when either party lever was pulled. This arrangement reflected the strength of the party organizations in Connecticut and was an important inducement to straight-ticket voting.[22] It also put a premium on the popu-

---

[22] Straight-ticket voting is considerably more common in states using the party column ballot, and the influence of differences in ballot form seems to be greatest on less educated voters. See Angus Campbell, Philip E. Converse, Warren E. Miller, and Donald E. Stokes, *The American Voter* (New York: John Wiley and Sons, Inc., 1960), pp. 275–76; and Jack L. Walker, "Ballot Forms and Voter Fatigue: An Analysis of the Office Block and Party Column Ballots," *Midwest Journal of Political Science*, 10 (November 1966), 449–50.

larity of the candidate at the head of the ticket. His appeal largely determined the fate of candidates for lesser municipal offices, who were usually put on the ticket for the extra votes that could be gained from their friends. Sometimes it seemed that the lever rather than the party was the object of campaign slogans, which customarily were phrased like this: "Vote Democratic— Pull Top Lever." The rate of participation in city elections was very high. In the five municipal elections from 1949 through 1957 the average turnout was 82 percent of all registered voters, compared to 47 percent for all comparable cities with more than 25,000 population.[23]

The two parties were on even terms in city politics for more than a century. Only twice in the hundred years prior to 1955 had a mayoralty candidate received more than 60 percent of the vote—a Republican in 1879 and a Democrat in 1937. In the first half of the twentieth century control of city hall passed from one party to the other seven times. The Lee administration was something of a departure from this pattern, for Lee was mayor from 1953 through 1969 and won five elections with more than 60 percent of the vote.

At the time of our study there were 33 aldermen representing wards ranging in size from 772 to 5,123 registered voters. Seventeen percent of all medium-sized American cities elect municipal legislators solely from wards; this proportion doubles in the Northeast. Among its other functions, the Board of Aldermen passes ordinances and approves the budget. The mayor can veto aldermanic ordinances and his veto can be overridden by a two-thirds vote.

There are no independently elected or financed public boards or commissions, hence all local public functions except the judicial system are concentrated in the municipal government.[24] But the city charter prescribes a "weak-mayor" form of governmental organization in which most municipal functions are the responsibility of boards whose members are appointed for fixed terms by the mayor. Nineteen municipal departments with more than 90 percent of all city employees were under the formal control of their respective boards. The realities of the situation, as well as many other aspects of local public agencies, are discussed in Chapters 4 and 7. Of the 3,100 municipal employees in 1959, 1,150 were in the Department of Education and 850 were firemen or policemen.

---

[23] The latter figure is for all municipal elections held in 1961 and 1962 not concurrently with a state or national election. Robert R. Alford and Eugene C. Lee, "Voting Turnout in American Cities," *American Political Science Review*, 62 (September 1968), 796–813.

[24] The Park Commission is a partial exception to this statement. See Dahl, *Who Governs?*, pp. 207–8.

The Media of Mass Communication

New Haven's two daily newspapers are jointly owned. The *New Haven Journal-Courier* appears every morning but Sunday. At the end of the 1950s it had a circulation of 23,885. The much more important *New Haven Evening Register* had a circulation of 94,453 on weekdays and about 10,000 more on Sundays.[25]

During the events described in this book both papers were owned by John Day Jackson, who died in 1961 at the age of 92. A very conservative Republican, Jackson acquired the *Register* in 1907. From that time forward he expressed, in both news and editorial columns, his hostility to liberal programs under consideration at all levels of government. Jackson seemed to be most outraged by policies that might increase taxes. Just as Samuel Gompers's motto was "More," Jackson's political byword was "Less." His thoroughgoing opposition to government spending cost his newspapers considerable influence in the community. While 90 percent of our sample of registered voters said that they read the *Register* regularly, more than half of them expressed a lack of confidence in the paper as a source of news.

A third local newspaper was the *Sunday Herald,* a scandal-oriented tabloid originating in Bridgeport whose New Haven edition appeared weekly. It presented a scanty ration of political news in a frantic, side-of-the-mouth style. The *Herald's* editorial policy was aggressively liberal. I have been unable to find New Haven circulation data for the *Herald,* but it was read by most political figures and by a sizable fraction of the working class.[26]

There were three radio stations in New Haven, one of which also operated a television station. These media were more or less neutral in local news reporting. The owner of one radio station, Daniel W. Kops, followed an enterprising news policy, including the use of "radio editorials."

The Case of Yale University

Yale is probably the most important economic resource in New Haven. It was the city's second largest employer and tenth biggest taxpayer, despite the tax-exempt status of most of its holdings. In 1957 the assessed value of its tax-exempt property was $71 million, more than three times the value of the biggest taxpayer's holdings. It is a major purchaser of goods and ser-

[25] Audit Bureau of Circulation data in *N. W. Ayer and Son's Directory of Newspapers and Periodicals* (Philadelphia: N. W. Ayer & Son, 1959).

[26] Hollingshead and Redlich said that the *Sunday Herald* was read in about a third of all working-class households (*Social Class and Mental Illness,* p. 112).

vices and its 8,000 students, together with alumni and visitors, spend more than $10 million annually in New Haven.[27]

Yet in the period of our study Yale had remarkably little direct impact on New Haven politics for several reasons, most of them rooted one way or another in New England social customs. For one thing, hostility to Yankees is endemic in New Haven. Since Yale is a Yankee institution and was popularly assumed to be a finishing school for the idle sons of millionaires, it was a natural target for these antipathies, which generally were reinforced by class consciousness. Manifestations of this hostility ranged from attacks on Yale students by street gangs to a political climate in which city officials felt they had to avoid giving the impression of being soft on Yale. This anxiety once caused a decision not to choose a blue letterhead for one of Mayor Lee's campaign organizations for fear that the color would give ammunition to those of Lee's critics who accused him of favoritism to Yale.

The university's local unpopularity and lack of political influence were illustrated in several ugly clashes between police and undergraduates in the late 1950s. The police, mainly from working-class Catholic homes, doubtless shared the local anti-Yale sentiment. The students, perhaps a bit snobbish, liked to taunt the police. As a result, wholly unpolitical student disorders were sometimes suppressed with inordinate and gratuitous force. The worst of these incidents occurred after the 1959 St. Patrick's Day parade when, probably in response to a snowball thrown from a crowd of undergraduates, several dozen policemen charged the students with nightsticks flailing. A number of bystanders were clubbed and dragged off to jail as the police pursued their victims into the recesses of the adjoining residential college. As a result of this and corollary disturbances, several students were suspended from Yale, two of them for expressing disrespect to the mayor with a casual catcall as Lee left a clothing store near the campus.

A university's presence might be reflected in local politics through its institutional actions or the participation of its faculty and staff as individuals. The University of Chicago furnishes the best known example of both forms of influence.[28] One reason for the difference in political impact between the two schools is nothing more profound than their respective physical environments. The social geography of the Chicago metropolitan area is such that no accessible area except the immediate vicinity of the university is an ac-

---

[27] This estimate on spending is from the Southern New England Telephone Company.

[28] For an extended discussion of the University of Chicago's political activities, see Peter H. Rossi and Robert A. Dentler, *The Politics of Urban Renewal* (New York: The Free Press, 1961). Rossi and Dentler do not indicate that the University of Chicago's bargaining position with its municipal administration was seriously damaged by the sort of town–gown hostility that so hobbled Yale. Doubtless the lack of an effective opposition to the Chicago Democratic organization and the university's less conspicuous position in that city minimized the political hazards of having the university for an ally.

ceptable residential neighborhood for most faculty, as many as 80 percent of whom lived within a mile of the campus. The need to conserve, improve, and protect this neighborhood was an immediate and pressing incentive for political action by the university, which felt that its survival as a major institution required massive action to achieve this end. Moreover, Chicago has long been a school where the predominant style is concern about political issues. The Hyde Park neighborhood is an avant garde enclave which attracts many nonacademic residents. This area not only had a distinctive activist tradition but was big enough to elect an alderman and sustain a lively reform Democratic organization, the Independent Voters of Illinois.

In contrast, New Haven proper has few congenial residential areas, and Yale professors and staff can find pleasant homes in a number of accessible suburbs. Far more readily than their Chicago colleagues, they can move away if they dislike their city neighborhood. In 1959 only 44 percent of Yale faculty lived in the city of New Haven, and they were not concentrated in a single section.[29] Very few of the Yale people who did live in New Haven participated in local politics in the 1950s. As we will see later, the New Haven parties had ample workers and money through conventional patronage channels and neither needed nor welcomed upper-middle-class intellectual activists. Moreover, the Yale style was very different from the atmosphere of excitement and engagement at Chicago. Until the mid-1960s one found at Yale that languid disengagement that was one of the more conspicuous traits of the Ivy League gentleman. This mood is fast disappearing, of course, for Yale is no exception to the general fashion of university activism, but during our study it was quite evident.

Again unlike the University of Chicago, Yale did not until recently display much interest in its local environment, although it too was affected, in lesser measure, by congestion, slums, and a shortage of room for expansion. Until 1958, for example, there was no coordination between the university's long-range capital improvement program and the city's planning activities. This political reticence is something of a puzzle if one regards local politics with any frame of reference that equates political interests and political actions. It might be thought, for instance, that as an institution enjoying a much-resented tax exemption, Yale might participate in community life in the same ways—and for much the same reasons—that public utilities do. In fact, A. Whitney Griswold, the university's late president, advocated just such a policy in 1957. But despite all the apparent reasons for playing an active part in New Haven's civic and political life, Yale eschewed such a role. The Yale Corporation (the university's board of trustees) was very reluctant to take steps toward this end. During the period of our study no one from the New Haven area was on the Corporation. In the mid-1960s William Horowitz, a local businessman and politician (see note 19), was elected to the Corpora-

[29] This figure is from analysis of a 25 percent sample of the 1959 *Yale Directory*.

tion by vote of the alumni after having been nominated by the unusual method of a petition. He was the first Jewish member of the Corporation.[30]

Inevitably, as a major land user, the university was involved in many dealings with local public officials. Its bargaining power was limited by its extraordinary unpopularity, which politicians pointed to as a reason for not daring to be more accommodating. For example, Mayor Lee persuaded Griswold to raise Yale's purchase price for some city property from the agreed-upon $2.7 million to $3 million because the rounder figure would "look better" to the allegedly suspicious Board of Aldermen (see Chapter 6). Because Yale's constituency covers the entire country, there are not many local alumni who could be persuaded to give their alma mater a break, and discouragement of middle-class political activity in New Haven reduces the influence of local alumni.

In short, there were few ties between the university and its community. Yale did not use its economic power as a means of influence in local politics, nor did it have much of a local "old boy net." It was rarely a significant source of political activists in local elections (national campaigns were sometimes another story), nor was its faculty's expertise often brought to bear on New Haven problems. Considering its national importance and sizable body of talents, Yale was a remarkably small active factor in New Haven's politics.

Nevertheless, the university's presence had certain very important consequences, mostly of a fortuitous nature. Edward J. Logue, now the country's foremost urban renewal official, would not have contributed his formidable talents to New Haven, where he began his career, had it not been for his ties to Yale (see Chapter 9). As I argue in Chapter 6, Lee's job as Yale's publicity director probably influenced the development of his political values. The university's special needs for housing and its willingness to be generous when asked helped the Lee administration through several sticky periods in its urban renewal program (see Chapters 9 and 10). These were all unique events. In addition, Yale could be used as an institutional ally and source of prestige (see Chapter 8), but only with great care and skill because of its unpopularity. For the same reason, plus perhaps the relative political talents of the people involved, the balance sheet of Yale's dealings with city hall gave little support to the durable town myth that New Haven was exploited by the great university in its heart.

How Typical Is New Haven?

New Haven was the locale for our study largely because its proximity to Yale made it the most physically convenient site and also gave us important political connections. One response to *Who Governs?* has been the suggestion

---

[30] No Catholic has ever been a member of the Yale Corporation.

that many of its conclusions about New Haven are of limited or dubious utility because New Haven is an unusual city. The argument seems to be that some persistent aspects of New Haven's political environment are not ordinarily found in American cities and therefore information about the city has only curiosity value for the student of local politics. The presence of Yale is one of the things that supposedly makes New Haven deviant. In point of fact, almost any American city has some unusual feature that could furnish ammunition for critics determined to argue that it was an inappropriate locale for research. Looking at other Connecticut cities, one notes that Bridgeport has a Socialist party whose durable leader, Jasper McLevy, was mayor for 24 years; Hartford has an economy in which the insurance industry plays an unusually important part; and so on.

As I have tried to show in this chapter, there is nothing unique about New Haven's political setting. Those of its political, social, or economic features that are not commonplace in other parts of the country, for example, partisan elections and an elected mayor, are found generally in the Northeast. In the next two chapters I discuss regional variations in two important aspects of New Haven politics: the prominent role played by nationality groups in local political perspectives, and the city's patronage-based machine politics. In these respects, as in many others, a truly "typical American city" cannot be found and the best that one can hope for is a research site that is typical of its type. New Haven meets this criterion; it is not a municipal freak.

3 ethnic politics

Mass immigration to the United States ended 50 years ago, but national origins continue to be a prominent dimension of many individuals' perceptions of themselves and others.[1] Where this awareness is widespread, as in New Haven and many other cities, it plays a major role in politics.[2] One aspect of ethnic politics is ethnic voting, that is, situations in which ethnic group membership is an important independent variable in voting behavior. It has two manifestations: (1) Members of an ethnic group show an affinity for one party or the other that cannot be explained solely as a result of other demographic characteristics. Irish Catholics, for example, are more likely than other voters to be Democrats. (2) Ethnic group members will cross party lines to vote for or against a candidate belonging to a particular group.[3]

The most striking example of ethnic voting in New Haven is the marked Republican affiliation of the city's Italians, the poorest segment of the white population. This Italian Republicanism is a development of the past 30 years,

[1] Much of the material in this chapter was published in two articles: "The Development and Persistence of Ethnic Voting," *American Political Science Review,* 59 (December 1965), 896–908; and "Some Consequences of Ethnic Politics" in *The Electoral Process,* eds. M. Kent Jennings and L. Harmon Zeigler (Englewood Cliffs, N.J.: Prentice-Hall, Inc., 1966), pp. 42–54. © 1966. Reprinted by permission of Prentice-Hall, Inc., Englewood Cliffs, New Jersey.

[2] Conflict among nationality groups is a central topic in descriptions of politics in the Northeast. See, for example, Duane Lockard, *New England State Politics* (Princeton, N.J.: Princeton University Press, 1959). For discussions of ethnicity in personnel appointments, see Theodore J. Lowi, *At the Pleasure of the Mayor* (New York: The Free Press, 1964), *passim*; and Daniel Patrick Moynihan and James Q. Wilson, "Patronage in New York State, 1955–59," *American Political Science Review,* 58 (June 1964), 296–301.

[3] Evidence to support these propositions will be found in this chapter and in Robert A. Dahl, *Who Governs? Democracy and Power in an American City* (New Haven, Conn.: Yale University Press, 1961), pp. 55–60; Lucy S. Davidowicz and Leon J. Goldstein, *Politics in a Pluralist Democracy* (New York: Institute of Human Relations Press, 1963); Robert A. Lorinskas, Brett W. Hawkins, and Stephen D. Edwards, "The Persistence of Ethnic Voting in Urban and Rural Areas: Results from the Controlled Election Method," in *The Ethnic Factor in American Politics,* eds. Hawkins and Lorinskas (Columbus, Ohio: Charles E. Merrill Publishing Co., 1970), pp. 124–33; and Gerald Pomper, "Ethnic and Group Voting in Nonpartisan Municipal Elections," *Public Opinion Quarterly,* 30 (Spring 1969), 79–97.

during which time the Italians have been the mainstay of Republican voting strength, even in elections with no Italian candidates. This situation suggests a general theory of ethnic voting different from the prevailing interpretation; this theory is developed later in this chapter. I then turn to a general discussion of some of the major consequences of ethnic politics, consequences of a political style in which appeals to nationality group loyalties are important and conspicuous. Finally, I will apply the propositions developed in this chapter about ethnic politics to the emerging phenomenon of black power.

Throughout this chapter I will use the terms *ethnic group* and *nationality group* interchangeably to refer to whites whose national origins or cultural heritage (in the case of Jews) differentiate them from the predominantly Protestant old American society. This terminological looseness may be semantically inconsistent, but it is in accord with the outlook of the politicians and voters whose behavior I will describe. The discussion of ethnic politics in this chapter is limited to the urban areas of the Northeast and the industrialized parts of the eastern Great Lakes states. It is not intended to cover the Cajuns of South Louisiana, the Czechs of Nebraska, the Russians of North Dakota, or the Italians of San Francisco's North Beach.

The Durability of Ethnic Consciousness

From the time of the first Irish immigration to the Northeast the Yankees greeted non-Protestant newcomers with hostility, religious bigotry, and economic exploitation. In some places this enmity erupted in rioting, killing, and burning of Catholic churches. Before the Civil War widespread feeling against immigrants led to the formation of the "Know Nothing" party, which drew impressive voting support during its brief career, particularly from the native urban working class.[4]

The immigrants generally were penniless and uneducated and could get only the worst jobs. While they may have been eager to shed their old national identities and become Americanized, the affronts of everyday life enhanced their sense of separateness, as did the obvious gap in well-being between them and the old settlers. Excluded from most associational aspects of the majority society, they developed their own society. Forces other than deprivation and Yankee hostility helped maintain ethnic solidarity. For European peasants living in an American city, a familiar language, religion, and culture were comforting when so much else was different. Thus members of each nationality group usually settled in the same neighborhoods, married their own kind, formed nationality associations, and worshiped in national churches.

[4] John H. Higham, *Strangers in the Land* (New Brunswick, N.J.: Rutgers University Press, 1955).

There are three dimensions of the absorption of the immigrants into American society.[5] One step is *acculturation*: assumption of the behavior patterns typical of the majority society, including speaking English, increases in education and income, and the development of skills, economic activities, cultural and social organization, and family relationships resembling those of the old settlers. The first signs of this acculturation came as the years passed and some of the immigrants and their descendants moved, in varying numbers, into the middle class.

A second aspect of Americanization is *association*: integration of behavior patterns with those of nonethnics, including the disappearance of segregation in economic, social, residential, marital, educational, and recreational behavior. This is by no means a necessary consequence of at least the first stages of acculturation. Often much of the new prosperity in a particular national community came from neighborhood-based enterprises like groceries and mortuaries that required a certain amount of proximity. Thus economic mobility did not result in an equal degree of geographical dispersion. This in turn helped maintain the associational separatism of the early days, particularly as the leaders of ethnic organizations usually were the more prosperous members of the local community. The institutionalization of nationality group segregation retarded association. Like all organizations, these fraternal, welfare, recreational, social, and religious bodies tended to persist, both creating and fulfilling the need for continued ethnic togetherness.

The third aspect is *assimilation*: the disappearance of ethnicity as a source of identity. The opposite pole of assimilation is ethnic consciousness, awareness of one's ethnicity. In this sense ethnicity may be considered a reference group, a collectivity with which people identify and which helps its "members" define themselves. It is most convenient in the present context for us to think of ethnicity as one of several identities that coexist and compete with other identities, one which is more prominent and relevant for some purposes and at some times. Thus ethnic consciousness may readily be submerged on the job, and then come to the fore when an individual thinks of neighbors or political candidates.

These three dimensions are not developmental stages, the first of which must be completed before the second one begins; all three can occur simultaneously. Nor does any one of them necessarily lead to the others, although clearly they are related. For example, education and widespread entry into the middle class do not eliminate ethnically-associated interaction patterns, although they do at least make physical and emotional departure from the

---

[5] For an earlier typology, defining two dimensions of ethnic group adaptation to American society, see Milton M. Gordon, "Social Structure and Goals in Group Relations," in *Freedom and Control in Modern Society,* eds. Morroe Berger, Theodore Abel, and Charles H. Page (New York: Van Nostrand Reinhold Company, 1954), pp. 151–57. Gordon's two categories are similar to what I have called acculturation and association.

immigrant culture more feasible. By the same token, if most members of an immigrant community remain poor, they will be more likely to retain their national solidarity.

Acculturation, association, and assimilation are not dichotomous, yes/no phenomena, but continuous dimensions at both the individual and aggregate levels. They also vary from group to group. Jews, for example, have attained a high degree of acculturation in that their income, educational, and occupational levels are higher than average. They are much less "associated," and their ethnic consciousness is high. The passage of time by itself does not reduce ethnic salience, for (aside from the Jews) nationality groups seem to vary in their rates of assimilation. Few Irishmen have ancestors who came to the United States after the turn of the century, yet from all indications there are many places where Irish self-consciousness is still very strong—notably in New York, for instance, as well as in New Haven, Boston, and many other cities. But most Germans, who immigrated to New York in considerable numbers about the same time as the Irish, no longer seem to be part of a self-conscious nationality group.[6]

Apart from physical characteristics, various factors retard the absorption of ethnic groups. One, of course, is majority-society hostility. It also appears that there may be differences in the modal cultural patterns of different ethnic groups that affect their ability to adapt to American forms of social and economic life.[7] Perhaps the most durable force maintaining ethnic consciousness is the memory of past hostility and rivalry. The immigrants naturally responded to Yankee rebuffs with a hatred that has not yet vanished and may readily be invoked. The "Irish Mafia" members of President Kennedy's White House staff sometimes found occasion to remind each other of the famous "No Irish Need Apply" signs of their Massachusetts heritage. In some cities members of each of the major nationality groups still regard the others with varying amounts of jealousy and suspicion. For their part, some Yankees continue to look down on the ethnics. The novelist James Gould Cozzens has one of his fictional heroes bemoan the political ascendance of Catholics in New England:

> Yet does any free man, without grief, without shame, without fear, see names so proud a hundred years ago in their birthright of liberty as New Hampshire, Massachusetts, Rhode Island, Connecticut, little by little in the past fifty years degraded to designate virtual papal states?[8]

6 On the "disappearance" of the Germans, see Moynihan and Wilson, "Patronage in New York State," pp. 299–300; and Nathan Glazer and Daniel Patrick Moynihan, *Beyond the Melting Pot* (Cambridge, Mass.: The M.I.T. Press and Harvard University Press, 1963), p. 311.

7 Glazer and Moynihan, *Beyond the Melting Pot*.

8 James Gould Cozzens, *By Love Possessed* (New York: Harcourt Brace Jovanovich, Inc., 1957), p. 229. Used by permission of the publisher and Longman Group Limited.

One result of this heritage of nationality group relations in New Haven (and in many other cities) is a persistent emphasis on ethnic differences, which continue to be a major organizing principle in the city's social structure and political culture. One study of New Haven concluded that nationality group identifications divided the social structure "horizontally" just as economic divisions organized it "vertically."[9] Ethnic and economic divisions are superimposed; while there is some overlap, their boundaries are far from coextensive. Thus to the bifurcation of the city's elites described in Chapter 2, we must add this portrait of ethnic consciousness, which defines another aspect of community segmentation.

Because they were initially excluded from society far more fully than the native working class, the immigrants and their descendants never developed the respect for the patricians that characterized the earlier, more homogeneous New Haven. The seasoned hostility between the Yankees and the ethnics not only reduces the "endorsement value" of big businessmen, but minimizes the potential political leverage of social status. Awe of the upper classes was not a feature of New Haven perspectives.

The intensity of ethnic consciousness and its accompanying community divisions seems to vary considerably from one part of the country to another. While it is difficult even to suggest objective measures for comparing ethnic consciousness, much less to find data on the subject, a wealth of impressionistic evidence suggests that interest in national origins is much greater in New England and the Middle Atlantic states than in most other parts of the country. The reasons for this regional difference are not immediately apparent. The numerical prevalence of ethnics does not account for it, for the major cities of the West Coast have sizable foreign stock populations.[10] San Francisco has about the same proportion of first- and second-generation residents as New Haven (43 as against 42 percent), but there is no comparison between the two cities with respect to ethnic salience, just as the West in general seems to display much less concern with national ancestry (except for Orientals and Mexican-Americans).[11]

9 August B. Hollingshead and Frederick C. Redlich, *Social Class and Mental Illness* (New York: John Wiley and Sons, Inc., 1958), p. 64.

10 Among cities with more than 500,000 population, San Francisco trails only New York and Boston in the proportionate size of its foreign stock population. Los Angeles has more first- and second-generation Americans per capita than Detroit, and Seattle more than Cleveland or Pittsburgh. There are some regional differences in the national origins of these ethnic populations. On the other hand, San Francisco, for one, has sizable Irish and Italian groups.

11 This description of regional variations in ethnic consciousness is based on my own observations and is affirmed by conversations I have had with social scientists who have lived on both coasts. For similar views on lower ethnic salience in the West, see Glazer and Moynihan, *Beyond the Melting Pot*, pp. 10, 250; and James Q. Wilson, "A Guide to Reagan Country: The Political Culture of Southern California," *Commentary* (May 1967), 39.

This regional variation may exist because in the Northeast the non-British immigrants came to settled communities with relatively stable class structures and systems of status ascription, where only menial jobs were open to them. The distribution of economic opportunities reinforced the unambiguous class system. On the other hand, European immigrants came to the West at the same time as the Yankees, or on their heels: "The Forty-Niners came from all parts of the world, and foreign accents were as common in the mining camps as American ones."[12] The two groups shared the same pioneering experiences, wildly fluctuating economies, and unsettled social systems characteristic of boomtowns. In subsequent, less tumultuous decades, labor was scarcer throughout the West Coast, wages were higher, many early immigrants were better off and better educated, and class distinctions were weaker and less stable.[13] Because economic advantage was not so closely associated with ethnicity and because there were greater economic advantages for newcomers, the various elements of social class were not so neatly lined up against immigrants in the West.

The Conditions of Ethnic Politics

The immigrants in New England were equal to the old settlers in only one respect: they could vote. Their previous experience in Ireland or continental Europe had not led them to believe that their opinions had much to do with what the government did, and so in America their votes had no abstract value to them. But these votes were valuable to American politicians, who solicited them with advice, favors, gifts, flattery, and jobs.

The politicians found it convenient and efficient to classify the electorate by national origins and to develop strategies and dispense rewards on this basis. The prominence of ethnic identifications encouraged this practice, which was also fostered by limitations in available political intelligence. Politicians need schemes for classifying voters and tend to look for such taxonomies

---

The only dissenter on this point of whom I am aware is Michael Parenti, but his thesis is apparently based on no evidence other than the indisputable fact that nationality groups and Jews have organizations in the West as in the East. On this subject, as elsewhere in his article, Parenti seems to believe that all manifestations of ethnicity are equally strong indices of ethnic consciousness. By this logic, Jews will be assimilated only when they have given up their temples, Catholics when the Knights of Columbus merge with the Masons, and so on. See his "Ethnic Politics and the Persistence of Ethnic Identification," *American Political Science Review*, 61 (September 1967), 721.

12 Louis Berg, "Peddlers in Eldorado," *Commentary* (July 1965), 64. Berg observes that "the early Jews in the West could boast that they were pioneers among pioneers" (p. 65).

Parenti suggests that the movement of immigrants to the West is a recent phenomenon, but offers no evidence or citations to support this remarkable assertion (p. 721).

13 Earl Pomeroy, *The Pacific Slope* (New York: Alfred A. Knopf, Inc., 1965).

in election returns. Because immigrants and their descendants clustered together in ghettos, wards and precincts were more homogeneous in ethnicity
than in any other characteristic. Before the development of reliable polling
techniques, voting returns were the best available source of information on
the preferences and voting patterns of different groups in the electorate, and
relying on them involved an implicit bias for ethnic explanations of election
outcomes. Sample survey research gave politicians an opportunity to escape
from this limitation by providing a way to analyze opinions and votes according to other categories.[14] Lee was one of the first politicians to use professional sample surveys, yet data from the polls he commissioned were analyzed
by ethnic group rather than income, occupation, or education.

The tangible rewards available to immigrants were limited. Not everyone
could be given a job or a Christmas basket, nor did everyone want one, or
need to get a son out of jail, or a relative into the United States, or a push-
cart license from city hall. Winning votes by such individually bestowed
gifts is called "retailing." Ethnic support could also be won by "wholesale"
tactics, most commonly by "recognizing" the merits of a particular group.
When, in the middle of the nineteenth century, the first Irishman was nominated for public office, this was "recognition" by the party of the statesman-
like qualities of the Irish, seen and appreciated by many Irishmen. Ethnic
solidarity let politicians economize on the indulgences they bestowed. It was
unnecessary to do a favor for every ethnic to win his vote, for rewards given
to the few were appreciated vicariously by the many. Thus money and jobs
given to a few leaders earned returns in two ways: (1) through the votes
that the recipient could deliver directly; and (2) through widespread appre-
ciation of his "recognition."

Public office is the most common currency of "recognition." Other techniques for enhancing ethnic self-esteem have produced some of the most
picturesque episodes in American politics. Conspicuous consumption of ethnic
food is a recurring minor campaign theme in some areas. In his 1964 senatorial campaign, for example, Robert F. Kennedy was photographed eating
pizza in what was considered an attempt to placate Italians angered by
his attacks on the Mafia while he was attorney general. A few years earlier
the two patrician candidates for governor of New York, Nelson Rockefeller
and W. Averell Harriman, courted votes and ulcers by ostentatiously eating
blintzes, salami, manicotti, and other ethnic foods.

---

[14] For this reason it is hard to accept Glazer and Moynihan's contention that
survey research has stimulated the use of ethnic appeals by politicians. Apparently they
came to this conclusion because the politicians who commission such research classify
the respondents by ethnicity instead of income or education. The important point is
that there is no intrinsic reason why survey data must be analyzed by ethnicity; a decision to do so would seem to depend on assumptions about what variables are related to
individual voting decisions. Glazer and Moynihan noted this point, but were unmoved by
it. See *Beyond the Melting Pot*, pp. 301–2, 305.

The same style of politics flourishes in New Haven. Lee became mayor by deposing William C. Celentano, the first Italian to be elected to the office. Even in defeat, Celentano had won more than three-fourths of the vote in Italian wards, and Lee was concerned to improve his popularity among the city's biggest voting bloc. Accordingly, one of his first official acts was to refurbish a statue of Columbus. That fall he inaugurated a Columbus Day Parade to parallel the traditional St. Patrick's Day Parade. In the next election the Republicans campaigned for their Italian candidate in Italian neighborhoods with the slogan, "Win our city back for us." Political discussion in New Haven, as in much of the Northeast, runs strongly to jealous comments about the unjustified rewards—jobs, testimonial dinners, and other forms of recognition—that one nationality group or another is enjoying. Even seemingly routine administrative decisions were made with ethnic considerations in mind. When ex-President Truman visited Yale for several days in 1958, a number of city policemen were assigned to a sort of honor guard for him. Mayor Lee personally selected the members of this detail, in order to be sure that it displayed the proper ethnic balance: so many Irishmen, Italians, Poles, and so forth. (Lee had planned to include one black policeman in this detail until he learned of Truman's strong personal antipathy to Negroes.)

The History of Ethnic Politics in New Haven

The first Irish member of the New Haven Board of Aldermen was elected in 1857. From that time forward Irishmen and other immigrants held municipal offices in increasing numbers. By the time later waves of immigrants arrived, the Irish had attained considerable influence, largely in the Democratic party. The election of 1899 marked the beginnings of ethnic dominance in local politics. Cornelius Driscoll, born in County Cork, was elected mayor on the Democratic ticket, deposing the Republican incumbent, a Yankee foundry executive. As the Irish subsequently strengthened their hold on the party, some Yankee Democrats defected to the Republicans.

The Irish were not reluctant to take the spoils of victory. By the early 1930s first- and second-generation Irishmen comprised 13 percent of a sample of 1,600 family heads in New Haven, but they held 49 percent of all governmental jobs. The Italians suffered most of all from Irish exclusiveness: there were *no* government employees among the Italians in the sample.[15] These data exaggerate the Italians' exclusion from political rewards, but not by very much. In 1930 the proportion of Italians in low-paying municipal jobs was

[15] John W. McConnell, *The Evolution of Social Class* (Washington, D.C.: American Council on Public Affairs, 1942), p. 214. The data are from the Sample Family Survey conducted by the Yale Institute of Human Relations in 1931–33.

only a quarter of the proportion of Italians in the total population; the ratio for better city jobs was much lower. By 1940 Italians had attained half their "share" of the poorer jobs and only about a fifth in white-collar positions. Subsequently their representation in both appointive and elective positions increased enormously; in the 1950s, during a period of Democratic success, Italians held slightly more than their share of municipal elective offices.[16]

The explanation of the New Haven Italians' Republicanism may then be thought to lie here: shut out of the Democratic party, they had no place to go but to the Republicans. This argument has two crippling limitations: (1) the Italians became more Republican during the period when they finally came closer to achieving their "fair share" of municipal jobs; and (2) Irish control of the local Democratic party is common in northeastern industrial cities, but the level of Italian Republicanism found in New Haven is not. The best present source of data on this subject is the series of national election studies conducted over the past 20 years by the Survey Research Center of the University of Michigan. I have compared the party identification of the Italian and Irish respondents who lived in the New England and Middle Atlantic states in the 1952, 1956, and 1958 studies. As Table 3-1 shows, the Italians were a little more inclined than the Irish to consider themselves Democrats.[17]

As the level of Italian Republicanism found in New Haven is not common in the Northeast, local history is more likely to provide an explanation. Two local causes can be identified. The first is the determined courting of the Italian vote by Isaac and Louis Ullman, two prominent German Jewish busi-

[16] Jerome K. Myers, "Assimilation in the Political Community," *Sociology and Social Research,* 35 (January–February 1951), 175–82; and Dahl, *Who Governs?,* pp. 43–44. Also see pp. 67–68 below. The Republicans lost control of city hall in 1932 to John W. Murphy, a Democrat of the old school.

As these findings suggest, there are impediments to a "rational" strategy of ethnic politics (1) Party leaders may refrain from cultivating ethnic groups out of prejudice. (2) Party activists may be reluctant to share political spoils with "outsiders." This seems to have been true of many Irish Democrats. Until a very few years ago, one Democratic ward organization in a New Haven Irish neighborhood would not let Italians participate in any form of campaign activity. (3) There may be principled objections to making appointments on the basis of ethnicity rather than merit. For examples of this attitude, see James Q. Wilson, *The Amateur Democrat* (Chicago: University of Chicago Press, 1962), pp. 282–88. It is very possible, however, that such scruples can easily be ignored when the men who hold them actually attain power. See Moynihan and Wilson, "Patronage in New York State."

[17] For other data casting doubt on the notion of Italian Republicanism, see Davidowicz and Goldstein, *Politics in a Pluralist Democracy,* pp. 11–12, 30–32; J. Joseph Huthmacher, *Massachusetts People and Politics 1919–1932* (Cambridge, Mass.: Harvard University Press, 1959), pp. 173, 179–84, 252, 260–61; Lockard, *New England State Politics,* pp. 210, 305–19; and Samuel Lubell, *The Future of American Politics* (Garden City, N. Y.: Doubleday & Company, Inc., 1956), pp. 225–26.

TABLE 3-1. Party identification of Italians and Irish in the Northeast, 1952, 1956, and 1958

Party identification	Irish	Italians
Democratic	51%	57%
Independent	18	13
Republican	32	30
	101%	100%
N	152	143

Source: Survey Research Center data obtained through the Inter-University Consortium for Political Research, with the assistance of Ralph Bisco and Richard T. Lane of the Consortium staff. I am solely responsible for computation and analysis of the data.

nessmen who led the New Haven Republican party in the first quarter of the twentieth century. The Ullman brothers realized that the large and hitherto passive Italian population was an untapped source of potential Republicans, and they set out to capture them. Using the familiar techniques of ethnic politics, they helped Italian immigrants take out citizenship papers, registered them as voters, found them jobs, used their considerable political influence to smooth over administrative and legal difficulties, subsidized Italian-American fraternal and political clubs, and so on.

It is not too much to say that the Ullman brothers' foresight and political skill kept the Republican party competitive in New Haven. Although the Italians were the poorest part of the population, they were, in the thirty years after 1910, less favorable to Democratic candidates than any other immigrant group, except perhaps the Jews.[18] In the tenth ward, with the city's heaviest concentration of Italians, the Democratic share of the presidential and mayoralty vote fluctuated around 50 percent. In fact, the tenth voted much like the city as a whole, a remarkable similarity in view of its residents' modest economic position.[19] The other wards in which Italians predominated were also less Democratic than one would expect from their low income levels. It seems likely that this situation was due largely to the proselytizing by the Ullman brothers.

[18] Jews in New Haven, as elsewhere, voted strongly Republican until the New Deal, and have been overwhelmingly Democratic since then. See Lawrence H. Fuchs, *The Political Behavior of American Jews* (New York: The Free Press, 1956), p. 56; and Angus Campbell, Philip E. Converse, Warren E. Miller, and Donald E. Stokes, *The American Voter* (New York: John Wiley & Sons, Inc., 1960), p. 159.

[19] Except for the 1928 election, when the tenth was 18 percent ahead of the city in its support of Al Smith, and the 1932 and 1936 elections, when Roosevelt ran about 10 percent ahead of the city-wide vote there. In other mayoralty and presidential elections before 1939, differences generally were minor; see Dahl, *Who Governs?*, pp. 48–50.

Although the Ullmans' efforts gave Republicans a certain advantage with Italian voters, for some 30 years the result was no more than a standoff. The Italians split their votes more or less evenly between the two parties until the end of the 1930s. The big shift in their voting habits began when William Celentano won the Republican mayoralty nomination in 1939. Celentano was the first New Haven Italian to win either party's nomination for a major office. He cut 10,000 votes from the enormous majority that the incumbent Democrat, John W. Murphy, had won two years earlier, and came close to winning the election. The Second World War kept Celentano off the ballot until 1945, for the city's Republican leaders did not think it prudent to nominate an Italian while Italy was fighting the United States. But in 1945 he defeated Murphy by 6,000 votes.

Celentano's candidacy brought thousands of Italians into the Republican party, as the voting history of the heavily Italian tenth ward illustrates. In 1937 Murphy received 52 percent of the ward's vote. Two years later, running against Celentano for the first time, he got 22 percent and fared almost as badly in other Italian neighborhoods.[20] Matters improved somewhat for the Democrats during the war, but Celentano's second candidacy produced an even greater Republican swing; in 1945 Murphy won only 17 percent of the tenth ward's vote.

In 1947 the Democrats tried to match Celentano's appeal by giving the mayoralty nomination to an obscure Italian dentist. They recouped most of their losses in Italian neighborhoods—their share of the tenth ward vote rose from 17 to 42 percent and was about this high in the other Italian wards—but lost heavily elsewhere in the city. Furthermore, a Socialist candidate won a sixth of the total vote and made his best showing in middle-class neighborhoods. As this was several times greater than any third-party vote in a generation, anti-Italian sentiment may have motivated many of these Socialist votes. The 1947 election was the only one in the city's history before 1969 in which both major party candidates for mayor were Italians.

Richard Lee was the Democratic mayoralty candidate in every election from 1949 through 1967. A Catholic of mixed English, Scottish, and Irish descent, he emphasized his Irish side. When speaking at a Knights of Columbus function he used a brogue that was not noticeable in other circumstances.[21]

---

[20] President Roosevelt's 1940 "stab-in-the-back" speech and World War II are supposed to have cost him some Italian votes in 1940 and 1944. Whatever the extent of this loss, it seems to have been recouped in the 1948 election; see Lubell, *The Future of American Politics,* pp. 225–26. For differing assessments of the impact of Roosevelt's speech, see V. O. Key, Jr., *Public Opinion and American Democracy* (New York: Alfred A. Knopf, Inc., 1961), pp. 271–72; and William F. Whyte, *Street Corner Society,* enlarged edition (Chicago: University of Chicago Press, 1955), pp. 230–31.

[21] Fred Powledge, "The Flight from City Hall," *Harper's Magazine* (November 1969), 77.

(This masquerade evidently was persuasive. In a memorandum about Lee's public image, Louis Harris reported that many Irish survey respondents "take a proprietary interest in him as one of their own.") Lee unseated Celentano in 1953 after two unsuccessful attempts. Celentano did not run for mayor again and subsequently Lee defeated a series of Republican candidates, usually by large margins.

Although Celentano has not been a candidate for public office for 20 years, his impact on the political allegiance of New Haven's Italians seems to have endured. In a well-known article some years ago the late V. O. Key suggested

> the existence of a category of elections . . . in which the decisive results of the voting reveal a sharp alteration of the pre-existing cleavage within the electorate. Moreover . . . the realignment made manifest in the voting in such elections seems to persist for several succeeding elections.[22]

Key called such contests "critical elections." As the following data show, Celentano's several mayoralty campaigns were critical elections with respect to the voting behavior and partisan loyalties of the Italians in New Haven.

Since 1947 the Italian wards have been the most Republican ones in the city. Table 3-2 shows the citywide Democratic percentage of the vote in mayoralty elections from 1949 through 1961 and the deviations from this vote of wards with the heaviest concentrations of Italians, Irish, and Negroes, respectively. As the table indicates, even a Yankee Republican made his best showing in the Italian wards. (In fact, until 1965 the Italian tenth ward was the only one that Lee had never carried. By then, however, much of its Italian population had been displaced by an urban renewal project and the people who moved into the neighborhood were neither so Italian nor so Republican as the old residents.) Because the Italian wards are among the poorest in town, it seems clear that their Republican voting record is not due to economic factors, but reflects a relationship between Italian identity and Republican loyalty. It is an example of ethnic voting.

I defined "ethnic voting" as situations in which ethnic group membership is an important independent variable in voting behavior. I do not claim that ethnicity is the only independent variable. An Italian (Irish, Jewish, etc.) voter is also a Democrat or a Republican, a member of a particular social class, engaged in a particular occupation (or unemployed), a resident of a particular neighborhood in a particular city, and so on; and each of these other reference groups may have an influence on his voting decisions. One corollary of this point is that ethnic voting cannot be detected by examining the voting behavior of a given group in isolation from the rest of the electorate. That Irish wards are 75 percent Democratic means one thing if the

[22] V. O. Key, Jr., "A Theory of Critical Elections," *Journal of Politics,* 17 (February 1955), 4.

TABLE 3-2. Deviations from New Haven citywide Democratic vote by selected wards with concentrations of various ethnic groups—mayoralty elections, 1949–61

Year and Ethnicity of Republican Mayoralty Candidate[a]	Citywide Democratic Vote[b]	10th and 11th Wards (Italian)[c]	16th and 17th Wards (Irish)[d]	19th Ward (Negro)[e]
	(%)	(%)	(%)	(%)
1949—Italian	46.6	−21.9	+ 8.5	+ 7.9
1951—Italian	49.9	−24.3	+ 8.0	+ 4.3
1953—Italian	51.9	−27.3	+ 9.0	+ 8.3
1955—Italian	65.3	−21.3	+ 8.1	+13.4
1957—Yankee	64.8	−14.4	+11.5	+14.2
1959—Italian	61.8	−20.2	+11.0	+16.3
1961—Yankee	53.5	−10.7	+15.9	+24.3
1950 median family income	$3,301	$2,660 $2,318	$3,174 $3,280	$2,117

a In all these elections Lee was the Democratic candidate.

b Percentages are of the total vote cast for mayor.

c In 1960 population shifts caused by an urban renewal project began to change the composition of the tenth and eleventh wards. By 1963 a substantial fraction of the old residents had been replaced by newcomers, most of whom were neither Italians nor Republicans.

d Since about 1958 these wards have had an influx of Negroes. Data from Harris surveys in 1957 show an increase in Irish support for Lee through the fall of that year.

e Negroes constituted 72 percent of the nineteenth ward in 1950. Increasing Democratic majorities there may be due in part to continued growth of the ward's black population.

Sources: Voting returns for 1949–57 are from official sources; for 1959–61 from newspapers. Choice of wards was based on a combination of Census data and political lore. (Census tracts do not coincide with wards. The 1950 Census data were matched with wards, but this was an expensive process and was not repeated for the 1960 Census.) One of the three wards with the highest proportion of Italian-born residents, the twelfth, had a dissident Democratic organization and was excluded for this reason. Since the first sizable numbers of Irish came to New Haven 120 years ago, Census data on the birthplace of present ward residents are an unreliable index of Irish predominance. I followed the advice of New Haven politicians in choosing the sixteenth and seventeenth as the most Irish wards.

rest of the city is only 40 percent Democratic, and another (virtually nothing) if the rest of the city is 70 percent Democratic. Thus my use of deviations from citywide voting patterns, rather than simple percentages, is based on the assumption that ethnicity is not the only factor affecting voting in New Haven. It is an attempt to control for the effects of independent variables other than ethnicity.

Italian support for Republican candidates was so lopsided that the customary relationship between Democratic voting and foreign birth was reversed in New Haven. The ward-by-ward correlation coefficient (Pearson's r) between percentage of foreign-born residents and percentage of the vote for Democratic mayoralty candidates was negative for most of the elections from 1939 through the late 1950s.[23]

While Italian Republicanism is a product of local politics, it is also expressed in state and national elections. The ethnic voting that resulted from Italian solidarity in New Haven is now manifested in elections where "recognition" of Italians is not an issue. As Table 3-3 shows, the tenth ward has been consistently more Republican than the city as a whole in elections where neither candidate was Irish or Italian. For example, the Democratic incumbent governor barely carried the tenth ward in 1958, while in the Irish seventeenth ward, with a $600 higher median family income, he won by a three-to-one ratio.

TABLE 3-3. Democratic vote for state and national candidates in New Haven and in selected wards

	Citywide Vote	10th Ward (Italian)	17th Ward (Irish)
	(%)	(%)	(%)
1956 Presidential	45	34	51
1958 Gubernatorial[a]	69	52	75
1962 Senatorial[b]	65	52	75

[a] The candidates were the incumbent Democrat, Abraham A. Ribicoff, and Fred Zeller.
[b] The candidates were Ribicoff and Horace Seely-Brown.
Source: Official voting returns.

Most Italians not only vote for Republican candidates but consider themselves Republicans; their party identification was changed and fixed by Celentano's several campaigns. Table 3-4 shows the percentages of blue-collar workers and of Democrats in various New Haven ethnic groups. Little more than a third of the Italians were Democrats, although they were second only to blacks in proportion of manual workers.

These tables show why New Haven politicians customarily explain the outcome of elections in terms of nationality groups rather than social classes: the most important lines of division in the electorate are ethnic rather than

[23] Except for the 1941 and 1943 elections, when Celentano was not a candidate, and 1947, when both candidates were Italians. Needless to say, this negative correlation does not measure a decline in ethnic voting in New Haven. Interpreting it this way treats all nationality groups as a homogeneous mass instead of distinguishing among different groups. Thus, far from signifying a drop in ethnic voting, this correlation reflects the opposite: the mobilization of the Italian vote.

TABLE 3-4.   Percentage in working-class occupations and percentage Democrats of a sample of New Haven voters, by ethnic groups, 1959

	Manual Workers		Democrats	
Ethnic group	Percentage	Rank	Percentage	Rank
Negroes	76	1	57	2
Italian Catholics	61	2	37	5
European Catholics	58	3	48	4
European Protestants	35	4	16	6
American Protestants[a]	27	5	9	7
Irish Catholics	20	6	64	1
Jews	15	7	52	3

[a] "American" here means parents and grandparents born in the U.S.

Source: The table is based on 474 persons (of the sample of 525 voters) who could be identified by religion and by place of birth of themselves, parents, or grandparents. The percentages of Democrats are those who identified themselves as Democrats in response to the question: "Generally speaking, do you usually think of yourself as a Republican, a Democrat, or what?"

economic. In fact, ethnic cleavages wash out the usual relationships between socioeconomic status and partisan preference. When New Haven wards are correlated by median income and Republican vote in the 1959 mayoralty election, the coefficient is $-.02$. Similarly, there is no relationship between the proportion of manual workers in an ethnic group and the percentage of the group's members who consider themselves Democrats, as Table 3-4 shows. Ethnic voting explains the apparent anomaly that the Republican party's stronghold was in the poorest parts of town, while the Democrats drew their greatest support from the largely middle-class Jews and Irish as well as poor Negroes.[24] Since the two best examples of ethnic voting are the Republican inclinations of working-class Italians and the Democratic loyalty of white-collar Irishmen, the political correlates of ethnicity clearly are not mere reflections of underlying economic differences.

Two Theories of Ethnic Voting

It was once generally believed that dwindling immigration and increased prosperity and education would reduce the political role of ethnic conscious-

[24] Dahl has an interesting table comparing the black nineteenth ward to the Italian eleventh. The two wards have similarly low occupational, income, and educational levels, yet the nineteenth is overwhelmingly Democratic and the eleventh is very Republican. This is the reverse of their partisan affinities in 1930. See Dahl, *Who Governs?*, p. 57.

ness. According to this view ethnic voting is strongest during a group's earliest residence in this country and subsequently declines as the group's members make their way out of the working class. This might be called an "assimilation theory." It sees a direct relationship between the proportion of a nationality group in the working class and that group's political homogeneity. As more and more of the group join the middle class, its political unity is progressively eroded. Along with middle-class status, group members are said to acquire different political interests and to identify more with the majority society and less with their nationality group; in short, they become assimilated. The assimilation theory assumes that ethnic consciousness dwindles rapidly as members of an ethnic group attain middle-class status. Presumably the end of the process is reached when group members are as occupationally differentiated as the whole population. At this point they are politically indistinguishable from the general population, and ethnicity is no longer a factor in their voting behavior.[25]

Despite its failure to distinguish between acculturation and assimilation, this is a plausible argument, but it clearly does not fit the development of Italian bloc voting in New Haven. The New Haven case can be explained by a different interpretation which suggests that New Haven is not as anomalous as it may first appear to be. I will call this different view the "mobilization theory" of ethnic voting. It can best be explained by reexamining the assumptions of the assimilation theory.

The assimilation theory is based on the assumption that the strength of ethnic voting depends on the intensity of the individual's identification with his ethnic group.[26] The theory supposes that ethnic identification is never stronger than in the early years of residence in this country[27] and declines thereafter as the immigrants gain some measure of well-being. The assimilation theory overlooks another prerequisite to ethnic voting: no matter how salient an individual's ethnic identification may be, it will not influence his voting behavior unless he sees a connection between this identity and the

---

[25] The assimilation theory is clearly and systematically stated in *ibid.*, pp. 34–36.

[26] For data on group identification and voting behavior see Bernard R. Berelson, Paul F. Lazarsfeld, and William N. McPhee, *Voting* (Chicago: University of Chicago Press, 1954), pp. 67–72; and Campbell et al., *The American Voter*, Chap. 12.

[27] This may be a dubious assumption, although it is not crucial to my argument. There are indications that the previous identification of many immigrants was not with the old nation, but the old village or province. In this view, it was not until the immigrants saw that Americans classified them by nationality that they themselves developed some sense of belonging to a nationality group.

One could also argue that, whatever the locale of his previous identity, the immigrant's first impulse was to forget this old identity and become an American, but he was forced into ethnic consciousness by old-settler prejudice. Recurring nativist phenomena like Know-Nothingism, the Ku Klux Klan, Prohibition, and the end of mass immigration probably increased many ethnics' self-consciousness.

choice he makes on election day.[28] How does the ethnically conscious Irishman know which candidate (if any) is friendlier to the Irish? The implications of this question are worth further exploration.

Established politicians appealed to immigrants with tangible rewards and recognition. While one party may have been more vigorous in its efforts, both parties usually made some attempt to win their votes. These campaign efforts posed a twofold communication problem of coverage and persuasion: how could the party get its message to every ethnic voter, and how could it make the message credible? Only some ethnics would receive a job or favor, and only some would know of the recognition given by one party or the other, or, confusingly, by both. How did the ethnic know which party was friendlier to his people?

Direct personal contact with the individual voter is the most effective means of electioneering, particularly with unacculturated and unassimilated people. As Oscar Handlin observed, "the immigrant might sometimes read an article on such a matter in his newspaper but was less likely to be persuaded by any intrinsic ideas on the subject than by the character of the persuader."[29] Agents of political persuasion typically included various kinds of immigrant leaders whose services could often be bought, as well as overt party workers. There are no systematic data on precinct workers' activity at the peak of the immigrant era, but contemporary accounts suggest that, in at least some cities, few prospective voters could escape the attention of the political organizations.[30] At present the level of precinct work is much lower. In northern cities with over 100,000 population, fewer than 20 percent of the adults reported contact with a party worker in the 1956 election.[31] In New Haven, where both parties have very strong and active campaign organizations, 40 percent of the registered voters said that they had never been reached by a precinct worker.

Let us assume that precinct organizations were able to contact almost every potential voter 60 years ago. What if both parties sent workers around? What if both parties had won—or bought—the support of some ethnic leaders? No matter how fervently the ethnic might identify with his group,

[28] See the discussion of "political proximity" in Campbell et al., *The American Voter*, p. 311 (emphasis in the original): "Groups as perceived objects may be located according to their proximity to the world of politics . . . at the individual level: *as perception of proximity between the group and the world of politics becomes clearer, the susceptibility of the individual member to group inflence in political affairs increases.*"

[29] Oscar Handlin, *The Uprooted* (Boston: Little, Brown and Company, 1952), p. 211.

[30] See, for example, Robert A. Woods, "Traffic in Citizenship," in *Americans in Process,* ed. Robert A. Woods (Boston: Houghton Mifflin Company, 1903), pp. 154–56.

[31] Source: data from the University of Michigan Survey Research Center national election study, reported in Fred I. Greenstein, "The Changing Pattern of Urban Party Politics," *The Annals,* 353 (May 1964), 8–9.

the appropriate political expression of this identification might not be clear to him.

First-generation ethnic groups seldom had many political resources aside from their votes. Many of their members were illiterate; except for the Irish, many could not speak English. At this stage it was easiest for the parties to compete for ethnic votes, because the enticements least in demand by party activists were most suitable for the immigrants. As time passed children went to school, men prospered, and the ethnic group produced representatives with the organizational skills necessary for political leadership. These leaders made stronger demands on both parties and grew more skilled at pressing their claims. The level of bidding between the parties for ethnic support rose, for now the ethnics were asking for rewards that were both scarcer and more highly prized by the people already established in the party organizations. The ethnics' ambitions were naturally resisted by those who would be displaced. Because of this resistance and the time it took to develop political skills, a generation or more went by before members of a new nationality group found their way into local party positions of any visibility and influence. Summarizing the pattern of immigrant political access in Providence, Elmer E. Cornwell, Jr., reported that "members of a new group are not likely to appear as ward committeemen at all until some three decades after their first arrival in substantial numbers" in the city.[32] Lowi, who studied top-level municipal appointments, found that "the representation of a new minority in places of power occurs long after it has reached considerable size in the population and electorate."[33] Mr. Dooley may have provided the most succinct explanation for the fact that political plums do not drop easily into the hands of new groups: "Politics ain't beanbag."

Sooner or later some ethnics will occupy party positions. One party will nominate an ethnic for a minor office. Such positions are unimportant, and if the bid seems to pull votes, the other party will soon match the offer.[34] Most ethnic voters continue to have trouble figuring out the "right" ticket to vote for, since it is still not evident which party is friendlier. The ethnic group may be given some unity if it has an unquestioned leader who can deliver its vote to the party with which he has made a deal, but this does not

[32] Elmer E. Cornwell, Jr., "Party Absorption of Ethnic Groups: The Case of Providence, Rhode Island," *Social Forces*, 38 (March 1960), 209.

[33] Lowi, *At the Pleasure of the Mayor*, p. 39. See also Lubell, *The Future of American Politics* (p. 79): "The key to the political progress of any minority element in this country would seem to lie in just this success in developing its own middle class." Lubell does not discuss the importance of candidacy for major office, which is the key point in any group's mobilization.

[34] For an interesting description of this competitive bidding process see Huthmacher, *Massachusetts People and Politics*, pp. 119–26. His account makes clear that such strategies are dangerous because of the jealousies aroused when newer groups are recognized.

appear to have been a common phenomenon. Customarily ethnic groups were fragmented, with several leaders, each telling his constituents about his exclusive inside track to the political bigwigs.[35]

The day will come when an ethnic will win a party nomination for a major elective office.[36] When this happens the problem of coverage and persuasion will be solved for many of his fellow ethnics. They will all see his name on the ballot and many will take this as proof that the party that nominated him is the right party for them because it has given the most recognition to their group. The bigotry from others that often accompanies a "first" candidacy is likely to enhance the political relevance of ethnicity for the members of the candidate's group.

It seems plausible that an ethnic group will get such a major nomination when adversity forces one party or the other to appeal to new sources of support. This seems to have been the case with Celentano's nomination. In the late 1930s the New Haven Republicans were in dire straits. Some of the state party's leading figures had been implicated in the spectacular "Waterbury scandals." In 1937 the local party had suffered its most crushing loss in any mayoralty election in a century. Coming on the heels of Roosevelt's overwhelming reelection victory, Murphy's 1937 landslide must have suggested to the city's Republicans the need for a new campaign strategy; they had little more to lose. It was in this desperate situation that a member of New Haven's most numerous nationality group was first nominated for mayor.

Celentano was chosen for the 1939 nomination by leaders of the Republican organization. The party came close to beating Murphy with non-Italian candidates in 1941 and 1943. By the summer of 1945 Murphy's administration had suffered such a decline in popularity that Republicans were confident of winning the fall election. Preferring a Yankee who would be more dependent on their support, the party leaders did not want to give the nomination to Celentano and he had to wage a hard fight in ward primaries to win a majority at the nominating convention.

A half century earlier the Democrats had nominated Driscoll, their first Irish mayoralty candidate, under similar circumstances. The great controversy over free coinage of silver had split the party and given the 1897 mayoralty election to the Republicans. The defection of Gold Democrats may well have

[35] Before Celentano's nomination the Italian community in New Haven was fragmented, with no single leader or hero. See McConnell, *The Evolution of Social Class,* pp. 159–60.

[36] For present purposes "major office" may be defined as any public elective office which is the central prize in a political system: mayor, governor, perhaps United States senator, and, of course, the presidency. Candidacy for minor office does not seem to produce so much ethnic impact, at least where candidates for such positions appear on the ballot below more important ones. This is particularly true in states like Connecticut, where one can vote for an entire party slate with a single choice.

driven the Democratic leaders of that day to adopt a strategy of maximizing their party's appeal to the Irish.

The mobilization theory of ethnic voting states that *the strength of ethnic voting depends on both the intensity of ethnic identification and the level of ethnic relevance in the election. The most powerful and visible sign of ethnic political relevance is a fellow ethnic's name at the head of the ticket, evident to everyone who enters the voting booth. Middle-class status is a virtual pre-requisite for candidacy for major office; an ethnic group's development of sufficient political skill and influence to secure such a nomination also requires the development of a middle class. Therefore ethnic voting will be greatest when the ethnic group has produced a middle class, in the second and third generations, not in the first. Furthermore, the shifts in party identification resulting from this first major candidacy will persist beyond the election in which they occurred.*

This is not to say that the growth of a middle class past the point of mobilization will necessarily increase ethnic voting. Nor does the theory state that the resulting alignment is impervious to other political and social developments, or that more than one such shift cannot take place. But it does say that, in a given political arena and for a given nationality group, the development of voting solidarity is a product of leadership; that such leadership requires a middle class; and that such alignments are more durable than the political candidacies that produce them.

The mobilization theory seems more useful than the assimilation theory in explaining ethnic voting at the national level. Most members of ethnic groups in cities are, by and large, Democrats, and the conventional wisdom holds that this merely continues the traditional immigrant pattern. It is often forgotten, however, that the current ethnic Democratic affinity is a fairly recent development and that at the turn of the century, in the era of massive immigration and minimum assimilation, the partisan allegiances of urban nationality groups were in fact more evenly divided. Before the party realignment of 1896 there seems to have been some inclination toward Democratic allegiance among most immigrant groups, but the extent of this tendency is not at all clear.[37]

While data are not readily available to establish with any clarity the extent of immigrant Democratic propensities before the watershed election of 1896, there is no doubt that William Jennings Bryan's capture of the Democratic

---

[37] Seymour Martin Lipset argues that the Democratic party has always had a greater attraction for most immigrants, but concedes that the lack of systematic comparative data makes it "difficult to be precise concerning the relation between party support and religious and ethnic group memberships from the Civil War to the Smith campaign in 1928." See "Religion and Politics in the American Past and Present," in Lipset, *Revolution and Counterrevolution,* rev. Anchor ed. (Garden City, N.Y.: Doubleday & Company, Inc., 1970), p. 325.

nomination in that year drastically eroded the party's attraction for city dwellers. The agrarian nostalgia epitomized by Bryan may also account for the national Democratic party's reluctance to exploit the economic grievances of urban workers in the long generation before Al Smith's nomination in 1928. The results of Bryan's candidacy established the Republicans as the majority party in the urban, industrial, ethnic Northeast. To most observers in this period the Republicans seemed likely to be the party that would take the lead in dealing with the socioeconomic problems of modern America.[38] In his recent history of the social bases of the American parties, Everett Carll Ladd, Jr., concludes that

> ...in the first twenty-five years of this century the Republicans made gains among Catholic Americans because of their status as the party of industrialism and the strength of the Democrats' rural Protestant wing.... It was the Democracy, the only partisan survivor from the Rural Republic, which gave the most consistent major party representation to the claims of agricultural America....[39]

During the early part of the twentieth century, when the populations of many big northeastern cities were predominantly foreign stock, these cities were won by Republican presidential candidates as often as not. In 1920, shortly before the end of unrestricted immigration, the Republicans carried most cities with big immigrant populations. Warren G. Harding swept New York, Cleveland, Boston, Chicago, Philadelphia, Pittsburgh, and Detroit by an aggregate plurality of 1,330,000 votes. The Republicans did almost as well in 1924. But in 1928 the aggregate Democratic margin in these seven cities was 307,000 and since then they have gone Democratic in every election, usually by substantial margins.[40]

The switch in ethnic partisan loyalties seems to be a result of a nationwide mobilization of foreign stock voters by Al Smith's presidential campaign in 1928. As the first Catholic presidential candidate, Smith provided a far higher level of ethnic political relevance than had been attained on a national scale up to that time. His influence on national ethnic voting was analogous to Celentano's local impact in New Haven. Smith's candidacy seems to have been particularly important with respect to partisan alignments in southern New England. Connecticut, Massachusetts, and Rhode Island, with the

---

38 Everett Carll Ladd, Jr., *American Political Parties: Social Change and Political Response* (New York: W. W. Norton & Company, Inc., 1970), pp. 152–57.

39 *Ibid.*, pp. 166, 178.

40 Samuel J. Eldersveld, "The Influence of Metropolitan Party Pluralities in Presidential Elections Since 1920: A Study of Twelve Cities," *American Political Science Review*, 43 (December 1949), 1196. As late as the mid-1950s the Northeast included an appreciably larger proportion of Republicans and a smaller share of Democrats than any other region. See Campbell et al., *The American Voter*, p. 158.

nation's heaviest ethnic concentrations, were also, until 1928, stoutly Republican in state and national elections. Since then they have more often been in the Democratic column. Key's article on critical elections demonstrates this point more precisely. Cities which underwent a sharp and durable pro-Democratic change in 1928 had large Catholic, foreign-born populations; cities which reacted in the opposite way were largely Protestant and native-born. In short, the ethnic population of southern New England has become more Democratic as the duration of its residence in this country has increased.

The Persistence of Ethnic Voting

I have argued that the importance of ethnicity in voting decisions does not diminish steadily from an initial peak, but instead increases during at least the first two generations. What next? While the assimilation theory may be inadequate for the first development of ethnic voting, what about succeeding generations? Does the importance of ethnicity diminish rapidly with more general acculturation? Or does it persist as a major independent variable, although perhaps declining somewhat in importance? I think that the latter alternative is more plausible; it has also been less popular.[41] Ethnic politics is one of those features of American political life that are often said to be on the point of disappearing, but that somehow continue to flourish. Journalists and scholars began to recognize the persistence of ethnic voting in the early 1970s. This development did not reflect a revival of ethnic consciousness, but rediscovery of a phenomenon that in fact had never faded.

Depending on whether they are talking in public or private, politicians are of two minds about the persistence of ethnic politics. As *Newsweek* observed of the 1964 senatorial campaign between Robert F. Kennedy and Kenneth Keating, "From the stump, New York politicians righteously deplore any suggestions that their red-blooded American constituents might be influenced by bloc voting patterns; off the stump they find it hard to discuss strategy in any other terms."[42] John M. Bailey, leader of the Connecticut Democratic party and chairman of the Democratic National Committee from 1960 to 1968, has been franker than most politicians on this issue. Replying to a suggestion that the Democrats abolish their "Nationalities Division" (the Republicans have a similar unit for ethnic appeals), Bailey said:

> Such an operation will not be needed when American citizens of foreign descent are fully assimilated into political activities and other phases of civic activity in their communities. Until they are, I believe our Nationalities Division is performing a useful service.[43]

[41] For a well-known statement on the decline of ethnic voting, see Dahl, *Who Governs?*, pp. 34–36, 59–62.

[42] *Newsweek* (12 October 1964), 35.

[43] Quoted in Louis L. Gerson, *The Hyphenate in Recent American Politics and Diplomacy* (Lawrence, Kansas: University of Kansas Press, 1964), p. 306.

While direct evidence on trends in ethnic voting is scarce, there are some clues. The data in Table 3-2 indicate that ethnic voting did not decline in New Haven in the postwar period. Deviation from the citywide vote by Italian and Irish wards was as great in 1959 as in the 1940s. The smaller Italian deviation in 1961 may be a sign of declining ethnic salience, but it may also reflect Italian coolness to a Yankee Republican candidate or the first wave of population changes resulting from the Wooster Square Urban Renewal Project. At least in New Haven, social change does not seem to have reduced the political importance of national origins.

Since religious affiliation is analogous to ethnicity as an independent variable in voting behavior, information on Catholic voting patterns is useful where trend data on ethnic voting are unavailable. Catholics tend to be more Democratic than Protestants. This difference persists when income, education, or occupation is controlled—it is not simply an artifact of Protestants' higher social status.[44] Like ethnicity, the strength of religion as a variable in voting behavior is subject to considerable short-term variation. For example, Catholicism was much more important in the 1960 presidential election than in 1956.[45]

Catholic preference for the Democratic party does not seem to be a result of the disproportionately heavy representation of Catholics among more recent immigrants. When generation of American residence is controlled, Catholic–Protestant differences do not diminish significantly.[46]

The passage of time is thought to be associated with weakening ethnic consciousness not just through attenuation of immigrant memories, but because members of any given ethnic group will obtain better jobs and, after two or three generations, be represented among all occupational levels more or less in proportion to their numbers.[47] Occupational mobility is believed to reduce the importance of ethnicity in voting decisions for two reasons: (1) it will produce economic interests inconsistent with ethnic voting; and (2) the mobile individuals will come into contact with a broader, socially heterogeneous environment that will dilute ethnic salience.

---

[44] Berelson et al., *Voting,* pp. 61–71; Angus Campbell, Gerald Gurin, and Warren E. Miller, *The Voter Decides* (Evanston, Ill.: Row, Peterson, 1954), p. 71; Campbell et al., *The American Voter,* Chap. 12; Angus Campbell et al., *Elections and the Political Order* (New York: John Wiley and Sons, Inc., 1966), Chaps. 5, 6; Lipset, "Religion and Politics," pp. 337–42; and Scott Greer, "Catholic Voters and the Democratic Party," *Public Opinion Quarterly,* 25 (Winter 1961), 611–25.

[45] Campbell et al., *Elections and the Political Order,* Chaps. 5, 6; and Lipset, "Religion and Politics," p. 339.

[46] Campbell, Gurin, and Miller, *The Voter Decides,* p. 79; Greer, "Catholic Voters and the Democratic Party," p. 621; and Lipset, "Religion and Politics," pp. 351–52.

[47] All ethnic groups are not, of course, equally represented in major occupational categories. In addition to Table 3-4, see Glazer and Moynihan, *Beyond the Melting Pot,* pp. 317–24.

While direct evidence for these propositions is unavailable, findings on related subjects strongly suggest that increased prosperity will not necessarily reduce ethnic voting. Although education and better jobs may produce changes in political outlook, they do so from a "base point" of previous habits; they do not obliterate existing predispositions. Partisan differences between Protestants and Catholics are as great in the middle class as in the working class. Indeed, several studies have found that the gap between the two religious groups in party identification and voting choice is actually greater in the middle class.[48] It appears that, if anything, social mobility heightens the importance of religion as an independent variable. In New Haven, the Democratic loyalty of the Irish seems to have been virtually impervious to their improved social status. Although they are almost all in the middle class, their present support for the Democratic party is so pronounced that it could not have declined substantially as they went from manual labor to white-collar jobs.

Data from research on social mobility demonstrate the power of political inertia—the tendency for changes in political preference to lag behind shifts in social and economic status. Upward-mobile members of the middle class display political characteristics intermediate between those typical of their old and their new class positions. While more Republican than their parents, they are far less likely to be Republicans than are people born into the middle class.[49] It appears that most people whose party identifications are "inconsistent" with their class position are following parental political preferences.[50]

There is every reason to think that the great majority of voters inherit their partisan loyalties from their parents. Most report that their party is the same as their parents', and few say that they belong to the opposite

[48] Berelson et al., *Voting,* p. 65; and Lipset, "Religion and Politics," pp. 337–40. Pomper found that ethnic motivations in partisan elections were more evident in middle-class neighborhoods. See his "Ethnic and Group Voting," p. 95.

[49] James A. Barber, Jr., *Social Mobility and Political Behavior* (Chicago: Rand McNally & Co., 1970).

[50] Berelson et al., *Voting,* p. 90; and Arthur S. Goldberg, "Discerning a Causal Pattern Among Data on Voting Behavior," *American Political Science Review,* 60 (December 1966), 913–22.

For a discussion of the varying strength and characteristics of the relationship between social class and voting behavior, see Campbell et al., *The American Voter,* Chap. 13. The most important distinction drawn in this analysis is between objective social class, as measured by an indicator like occupation, and subjective class, the status position to which each individual assigns himself. When objectively middle-class people identify with the working class their political attitudes and behavior tend to resemble those of members of the working class. Perhaps middle-class ethnics are more likely to consider themselves working class than are middle-class Yankees. This suggests one mechanism that would modify the political impact of social mobility.

party.[51] Yet while parents seem to pass on their party affiliation, the same is not true of their opinions on political issues. Research on high school seniors reveals very weak relationships between the students' attitudes and those of their parents.[52]

Two easily compatible interpretations can be made of the findings on social mobility and intergenerational political patterns. One is that ethnic consciousness is transmitted by parents to children, reinforced by a host of associational factors. Despite social mobility, many people continue to view political phenomena and allegiances from a conscious ethnic perspective. Italians (Irish, Poles, and so on) may regard at least some political choices and loyalties differently from non-Italians. A second interpretation, stressing the habitual character of party identification, is based on "the functional autonomy of party loyalties, which maintains political differences even in periods when the perceived political relevance of the originating group is low."[53] In this view, the intergenerational transmission of partisan affiliations will long survive the disappearance of the causes of the affiliation.

Thus even when ethnic salience has faded, its political effects will remain. One of the most remarkable tendencies in political behavior is the persistence of party loyalties for generations after the reasons for their formation have become irrelevant to contemporary society. Gratitude to the "party of Lincoln" kept blacks in the Republican party until the New Deal. The dogged Republicanism of the impoverished mountaineers in eastern Tennessee reflects their ancestors' dissent from the majority Confederate feeling in that state. The best-known demonstration of this proposition is V. O. Key and Frank Munger's article on county voting patterns in Indiana. Some Indiana counties have been consistently Democratic while others, apparently identical economically, are Republican strongholds. The roots of these durable alignments seem to be the origins of the counties' first settlers—New England or the South: "If one plots on the map of Indiana clusters of underground railroad stations and points at which Union authorities had difficulties in drafting troops, he separates, on the whole, Republican and Democratic counties."[54]

---

[51] Robert D. Hess and Judith V. Torney, *The Development of Political Attitudes in Children,* Anchor ed. (Garden City, N.Y.: Doubleday & Company, Inc., 1968), p. 103; and M. Kent Jennings and Richard G. Niemi, "The Transmission of Political Values from Parent to Child," *American Political Science Review,* 62 (March 1968), 172–74.

[52] Jennings and Niemi, "The Transmission of Political Values from Parent to Child," pp. 174–76, 183.

[53] Campbell et al., *Elections and the Political Order,* p. 100.

[54] V. O. Key, Jr., and Frank Munger, "Social Determinism and Electoral Decision: The Case of Indiana," in *American Voting Behavior,* eds. Eugene Burdick and Arthur J. Brodbeck (New York: The Free Press, 1959), p. 457n.

Walter Dean Burnham argues "that there are also latent or suppressed cleavages which may endure for decades...[and] can suddenly be brought into clear view after they were thought to have become extinct,... and with little regard to intervening, even long-standing, partisan balances...." See his "American Voting Behavior and the 1964 Elec-

Key and Munger conclude that for many voters elections are merely "a reaffirmation of past decisions." It seems likely that this will be the legacy of ethnic politics: when national origins are forgotten, the political allegiances formed in the days of ethnic salience will be reflected in the partisan choices of many totally assimilated descendants of the old immigrants.

Variations in Ethnic Voting

The major theme of the previous section is that the importance of ethnicity as a factor in voting behavior may not be markedly reduced by changes in the economic fortunes of the individuals affected. This is not to say that perspectives formed in the first generations of American residence will persist forever. Ethnic consciousness is already faint in some parts of the country and for some ethnic groups.[55] Continuing education, regional migration, intermarriage, and assorted intergroup contacts are all likely to hasten assimilation.

I have not mentioned one particular contemporary trend of great consequence for ethnic salience. This chapter has discussed mainly those ethnics who have chosen to remain in the old core cities. Their neighborhoods tend to be ethnically homogeneous but economically diverse, with working-class and middle-class families intermingled. It is plausible that people who have decided to stay in such neighborhoods despite their financial ability to move away have stronger ethnic identifications, whether as a consequence or as a cause of continued proximity. What about the ethnics who have moved to the suburbs? They should be less ethnically conscious. Suburbs tend to be economically homogeneous and ethnically diverse; in these respects they are the reverse of the old city neighborhoods. It seems likely that many of these new suburbanites break off, either deliberately or by necessity, the interpersonal and institutional relationships that sustain and transmit ethnic consciousness. Since group solidarity is maintained by personal contact, geographical dispersion will dilute ethnic salience.[56] At the same time, how-

---

tion," *Midwest Journal of Political Science,* 12 (February 1968), 30. Thus, like mushroom spores, forgotten and inoperative ethnic perspectives may be reactivated by unanticipated future stimuli.

[55] On the other hand, at least one major nationality group, the Mexican-Americans, is still in an early stage of mobilization and appears just now to be developing greater solidarity and political self-consciousness.

[56] For data supporting this proposition see Stanley Lieberson, "The Impact of Residential Segregation on Ethnic Assimilation," *Social Forces,* 40 (October 1961), 52–57.

Ethnic groups may differ in their willingness to move from old urban habitats. Glazer and Moynihan report that Italians in New York, unlike some other groups, seem to remain, generation after generation, in the same areas where they first settled. The areas of Italian concentration in 1920 and 1960 were substantially the same except where land clearance had displaced people. See *Beyond the Melting Pot,* pp. 186–87.

ever, it will help retard the assimilation of the urban survivors by draining off those with the weakest ethnic identifications. Moreover, immigration continues to provide a diminished but by no means negligible fresh supply of first-generation Americans. Most of the 5.8 million people who entered the United States as immigrants between 1950 and 1970 probably settled in neighborhoods inhabited by earlier arrivals from their respective countries. These newcomers, of course, provide a fresh clientele for nationality group organizations as well as a reminder of ethnic identities.

The available evidence on this subject is not very extensive, but it does support the proposition that ethnic voting is stronger in the core cities than in the suburbs.[57] Robert A. Lorinskas and his associates showed a sample ballot with fictitious names to Polish respondents in Chicago and in an outlying area.[58] The Chicago respondents were considerably more likely to indicate a preference for candidates with Polish names. Evidently rural life, with its more heterogeneous social relationships and lack of ethnic institutions, reduced ethnic consciousness. Scott Greer found that in the St. Louis metropolitan area, with education and generation of American residence controlled, suburban Catholics were more likely than urban Catholics to defect to the Republicans, although they were also consistently more Democratic than suburban Protestants of similar social class.[59]

One hypothesis of the mobilization theory is that ethnic voting increases in electoral situations where ethnicity is more relevant to the choices the voter makes. *Ethnic voting is more likely when other cues to guide the voter's decision are weak or absent.* If we think of ethnic consciousness as an example of reference group behavior, then we should expect that its impact on political choices will depend not only on the politically-relevant salience of ethnicity, but also on the prominence of other reference groups in the individual's affective configuration.

The most important political reference group is the party.[60] Ethnicity will be more strongly associated with voting behavior in nonpartisan elections, where voters cannot rely on the party label and where party identification does not compete with ethnic consciousness. This proposition is confirmed

[57] Parenti took issue with this proposition when it was stated in my earlier article, offering as evidence for his position a variety of anecdotes and citations to the effect that suburban members of ethnic groups sometimes cluster together physically and socially. This is difficult to dispute, but it is beside the point, which is whether ethnic consciousness is *as strong* in the suburbs as in the old core-city neighborhoods. As before (see note 11), his mistake is to assume that all symbols of ethnic distinctiveness, ranging from pizza parlors to chapters of Hadassah, are of equal weight as indices of nonassimilation.

[58] Lorinskas et al., "The Persistence of Ethnic Voting in Urban and Rural Areas."

[59] Greer, "Catholic Voters and the Democratic Party," p. 621.

[60] For a summary of the literature on party identification, see Benjamin I. Page and Raymond E. Wolfinger, "Party Identification," in *Readings in American Political Behavior,* 2nd ed., ed. Raymond E. Wolfinger (Englewood Cliffs, N.J.: Prentice-Hall, Inc., 1970), pp. 289–99.

by Pomper's study of Newark: the tendency for ethnically distinctive wards to support a fellow ethnic was far more prevalent in nonpartisan municipal elections than in state legislative elections where party labels were on the ballot. Similarly, Lorinskas and his associates reported that their respondents' preferences for fictitious Polish-named candidates were considerably greater when no partisan designations appeared on the sample ballot.[61] While party identification impedes the electoral expression of ethnic solidarity, it also stabilizes and prolongs ethnic voting by providing a vehicle for continuing perception of ethnic relevance. Celentano's candidacy won Italian support not only for him, but also for the Republican party in subsequent elections, because his association with the party led Italians to think that it gave them more recognition. Once established on this basis, their party identification continued.

It also appears that ethnic voting may decline when substantive issues capture attention and provide alternative cues (although doubtless such events may be interpreted to some extent in an ethnically-relevant frame of reference, along the lines of the famous joke, "The Elephant and the Jewish Question"). Such events are difficult to detect at the individual level, but when some great substantive issue dominates political perspectives, as the Depression did in the 1930s, there seems to be a decline in ethnic voting. This, then, may explain the pro-Democratic voting of New Haven Italians in the 1932 and 1936 presidential elections: unemployment and the New Deal offset the Republican sympathies elicited by the Ullman brothers' efforts.[62] It should be emphasized that ethnicity is only one independent variable; it does not cancel other influences on the voting decision.

Some Consequences of Ethnic Politics

One important social consequence of ethnic political appeals is suggested by much of the foregoing: structuring politics as ethnic conflict heightens and maintains separate nationality group perspectives and so retards assimilation of immigrants and their descendants into American society. This may seem so obvious as to be not worth saying, but in fact many writers have said that ethnic politics has *aided* the immigrants' assimilation.[63] It is difficult to sup-

---

[61] Pomper, "Ethnic and Group Voting"; and Lorinskas et al., "The Persistence of Ethnic Voting in Urban and Rural Areas."

It seems probable that the form of the ballot will affect responses to an ethnic running for a lesser office, in that a party column ballot would discourage split-ticket voting. See note 22, Chap. 2.

[62] See note 19; and Dahl, *Who Governs?*, pp. 49–51.

[63] See, for example, Dahl, *Who Governs?*, pp. 33, 59; and Elmer E. Cornwell, Jr., "Bosses, Machines, and Ethnic Groups," *The Annals,* 353 (May 1964), 31–34. Dahl seems to be of two minds on this point, as he also says that by treating ethnic distinctions as fundamental, politicians made them fundamental (p. 54).

port this proposition, for just as the feasibility of class-based political appeals depends on class consciousness, so ethnic politics depends on ethnic salience. The proposition that ethnic politics hastens assimilation is analogous to saying that class consciousness would be minimized if politicians treated class distinctions as fundamental, if individuals made their voting decisions by calculating class advantage, and if public jobs were filled on the basis of appointees' class origins.

As I argued earlier, ethnic voting is a product of both ethnic salience and an "ethnic stimulus." Where voters are mindful of nationality group differences, such stimuli are inherent in the ethnicities of candidates for elective office. But the kinds of appeals made by candidates also contribute mightily not only to the persistence of ethnic voting, but to maintenance of ethnic consciousness generally. Like everyone else, politicians tend toward inertia in the ways they approach their problems. Accustomed to categorizing the electorate ethnically and devising campaign strategies in the same terms, they are likely to continue doing so. There is a self-confirming quality to politicians' uses of ethnic frames of reference: their continuing appeals to nationality group chauvinism contribute to the persistence of that chauvinism. Consider the entertaining and instructive controversy that arose in 1965 over the "Vinland map," a document that, if genuine, implied that Christopher Columbus, far from being an intrepid explorer of unknown oceans, in fact made use of a Norse map of the Atlantic approaches to America. Shortly before Columbus Day, the Yale library announced that the Vinland map's authenticity had been verified. The chairman of one Columbus Day parade said that the whole business was just a "Communist plot." It fell to John V. Lindsay, running for mayor of New York, to make the classic comment. Perhaps reflecting on the fact that New York City contained over 860,000 Italians and only 37,000 Norwegians, Lindsay observed, "Saying that Columbus did not discover America is as silly as saying that DiMaggio doesn't know anything about baseball, or that Toscanini and Caruso were not great musicians."[64]

It is significant, of course, that Lindsay, a widely-heralded apostle of "the new politics," felt called on to make this remark. Since continued enjoyment of the benefits of ethnic politics depends on the maintenance of ethnic consciousness, it would appear that politicians will continue to use strategies that reinforce their constituents' consciousness of their national origins. Where assimilation of immigrants is most advanced, on the Pacific Coast rather than in the Northeast, political appeals to ethnic identifications are far less common and conspicuous. In the polyglot state of California, most politicians consider such appeals both unethical and ineffective.[65] In short,

---

64 The population figures and quotations are from *Time* (22 October 1965), 25B.

65 See James Q. Wilson and Harold R. Wilde, "The Urban Mood," *Commentary* (October 1969), 59.

it is unlikely that political calculations and strategies emphasizing ethnic identity will hasten the submergence of that identity.

These continued politically-related reminders of nationality group membership have had a profound impact on the character and direction of American politics. Ethnic politics diverted the immigrants from radical or even vigorously progressive political action. It continues to have the same effect on many of their children and grandchildren.

Most immigrants, particularly in the cities of the Northeast (the focus of discussion throughout this chapter), were poor, uneducated, ignorant of American customs and language, and victims of religious bigotry. They were exploited by businessmen and scorned by old settlers of all classes. They lived in miserable housing and experienced massive social disorganization. The cultural traditions, authority patterns, forms of social interaction, and personal habits formed in centuries of European village life were incompatible with American industrial cities, yet the immigrants were discouraged from identifying with the majority society and did not approach an equal share of its prosperity. As they had come to America seeking the Promised Land of prosperity and equality, their treatment in the slums of the Northeast must have been bitterly disillusioning. Such deprivation, alienation, and disappointment are supposed to be fertile soil for radical political appeals, yet the immigrants and their descendants have been largely unresponsive to protest ideologies and class-conscious political organizations.

While American radical parties have been small, have their supporters been mostly ethnics? It appears that the immigrant proportion of radical party membership varied enormously from party to party and from one decade to the next. Most members of the late nineteenth century Socialist Labor party were born abroad. On the other hand, the Socialist party was largely native until the First World War; in 1912 its presidential ticket ran far better in the West than in the East. The subsequent immigrant majority among the Socialists appears to have been a result more of antiwar sentiment arising from old-country politics than of socioeconomic ideology. (Indeed, it is likely that more immigrants came to this country as radicals than became Socialists or Communists after exposure to the miseries of tenement life.) During the 1920s the Communist party was overwhelmingly foreign-born, but the most heavily represented nationality groups were among the smallest immigrant communities in the United States: Finns, Lithuanians, and the like. At no time during this period did the party have as many as 20,000 members. In the 1930s and '40s, when its membership rose to more than three times this figure, the proportion of foreign stock declined steeply. The essential point, however, is that at no time was more than a tiny fraction of any nationality group (with the possible exception of the Finns) attracted to radical parties.[66]

[66] This paragraph is based on Nathan Glazer, *The Social Basis of American Communism* (New York: Harcourt Brace Jovanovich, Inc., 1961), Chaps. 1–3.

Lack of interest in radical politics has characterized virtually all elements in American society. Many of the familiar explanations of this phenomenon were least relevant to urban immigrants. The prospect of homesteading on the frontier was never important to them. (Considerable numbers of immigrants were pioneers, homesteaders, miners, cowboys, and so on. These people had very different experiences from the immigrants with whom I am concerned here—those who settled in the industrial cities of the Northeast and Great Lakes states.) Given their intrinsic handicaps and the prevailing prejudices, they did not have the same chances of making money as other groups in industrial cities. Even the *myth* of social mobility must have been vitiated for many of them.

Such explanations do not go to the heart of the matter. The immigrants not only eschewed radical politics, but before the New Deal they were not notably strong supporters of milder forms of political protest. As Marcus Lee Hansen concluded, "the weight of immigrant political influence has historically been felt on the side of conservatism."[67] Their votes often were cast predominantly against Populist and Progressive candidates, who represented the main expressions of moderate social protest between the Civil War and the New Deal. True enough, urban workers generally found little specific appeal either in Populist demands for cheap money, easy credit, low tariffs, and railroad regulation; or in Progressive remedies like trust busting and civil service reform. Yet these movements represented the principal expressions of protest against an onerous status quo. The ethnics in their tenements had more grievances than the agrarian Populists and the genteel middle-class Progressives, yet they neither made common cause with these movements nor generated any consistent reformist demands of their own.[68] Later, after the Democratic swing produced by Al Smith's candidacy, they supported the New Deal, but their political leaders were far from the most progressive element in that coalition, and since then they have not lived up to their reputation as radical urban masses.

Democratic politicians from ethnic milieux have often been relatively conservative. The Irish, being the first to take over from the Yankees, were also the first to reveal how mild their substantive policy demands were. As Glazer and Moynihan put it, "the Irish did not know what to do with power once they got it. . . . The main thrust of Irish political activity has always been moderate or conservative in New York."[69] In part, this is because for

67 Marcus Lee Hansen, *The Immigrant in American History,* ed. Arthur M. Schlesinger (New York: Harper & Row, Publishers, 1964), p. 82.

68 Both Populism and Progressivism displayed a good deal of hostility to immigrants. The fundamentalist, dry Populists saw in the Catholic, wet immigrants a cosmopolitan threat to their lost Arcadia. The Progessives kept their distance from the ethnics, whom they considered the raw material of civic depravity.

69 Glazer and Moynihan, *Beyond the Melting Pot,* pp. 229, 264.

many Irishmen loyalty to the Democratic party is part of their heritage. A joke from New Haven City Hall makes this point nicely: Two Irish ladies are sitting on a front porch gossiping. One asks the other, "Did you hear that Paddy Murphy turned Republican?" The second lady gasps, "Why, that can't be true; I saw him at mass just last Sunday." For those who are Democrats "because they are Irish" (or Italian, Polish, or the like), attitudes on issues may not be as liberal as one would expect if ethnicity were not the source of their party identification. While direct evidence for this proposition is unavailable, there is an analogy with Catholics, whose disproportionate affiliation with the Democratic party is not accompanied by concomitant differences from Protestants on attitudes toward public policy.[70] And as we have seen, party loyalties often persist long after the originating issue has become irrelevant.

Oscar Handlin has suggested that the source of the ethnics' conservatism was their largely Catholic peasant origins.[71] This argument is given added plausibility by the fact that of all the immigrants, Jews were by far the most liberal. But Handlin's argument is less persuasive when one remembers that millions of these same Catholic peasants also migrated to European industrial cities, where their religious heritage has not kept them from enthusiastic support of communist and socialist parties.

A more tenable proposition is that *ethnic politics tended to make economic and social issues less relevant in party competition by emphasizing nationality group membership rather than social class.*[72]

Irrespective of the effect of politics, ethnic salience inhibited the development of class consciousness. For one thing, working-class solidarity was impeded by the existence of a Yankee proletariat, who could hate the immigrants for their wage-cutting competition as well as for their strange habits. Thus, native workers were among the strongest supporters of the Know-Nothing party and the post–Civil War American Protective Association.[73] Until the present generation labor unions generally were opposed to unrestricted immigration because it increased the supply of labor and thus depressed wages. Hostilities among different nationality groups—sometimes fomented by employers—also contributed to worker disunity.[74]

70 Robert A. Dahl, "The American Oppositions: Affirmation and Denial," in *Readings in American Political Behavior,* ed. Wolfinger, pp. 420–21. The present discussion assumes a weak relationship between issue attitudes and party identification under any circumstances (see Page and Wolfinger, "Party Identification," pp. 294–95).

71 Handlin, *The Uprooted,* pp. 217–18.

72 Dahl has developed this point at some length. See *Who Governs?,* Chaps. 4, 5.

73 See Higham, *Strangers in the Land,* p. 181.

74 W. Lloyd Warner and J. O. Low, *The Social System of the Modern Factory* (New Haven: Yale University Press, 1947); and James B. McKee, "Status and Power in the Industrial Community: A Comment on Drucker's Thesis," *American Journal of Sociology,* 58 (January 1953), 364–70.

Class-based political appeals were also made more difficult by immigrant economic achievements. As some members of a nationality group became prosperous, their success gave vicarious pleasure and self-respect to their fellows by showing that, given half a chance, Irishmen (or Italians or Poles) could do as well as Yankees. But once this happened, working-class solidarity meant turning one's back on fellow ethnics who had made good. To put it more formally, class consciousness and ethnic salience posed the problem of conflicting reference groups, a problem that increased in scope with the size of a nationality group's middle class. Apparently the ethnic group often was a more satisfying and tolerable reference group than membership in the proletariat. Ethnic separatism even appeared in the American Communist party, which was organized in nationality group federations in the 1920s.[75]

The ways the immigrants were introduced to American politics also encouraged the submergence of class-based political demands. One typical agent of immigrant politicization was bosses of casual labor gangs on public works projects, who owed their positions to their ability to deliver their gangs' votes and their vote-getting ability to their command of jobs. Another important political linkage came through the heads of nationality group associations, usually men who had been among the first to make some money.[76] In either case these leaders' economic interests seldom coincided with those of their fellow ethnics. Local party organizations often could effectively create spokesmen by the judicious use of appointments, contracts, and other favors. These men, of course, were even less likely to make serious demands on behalf of their constituents.

Such leaders, with one foot in the outer world, rarely led their deprived followers in search of social justice. William F. Whyte described this double allegiance in his famous study of the Italian community in Boston's North End:

> He [the candidate] tries to convince his listeners that he is so well qualified by education and experience that he will be able to meet the "big shots" of politics on an even footing, but at the same time he points out that he is still of the common people and will be loyal to them no matter how far he advances. The most important qualification a politician can claim is that he has been and will always be loyal to his old friends, to his class, and to his race.... They seek to show people that they have such good connections that they will be able to do favors, win or lose.[77]

Electoral competition is often described abstractly as a process in which candidates offer inducements to individuals in hopes of winning their votes.

---

[75] Theodore Draper, *The Roots of American Communism* (New York: The Viking Press, Inc., 1957), pp. 392–93.

[76] For a description of these prototypical patterns, see Handlin, *The Uprooted,* Chaps. 7, 8.

[77] Whyte, *Street Corner Society,* p. 232. Here "race" means nationality group.

The nature of the inducements varies with the salient reference group memberships of the voters. Where social class consciousness is high, politicians compete by offering substantive programs to satisfy class-based policy demands. Group success in class-oriented politics is expanded educational, welfare, and recreation programs, progressive taxation, liberal labor laws, and so on. In Dahl's terms these are "indivisible benefits," in that they "cannot be or ordinarily are not allocated by dividing the benefits piecemeal and allocating various pieces to specific individuals."[78]

In ethnic politics politicians try to get votes by offering jobs, favors, and more symbolic gratifications on the basis of ethnicity. "Divisible" benefits— patronage, favors, and the like—go to leaders, generally in exchange for delivering blocs of votes. Group success in ethnic politics is "recognition," an indivisible, intangible, and highly important emotion. "Recognition" is pride that members of a nationality group feel when one of their own gets a political reward that reflects honor on the entire group, or when the group is glorified by public homage to a hero, custom, or event. In contrast to its importance in ethnic politics, recognition is an inappropriate strategy in class politics, for no one thinks of appointees in terms of their social status, and this is seldom an important criterion in evaluating candidates.[79] Appointees and candidates symbolize ethnic groups, not social classes. Most public positions, whether elective or appointive, require qualifications that tend to eliminate most proletarians from consideration.

By shaping political competition so that voters' expectations center on recognition, ethnic strategies divert working-class political expectations away from substantive policy questions. If the political demands of a worker who happens to be of Italian descent are satisfied by putting an Italian on the ticket or by gilding a statue of Columbus, why should a party try to win his vote by promising better schools? Nationality group leaders all too often can fulfill their followers' expectations through the "recognition" that is bestowed on them rather than by means of tangible policy results. This process makes it easier to buy off ethnic leaders as they become visible, since their followers will appreciate the "recognition."

Glazer and Moynihan offer a different interpretation of the relationship between ethnic politics and substantive social class interests. They argue that since any nationality group has distinctive economic characteristics, ethnic consciousness is a shorthand way of referring to social class that avoids American distaste for the idea of class distinctions. Thus ethnic politics is a way of having class politics without offending egalitarian myths.[80] This thesis leaves some important loose ends unexplained: Why is the myth of classlessness more sacrosanct than the myth of the melting pot? Why do

[78] Dahl, *Who Governs?*, p. 52.

[79] Lowi, *At the Pleasure of the Mayor*, p. 51.

[80] Glazer and Moynihan, *Beyond the Melting Pot*, pp. 17, 301–2.

groups with similar economic characteristics often cast their votes in very different ways?[81] But most fundamentally, Glazer and Moynihan are wrong in arguing that ethnic and class lines coincide. Any single ethnic group is now so occupationally differentiated that its members have diverse economic interests. While different groups may predominate in some occupations, all groups are distributed across the economic spectrum. For example, while many shopkeepers are Jews, most Jews are not shopkeepers.[82]

Instead of being a surrogate for economic differences, ethnicity provides a set of cleavages that cut across class lines. As Dahl points out in his study of political opposition in America, these competing identifications help prevent American society from splitting into two neatly polarized socioeconomic divisions and thus militate against widespread and fundamental conflict.[83] Depending on the particular group in question, "ethnic identity may either amplify the effects of class and status on voting, . . . [or] depress the significance of class and status by providing a crosscutting cleavage, as in the case of middle-class Catholics. . . ."[84] But looking beyond voting behavior to the inducements offered voters, and thus at the role of party competition as a means of stimulating substantive government programs, one can see that ethnic politics will *uniformly* tend to minimize working-class interests as a basis of political demands. Even when ethnicity and status coincide, the effect of ethnic political appeals is not to heighten the political thrust of class-based demands, but to muffle and divert them. Thus, irrespective of the lines of coincidence between ethnicity and class, ethnic consciousness retards the political expression of class-based interests.

All political issues are not class-based, of course, and thus it is possible that other sorts of substantive issues are implicated in ethnic politics. It appears, however, that nationality groups have rarely been interest groups as far as substantive policies are concerned; they seldom make policy demands on the basis of their ethnicity. One of the most important exceptions to this generalization is in foreign policy, although most activity in this field seems to be a thing of the past. Central European immigrants played a role in the creation of the Succession States at the end of the First World War, both by pressuring the Wilson administration and by financing national independence movements. Similarly, America was (and is) a source of refuge, money, and weapons for the Sinn Fein and the Irish Republican Army. Since 1922 legislators from Boston and other centers of Irish strength have taken the lead in introducing congressional resolutions deploring the partition of Ireland. It is said that German, Italian, and Irish voters registered their

---

81 See note 24.

82 See note 47.

83 Dahl, "The American Oppositions," pp. 418–21.

84 *Ibid.*, p. 420.

disapproval of Franklin D. Roosevelt's foreign policies by voting Republican, and that their fathers did the same in response to Woodrow Wilson's diplomacy. The major remaining example of consequential ethnic impact on foreign policy seems to be the relation between Jews and official policy toward Israel. President Truman's speedy recognition of Israel and continuing American military and diplomatic aid reflect, apart from strategic considerations, the influence of Jewish votes and campaign contributions. Jewish concern for Israel is also manifested in more frivolous activities, such as ritual attempts by congressmen from Jewish constituencies to end American aid to Egypt.

Israel aside, ethnic interest in foreign affairs seems to focus mainly on symbolic questions of no real importance. Politicians are eager to give voice to such concern, since in doing so they can cater to their constituents' emotions without worrying that they may have any influence on the actual conduct of foreign policy. For example, in the election year of 1964 Senator Kenneth Keating of New York demanded, in a speech on the Senate floor, that both the State Department and the United Nations intervene in the affairs of the Soviet Union, for "if pressure is not promptly brought to bear, there will not be an adequate supply of matzoth for Passover" for Russian Jews.[85] The *Congressional Record* is a particularly rich source of proof that millions of Americans continue to be emotionally involved in past and distant political events, and that their senators and representatives are willing to indulge that interest. Memorials to national heroes, triumphs, and calamities can be found in almost every issue of the *Record,* with speeches of praise, lamentation, and denunciation reaching crescendoes during the most important anniversaries.

In domestic politics most issues of public policy that might be called "purely ethnic" generally are substantively trivial, although the passions they arouse can be anything but trivial. Some years ago in New York City there was a notable squabble over the color of the center line to be painted on Fifth Avenue for the Columbus Day Parade, with different colors advocated by, among others, representatives of Italian and Spanish loyalties. One of the parties to the dispute grumbled that the city traffic commissioner had handled the affair in a "very provincial, very parochial and out-of-town manner." The commissioner, a newcomer to East Coast ethnic politics, remarked "I can't understand why a city as great as New York should get so excited over a line in the street."[86]

An institutionalized manifestation of ethnic consciousness is the Italian-American Civil Rights League, which succeeded in mobilizing almost 100,000 people at one demonstration, raised nearly $500,000 at a single benefit dinner,

---

[85] *Congressional Record* (daily edition), 19 March 1964, p. 5533.

[86] Charles West, "Symbolic Rewards and Interest Groups," in *American Governmental Institutions,* eds. Aaron Wildavsky and Nelson W. Polsby (Chicago: Rand McNally & Co., 1968), pp. 472–73.

and boasted 45,000 members in 1971. The principal organizer and leading spirit of the IACRL was Joseph Colombo, Sr., widely thought to be a prominent figure in the Mafia. For all its numerical and monetary strength, the IACRL's accomplishments seem to be largely symbolic: the attorney general of the United States ordered the Justice Department and the Federal Bureau of Investigation to stop using terms like *Mafia,* and various other public officials have followed suit. Indeed, the incidental relationship (real or imaginary, as one likes) between Italo-Americans in general and the Colombo family in particular and organized crime seems to have precipitated the formation of the IACRL, which first attracted public attention by picketing the New York office of the FBI and distributing a leaflet claiming, among other things, that "MANY ITALIAN-AMERICANS HAVE SUFFERED TRAVESTIES THAT MAKE DREYFUSS [sic] LOOK LIKE A SISSY."[87]

There is a range of serious political concerns in which ethnicity is not explicitly involved in the substance of the issue, but where the ethnic composition of one party at interest gives controversies an incidental ethnic coloration. These issues generally are those in which the Catholic Church has an interest, such as birth control, education, and censorship.[88] Disputes on these topics often pit Protestants and Jews against Irishmen and Italians. National origins are not the basis of the claims made by either side, but where religion and ethnicity coincide, some of the contestants may think

[87] For a description of the IARCL, see *Newsweek* (5 April 1971), 22–23. The quotation about Dreyfus is taken from a leaflet distributed by the pickets at the FBI office. The IARCL seems to have gone into an eclipse since late 1971, when Colombo was paralyzed in a gangland shooting.

[88] There was a great deal of gossip among Protestants and Jews in New Haven about the pervasive political influence of the Catholic Church. (Dahl, Polsby, and I once lunched with two Yale sociologists who dwelt alternately on the local political omnipotence of the Roman Catholic Church and of Yankee bankers—without the slightest sign of self-consciousness. A few months later one of the sociologists had a new candidate for "the real power" in New Haven: the Mafia.) Despite considerable vague talk about Catholic Church influence in the public school system, we could find no concrete evidence on this subject—other than the unsurprising fact that most teachers and administrators were Catholics.

There was some Catholic Church involvement in the 1957 municipal election campaign, in which Mayor Lee, a Catholic, was opposed by Mrs. Edith Valet Cook, a Republican state legislator. Mrs. Cook, also a Catholic, had voted against her church's position on bills about birth control and state aid for parochial school buses. During the campaign local priests read from their pulpits a letter from the archbishop instructing their congregations to remember how their representatives in Hartford had voted on the bus issue. At a Communion breakfast for city policemen and firemen that fall, the priest attacked Mrs. Cook for her votes on both issues, and praised Lee.

We found no evidence that the Catholic Church participated in any decisions on urban renewal, except that a priest who was a member of a neighborhood committee was influential in vetoing a proposed outdoor café in the Wooster Square Renewal Project. As is usually the case in local politics, officials treated *any* church with great delicacy and generosity (see Chapter 9).

that their ethnic group as such is under attack. Controversies of this sort often involve important and deeply emotional issues and can be exceptionally bitter. Another major issue area of this type has to do with land use: where to locate a freeway or housing project, where new schools should be built, and so on. Such issues, which are among the most important and common in local politics, generally define interest geographically. Because of the ethnic homogeneity of many neighborhoods, land-use issues often take on an ethnic overtone. If a block of houses to be razed for a new school is inhabited largely by, say, Poles, it is not uncommon for the protesting residents to see in the plan evidence of a pervasive anti-Polish sentiment on the part of "them" at city hall. The increasing importance of urban renewal, Model Cities programs, and assorted other government interventions in land-use decisions is likely to mean a new source of ethnic political involvement, since projects of this kind usually have a limited and specific geographical focus.

These caveats aside, it appears that political appeals invoking ethnic consciousness tend to substitute emotional for tangible gratifications. The tangible benefits of this political style exist largely in the form of patronage and government contracts, which, desirable as they may be, inherently cannot be bestowed on more than a small minority. In those regions where ethnic politics flourishes, most government and party leaders are members of nationality groups.[89] This is clearly the case in New Haven. In 1959 members of the three major groups, Italians, Irish, and Jews, comprised 57 percent of the city's registered voters, but accounted for 82 percent of all elected municipal officials, as Table 3-5 shows. Similar patterns are found in most of the Northeast and the industrial areas of the Midwest. This has led many writers to acclaim the virtues of the political system as a channel of occupational mobility for the immigrants. This is true, but only with respect to government jobs and other patronage. Political success has not been accompanied by parallel achievements in other areas; politics has not been the path to equality for the ethnics in social and economic life. As Glazer and Moynihan observe, "Instead of profiting by their success in the all-but-despised roles of ward heeler and policeman, the Irish seem to have been trapped by it."[90] New Haven's three major ethnic groups (at the time of our study, and for many years before that) are overrepresented in political positions and drastically underrepresented in the city's social and economic elites, as indicated in Table 3-5. In fact, with the exception of Jews in the economic elite, these two nonpolitical leadership groups are almost wholly Yankee. Being at the pinnacle of a city's social or economic life is a demanding test of upward

[89] This is truer for the Democrats, but the Republican party is by no means a Yankee monopoly. See, for example, Cornwell, "Party Absorption of Ethnic Groups"; and Lockard, *New England State Politics,* Chap. 11.

[90] Glazer and Moynihan, *Beyond the Melting Pot,* p. 256.

mobility, since only a few people can find room at the top. Clearly New Haven's middle class is not a Yankee monopoly. The point of this comparison is that the attainment of political prominence by ethnics should not be interpreted as evidence that they have been equally mobile outside politics. The direct benefits of political success cannot be shared by masses of people—there are only so many jobs and contracts to pass around.

TABLE 3-5.   Representation of ethnic groups among registered voters, major elected officials, economic elite, and social elite in New Haven, 1959

Ethnic Group	Registered Voters	Major Elected Officialsa	Economic Elite	Social Elite
Italian	31%	34%	4%	1%
Irish	11	29	4	2
Jewish	15	19	20	1
Other	43	17	72	96
	100%	99%	100%	100%
N	525	41	123	198

a Includes aldermen and citywide officials, almost all of whom were Democrats. Because most defeated Republican candidates for these offices were ethnically similar to their respective victors, a change in regime would not greatly change the ethnic proportions among officials.

It has been argued that the achievement by ethnics of political dominance provides tangible benefits to members of ethnic groups because their interests are looked after by "their" officials. It does not appear that group ties are much of a guarantee in this respect, given the issueless quality of ethnic politics. Such appointments are often made because it is expected that voters will be content with the "recognition" and will not press substantive demands as well. In the useful typology developed by Hanna F. Pitkin, "recognition" can be considered "symbolic representation [which] seems to rest on emotional affective, irrational psychological responses rather than on rationally justifiable criteria." This kind of representation "need have little or nothing to do with...enacting laws desired by the people."[91] The appointees or nominees often owe their positions to "outside" selection, with the implicit understanding that they will dissuade their fellow ethnics from making policy demands. Thus while patronage does indeed further the social mobility of those who actually obtain jobs, it buys off leaders who might otherwise mobilize demands for substantive welfare policies. In this connection it is

[91] Hanna F. Pitkin, *The Concept of Representation* (Berkeley and Los Angeles: University of California Press, 1967), pp. 100, 106.

noteworthy that liberal municipal administrations in New York City have had more Protestant and Jewish high officials than the status quo regimes, which make more upper-level appointments from the poorer Catholic ethnic groups.[92]

In short, the consequences of ethnic politics are monetary rewards for a few and symbolic gratification for the rest. This political style has advantages for politicians and for the rich. When the working classes, whose prime political resource is their vote, cast their ballots on the basis of ethnicity rather than policy considerations, they deprive themselves of their best means of seeking political remedies. On the other hand, the better-off, who can use money, skill, and organizational relationships as resources, are not so handicapped by such diversion of political attention. In fact, they benefit from it. Recognition might affront Yankee businessmen, but it is far less offensive than economic reform. The public jobs that are the payoffs in ethnic politics were not coveted by the wealthy. Thus as long as vast numbers of new jobs were not created, the main losers were the former jobholders. While the eventual political ascendance of the ethnics deprived Yankees of one arena of power and status, this loss was made easier to bear by the restraint of the new rulers. For their part, politicians found ethnic strategies convenient because they elicited less opposition from conservatives than would have resulted if substantive appeals had been widely employed. To the extent that they could exclude economic and social issues from political competition by diverting attention to ethnic questions, there was less pressure on them to make indivisible policy commitments to win votes. Racist appeals in the South generally are calculated to have had the same effect: taking poor white voters' minds off more tangible grievances.[93]

While ethnic politics generally has been a conservative force in the United States, there is one important sense in which this political style can be used for liberal ends. The ability to appeal to national loyalties is a political resource, similar to such other resources as money, social status, and legal skill. Ethnic-oriented political systems sometimes produce politicians who use nationality group solidarity to build support for innovative policies. Such leaders as Lee, Al Smith, and Fiorello LaGuardia have tried to build reputations for achievement and electoral popularity as a strategy for proceeding to a higher political level. We have seen already, as in the case of Irish support for Lee, how ethnic loyalties *can* be manipulated in the service of liberal policies. While the incentive system of ethnic politics is more congenial to

[92] Lowi, *At the Pleasure of the Mayor,* pp. 197–98.

[93] V. O. Key, Jr., *Southern Politics* (New York: Alfred A. Knopf, Inc., 1949), especially Chap. 7. For a more recent and immediate description of the diversionary merits of race-baiting, see A. J. Liebling, *The Earl of Louisiana* (New York: Balantine Books, Inc., 1961).

maintenance of the status quo, it can, when controlled by innovators, become a means for progress.

Up to this point, my assessment of ethnic politics has been a negative verdict on two counts, fulfillment of substantive policy needs and reduction of nationality group consciousness. On a third criterion, however, the classic ethnic political style does not come off so badly: it helped articulate the immigrants to American society, not by ending separate ethnic identity, but by giving them a stake in that society. This integration-without-assimilation came about in two ways. First, the strategy of "recognition" brought ethnic leaders into the political mainstream and rewarded them for staying there. Second, the fact that some ethnics attained public office showed their fellows that immigrants could succeed in the United States. In terms of tangible benefits, "recognition" may have been a poor substitute for progressive legislation, but it did demonstrate that immigrants could share in the honor and glory of political success. From all accounts, this is a powerfully compelling symbolic achievement for members of any minority group. "Recognition" established a sort of political Horatio Alger myth, thus fulfilling one promise of the American dream.

The main consequence of this development has been protection of the American political system from a potentially disastrous loss of popular support. Whatever its deficiencies, nationality group "recognition" militated against rejection of predominant political values by disadvantaged ethnic groups. In other countries fundamental challenges to the legitimacy of the prevailing political system have often drawn their strongest support from members of disadvantaged minorities.[94] Extremist movements of both left and right commonly are led by arrivistes whose newly attained wealth or education has not been matched by commensurate political and social status.[95] Such men readily question the legitimacy of a political order that denies them the respect to which they consider themselves entitled. Exploited and rejected minority groups led by embittered nouveaux riches can pose a formidable challenge to political stability.

The successful second- and third-generation members of American ethnic groups surely could have played such a leadership role, since they generally were not socially accepted by the established Yankee society. Joseph Kennedy is an extreme example of this type. Yet, as Kennedy's life demonstrates, such men could find distinction in politics. Not only did political success prevent the possible development of a politically alienated counterelite, but the vicarious pleasure drawn from their leaders' "recognition" demonstrated to the masses of ethnics that power and glory were not denied to them. In view of

[94] For a recent survey of evidence on this point, see Andrew C. Janos, "Ethnicity, Communism, and Political Change in Eastern Europe," *World Politics*, 23 (April 1971), 493–521.

[95] Lipset, *Revolution and Counterrevolution*, Chaps. 5, 6.

the politically disruptive role played by alienated minorities in other countries (and perhaps also in the future by blacks in the United States), this
is no mean achievement.

In early 1965, when I wrote the final draft of the earlier published version
of this discussion, this third consequence of ethnic politics, while noteworthy,
did not seem as important as it did at the beginning of the 1970s. The
legitimacy of the major institutions and procedures of American politics was
not under widespread attack.[96] "Working within the system" was taken for
granted in 1965; by the end of the decade it was a widely debated alternative
tactic that many writers scorned. Doubts about the value and the survival
of representative government, open political competition, elections, civil
liberties, and peaceful resolution of political disputes were not expressed by
numerous politicians and political writers in 1965. By the 1970s such doubts
were commonplace.

In that earlier time I took it for granted that political stability was assured,
with little more thought than goes into the assumption that tap water is safe
to drink. Now, of course, it is easy enough to see that the legitimacy of
American political values, institutions, and processes is not permanently
established. With the benefit of this hindsight, I think now that a somewhat
more ambivalent verdict about the consequences of ethnic politics is in order:
whatever its faults, this style did protect the existing political system from
disruptive influences that could have had exceedingly violent outcomes.

These conclusions about ethnic politics have a good deal of relevance to
current trends in black political action. When the slogan "black power"
became popular, it was often interpreted to mean that blacks wanted only
what European immigrants had gotten from politics, and thus that black
power was just like Irish or Italian power.[97] While this is by no means the
only definition of *black power*, it is a fairly common one. For example, summarizing her interviews with 84 Negro political leaders in New York, Joyce
Gelb reported that "what the black politician means by his use of the term
'Black Power' is the kind of ethnic organization utilized by other groups in
our political system."[98]

[96] It is important to distinguish between (a) the current onslaught on "the system,"
which represents a cyclic change of some magnitude, and (b) opposition to prevailing
political values by people who do not actively question and attack the procedural status
quo. Opposition of the second type was widespread even before the turmoil of the late
1960s. See Herbert McClosky, "Consensus and Ideology in American Politics," *American
Political Science Review*, 58 (June 1964), 361–79.

[97] This comparison was often made by Stokely Carmichael, who coined the term
black power, and it also appears in the book he quickly coauthored. See Stokely Carmichael and Charles V. Hamilton, *Black Power*, Vintage ed. (New York: Random House,
Inc., 1967), pp. 44–45, 51.

[98] Joyce Gelb, "Blacks, Blocs and Ballots: The Relevance of Party Politics to the
Negro," *Polity*, 3 (Fall 1970), 55.

In fact, this is a fairly accurate characterization of one major aspect of black politics. Increasingly, the aims of many black leaders are strongly reminiscent of nationality group politics. Since the passage of civil rights legislation ended officially sanctioned discrimination and produced a change in the direction of black political action, one major emphasis in black goals has been the same sorts of patronage and recognition sought by nationality groups. Government is thus seen essentially as a source of divisible spoils, not an instrument to formulate policies for greater social and economic equality for the masses.

This phenomenon can be seen with particular clarity in the statements of black student groups in universities, which have been labeled a major manifestation of "black power."[99] As many readers of this book may have noticed, the "demands" made by black student unions are concerned almost entirely with the academic equivalent of patronage: more admissions, jobs, and financial aid for blacks; black control of funds going to blacks; autonomous black studies departments; and so on. Conspicuously missing from these demands is a concern that the intellectual resources of universities be mobilized to attack the problems afflicting masses of blacks: unemployment, dope addiction, substandard housing, inadequate schools, and the like. In practice, "black studies" is not a way to help black communities, but a vehicle for jobs for a few and "recognition" for all. Like the government, the university becomes a source of patronage, not a means by which the welfare of the black community as a whole can be improved. Thus controversies about black studies programs usually seem to be about control over appointments, with black power advocates claiming that they rather than university authorities should name and remove teachers and administrators. In one such struggle on the Berkeley campus of the University of California, a spokesman for this viewpoint argued that "we of the black community have a right to receive our share of the University's goods and services."[100]

Scholarly comments about this aspect of black power are also similar to the conventional wisdom about nationality groups: "At the very least, party politics provides a route of upward mobility for New York Negroes, permitting them entry to the middle class; the politicians, in turn, provide increased employment opportunities for other Negroes in government."[101] This is, of course, the familiar "channel of mobility" line followed by writers celebrating the advantages of ethnic politics. The argument is unquestionably true, as far as it goes. The parties (and other sources of racially determined spoils) do indeed offer the beneficiaries a route to prestigious and relatively secure positions, just as they have for the European immigrants.

[99] Charles V. Hamilton, "An Advocate of Black Power Defines It," *New York Times Magazine* (14 April 1968), 23.

[100] Quoted in the *Daily Californian,* 2 October 1972, p. 8.

[101] Gelb, "Blacks, Blocs and Ballots," p. 63.

There is no doubt that this kind of black power is good for black politicians. Just as Irish power was a way to unite middle-class and working-class Irishmen, so black power provides causes which make it easier for working-class and middle-class blacks to agree. Black power, then, is a means of maintaining black political unity by ignoring diversities of interest among blacks in different social classes. Because black politicians, like Polish or Irish politicians, rely heavily on ethnic solidarity, it is in their interests to maintain the unity of their ethnic coalition, and an emphasis on recognition and symbolic gratification is an important way to do this. Such a strategy is also less costly. It is a good deal cheaper and easier to gratify Negroes by closing the schools on Martin Luther King's birthday than it is to devise and enact programs to make the schools adequate educational institutions for poor black children.

To the extent that black power is a continuation of ethnic politics, it is a way to bring black leaders into the political mainstream by giving them a stake in the system. It will divert black demands for social justice into the same concern for patronage and recognition that absorbed nationality groups. Thus this form of black power will have important benefits for whites.

The integration of the immigrants into the American political system was accomplished by processes that sacrificed social justice to emotional gratifications. The parallel to the contemporary racial situation is clear: the paths to black acceptance of the legitimacy of "white man's rules" and to attainment of genuine racial equality may be very different. Reduction of black alienation may well take place independently of, if not at the cost of, social justice for blacks.

4 *machine politics*

Citizen participation in politics is often thought to reflect public spirit, ideological enthusiasm, or a desire to influence governmental decisions on a particular issue. Some people in New Haven were moved to political activity by such civic-minded concerns. For hundreds of the city's other residents, however, participation in politics was a matter not of issues or civic duty, but of bread and butter. The law permitted and custom provided a variety of material rewards for political activity. Service to the party or influential connections were prerequisites for appointment to hundreds of municipal jobs, and the placement of government contracts was often affected by political considerations. Both parties had what journalists like to call "old-fashioned machines," of the sort whose disappearance has been heralded for most of the twentieth century.

This chapter begins with a description of party organization and activity in New Haven. Analysis of this behavior in the light of contemporary literature suggests new perspectives on machine politics. The latter part of the chapter goes beyond New Haven, to the conditions associated with the growth and alleged decline of machine politics, the consequences of this political style, and a reformulation of customary definitions in this field.[1]

Since the subject of machine politics is so heavily freighted with moral judgments, it may be well to begin with several disclaimers. Few of the practices I will describe are illegal in Connecticut; if those examples of illegality were removed, the effect on New Haven political life would be trivial. Compared to the conditions described early in this century by muckrakers like Lincoln Steffens,[2] there is little dishonesty in New Haven government. There is no plundering of the treasury, nor is outright bribery common or important. As the famous Tammany sage George Washington Plunkitt is supposed to have said, "With the grand opportunities all around for the man

---

[1] Portions of this chapter were published in "Why Political Machines Have Not Withered Away and Other Revisionist Thoughts," *Journal of Politics,* 34 (May 1972), 365–98.

[2] *The Autobiography of Lincoln Steffens* (New York: Harcourt Brace Jovanovich, Inc., 1931).

with a political pull, there's no excuse for stealin' a cent."[3] Leading political figures can make money by taking advantage of business opportunities through inside information, or from business given to them by government favoritism or a desire on the part of customers to be well regarded by the party organization. We could find no indications that the underworld had a hand in local politics; the closest thing to racketeering in New Haven seemed to be penny ante numbers operators, who were harried and arrested by the police.[4]

There is no reason to think that the style of organization politics found in New Haven is particularly atypical of American cities. In some parts of the country, notably the West, it is uncommon; elsewhere, particularly in the Northeast and some of the industrial cities of the Great Lakes states, it is very much in evidence.

The Sources of Political Participation

There is an election for high stakes in New Haven every fall. In odd-numbered years the greatest prize—control of city hall—is at stake. State officials come up for election every other even-numbered year. Finally, and least important in the local scheme of things, there are presidential and congressional elections. The state and local campaigns produce the most intense electioneering by the city's political parties. The Democrats, who enjoyed an unprecedented period of success in both city and state for almost 20 years, had active organizations in all of the city's 33 (now 30) wards. The Republicans were generally supposed to have fallen on hard times, yet by the standards of many American cities, they were not so badly off. A disconsolate Republican leader complained during an interview that even in a strong ward his party could count on only 14 or 15 "really good, active workers."

More than a third of our sample of registered voters (37 percent) reported that they had engaged in at least one type of campaign activity other than voting—giving money, belonging to a club, attending any kind of political function, or doing "any other work for one of the parties or candidates." Twenty-six percent had given money and 23 percent said that they went to "political meetings, rallies, dinners, or things like that." These figures indicate a high level of political action, particularly for a relatively uneducated

[3] William L. Riordan, *Plunkitt of Tammany Hall* (New York: McClure, Phillips & Co., 1905), p. 60.

[4] In his generally favorable review of *Who Governs?* in *Commentary* (May 1962), Lewis A. Coser deplored Dahl's failure to discuss the underworld (p. 455): "Given our general knowledge of the manifold ways in which criminal elements have been able to influence political decisions in municipal affairs, is it likely that in New Haven such elements have no influence worth discussing?" Likely or not, criminal elements had no influence in the decisions described in this book.

population, but unfortunately they cannot be compared with normative data from nationwide studies of citizen participation. The same questions were asked in our survey and in the University of Michigan Survey Research Center national election studies, but the SRC questions ask only about the election under study, while our questions were phrased in the present tense and so had no specific time reference. The SRC data for two successive campaigns reveal considerable circulation into and out of the ranks of the active; about half the people who participated in the 1956 election were not active in 1960, and vice versa.[5]

Other evidence suggests that electioneering in New Haven is much above the national norm. Fully 60 percent of our respondents were contacted by one party or the other (or both parties) during campaigns, compared to only 10 percent of the national adult population who were canvassed during the 1956 presidential race.[6] In most New Haven wards precinct workers do a good deal more than call on potential voters. They record every resident's preference and on election day track down all favorably inclined persons who have not yet voted. In addition to a good deal of highly effective personal persuasion (see Chapter 11), both parties follow the usual practices of offering transportation to the polls, baby-sitting services, and so on. In some wards party workers were able to accompany the voter into the booth. This was possible only where the other party's poll watchers had been bought off, which was another reason for high "election day expenses." (The day before the 1957 election I saw the chairman of one of the parties, accompanied by bodyguards, carrying two bulging satchels. That evening in a bar one of his companions asked if he were ready for the election on the morrow and the chairman jovially replied by pulling back his jacket to reveal enormous wads of currency in his pockets.) In the late 1950s voters in at least one ward were paid to go to the polls. One important consequence of all this activity was a very high turnout. As reported in Chapter 2, 82 percent of New Haven's registered voters went to the polls in municipal elections in the 1950s, almost double the 47 percent rate for all comparable cities.

Such a high level of precinct work requires money and organization. After the 1957 mayoralty campaign the Republicans officially reported election day

[5] These data are from Carolyn Ban, "The Party Activist, 1956–68" (unpublished doctoral dissertation, Stanford University, 1973).

For what it is worth, 20 percent of the registered voters in the 1960 SRC study who lived outside the South did some kind of campaign task other than voting. (These data were obtained from the Inter-University Consortium for Political Research, with the assistance of Mrs. Maxene S. Perlmutter of the Consortium staff. Responsibility for interpreting and computing the data is solely mine.)

[6] The source for the figure on the 1956 campaign is Angus Campbell et al., *The American Voter* (John Wiley & Sons, Inc., 1960), p. 427. Here again the SRC question was phrased in the past tense and ours in the present tense, but the difference between 10 percent and 60 percent cannot be completely discounted because of the change in tense.

expenses of $10,700 and the Democrats listed $18,000.[7] In both parties the going rate of pay for drivers and poll watchers was $25. A good deal of money is given to ward chairmen at election time, ostensibly for hiring workers. It is understood that some portion of this money is compensation for the chairman's efforts, although many chairmen have other political sources of income, as I will show. Campaign expenditures for other purposes also seem to be very heavy in New Haven, although there are no reliable systematic data with which they can be compared because of the general weakness of laws requiring disclosure of campaign finances. In 1957 the Democrats spent about $13,000 on newspaper advertising and a similar amount on radio and television time. Some other expenses include printing and mailing costs, research, campaign staffs (although the ruling party makes liberal use of public employees for this purpose), and entertainment. Mayor Lee, for instance, customarily financed a lavish reception staged by Negro ministers in a church. On the Sunday before election day in 1957 the Democrats brought to town a former heavyweight boxing champion of Italian descent, Rocky Marciano; a prominent Broadway singer, Martha Wright; and Senator John F. Kennedy. The latter two celebrities paid their own way, but Marciano cost $1,000 for one day's appearances. Altogether the Democrats reported campaign expenditures of $75,000 for that election and the Republicans said that they spent $43,000; two years later Democratic spending was up to $100,000.

A good deal of the money and labor sustaining these elaborate campaigns is drawn from governmental employment and purchasing practices. Before looking directly at the sources of the money, it may be well to describe these practices. A new administration taking over New Haven's city hall had at its immediate disposal about 75 politically-appointed, non–civil service, policy-making positions; about 300 lower-level patronage jobs; and about the same number of appointments to various citizen boards and commissions. The latter positions varied in importance; some of them included stipends ranging up to $25 per meeting or several hundred dollars a year, and they all conferred "recognition." Summer employment was an additional source of patronage. Every year the city hired 100 to 150 young men for unskilled labor at outside jobs, mainly with the Parks, Public Works, and Parking Departments. These positions were a more flexible type of incentive because they were recurring and revocable, and required no qualification but reasonable physical health and political connections. In recognition of the city's religious composition, as well as the sentiments of most of its political leaders, students in Catholic

---

[7] The Democratic report on expenses and contributors was summarized in the *New Haven Journal-Courier*, 4 December 1957. The Republican report was in the same paper on 6 December 1957. These are probably accurate reports of the total *amount* of money spent and collected, although, as indicated in the text, they are not always correct about sources and purposes.

seminaries were usually given summer jobs automatically. Beyond this, the jobs were given out so as to reward the maximum number of political supporters. Regardless of political considerations, the jobs were also used to help students working their way through college and as a step toward rehabilitating juvenile delinquents. In the winter, snowstorms were a bonanza for the ruling party organization, as snow removal required the immediate attention of hundreds of men and dozens of pieces of equipment. It is estimated that two bad blizzards in the winter of 1958 cost the city $70,000.

The county sheriff appointed several dozen deputies, usually with the advice of the party leaders who sponsored his nomination. A hundred or more jobs in field offices of the state government were filled with the help of the relevant party's leaders. The City Court, appointed by the governor with the advice of the local dispensers of his patronage, had room for two or three dozen deserving people.

The New Haven Probate Court had a 1958 payroll of more than $67,000,[8] but its real political significance was the Judge of Probate's power to appoint appraisers and trustees of estates. Except in difficult cases, little technical knowledge was necessary for appraising, for which the fee was $1 per $1,000 of appraised worth. Probate patronage was sometimes used to meet specific party needs. Some years ago a losing candidate's campaign fund showed a considerable deficit. One of his political associates was given a number of lucrative appraiserships, and a good portion of the fees was used to make up the deficit. The probate judge during our research, a popular Democrat, had been supported for election by Republicans and in return gave Republican attorneys a share of the ample rewards at his disposal.

Businessmen with close relations with one party or the other—notably building contractors—would sometimes hire a man at the request of an influential politician. This "private patronage" was of some importance, but I do not know how much. As we will see, some businesses were anxious to stay on good terms with city hall.

The desideratum for all these appointments was campaign work for the party, contributions, control of a bloc of votes, or influential friends or relatives. In calculating the relative advantages of different possible appointments, leaders took into consideration such matters as to whom each man owed allegiance, what ethnic group would be "recognized" by his appointment, and whose aspirations could be satisfied or frustrated. In promotions and transfers the mayor would be concerned with the influence of each man's "sponsors" and how strongly they were committed to their candidates, clearing with one or two other ranking politicians, and making sure that in the aggregate the appointees were ethnically balanced. Ethnicity is an important factor

8 Source: *New Haven Evening Register,* October 12, 1959, p. 3. There have been recurring efforts to reform the probate court system, which was considered vulnerable to abuses of various kinds.

in such matters; each group presses for maximum representation and the top leaders strive for balance.[9]

Many patronage jobs did not require much skill. (Where they did, the rationalization was the organization politician's familiar and not unpersuasive rhetorical question, "If two people can do the job and one of them is a friend of yours, why not take the friend?") Generally, the importance of political considerations in personnel decisions varied inversely with the level of training required for the job. For this reason, as well as for its dealings with contractors, the Public Works Department was usually the most important source of mass patronage.

While most city employees would not lose their jobs if the regime were turned out of office, their political affiliations and activities were relevant to their chances of advancement. In the police and fire departments, for instance, promotions were based on grades, which were determined 55 percent by a written examination and 45 percent by "efficiency ratings" by the commissioners. These ratings gave ample room for political pull. Each fireman and policeman had his "sponsors," politically relevant individuals whose support was important.

The extent of political connections among city employees varied from group to group. In addition, some groups participated in politics on the basis of their group identity, for example, the policemen made demands as policemen. They and the firemen were probably the most consistently and intensely politicized groups of city employees. The members of each department belong to unions that cooperate in collective bargaining with the municipal administration; in addition to working for the party, they also work for themselves. In contrast, the school teachers ordinarily did not engage in political action *as teachers,* although on occasion they participated actively in politics as a group, notably in 1945, when they played an important part in deposing the incumbent mayor. While teachers had to be qualified to be hired, political and ethnic considerations were important in promotions and transfers. (The political involvements of city employees are discussed further in Chapter 11.)

Public employment is only part of the rewards of machine politics, and it is relatively unimportant for the more important people in the party organizations. Some top-ranking public posts, especially those that could be held by lawyers on a part-time basis, went to leaders. But patronage includes government contracts, court appointments, and other spoils. Much of the city's business is done with men active in organization politics, particularly in such "political" businesses as printing, building and playground supplies, construction, and insurance. The city charter required that any municipal contract budgeted for more than $1,000 be put out for bids, but this provision

---

[9] For an excellent discussion of the different uses of patronage, see James Q. Wilson, "The Economy of Patronage," *Journal of Political Economy,* 69 (August 1961), 369–80.

was often ignored until 1960. In any event, the method of competitive bidding does not seriously increase the uncertainty of the outcome if the administration wants a certain bidder to win.[10] As in many places, it was commonplace for city officials to "advise" a prime contractor which local subcontractors, suppliers, and insurance agencies he should patronize. Given the numerous ways city hall could make a contractor's path smoother or rougher, such hints were usually accepted, if not anticipated.

Furthermore, many government purchases were for one reason or another exempt from competitive bidding. Decisions about these items could be made politically without formality. The prices of some things, like insurance, are fixed. Thus the city's insurance business could be (and was) given to politically deserving agencies. Other kinds of services, particularly those supplied by professional men, are inherently unsuited to competitive bidding. Architects, for instance, are not chosen by cost. Indeed, some professional societies forbid price competition by their members.

Even when a supplier of goods or services was not active in local politics (except as a campaign contributor), political considerations affected his selection. For a long time, for example, it was customary to hire only local architects for municipal construction projects. The Lee administration, seeking greater aesthetic distinction in its numerous building endeavors, began to look to out-of-town architects, but with the understanding that a local man would still get a fee of one-half percent as a "consulting architect."

The income that some party leaders received directly from the public treasury was dwarfed by trade from people who hoped to do business with the city or wanted friendly treatment at city hall, and thus sought to ingratiate themselves with the influential. A contractor hoping to build a new school would be likely to do business with John M. Golden, a powerful Democratic leader who was senior partner in a bond and insurance agency. Similar considerations apply to attorneys with part-time government jobs; their real rewards came from clients who wanted to maximize their chances of favorable treatment in the courts or by public agencies. In addition to all these rewards for political influence, some people could profit from inside information to which they had access, for example, about the right-of-way for a new freeway.

Some politicians, having attained influence in their party, then go into business in a line that permits them to make money from their political power. (Such a change in occupation is not necessary for lawyers.) Money thus earned is useful politically, of course, but the essential causal connection should not be confused: in these cases political power is not the result of the man's income, but the cause of it. One implication of this pattern is that

10 Commenting on my dissertation in 1965, Mayor Lee denied that political considerations affected the placement of government contracts. This is not consistent with information we gathered during our study, nor with the large campaign contributions made by these contractors.

studies of the occupations of political leaders should be interpreted with caution.

Control of city or state government, then, provides either local party with a formidable array of resources that by law, custom, and public acceptance can be exploited for money and labor. Party leaders reward the faithful and useful by giving them jobs, and then assess these jobholders for sizable contributions to pay the costs of maintaining power. Holders of the 75 or so policy-making jobs were assessed 5 percent of their annual salary in municipal election years and 3 percent in other years. A few of these officials were later reimbursed quietly from funds given by people who wanted their contributions to be confidential. At the lower patronage levels employees and board members gave (in the 1950s) from $25 to $100 or more. Mayor Lee was assessed $5,000 by the party in the same year, and in fact gave much more than this, raising the money in turn from his "personal" contributors.

Politically-appointed employees also were expected to contribute their time during campaigns. The following letter illustrates this, and also something of the style of machine politics in New Haven. It was written by Arthur T. Barbieri, at the time both municipal Director of Public Works and chairman of the Democratic Town Committee, and addressed to "27th Ward Workers":

> I have been to two of the 27th Ward meetings at the Italian-American Club on James Street during the past couple of weeks. It has been extremely disappointing to me to observe that most of the people who are working in the Public Works Department and who belong to the 27th Democratic Ward Organization were among the missing at these meetings.
>
> All of you came to me prior to your employment telling me of your great political activity in behalf of the Democratic party. It appears as though that activity ceased when you received your share of the so-called "spoils."
>
> Please be informed that there is to be a meeting at the same Italian-American Club on James Street on Wednesday evening at 8:00 P.M. I intend to be there and check off the names of those present.
>
> It is my intention in the future to deal with those who are missing, as I feel they should be dealt with.
>
> This letter is a general letter sent to all Public Works employees of the 27th Ward. It may include some of you who have attended every meeting. If you are in that category, please disregard the above statement. If you are not, please take heed.

This remarkable letter was written in 1956. A copy fell into the hands of the Republican candidate for mayor in 1957. She publicized it widely and reproduced it in a full-page advertisement in the *Register*.[11] The Democratic

---

[11] *New Haven Sunday Register,* 4 November 1957, p. 7.

alderman from the twenty-seventh ward admitted that employees of the Public Works Department made up a "large part" of his ward organization.[12] Yet no public outcry followed the letter's publication, which made no discernible impression on New Haven voters, who shortly thereafter gave the mayor the largest electoral margin in the history of New Haven.

Men who sell to the city, or who may want favors from it, are another important source of funds. The party in control of city hall—and often the opposition party as well—sends letters of solicitation at election time to all concerns that have done business with the city. If the local party has helped someone get business with the state government, this too is a basis for claiming a contribution. Usually a mutual assumption that a contribution will be made was implicit in public contractual relationships in New Haven, but firms doing a good deal of business with the city were approached directly and vigorously. During one mayoralty campaign a party official asked a businessman reluctant to contribute: "Look, you son of a bitch, do you want a snow removal contract or don't you?" Construction is a particularly political business. Not only is there a good deal of public construction, but the local government exercises numerous regulatory powers over building. Some big contractors tend to be associated with one party or another, but generally they make substantial contributions to both parties and favor the one in office: "We always contribute to both parties. It's a form of insurance. We don't know who is going to win."

Tax assessment procedures in New Haven were reformed a few years ago, but before that time they were used to produce contributions. One prominent politician associated with the Republican administration deposed in 1953 explained to Dahl and me how the system worked: If a taxpayer felt his assessment was being set too high he could protest to the Board of Tax Review, whose members could be expected to be responsive to city hall. If he were dissatisfied with the board's finding, the taxpayer could take his case to court, but in most cases the amounts involved were too small and the procedures too expensive and forbidding for litigation. Even substantial firms might find litigation so expensive and uncertain that they preferred to compromise with the city. In fact, this commonly happened and court fights on assessments were rare. The customary procedure when a concern judged its assessment excessive was to seek a negotiated settlement with the city before the figure was formally recorded. One concomitant of a satisfactory settlement often was a subsequent campaign contribution, usually made by an executive who was duly given an equivalent bonus. The quid pro quo was not demanded by the city; rather there was a tacit understanding that it was part of the settlement. Needless to say, this practice gave the regime opportunities that had to be grasped with delicacy and a nice sense of the

12 *New Haven Journal-Courier*, 30 October 1957, p. 3.

possible, else the taxpayer would find it worth his while to sue rather than settle. This happened in 1959, when the city lost such a court appeal and had to refund over $200,000 to a large manufacturer.

It is difficult to report with any completeness what amounts of money were involved in these various categories of campaign contributions because specific information is elusive. Many contributors do not wish their generosity to become known. This was notably true of many of the men in less "political" lines of business whose support Mayor Lee won by the end of his first term. Yet the law requires that campaign contributions be listed. With bashful donors, the recipient often insisted that names as well as money be contributed; if not the real name, then, say, the first names of two grandchildren, which would be combined and put down as the legal contributor. Another common practice was to attribute such gifts to city or party officials, often policy-making officials who did not owe their positions to patronage and so were exempted from the usual levy. Contributions from city contractors varied not only with the size of the contract, but with the importance of political considerations in awarding it.

Some idea of the sums involved can be had from the official reports made by each party to the town clerk after an election.[13] In 1957 the biggest individual donor, who gave $1,500, was a partner in the architectural firm that designed two new high schools. A contractor closely associated with a top-ranking Democratic politician gave $1,000. A partner in the firm that built the new high schools and an apartment building in a redevelopment project gave $900. Dozens of city, court, and party officials were listed as contributors of sums ranging from $250 to $1,000.

The expression *campaign contribution* is something of a misnomer, for there are also political expenses at other times. For instance, the mayor commissioned a public opinion survey of New Haven from Louis Harris Associates every six months or so. Contributions to his personal campaign fund paid for these surveys, for lunches for political purposes (the mayor did not have an expense account), and for innumerable other things. Either surpluses from campaign funds or extra solicitation were necessary for these expenses. Any active politician's needs along these lines should make us all view in a kinder light such old "scandals" as Richard M. Nixon's celebrated fund to pay political expenses not covered by his congressional allowances.

Besides jobs and politically influenced selection of contractors, the third sign of machine politics is "favors": for parents of school children, owners of houses that may have code violations, people wanting zoning changes, taxpayers wanting lower assessments, traffic violators, and so on. In these and numerous other categories of citizen relationships with government, machine politicians are prepared to be obliging, but quids pro quo are implicit.

---

[13] These reports were summarized in the newspapers; see note 7.

The right friendship, a contribution, or some other token is helpful in getting favorable consideration, either by direct approach by the petitioner to the favor-giver or by means of an intermediary. Indeed, being the "man to see" is an important aspect of political power. Being able to fix traffic tickets seemed to have special symbolic value in New Haven; one rather unimportant party stalwart whom I knew was so proud of the reputation for influence that would come in this manner that he took his friends' tickets to fix and then paid for them himself, preferring the reputation to the cash.

A great deal of cant has been written about machine politics, including emphasis on the "warmth" and generosity of its leading practitioners. The cash nexus is supreme in organization politics, but this is not to say that less tangible considerations have no place at all. For one thing, the money and power generated by this style of politics can be used to do favors for people whose only resources are their votes and those of their families. One prominent New Haven politician reminisced on how he accumulated gratitude which could be exploited later:

> I do a lot of things for people. I keep working at it. . . . People come to see me, call me at my home at night. For instance a woman calls me, her husband has gone out and got drunk, and he's been arrested for drunken driving. She can't meet bail. She calls me up and I go down and bail him out. Or a colored fellow gets in trouble, uses some of his employer's money; I go to his employer and write out a personal check covering the loss so the employer won't press charges. I just keep piling up good will. . . . I'm always building up loyalty. People never forget.

When the organization built up by machine politics develops a fairly stable interaction pattern, it provides its members a variety of intangible gratifications. Even if there is no formal club, at election time the organization is a locus of social life for its lowliest workers—often middle-aged women doing clerical chores—and a source of vicarious status through contacts with prominent personages. For the slightly more important members, the organization is a social system in which status is conferred by such things as "closeness" to leaders, as suggested in these remarks by "Labovitz," a city councilman in the city resembling New Haven studied by Rufus Browning:

> You see, recognition by the party leaders is very important to the rank and file of the party. For instance, at a recent city committee meeting, Delaney [an important leader] came up to me and talked with me for five minutes. Then Casella [another important figure] asked me to make the motions for this meeting, and he told me what motions to make and when, so the meeting would run smoothly, you know. In fact, I've made the motions during the last two meetings. I know these are small and silly things, and they must seem so to outsiders, but they are also important to people in the party because this is the way you know how you stand in the party.

People watch this sort of thing. When Delancy came up to me at the meeting, people saw it and wondered, what are Delaney and Labovitz talking about? And they look to see who makes the motions and who sits down in the front row with Delaney.[14]

Several of these generalizations about machine politics can be illustrated by a brief description of the career of John M. Golden, the Democratic National Committeeman from Connecticut at the time of our study and generally considered the area's prime example of an "old-time" machine politician. An Irish Catholic, he was born and raised in the outlying town of Old Saybrook, where his father was a telegrapher and station agent for the New Haven Railroad. Golden quit high school and took a job at the Greist Manufacturing Company in New Haven; before he was 25 he was the superintendent of the Greist factory. His appetite for hard work also helped his concurrent political career. Golden became Democratic chairman of his ward in 1924 (he was still chairman in the late 1960s) and was recognized as a man with a future in the party. In 1932 he became Director of Public Works in the Democratic regime of John Murphy and left Greist to open a bond and insurance business, to provide himself with "adequate compensation." His firm prospered, aided not so much by government business as by performance bonds for government contractors, insurance, and, generally, the patronage of people who wanted to demonstrate their support for the party, most often as a step toward doing business with the city (or avoiding trouble from building inspectors and the like).

Along with Murphy and a former mayor, Golden formed a triumvirate that dominated the New Haven Democratic party for more than a decade. When Murphy was defeated in 1945 Golden moved to a kind of shaky preeminence, a position he maintained and strengthened by defeating candidates for various public offices sponsored by challengers to his leadership. Golden's mayoral candidate, Richard C. Lee, was elected in 1953; as he became more popular and successful, he attained power in the party comparable to Golden's, although based on very different foundations. The two men found it possible to work together, however, and were two-thirds of a new troika. The third man was Arthur T. Barbieri, a former post office worker, nightclub

---

[14] Rufus Browning, "Businessmen in Politics" (unpublished doctoral dissertation, Yale University, 1960), pp. 145–46.

Asking the right question at the right moment in a public meeting is not always a simple job. While working in city hall I once had to arrange that a particular question be asked in a certain contingency during a meeting of the League of Women Voters. Mayor Lee had many strong supporters among the League's members, but these upper-middle-class liberal women thought that asking planted questions was beneath them and so I had to turn to the Democratic organization, which produced a willing working-class lady. In the event, she failed to understand the situation, or I failed to explain it adequately, and her performance was a spectacular fiasco, bringing on the very embarrassment it was meant to preclude.

proprietor, and ice cream salesman who has been the efficient chairman of the Democratic Town Committee since the early 1950s.

Golden's indefatigable activity in party, fraternal, and lay religious circles earned him thousands of friends and also gave him innumerable opportunities to use his political influence to do favors, thus accumulating gratitude and hence more influence. As his insurance business made him wealthy, he could also make friends by financial generosity: bailing out petty violators, contributing to charities, and so on. This network of friendship and obligation established his leadership position in the party, which in turn further helped his business. At the time of our study Golden had an annual income well over $60,000 and spent considerable sums on political and charitable causes. For instance, he was officially listed as a contributor of $2,000 in the 1957 mayoralty campaign.

Relations between Golden, Lee, and Barbieri were amicable, wary, and a bit unstable. The three men had complementary but potentially divergent ambitions, talents, and roles. They were able to establish mutually satisfactory spheres of influence (with a good deal of skirmishing along the boundaries) and maintained an effective alliance for many years. Each needed the other two, although the extent to which this was true varied over the years, especially during the 1960s when Barbieri's growing power pushed Lee and Golden closer together. Occasionally the three were on opposite sides, as in Lee's abortive attempt in 1958 to amend the city charter, but for the most part what was good for one was good for the other two. Lee and Barbieri eventually became open enemies, and with Lee's retirement Barbieri's power increased further.

This relationship reflects an enduring feature of machine politics in New Haven (indeed, in many other cities): political spoils came from several jurisdictions, chiefly the municipal government, the probate court, and the state government. The more sources of patronage, the lower the probability that all of them will be held by the same party, and hence the easier it is for both parties to maintain their organizations through hard times. When one party was triumphant everywhere in the state, as the Democrats were in the 1960s, there was considerable potential for intraparty disunity because the availability of more than one source of rewards for political activity made it difficult to establish wholly unified local party organizations. Inevitably state leaders would deal with one or more local figures in dispensing state patronage (including, it should be remembered, the city court system). This local representative need not be the same man who controlled probate or municipal patronage. Although the mayor had the power to give out city patronage, either directly or by telling his appointees what to do, he found it prudent to exercise this power in concert with those leaders who could control campaign organizations in New Haven through their access to state and probate patronage. In good measure because of the multiple sources of patronage, the loyalties of Democratic party workers went to different leaders. All this was also true of the Republican party.

One problem faced by any mayor of New Haven was gaining the support of those elements of his local party that were not dependent on municipal patronage. Unlike other local party leaders, the mayor had governmental responsibility and thus had to win at least intermittent support from the Board of Aldermen and other agencies that might be controlled by his intra-party rivals. Lee solved this problem very well during the period covered by our study. (Aspects of relations between Lee and the Democratic organization are discussed in Chapters 6, 7, 9, and 11.) His predecessor, Celentano, took office over the opposition of the organizationally stronger faction of the Republican Party and was cursed throughout his administration with a dis-united party (see Chapter 6).

Thus neither local party organization was monolithic, although there were occasions, such as state conventions, when at least the Democrats displayed impressive and unquestioning unanimity. From 1945 through the period of our study the Republicans were badly split. The Democrats maintained a working coalition, but not without a good deal of competition and fairly constant vigilance on the part of Lee, Golden, Barbieri, and their associates.

Machine Politics Elsewhere

How common is the New Haven style of party politics? Among both academics and journalists the consensus seems to be that machine politics is a thing of the past, extant only in a few temporary survivals of which Chicago is, by acclamation, the prototype. There is a good deal to be said for this view and many writers have been saying it for a generation or more.[15] On the other hand, there are indications that machine politics continues to flourish in many places. I think that this side of the case is closer to the mark.

Writers on the subject tend to confuse and combine very different things: bosses, strong party organizations, machine politics, and corruption.[16] The result is to mistake isolated events for historical trends and to propose false tests about the current level of machine politics. There can be no doubt that corruption and other forms of municipal dishonesty have decreased markedly

[15] For a cautious, qualified, and widely reprinted synthesis of the orthodox position, see Fred I. Greenstein, "The Changing Pattern of Urban Party Politics," *The Annals,* 353 (May 1964), 2–13. Another presentation of the conventional wisdom, with fewer caveats, may be found in Thomas R. Dye, *Politics in States and Communities* (Englewood Cliffs, N.J.: Prentice-Hall, Inc., 1969), pp. 256–72.

[16] For a remarkable example of this confusion, see Eric L. McKitrick, "The Study of Corruption," in *Sociology, The Progress of a Decade,* eds. Seymour M. Lipset and Neil Smelser (Englewood Cliffs, N.J.: Prentice-Hall, Inc., 1961), pp. 449–56.

in scope. It is uncommon now for people to vote more than once, although "repeaters" were a staple feature in many cities a generation or two ago. Votes are usually counted honestly now. But dishonesty is not necessary to machine politics and can be found where patronage is relatively uncommon. By the same token, strong political organizations are not a concomitant of corruption; indeed, sometimes a strong boss inhibits the greed of his subordinates.

The level of municipal honesty is one bad test of the decline of machine politics. Another false harbinger is the defeat of a particular political leader, often interpreted as symptomatic of an historical trend when all it really means is that one faction has lost and another has won. In an amusing profile —first published in 1946—of a Brooklyn leader named Peter J. McGuinness, whom he called "the last of New York's oldtime district bosses," Richard H. Rovere explained how McGuinness first became district leader by attacking the incumbent boss: "Like all good politicians, McGuinness pretended to be scornful of politicians in general and presented himself merely as a long-suffering private citizen who had been driven to action by corruption and abuse."[17]

New York City politics offers innumerable temptations to mistake one swallow for the onset of summer. Since the nineteenth century, genuine and bogus reformers have been elected mayor over the opposition of various political organizations, to the accompaniment of public death rites for Tammany Hall and the less celebrated but more potent organizations in the other boroughs. Yet just as regularly such mayors have been succeeded by organization politicians.[18] Indeed, the incumbent himself is often recast in the role of organization man, so that in turn *his* departure from city hall can be hailed as a symptom of the decline of machine politics. Thus Mayor Robert Wagner's renomination in 1961 over "the organization candidate" signaled "the machine's" decline. The same interpretation was offered four years later when Wagner, reading the portents as unfavorable to his reelection, withdrew and was succeeded by John V. Lindsay. It appears that one of the reasons we know that Tammany is dead is that it has been killed so many times.

The life cycles of contemporary party organizations in other major cities also cast doubt on the view that twentieth century urban history has been a process of the steady enfeeblement of strong machines. The Democratic machine in Chicago was not assembled until the 1930s, following an era in

17 Richard H. Rovere, "The Big Hello," in Rovere, *The American Establishment and Other Reports, Opinions, and Speculations* (New York: Harcourt Brace Jovanovich, Inc., 1962), pp. 25, 50.

18 On the alternation of reform and regular administrations in New York, see Theodore J. Lowi, *At the Pleasure of the Mayor* (New York: The Free Press, 1964).

which the party there was vastly more chaotic, if not a whit more honest.[19] The ruling Democratic organization in Philadelphia is a product of the 1950s. It replaced an entrenched (67 years) and corrupt Republican organization which was deposed by liberal reformers led by Joseph S. Clark and Richardson Dilworth, who in turn lost control of the Democratic party to "regulars" headed by the late Congressman William Green.[20]

Systematic trend data about the persistence of machine politics are scarce. Ideally, one would develop various measures of the incidence of machine politics and then compare these indicators, both over time and from city to city. One such index might be the proportion of city employees covered by civil service regulations, a figure that is reported annually for all cities in *The Municipal Year Book*.[21] As this source reveals, formal civil service coverage is fairly widespread in cities over 50,000 population. The states of Iowa, New York, and Ohio require their cities to use merit systems and in Massachusetts local employees come under the jurisdiction of the state civil service commission. In 1963, 51 percent of cities in the other states had complete civil service coverage for their employees, 6 percent covered all but manual workers, 27 percent covered only policemen and firemen, and 16 percent (mostly in the South) did not have merit systems.[22] One might assume that patronage is more abundant in places where formal civil service coverage is low. The reverse probably is true also, but only in a very general way, for there are many cities where political realities or administrative loopholes weaken the impact of the regulations. Cities in New York, for example, can keep jobs from being covered by civil service by classifying them as "provisional," that is, temporary, or "noncompetitive," which means that satisfactory tests cannot be devised. In Chicago all municipal workers except those in public utilities are "covered" by civil service, but as a matter of political reality, a great many city jobs can be used for patronage purposes with little difficulty.

Information on other kinds of patronage is equally elusive. Two students of the subject in New York report that judicial patronage (receiverships, refereeships, and the like) is "almost impossible even to research" and for

---

[19] Donald S. Bradley and Mayer N. Zald, "From Commercial Elite to Political Administrator: The Recruitment of the Mayors of Chicago," in *The Structure of Community Power,* eds. Michael Aiken and Paul E. Mott (New York: Random House, Inc., 1970), pp. 53–60.

[20] For an account of these events in Philadelphia, see James Reichley, *The Art of Government* (New York: The Fund for the Republic, 1959).

[21] Published in Chicago by the International City Managers' Association.

[22] Raymond E. Wolfinger and John Osgood Field, "Political Ethos and the Structure of City Government," *American Political Science Review,* 60 (June 1966), 314–15.

this reason "its value as political gifts is unquestionably priceless."[23] Because of the moral and legal delicacy of the subject, systematic and realistic evidence on machine politics is scanty, and thus comparisons are difficult. Nevertheless, journalists and scholars have turned up useful information.

A *New York Times* survey of city and state government in New York concluded that "patronage has vastly expanded in the last several decades because of the tremendous growth of government, spiraling government spending, and the expansion of government's discretionary powers to regulate, control, and supervise private industry."[24] The same story reported that the annual payroll in city jobs exempt from civil service regulations, which had been $10 million in the Wagner administration, soared to $32.8 million under Mayor Lindsay in poverty program jobs alone. During the first three years of Mayor Lindsay's regime the number of "provisional" employees increased from 1,500 to 12,800. Under Mayor Wagner the City of New York also had 50,000 "noncompetitive" jobs; 24,000 more such positions were added after Lindsay took office.[25] In the last year of the Wagner administration the city let $8 million in consulting contracts, without competitive bidding. By 1969, the city's annual expenditure for outside consultants had risen to $75 million, with many indications that Lindsay was using these contracts as patronage.[26] In addition to the jobs and contracts at his disposal, the mayor of New York also can wield tremendous patronage power through his control of the agencies that grant zoning variances. Lindsay made good use of this power for political purposes.[27]

The patronage resources of the New York mayoralty are not much greater than those of the Manhattan Surrogates' Court, a little-known agency that oversees the distribution of about $1 billion worth of estates each year. (There is a Surrogate's Court in each New York county.) The court's chief patronage is the appointment of guardians for the estates of minors and other heirs who are held to need such supervision. These appointments, both undemanding and lucrative, are generally made on the basis of political considerations.[28] The two Manhattan Surrogates are effectively elected in obscure primaries in which as few as 60,000 voters participate.

Other courts in New York City name referees, trustees, guardians, and

[23] Martin Tolchin and Susan Tolchin, "How Judgeships Get Bought," *New York Magazine* (15 March 1971), 34.

[24] *New York Times* 17 June 1968, pp. 1, 30.

[25] Martin Tolchin and Susan Tolchin, "How Lindsay Learned the Patronage Lesson," *New York Magazine* (29 March 1971), 48.

[26] *Ibid.*, pp. 47–48.

[27] *Ibid.*, pp. 43–46.

[28] *New York Times,* 17 June 1968, p. 30; and Wallace S. Sayre and Herbert Kaufman, *Governing New York City* (New York: Russell Sage Foundation, 1960), pp. 540–41.

receivers in a variety of situations. These appointments also are rewarding and politically determined. In one case, a fee of $445,000 was paid to a trustee, a veteran political figure.[29] Trustees, in turn, may decide where to bank the funds for which they are responsible, and their power in this respect constitutes another form of patronage if decisions are made politically—as they seem to be.

The governor of New York controls almost 40,000 patronage jobs, as well as a variety of other spoils.[30] The state controller, an elected official and often not a member of the governor's party, decides where to deposit the state's funds, which amount to more than $4 billion. During the 1960s, when the governor of New York was a Republican, the controller, a Democrat, deposited state money in about 75 percent of the state's banks. The controller is also responsible for investment of retirement funds,[31] and here again his decisions can have political impact in a setting where partisan advantage is assumed to be a consideration in such matters.

Other cities than New Haven and New York have political systems in which patronage plays a crucial part. Mayor Richard Daley of Chicago is also chairman of the Cook County Democratic Committee. These two positions together give him control of about 35,000 patronage jobs.[32] Daley reportedly scrutinizes each job application personally. As there are 3,412 voting precincts in Chicago, the Democratic organization can deploy an average of ten workers to each precinct on the basis of job patronage alone.

Over 8,000 state employees in Indiana owe their jobs to patronage and are assessed 2 percent of their salaries for the coffers of the ruling party's state committee.[33] "Macing" public employees is not uncommon in some locales, including New Haven, but the Indiana method of issuing automobile and drivers' licenses and automobile titles is unique. These matters are handled by a franchise system, rather like service stations or Kentucky Fried

[29] Tolchin and Tolchin, "How Judgeships Get Bought," p. 33. Presumably because of the very large amounts of money involved in numerous cases where judges appoint referees, trustees, guardians, and so on, and the custom of making these appointments politically, judgeships of all sorts in New York are highly prized. Although most judges are elected rather than appointed, the parties effectively control the appointment process. A man who wants to be a judge usually must have connections in one party or the other, and must also make a sizable payment to the appropriate party leader. Sayre and Kaufman estimated that a minimum payment for the lowest-level judgeship was $20,000 (p. 542). Tolchin and Tolchin suggest that the payments usually are higher than this ("How Judgeships Get Bought," pp. 21, 31).

[30] Tolchin and Tolchin, "How Lindsay Learned the Patronage Lesson," p. 49.

[31] *New York Times,* 1 June 1970, p. 27.

[32] *Newsweek* (5 April 1971), 82.

[33] Robert J. McNeill, *Democratic Campaign Financing in Indiana, 1964* (Bloomington, Ind. and Princeton, N.J.: Indiana University Institute of Public Administration and Citizens' Research Foundation, 1966), pp. 15–16.

Chicken outlets. Local "license branches" are "awarded to the county chairman of the Governor's party, or the persons they designate."[34] The branch pays the state party committee four cents for each license sold; otherwise, it retains all fees up to $10,000. Above that figure, half the take must be returned to the state Bureau of Motor Vehicles.

This brief survey shows that formidable patronage resources are available as rewards for political participation in various cities, and thus that New Haven's political practices are not an anachronistic survival. To put it another way, the dependent variable—machine politics—is still a common phenomenon.

The Plebeian Quality of Machine Politics

Like most forms of associational behavior, work for a political party is usually a middle-class pastime. But one of the striking features of the New Haven political scene was the relatively low socioeconomic status of most party organization activists. This was apparent from observation of Democratic or Republican gatherings, and is confirmed by our more systematically gathered information. In addition to our sample of registered voters, we defined a group of party "subleaders," a category that included all partisan local office holders; officials of both parties at the city, ward, and state senatorial district levels; and delegates to the municipal nominating conventions in 1957. (The Democrats assign the nominating function to their Town Committee, whose members are included among the subleaders.) All told, there were 497 party subleaders, of whom we interviewed 120. The distribution of occupations and incomes among these officials resembled the demographic profile of the city's population. The subleaders were remarkably representative of their constituents, with only a slight tendency to greater incomes and higher-status occupations. For example, 42 percent of the party officials held clerical or blue-collar jobs, compared to 60 percent of the voters. The same was true of income; 39 percent of the subleaders and 47 percent of the voters made less than $5,000 a year. These data are presented in Table 4-1.

These findings cannot be directly contrasted to data about other cities because the positions held by the party officials studied in other research are not comparable. But a direct comparison of campaign activists in New Haven and in the northern United States can be made by means of our sample of registered voters and the Michigan Survey Research Center national election studies. The New Haven respondents who say that they have engaged in some form of electioneering are much less likely to be middle class than are those people outside the South who report participation in the 1960 national election campaign. These data, outlined in Table 4-2, show that political

[34] *Ibid.*, p. 19.

TABLE 4-1. Social status of party subleaders and registered voters

Status	Party subleaders	Registered voters
Occupation		
Major professionals, higher executives, etc.	12%	5%
Managers, administrators, small businessmen	24	20
Clerks, wage earners	42	60
No answer	22	15
	100%	100%
N	120	525
Income		
Above $10,000	12%	6%
$5,000–$10,000	34	39
Below $5,000	39	47
No answer	15	8
	100%	100%
N	120	525

TABLE 4-2. Educational level of the politically active in New Haven and in the northern United States[a]

	Educational level	New Haven	U.S.
Of those giving money:[b]	No high school	42%	30%
	Attended high school	32	34
	Attended college	26	35
		100%	99%
Of those going to political rallies:	No high school	47%	27%
	Attended high school	32	39
	Attended college	20	34
		99%	100%
Of those belonging to a political club:	No high school	41%	23%
	Attended high school	32	31
	Attended college	27	46
		100%	100%

a Data for the United States exclude the 11 former Confederate states, Kentucky, Maryland, and the District of Columbia.

b Questions on the first two items were phrased in the past tense in the SRC survey and in the present tense in New Haven.

Source: The national data are from the 1960 National Election Study of the Survey Research Center of the University of Michigan, obtained through the Inter-University Consortium for Political Research with the aid of Mrs. Maxene S. Perlmutter of the Consortium staff. Responsibility for computing and interpreting these data is solely mine.

activity in New Haven is conducted by a far humbler and broader segment of the electorate than is the case in the North as a whole. Forty-seven percent of those attending political rallies and meetings in New Haven had not been to high school, compared to 27 percent in the national sample (with the South excluded). In the country as a whole campaign participation increases with education. In New Haven this relationship is much weaker, and at the highest levels of participation the proportion of better-educated participants drops off markedly.[35]

The plebeian character of party politics in New Haven does not reflect Democratic party dominance. Officials of the two parties are drawn from the same economic strata. Exactly similar proportions of Republican elected and appointed municipal officials (in 1950) and Democratic ones (in 1957) were executives, proprietors, managers, and professionals. Substantially the same was true for manual workers (with a Democratic edge) and white-collar workers and small businessmen (here the Republicans were slightly more numerous). Scarcely anyone from the city's social and economic elites is in either party's organization. The Republican subleaders included only two members of the social elite and two from the economic elite. Golden was the only person from the latter group in the Democratic organization.

One important cause of the class composition of the New Haven party organizations is the nature of the most common incentive to participation in municipal elections: not citizen duty or a desire to change public policy, but the discipline imposed by a patronage job or the hope of getting one. These positions are not so attractive to the middle class. They usually do not pay well, but this is not the sole explanation. Our survey sample was asked, "Assuming the pay is the same, would you prefer a job with the city or with a private firm?" Half the respondents who had not gone past elementary school preferred the city job, compared to only 31 percent of those who had gone to college. The findings were similar among different income and occupational groups. Apart from the compensation, then, the commonest rewards of machine politics were most effective with poorer people, the line soldiers of both party organizations.

Numerous higher-ranking municipal positions do go to members of the middle class, who are also the primary beneficiaries of favoritism in the courts and in the letting of contracts. Activity in one party or the other as a means of developing contacts and influence in the courts is a common career pattern for young lawyers, generally Catholics and Jews who have attended second-rank law schools and practice by themselves or in small firms. Lawyers in the city's prominent law firms were unlikely to be party regulars or to have much to do with the machine-courthouse circuit.

---

[35] Sources: for New Haven, Dahl, *Who Governs?*, pp. 285–87; for the United States, Campbell et al., *The American Voter,* p. 476.

Although the dominance of local politics by ethnic groups may reduce the prestige of municipal office below what it is in different kinds of cities, or what it is said to have been in the nineteenth century,[36] it would be a mistake to conclude that "recognition" has no attraction for the middle class. One of my most vivid memories from city hall is of the ecstasy displayed by a dentist when he was sworn in as a member of the New Haven Board of Health, the first member of his profession to be so honored. Surrounded by his large, overjoyed extended family, he pressed cigars on everyone within reach, posed happily for his relatives' cameras, and, all in all, made abundantly clear that there was a place in the patronage system for the well-off. (The appointment had been carefully planned by the mayor to strengthen his position vis-à-vis Golden and Barbieri.) But while this mark of distinction was important to the dentist, as similar honors seemed to be to a variety of other middle-class people, it was neither crucial to his livelihood nor likely to give the party a hold strong enough to control his behavior as it could an employee of the Public Works Department.

A great many people in New Haven must be politically active to keep their jobs or other rewards of political favoritism.[37] Patronage inevitably creates a cadre of activists for whom politics is a way to make money, not a means of striving for the good, true, and beautiful. Patronage then has the effect of drawing into political action people who would not participate out of a sense of civic duty; such people are likely to be of lower social status than activists with less tangible motivations. Of course, everyone in New Haven with political interests does not share this outlook; many people are interested in issues and government policy, in public service as a calling, or in politics as an interesting avocation. People like this tend to be educated members of the middle class. Apart from disparities in social style, they are likely to find the party regulars' political perspectives uncongenial. Such sentiments are by no means one-sided; many ward organizations of both parties prefer having no truck with "outsiders." In the 1950s Henry Townshend, a very wealthy member of one of the city's oldest families, tried to get

---

36 This assertion is often made in writings on local politics and "community power," without benefit of evidence. It would be interesting to know if the prestige of municipal office is lower in cities where nationality groups have wrested political control from Yankees than in places where this ethnic conflict is unimportant. One might also speculate whether the prestige of local governmental posts rose in those places where the city manager movement returned control of city hall to businessmen. For a brief discussion of the latter trend, see Samuel P. Hays, "The Politics of Reform in Municipal Government in the Progressive Era," *Pacific Northwest Quarterly,* 55 (October 1964), 157–69.

37 The data and conclusions in this chapter contradict Dahl's proposition that "political associations...in New Haven are more nearly avocational than vocational" (*Who Governs?*, p. 99). Dahl's conclusion does justice neither to the mainspring of party activity in New Haven nor to the difference between New Haven and cities where patronage is less important.

the Republican aldermanic nomination in his ward and was rebuffed. He succeeded some years later only after forming his own organization and threatening a primary. (Townshend subsequently persisted in his political career and made unsuccessful races for mayor in 1961 and 1963.) Townshend's perseverance is unusual, however, and the common run of the ideologically-oriented middle class seldom found the bulk of either party's workers to their taste, except in a few relatively prosperous wards. The net effect of patronage, then, is both to increase the number of working-class political activists and to reduce the middle-class component.

Middle-class abstention from politics was not just a matter of taste and conflicting perspectives. One common incentive drawing the middle classes into politics was weak in New Haven. The relatively high level of social and ethnic distance in New Haven (and in much of the Northeast) was manifested in the preferences of the well-off for private rather than public education. In 1955 about a fifth of all school-age children attended private schools, but in the best neighborhoods the figure was 43 percent.[38] The parents of these children will not care much about the public schools, and for this reason a major stake in municipal affairs was missing from the lives of people who in other settings are often engaged in political action.

When the participation of issue-oriented people in municipal campaigns was desired, ad hoc organizations were formed. Mayor Lee made good use of "Citizens for Lee" groups, exploiting his considerable appeal to intellectually inclined liberals who ordinarily would eschew any contact with the local Democratic organization. These groups were especially important to Lee in his first campaigns, when he was an underdog lacking the powers and prestige of the mayoralty and had no hold on the organization but his popularity and public relations skills. In these circumstances Citizens for Lee was a viable political force and a useful counterweight to the party regulars. As Lee was able to make use of municipal patronage to establish himself in the party and build his own organization, this vehicle became less important to him. The officers of Citizens for Lee typically were upper-middle-class, representing various categories of local residents (Yankees, Jews, Yale, and so on) with no connection with the regular organization. The group was a platform for public statements, an attributable source for campaign propaganda mailed to voters in more prosperous neighborhoods, and a vehicle for the efforts of people other than organization members. It had its own decorous election night victory party, carefully separated from the regulars' rowdy celebration.

The conflict in goals between "citizen" supporters and the regulars was neatly expressed in an encounter between a veteran machine politician and two prominent Yale officials who had been active in Lee's behalf during his

38 For the source of these data and further discussion, see Dahl, *Who Governs?*, pp. 143–47. Most of the citywide private school students attended parochial schools, but this was not the case with children from wealthy families.

first successful mayoralty campaign. The three men had lunched well together and, mellowed by several martinis, the politician addressed the academics somewhat as follows:

> You know, we've worked pretty hard on this campaign and gone through a lot together. I like you fellows and appreciate your help, but there's something I can't figure out: what are you after?
> Why, we want to see Dick elected.
> I know, we all do, but what's in it for *you?* We're friends, you can be frank with me.
> That's all we want, just to put Dick in city hall.
> Aw, come on, you guys don't have to give me that. What do you want? Jobs? Contracts?

And so it went. The two intellectuals were unable to persuade the politician that their only aim was to elect Lee. The politician was unable to believe that two grown men, much less such distinguished ones, would devote all that time and energy to a cause from which they did not expect to profit personally.

Such disparities in background, style, and goals have been ably described in James Q. Wilson's *The Amateur Democrat,* which also makes clear that "amateurs" are important in local Democratic parties only in the absence of patronage—as in California—or in atypical places like Manhattan or around the University of Chicago, where there are very large proportions of well-off Jews and/or bookish business and professional people.[39] New Haven meets none of these criteria and in fact the amateurs there are generally unimportant in local politics.

Machine politicians prefer not to rely on amateurs any more than they have to, for ideologically motivated people are harder to control. Being able to turn the flow of spoils on and off gives leaders a means of discipline that is lacking with workers whose political rewards are not as tangible and divisible as jobs or contracts. Moreover, activists who care about issues are concerned about the positions their leaders take on substantive policy; activists who care about their jobs either are not interested in issues or cannot afford to express their opinions. These leadership preferences are nicely illustrated in the following remarks by a Democratic organization politician in Chicago:

> What I look for in a prospective [precinct] captain is a young person—man or woman—who is interested in getting some material return out of his political activity. I much prefer this to the type that is enthused about the party cause or all hot on a particular issue. Enthusiasm for causes is short-lived, but the necessity of making a living is permanent.[40]

[39] James Q. Wilson, *The Amateur Democrat* (Chicago: University of Chicago Press, 1962), pp. 13–16, 35, 68.

[40] Quoted in Martin Meyerson and Edward C. Banfield, *Politics, Planning and the Public Interest* (New York: The Free Press, 1955), pp. 70–71.

As this observation suggests, amateurs are not only less amenable to control, but less consistently interested in party work. Their enthusiasm tends to be unstable—intense in national campaigns or when some great issue grips public attention, and then fading away or finding a focus in some area other than electoral politics. Political action seldom is central to the amateurs' primary economic needs; it may be psychologically important to them, but psychic needs can more easily be met by alternative activities. While the amateurs are, as Plunkitt observed, only "mornin' glories," the party regulars' attention to politics can be far more constant, because their jobs are at stake. This is particularly important because the elections most important to party organizations are primaries which often, as in New Haven, are held on the ward level and are very obscure. Because attention and turnout in these elections are so low, the outcome can more easily be controlled by the organization.

Amateurs seem to be interested chiefly in national and international affairs, and thus are more active and successful in presidential primaries and elections, where their policy concerns are salient.[41] While the stakes in these contests may be global, they seldom include the topic of prime interest to organization politicians—control of patronage—and hence the regulars will exert less than their maximum effort in them.

Conveniently for both amateurs and machine politicians, the two sorts of elections are held at different times and generally in different years, not only in New Haven but in most other cities as well. When the amateurs' enthusiasm is at its peak, the professionals will be less interested; when the machine's spoils are at stake, the amateurs are less involved. Thus in the 1968 Democratic presidential primary the regular organization's convention delegate slate, pledged to Hubert Humphrey, was defeated in New Haven by a slate pledged to Eugene McCarthy and backed by fervent amateurs. But the following year the amateurs were easily defeated by the regulars over the nomination of a Democratic mayoralty candidate to succeed Lee.

Participation in election campaigns is not the only form of political action. It is important to distinguish between electioneering and other types of political activity. In New Haven there was a major divergence between campaign and noncampaign activities. The likelihood that richer people would engage in noncampaign activity was far greater than the corresponding probability for campaigns.[42] This divergence reflected the probability that

---

41 According to Wilson, in New York City amateur interest in local government seemed limited mainly to procedural housecleaning ("reform") and did not extend even to development of specific substantive policy proposals. See his *The Amateur Democrat*, pp. 134–37.

42 The tendency for the better-off to participate less in campaigns than in other arenas is discussed at length in *Who Governs?*, Chap. 26. Dahl explains this as a result of the plebeian dominance of the city's political parties, and says that the affluent can

participation in a campaign is less autonomously motivated, for in New Haven, as Barbieri's letter to the Public Works employees shows, the discipline of patronage compels campaign work. There are no such external inducements for most noncampaign political action. Indeed, because such activity usually consists of trying to exert pressure on public officials, it is likely to be viewed with apprehension or disfavor by those machine politicians who dispense patronage. A sense of political efficacy, education, a white-collar job, and higher income are all thought to be associated with those personal qualities that lead people to try to influence the outcome of government decisions. In many parts of the country, these traits are also associated with electioneering. Some people participate in New Haven elections—particularly for national office—from such motives, but most activists, including party regulars, do not. The essentially involuntary character of much political participation in cities dominated by machine politics has received scant attention from students of participation, who customarily treat the phenomenon they study as a manifestation of solely internal stimuli.

Machine Politics Defined

I have discussed "machine politics" in New Haven and described the power of the Democratic "machine" there without defining these terms, although my use of them has been consistent with common usage in the social sciences. But it is also common to use these terms so as to mingle two very different phenomena, and it would be helpful to disentangle these two meanings.

Machine politics is the manipulation of certain *incentives* to partisan political participation: favoritism based on political criteria in personnel decisions, contracting, and administration of the laws. A *political machine* is an organization that practices machine politics, that is, that attracts and directs its members primarily by means of these incentives.[43] Unfortunately, the term *machine* is also used in a very different sense to refer to the *centralization* of power in a party in a major political jurisdiction: a "machine" is a united and hierarchical party organization in a state, county, or city. There is no

---

influence city officials through other channels than the parties. This assumes that political participation reflects primarily a desire to influence public policy, a proposition I consider insufficient for New Haven and cities like it.

The distinction between campaign and noncampaign participation is also germane to those radicals who reject American society so thoroughly that they disdain electioneering as a futile example of "working within the system."

[43] This definition is similar to James Q. Wilson's. See his "Politics and Reform in American Cities," in Thomas Landon Thorson et al., *American Government Annual, 1962–63* (New York: Holt, Rinehart and Winston, Inc., 1962), p. 38. But see also note 49 below.

necessary relationship between the two dimensions of incentives and centralization. Machine politics (patronage incentives) need not produce centralized
organizations *at the city level or higher*; the highest level at which cohesive
party organizations are found may be the ward, assembly district, or some
other geographical subdivision. Thus for purposes of citywide decision making a party may be fragmented despite the prevalence of machine politics.
Patronage and other such incentives, then, are by no means identical to
hierarchical party structure.

The availability of patronage makes it easier to centralize influence in a
cohesive party organization, since these resources can be distributed so as
to discipline and reward the organization's workers. Often, however, all
patronage is not controlled by the same people. The boundaries of a patronage-based organization need not coincide with those of any governmental
unit. Even if they do, there may be competing organizations or factions
within each party in the same area, for where patronage is plentiful, it
usually is available from more than one jurisdiction. In New Haven, city
hall had no monopoly on the spoils of government, which were also dispensed
by the probate court and the state government. Thus the existence of a
cohesive local organization in either party did not automatically follow from
the use of patronage to motivate party workers.

The distinction between machine politics and centralized local machines
is far from academic, for the former is found many places where the latter
is not. Chicago presently exhibits both machine politics and a very strong
Democratic machine. Forty years ago it had the former but not the latter.[44]
In Boston and New York there are the same kinds of incentives to political
activity as in Chicago, but no cohesive citywide organizations. Instead, these
cities have several contending party factions. In New York "the party"
includes reform clubs with considerable influence as well as a variety of
"regular" organizations. The frequently celebrated—and deplored—"decline"
of Tammany Hall is not so much the subjugation of the regulars by the
reformers, nor the disappearance of patronage and corruption (neither has
happened yet), as the decentralization of the city's old-line Democratic organization. As Sayre and Kaufman describe the situation:

> Party organizations in New York City are not monolithic in character. Each
> Assembly District is virtually an independent principality.... The parties are
> aggregations of segments rather than organic entities. They are decentralized
> and fragmented and undisciplined, but they achieve sufficient unity of purpose
> and action and leadership to identify them as organizations.[45]

Multiple sources of patronage are one of the factors maintaining organizational fragmentation. In the 1930s, when hostile organizations controlled

[44] See, for example, Bradley and Zald, "From Commercial Elite to Political Administrator."

[45] Sayre and Kaufman, *Governing New York City*, pp. 140, 141.

city, state, and federal government, Tammany Hall was sustained by patronage from the Surrogates' Court in Manhattan, which is thought to have about as much patronage as the mayor of New York.[46]

While the distinction between incentives and centralization is useful for accurate description and definitional clarity, it also has important theoretical ramifications. Robert K. Merton's influential explanation of the persistence of machine politics (patronage) points to the presumed coordinating function of centralized political machines:

> The key structural function of the Boss is to organize, centralize and maintain in good working condition the "scattered fragments of power" which are at present dispersed through our political organization. By the centralized organization of political power, the Boss and his apparatus can satisfy the needs of diverse sub groups in a larger community which are not politically satisfied by legally devised and culturally approved social structures.[47]

Yet machine politics exists many places where, as in New York, the party "organization" is a congeries of competing factions.[48] In fact, cohesive organizations like Chicago's or New Haven's may be fairly uncommon, while pervasive favoritism and patronage—machine politics—are much less so. Hence Merton explained the persistence of the incentive system by referring to functions allegedly performed by an institution (a centralized, citywide party organization) that may or may not be found where machine politics flourishes.

The rewards that create the incentives in machine politics are not only tangible but divisible. Moreover, they typically result from the routine operation of government, not from particular substantive policy outcomes.[49] Any regime in a courthouse or city hall will hire roughly the same number of people, contract for roughly the same amounts of goods and services, and enforce (or fail to enforce) the same laws, irrespective of the differences in substantive policies advocated by one party or the other. The measures adopted by an activist, enterprising administration will generate a higher level of public employment and contracting than the output of a caretaker gov-

[46] *Ibid.*, p. 541n; Tolchin and Tolchin, "How Judgeships Get Bought," p. 32.

[47] Robert K. Merton, *Social Theory and Social Structure,* rev. ed. (New York: The Free Press, 1957), p. 73. This view of the "functions of the machine" has been expressed by a number of writers. Whether political machines actually do serve as mechanisms for coordinating government policy is discussed in Chapter 7. The following section of the present chapter discusses relationships between governmental fragmentation and machine politics.

[48] For a description of a city with decentralized governmental institutions, fragmented party organizations, ample patronage, and major corruption, see John A. Gardiner, *The Politics of Corruption* (New York: Russell Sage Foundation, 1970).

[49] This point distinguishes my definition from that of Edward C. Banfield and James Q. Wilson. See their *City Politics* (Cambridge, Mass.: Harvard University Press and The M.I.T. Press, 1963), p. 115.

ernment. Yet the differences are not such as to change the generalization that they will flow regardless of what policies are followed. This excepts, of course, reform of personnel, judicial, and contracting practices.

One can, then, distinguish two kinds of tangible incentives to political participation. The incentives that fuel machine politics are inevitable concomitants of government activity, available irrespective of the policies chosen by a particular regime. A second kind of tangible incentive results from a desire to influence the outcome of specific policy decisions. This second type includes those considerations that induce political participation by interest groups that do not want patronage, but do want the government to follow a particular line of action in a substantive policy area: lower tax rates, antidiscrimination legislation, minimum wage laws, conservation of natural resources, and the like. A particularly pure example of a political organization animated by substantive incentives would be a taxpayers' group that acted as a political party—naming candidates, getting out the vote, and so on—to capture city hall for the purpose of enacting a policy of minimal expenditure. The ideal type of such a group would not care who was hired or awarded contracts, so long as a policy of economy was followed.

Incentives to political activity can be classified along two dimensions: tangible/intangible and routine/substantive. The matrix in Figure 4-1 shows

FIGURE 4-1. Incentives to political participation

	Routine	*Substantive*
Tangible	I. Patronage ——— Political machine	II. Favorable policy ——— "Main Street"
Intangible	III. Sociability Intrinsic enjoyment of politics Loyalty to a leader ——— Any kind of organization	IV. Ideology ——— "Amateur" club

the possible combinations, and examples of organizations in which each incentive system predominates. These categories are ideal types, of course; in any city people will be drawn to party activity by each kind of incentive and therefore few cities will display only one incentive system. But cities do vary enormously in the prevailing types of incentive systems according to the resources available, the stakes of electoral outcomes, and the attitudes of their citizens. As I mentioned earlier, there is also a Gresham's Law effect here: in cities with ample patronage resources, ideologically motivated people tend not to participate as actively in local elections, except perhaps in enclaves where they are numerous.

A word should be said about Category III, routine intangible incentives. This includes several different motivations, all of which have in common certain negative characteristics: they do not involve material rewards for political action, nor do they depend on the anticipation of preferred policy outcomes. Among these are "solidary" rewards for party work: gratification from membership in an organization or from social contact with other party workers. In principle, there is no reason why such pleasures could not be enjoyed by members of any sort of party organization. In practice, it may be the case that patronage-based organizations are more likely than other kinds to provide solidary rewards.

This has led some observers to suggest that at present, machines are sustained as much by these nonmaterial returns as by monetary considerations.[50] It is more plausible, however, that the solidary gratifications are essentially a by-product of a material incentive system that produces more stable and frequent interactions than is the case with amateur politics. One would expect that these interactions would not be wholly instrumental in character and that they would have emotional and social dimensions which would provide a framework of relationships that could be satisfying to many of the participants. (For an example, see the remarks of Alderman "Labovitz" on pp. 84–85 above.) As these politically-based social relationships are seldom exclusionary for the "right kind of people," people who are not reformers, one might also expect that political clubhouses would offer social pleasures to people who were not at the patronage trough (as "Labovitz" was). Some of these people may work for the machine. It would, however, be a serious error to confuse this incidental *effect* with the tangible rewards that *cause* the machine to exist. Consider an analogy: Many people derive important emotional sustenance from the social relationships at their jobs. These rewards, as "morale," may contribute to efficiency, easier recruitment, and low employee turnover. It does not appear useful, however, to argue that the firm exists because of the social benefits that may be a by-product of work.

Substantive policy issues are not normally among the incentives animating machine politics. They are irrelevant to this political style and more an irritant than anything else to its practitioners. One student of Chicago politics said that for the Democratic organization there "Issues are obstacles to be overcome, not opportunities to be sought."[51] Daniel Patrick Moynihan observed that in New York, "in the regular party, conferences on issues are

---

[50] *Ibid.,* p. 120.

[51] James Q. Wilson, *Negro Politics* (New York: The Free Press, 1960), p. 117.

regarded as women's work."[52] In California, on the other hand, conferences and resolutions about issues are meat and drink to the earnest middle-class activists who man both political parties. By the same token, local campaigns feature debate about issues in inverse ratio to the prevalence of machine politics, as James Q. Wilson noted:

> In Chicago, issues in city elections are conspicuous by their rarity. In New York, they are somewhat more common. In Detroit and Los Angeles, candidates often must go to considerable lengths to *generate* issues in order to attract interest to their campaigns for public office.[53]

In New Haven, also, the party organizations did not play an important role in developing alternative courses of municipal governmental action. Indeed, since machine politicians drew their resources from the routine operations of government, they did not concern themselves with policy formulation. Golden and Barbieri were seldom present at meetings where decisions about municipal policy were made, nor did they play an active part in these matters. On strictly party topics like nominations they were, with Mayor Lee, a triumvirate. Appointments, contracts, and the like were negotiated among the three, with Lee delegating a good deal of routine patronage administration to Barbieri.[54] But substantive city affairs were another matter; here the organization leaders were neither interested nor consulted on the outlines of policy.[55] Golden, Barbieri, and their associates were not excluded against their will; they were largely indifferent. This does not seem to be an unusual situation. In New York, for example, Sayre and Kaufman report that "the most distinctive characteristic of the party leaders as participants in the city's political process is their relative neutrality toward the content of public policy."[56]

The concerns of machine politicians are not irrelevant to substantive policy

---

[52] Daniel P. Moynihan, " 'Bosses' and 'Reformers': A Profile of the New York Democrats," *Commentary* (June 1961), 464.

[53] Wilson, *Negro Politics*, p. 37 (emphasis in the original).

[54] Most appointments in urban renewal and related fields were made by Lee without accommodating the Democratic organization's interests. See Chapters 7 and 9 for more on this point.

[55] By the same token, officials influential in urban renewal policy did not, with the exception of Mayor Lee, participate in nominations or other activities of the Democratic organizations.

[56] Sayre and Kaufman, *Governing New York City*, p. 474.

Robert H. Salisbury reports two coexisting elements in St. Louis politics, a policy-oriented faction and a patronage faction: "These two groupings are a durable part of the political scene and although they pursue different interests, they are not in perpetual conflict...each side can achieve its key values without interfering with the objectives of the other." Salisbury, "The Dynamics of Reform: Charter Politics in St. Louis," *Midwest Journal of Political Science*, 5 (August 1961), 263.

formation, for while the politicians are neutral "toward the content of public policy," they are very much interested indeed in the details of its execution; and in many policy areas the aggregate of their influence on all the details can be important. In Newark the politicians were not concerned about general policy in the city's urban renewal program, but they did scrutinize

> with great care all actions of the staff involving hiring, classification, and compensation of [Newark Housing] Authority personnel, the appraisal and acquisition of properties, the awarding of contracts, the maintenance of NHA-owned property, the selection of public housing tenants, the rents charged, and the relocation of displaced families.[57]

Sayre and Kaufman explain the considerations that lead to party interest in the execution of policy:

> Party leaders give most of their energy and attention to the decisions governing nominations, elections, and appointments—that is, to the decisions determining who shall hold office. But they are not indifferent to other types of governmental decisions, especially any that affect their influence over the nominating, electing, and appointing processes. The interest of party leaders in public policy seems to vary directly with its possible effect upon their role in choosing officials. In fact, this perception of their relation to public policy impels party leaders to be most concerned with discrete aspects of policy and its application rather than its range and content.[58]

There are two interesting aspects of this general tendency for machine politicians to be interested in the details of public policy rather than its basic outlines. One implication concerns Dahl's portrait of the ideal politician, whom he called *homo politicus*. In Dahl's view, "Political man...deliberately allocates a very sizable share of his resources to the process of gaining and maintaining control over the policies of government."[59] This may be an accurate characterization of many political leaders, but it is not suitable for machine politicians, who are relatively indifferent to public policy, do not consider issue appeals important or desirable elements of electoral strategies, and are primarily interested in control over the sources of patronage. Thus a political taxonomist could identify two subspecies of *homo politicus*. One of these fits Dahl's description and might be called *h. politicus substantus*. The other, the machine politician, is *h. politicus boodelus*. Forerunners of this classification can be found in the literature. In his autobiography the late "Boss" Flynn, the famous Democratic leader in the Bronx, persistently

---

[57] Harold Kaplan, *Urban Renewal Politics* (New York: Columbia University Press, 1963), pp. 47–48.

[58] Sayre and Kaufman, *Governing New York City,* p. 452.

[59] Dahl, *Who Governs?,* p. 225.

distinguished between "Democrats," whom he admired, and "New Dealers," whom he scorned as impractical, rigid meddlers.[60]

A second implication of the tendency for machine politics to slight issues concerns theorizing and research on relationships between the level of inter-party competition and the character of public policy. The classic position on this topic, generally associated with the work of V. O. Key, was that policies beneficial to the lower classes were more likely with evenly matched parties, while one-party domination tended to profit the rich.[61] Early quantitative research showed that competition and per capita spending for various welfare measures were very weakly related at the state level, and thus seemed to disconfirm the old belief about the policy consequences of party competition.[62] Both the original proposition and the subsequent research assumed that electoral competition would be "programmatic," that is, based on alternative policy platforms. But where machine politicians regard issues as "women's work" and "obstacles to be overcome," campaign appeals are likely to include far less issue content. The importance of issues in voters' perspectives might reflect in some degree the political stimuli presented by the campaign.[63] Thus a fair test of Key's proposition would separate "policy competition" from "patronage competition."[64]

Why Machine Politics Has Not Withered Away

Some people believe that our political system cannot work without the incentives inherent in machine politics. Martin and Susan Tolchin maintain that

[60] Edward J. Flynn, *You're the Boss* (New York: The Viking Press, Inc., 1947).

[61] See especially V. O. Key, Jr., *Southern Politics* (New York: Alfred A. Knopf, Inc., 1949), Chap. 14.

[62] Research of this kind was published by economists as early as 1952, but the first such study that attracted much attention from political scientists was Richard E. Dawson and James A. Robinson, "Inter-Party Competition, Economic Variables and Welfare Policies in the American States," *Journal of Politics,* 25 (May 1963), 265–89. For a review and critique of the ensuing literature, more sophisticated measures, and somewhat different findings, see Brian R. Fry and Richard F. Winters, "The Politics of Redistribution," *American Political Science Review,* 64 (June 1970), 508–22.

[63] There is some evidence to support the analogous proposition that the number of voters who see a campaign in ideological terms increases as the candidates emphasize ideological appeals. See John Osgood Field and Ronald E. Anderson, "Ideology in the Public's Conceptualization of the 1964 Election," *Public Opinion Quarterly,* 33 (Fall 1969), 380–98.

[64] For one example of such a separation, see John H. Fenton, *Midwest Politics* (New York: Holt, Rinehart and Winston, Inc., 1966). Fenton's findings tend to confirm Key's hypothesis.

These remarks about the feeble issue content of machine politics are, of course, analogous to my discussion of ethnic politics in Chapter 3.

"the mainspring of American politics. . .is patronage." "Patronage power is a necessary and legitimate extension of the power of elected officials."[65] The *New York Times* quotes a state senator as saying that "patronage is essential to the two-party system."[66] The weakness in this position is that many cities (and states) seem to be governed as well as New York or Chicago, with only a tiny fraction of the patronage available in these cities, and with very different incentive systems for political participation.

A second school of thought, far more influential in American social science, interprets machine politics as a product of the social needs and political techniques of a bygone historical period. Advocates of this position attempt to explain both the past existence of machines and their putative current demise in terms of the functions that the machines performed. In analyzing the functions—now supposedly obsolete—that machine politics served, it is useful to consider four questions:

1. Did political machines actually perform these functions in the past?
2. Do machines still perform them?
3. Has the need for the functions diminished?
4. Is machine politics found wherever these needs exist?

It is commonly argued that various historical trends have crucially diminished the natural constituencies of machines, people who provided votes or other political support in return for the machine's services. The essential machine constituency is thought to have been the poor in general and immigrants in particular. The decline of machine politics then is due to rising prosperity and education, which have reduced the number of people to whom the machine's rewards are attractive or necessary. These trends have also, as Thomas R. Dye puts it, spread

> middle class values about honesty, efficiency, and good government, which inhibit party organizations in purchases, contracts, and vote-buying, and other cruder forms of municipal corruption. The more successful machine [*sic*] today, like Daley's in Chicago, have had to reform themselves in order to maintain a good public image.[67]

One function that machines performed was furnishing needy people with food, clothing, and other *direct material assistance*—those legendary Christmas turkeys, buckets of coal, summer outings, and so on. There is no way of knowing just how much of this kind of help machines gave, but it seems to have been an important means of gleaning votes. From the time of the

---

[65] Tolchin and Tolchin, "How Judgeships Get Bought," p. 29; and " 'Honest Graft' —Playing the Patronage Game," *New York Magazine* (22 March 1971), 41.

[66] *New York Times,* 17 June 1968, p. 30.

[67] Dye, *Politics in States and Communities,* p. 271.

New Deal, government has assumed the burden of providing for the minimal physical needs of the poor, thus supposedly preempting a major source of the machines' appeal. The growth of the welfare state undeniably has limited politicians' opportunities to use charity as a means of incurring obligations that could be discharged by political support. Some political clubs still carry on the old traditions, however, including the distribution of free turkeys to needy families at Christmas time.[68] One might also note that the Black Panther party seems to be fulfilling a genuine need with its well-publicized program of breakfasts for hungry school children.

Machines supposedly provided other tangible rewards, the need for which has not been met by alternative institutions. The most obvious of these benefits is employment. The welfare state does not guarantee everyone a job and so the power to hire is still an important political resource. It has been argued, most ably by Frank J. Sorauf, that patronage jobs, mainly at the bottom of the pay scale, are not very attractive to most people.[69] But these positions are attractive to enough people to maintain an ample demand for them, and thus they still are a useful incentive.

A second major type of constituent service supplied by machine politics was *helping poor and unacculturated people deal with the bureaucratic demands of urban government.* Describing this function, some writers have stressed its affective dimension. Robert K. Merton put it this way: "The precinct captain is ever a friend in need. In our increasingly impersonal society, the machine, through its local agents, fulfills the important social *function of humanizing and personalizing all manner of assistance* to those in need."[70] In Dye's view, the machine "personalized government. With keen social intuition, the machine recognized the voter as a man, generally living in a neighborhood, who had specific personal problems and wants."[71] William F. Whyte saw a more cognitive element in politicians' services to the common man: "The uninitiated do not understand the complex organization of government and do not know how to find the channels through which they can obtain action."[72] Whyte's view of the relationship between the citizen and

---

68 Tolchin and Tolchin, " 'Honest Graft,' " p. 42.

69 See especially his "Patronage and Party," *Midwest Journal of Political Science,* 3 (May 1959), 115–26. In this and other articles Sorauf has argued not only that patronage is unattractive, but that it is inefficiently exploited by party leaders. His direct observations are limited to his study of the consequences of the 1954 Democratic gubernatorial victory for the highway maintenance crew in one rural county in Pennsylvania. Sorauf is more persuasive about the ineffectuality of Democratic leaders in Centre County than about the generalizability of his findings. He concludes, moreover, that "the parties need the strength of patronage, however minor and irregular it may be..." (*ibid.,* p. 126).

70 Merton, *Social Theory and Social Structure,* p. 74 (emphasis in the original).

71 Dye, *Politics in States and Communities,* p. 257.

72 William F. Whyte, *Street Corner Society,* enl. ed. (Chicago: University of Chicago Press, 1955), p. 241.

his "friend in need," the precinct captain, is a good deal less innocent than Merton's: "Everyone recognizes that when a politician does a favor for a constituent, the constituent becomes obligated to the politician."[73]

If machine politics was a response to "our increasingly impersonal society," it would seem to follow that continuing growth in the scope, complexity, and impersonality of institutional life would produce *greater* need for politicians to mediate between individuals and their government. The growth of the welfare state, therefore, has not diminished this need but increased it and presumably offers the machine politician new opportunities for exercising his function of helping citizens get what they want from the government. Describing the advent of New Deal social services in a poor Boston neighborhood, Whyte made it clear that the new welfare policies did not so much subvert machine politics as rearrange the channels of access while presenting some politicians with a new opportunity to accumulate obligations. Whyte quotes the wife of a state senator: " 'If you're qualified, you can get on [WPA] without going to a politician. But it will be four weeks before you get certified, and I can push things through so that you get on in a week. And I can see that you get a better job. . . .' "[74]

As far as local politicians are concerned, new public services may be new prizes which covetous citizens can more easily obtain through political influence. Writing a generation after Whyte, Harold Kaplan reported that in Newark

> A public housing tenant, therefore, may find it easier to secure a public housing unit, prevent eviction from a project, secure a unit in a better project, or have NHA [Newark Housing Authority] reconsider his rent, if he has the right sponsor at City Hall.[75]

There is no necessary connection, then, between expanded public services and a decline in the advantages of political help or in the number of people who want to use it. While the expansion and institutionalization of welfare may have ended "the party's monopoly of welfare services,"[76] one would think that this trend has vastly expanded the need for information, guidance, and emotional support in relations between citizens and government officials, and thus that there is no shortage of services that machines can provide the poor and unacculturated, who are still with us.[77]

---

[73] *Ibid.,* p. 240.

[74] *Ibid.,* p. 197.

[75] Kaplan, *Urban Renewal Politics,* pp. 42–43.

[76] Dye, *Politics in States and Communities,* p. 271.

[77] Some contemporary political organizations do give advice and legal aid, mediate disputes, and serve as clearinghouses for information. See Wilson, *The Amateur Democrat,* p. 176; and Tolchin and Tolchin, " 'Honest Graft,' " p. 42.

There is no doubt that in the past 50 years income levels have risen and the flow of foreign immigrants has dwindled considerably. But there are plenty of poor people in the cities, the middle classes have been moving to the suburbs for the past two generations, the European immigrants of yester-year are far from assimilated and acculturated, foreign immigration continues at a reduced rate, and these immigrants are accompanied by millions of blacks, Puerto Ricans, Mexican-Americans, and poor rural whites. Thus the familiar argument that affluence and assimilation have choked machine politics at the roots may now look a bit more threadbare. Yet the recent rediscovery of poverty and cultural deprivation has not had a discernible impact on thinking about trends in the viability of machine politics.

Along with the new interest in the urban poor has come a realization that existing institutions do not meet their needs. Among these inadequate insti-tutions is the political machine, which, in the traditional view, should be expected to do for today's blacks, Chicanos, Puerto Ricans, and poor whites just what it is supposed to have done for yesterday's immigrants. But even in cities with flourishing machine politics there has been a tremendous devel-opment of all kinds of community action groups for advice, information ex-change, and the representation of individual and neighborhood interests— just the functions that the machines are said to have performed. The gap between the disoriented poor and the public institutions serving them seems to be present equally in cities like Chicago, generally thought to be political anachronisms, and in places like Los Angeles that have never experienced machine politics.[78] This leads to an important point: most American cities have had the social conditions that are said to give rise to machine politics, but many of these cities have not had machine politics for a generation or more.

This fact and the evident failure of existing machines to perform their functions cast doubt on the conventional ways of explaining both the func-tions of machines in their supposed heyday and the causes of their "decline." One conclusion is that the decline is real, but that the causes do not lie prin-cipally in affluence and assimilation. A second possibility is that the machines persist, but have abandoned the beneficent functions they used to perform. A third is that they are still "humanizing and personalizing all manner of assistance to those in need," but cannot cope with a massive increase in the

[78] "The demise of the historic urban political machines...has eliminated an important political link between city government and low-income residents" and therefore con-tributed to black unrest. See the *Report of the National Advisory Commission on Civil Disorders* (New York: E. P. Dutton & Co., Inc., 1968), p. 287. While this argument by the President's "Riot Commission" is faithful to the conventional wisdom of political science, it overlooks the inconvenient fact that lethal racial uprisings occurred both in "good government" cities like Los Angeles and in places with "old-fashioned machines" like Newark. Although Chicago was spared a convulsion like the Watts tragedy, it has had several smaller riots as well as a continuing situation of tense racial confrontation.

needs of their clienteles. And a fourth alternative is that the extent to which they ever performed these functions has been exaggerated.

It does seem that a whole generation of scholarship has been adversely affected by overreaction to the older judgmental style of describing machine politics. Until a decade or two ago most work on this subject was moralistic and pejorative, dwelling on the seamy side of the subject and concerned largely with exposure and denunciation.[79] More contemporary social scientists have diverged from this tradition in two respects. One, apparently a reaction to the highly normative style of the old reformers, is a tendency to gloss over the very real evils they described. The other, addressed to the major problem of explaining the durability of machine politics, is the search for "functions": acculturating immigrants and giving them a channel of social mobility, providing a link between citizen and city hall, and coordinating formally fragmented government agencies. Some writers suggest that urban political organizations were a rudimentary form of the welfare state. While the tone of these later works has been realistic, some of them leaned toward idealizing their subject, perhaps in reaction to the earlier moralism or because functionalism has not been accompanied by an inclination to confront the sordid details. Thus the development of a more dispassionate social science has produced, on the descriptive level, a retreat from realism. The functionalists seem to have been somewhat overcredulous: "the precinct captain is ever a friend in need."

The innocence of the functionalist view may explain the popularity in recent textbooks of a pious declaration by a celebrated and unsavory ward boss in Boston: " 'I think,' said Martin Lomasny [*sic*], 'that there's got to be in every ward somebody that any bloke can come to—no matter what he's done—and get help. Help, you understand; none of your law and your justice, but help.' "[80] The kind of "help" that could be expected is suggested by the remarks of another local leader in Boston that convey, I think, a more realistic sense of the priorities in machine politics:

> When people wanted help from the organization, they would come right up here to the office [of the political club]. Matt [the boss] would be in here every morning from nine to eleven, and if you couldn't see him then, you could find him in the ward almost any other time. If a man came in to ask Matt for a job, Matt would listen to him and then tell him he'd see what he could do; he should come back in a couple of days. That would give Matt time to get in touch with the precinct captain and find out all about the man. If he didn't vote in the last election, he was out. Matt wouldn't do anything

[79] For a description of trends in the study of city politics, see Wallace S. Sayre and Nelson W. Polsby, "American Political Science and the Study of Urbanization," in *The Study of Urbanization,* eds. Philip M. Hauser and Leo F. Schnore (New York: John Wiley & Sons, Inc., 1965), pp. 115–56.

[80] Originally quoted in *The Autobiography of Lincoln Steffens,* p. 618.

for him—that is, unless he could show that he was so sick he couldn't get to the polls.[81]

"Helping" citizens deal with government is, in this context, usually thought to be a matter of advice about where to go, whom to see, and what to say. The poor undeniably need this service more than people whose schooling and experience equip them to cope with bureaucratic institutions and procedures. But in some local political cultures, advice to citizens often is accompanied by pressure on officials. The machine politician's goal is to incur the maximum obligation from his constituents, and merely providing information is not as big a favor as helping bring about the desired outcome. Thus *"help" shades into "pull."*

There is no reason why the advantages of political influence appeal only to the poor. Where the political culture supports expectations that official discretion will be exercised in accordance with political considerations, the constituency for machine politics extends across the socioeconomic spectrum. People whose interests are affected by governmental decisions can include those who want to sell to the government, as well as those whose economic or social activities may be subject to public regulation.

Favoritism animates machine politics, favoritism not just in filling pick-and-shovel jobs, but in a vast array of public decisions. The welfare state has little to do with the potential demand for favoritism, except to expand opportunities for its exercise. The New Deal did not abolish the contractor's natural desire to minimize the risks of competitive bidding, nor the landlord's equally natural desire to avoid the burdens of the housing code. It is all very well to talk about "middle-class values of efficiency and honesty," but the thousands of lawyers whose political connections enable them to benefit from the billion-dollar-a-year case load of the Manhattan Surrogates' Court are surely not members of the working class.

While "help" in dealing with the government may appeal primarily to people baffled by the complexities of modern society and too poor to hire lawyers, "pull" is useful in proportion to the size of one's dealings with government. Certain kinds of business and professional men are *more* likely to have interests requiring repeated and complicated relations with public agencies, and thus are potentially a *stronger* constituency for machine politics than the working classes. The conventional wisdom that the middle classes are hostile to machine politics rests on several types of evidence: (1) the undeniable fact that reform candidates almost always run better in well-to-do neighborhoods; (2) the equally undeniable fact that machine politics provides, in patronage and petty favors, a kind of reward for political participation that is not available in other incentive systems; and (3) the less validated proposition that middle-class people think that governments should be run

[81] Quoted in Whyte, *Street Corner Society*, p. 194.

with impartial, impersonal honesty in accordance with abstract principles, while the working classes are more sympathetic to favoritism and particular-istic criteria. These characterizations may be true in the aggregate for two diverse categories like "the middle class" and "the working class," although this has not yet been established. Even if these generalizations are true, however, they would still leave room for the existence of a sizable subcategory of the middle class who, in some political cultures, benefit from and endorse machine politics.

Textbook interpretations recognize these middle-class interests in machine politics, but generally relegate them to an hypothesized earlier stage in urban history. This was the era when America changed from a rural to an urban society, a shift that created a vast need in the new cities for municipal facilities and services: streetcars, electricity, paved streets, and so on. These needs were met by businessmen who corrupted officials wholesale in their eagerness to get franchises. Since the businessmen wanted action, they profited from political machines that could organize power to get things done by cen-tralizing the formally fragmented agencies of government. Thus machine politics served the needs not just of poor immigrants, but also of the genera-tion of businessmen exploiting the foundation of urban America. But after the first great rush of city building, the essential facilities and utilities had been supplied and business interest in local government declined. Machine politics no longer performed a coordinating function for the franchise seekers and so lost an important constituency.

While this may be an accurate description of relations between business greed and governmental corruption in the Gilded Age, it has a number of deficiencies as an explanation of the rise and fall of machine politics. Three of these flaws have already been discussed in other contexts: (1) Like poverty, urban growth is not a bygone phenomenon, but continues to this day. (2) Machine politics does not occur wherever cities have experienced sudden and massive needs for municipal services. (3) This explanation confuses patron-age and centralization of party organizations at the city level, two phenomena that may not be found together.

There are other difficulties with this line of thought. First, uncoordinated public agencies and jurisdictions continue to proliferate. If machine politics were a response to the formal decentralization of government, one would think that it, too, would increase, and that party organizations would grow stronger rather than weaker. It may be that one or more unstated intermediary condi-tions are preventing the latter trends from occurring; if so, no writer has, to my knowledge, shown what this interactive relationship is.

If it were true that "the key structural function of the Boss is to organize, centralize, and maintain in good working condition the 'scattered fragments of power'" typical of American local government, one would expect to find a positive relationship between the prevalence of machine politics and municipal institutions that maximize fragmentation. "Strong-mayor" cities should be least ridden by patronage, and commission and council-manager cities should have the most. There is no systematic evidence available about these relationships, but what data there are do not support the proposition: (It is also not supported by another piece of the conventional wisdom, which associates city managers with reformism.) Machine politics seems to be far more common on the East Coast than in the West, but so are cities with elected mayors. Cities with mayors and cities with managers are equally likely to have merit systems for their employees, which could be considered an index of the weakness of machine politics.[82]

Finally, political centralization may not be conducive to the interests of businessmen who want prompt and affirmative action from local government. Whether centralized power is preferable depends on what the businessman wants. If he wants a license or franchise, to sell goods or services, or to buy something belonging to the government, it might be in his interests to deal with an autonomous official or agency, not with a governmentwide hierarchy. John A. Gardiner's study of the notoriously corrupt city of "Wincanton" provides evidence for the proposition that decentralized political systems are *more* corruptible, because the potential corrupter needs to influence only a segment of the government, and because in a fragmented system there are fewer centralized forces and agencies to enforce honesty. The "Wincanton" political system is formally and informally fragmented; neither parties nor interest groups (including the criminal syndicate) exercise overall coordination. The ample patronage and outright graft in "Wincanton" are not used as a means of centralization.[83] Indeed, governmental coordination clearly would not be in the interests of the private citizens there who benefit from corruption, nor of the officials who take bribes. Attempts by reformers to stop graft or patronage founder on the city's commission form of government, which is both the apotheosis of local governmental fragmentation and a hospitable environment for machine politics.

The conventional wisdom also holds that the machines' electioneering techniques are as obsolete as the social functions they used to perform. According to this interpretation, "the old politics" based its campaigns on divisible promises and interpersonal persuasion, and these methods have been outdated by the mass media, particularly television, the growing importance of candidates' personalities, and the electorate's craving for ideological or at least programmatic promises.[84]

[82] Wolfinger and Field, "Political Ethos," pp. 314–16.

[83] Gardiner, *The Politics of Corruption,* pp. 8–12.

[84] Interviewing a number of party officials in New Jersey, Richard T. Frost found that "old-fashioned" techniques like door-to-door canvassing were considered more effective, and used more frequently, than newer methods like television advertising. See his "Stability and Change in Local Party Politics," *Public Opinion Quarterly,* 25 (Summer 1961), 221–35.

Like the other explanations of the machines' demise, this argument has serious factual and logical deficiencies. As we have seen, machine politics is an effective way of raising money for political purposes. There is no reason why the money "maced" from public employees or extracted from government contractors cannot be spent on motivational research, advertising copywriters, television spots, and all the other manifestations of mass media campaigns.

Similarly, there is no inconsistency between machine politics and outstanding candidates. Just as machine politicians can spend their money on public relations, so they can bestow their support on inspirational leaders exuding integrity and vitality. Many of the most famous "idealistic" politicians in American history owe their success to the sponsorship of machine politicians. Woodrow Wilson made his first venture into electoral politics as the gubernatorial candidate of an unsavory Democratic organization in New Jersey. (Once elected governor, Wilson promptly betrayed his sponsors.) In more recent times, such exemplars of dedicated public spirit as the elder Adlai Stevenson, Paul H. Douglas, and Chester Bowles were nominated for office as the candidates of the patronage-based party organizations in their respective states.[85]

Sayre and Kaufman explain organization willingness to support blue ribbon candidates: "They [machine leaders] have also learned the lesson of what retailers call the loss leader—that is, the item that may lose money for the storekeeper but which lures customers in and thereby leads to increases in purchases of profitable merchandise."[86] Generally, party regulars turn to blue ribbon "loss leaders" when they think that their popularity is necessary to carry the ticket to victory. Otherwise, machine politicians eschew candidates

---

[85] Bowles is sometimes depicted as a high-minded victim of crasser and smaller men in the Connecticut Democratic party. The principal event presented as evidence for this viewpoint is his defeat by Thomas J. Dodd for the senatorial nomination at the 1958 Democratic convention. Dodd had long been an opponent of the regular Democratic organization headed by then-Governor Abraham A. Ribicoff and state chairman John Bailey. Bowles, on the other hand, had been the organization's gubernatorial candidate in 1950. After his defeat for the senatorial nomination in 1958, he accepted the organization's offer of a congressional nomination and was elected to Congress in the fall. Ribicoff and Bailey thought that Bowles's popularity would help win the seat, then held by a Republican, and brushed aside the claims of the announced candidates for the Democratic nomination, who "voluntarily" withdrew their names from consideration by the convention.

One of the seconding speeches in support of Bowles's unsuccessful try for the senatorial nomination was by Arthur Barbieri, who later became a close ally of Dodd's. It was devoted to praising Bowles's willingness, when governor, to accede to the party's wishes in matters involving patronage. The disciplined New Haven delegation voted unanimously for Bowles, a Yankee patrician. Dodd, an Irish Catholic, was the sentimental favorite of many delegates, but almost all of them were city employees or financially dependent on city hall in some other way.

[86] Sayre and Kaufman, *Governing New York City*, p. 155.

with independent popular appeal, since popularity is an important bargaining resource in intraparty negotiating; without it, an elected official is more dependent on organization politicians.

In addition to candidates who have been the beneficiaries of machine favor, other compelling figures like Fiorello La Guardia and the Kennedys have built campaign organizations and then forced the party regulars to come to terms with them. The Kennedy brothers were not originally organization candidates the way Bowles or Stevenson were, but once they had formed coalitions with machine politicians, their own image-dominant style nicely complemented the kinds of electoral techniques generally associated with "the old politics." The Kennedys, of course, were skilled at machine politics as well.

The new politics is an ambiguous term. It is used to describe increasing campaign emphasis on the mass media and professional public relations, and is also applied to popular participation in party affairs and direct contact with the voters by campaign workers. In the 1968 and 1972 elections "the new politics" was associated with peace advocates and the young enthusiasts who gave so much tone to the presidential bids of Eugene McCarthy and George McGovern. Except for the age of the activists, there was little to distinguish this aspect of the McGovern and McCarthy campaigns from the idealistic appeal of such previous and diverse presidential candidates as Adlai Stevenson and Barry Goldwater, both of whom projected an image of altruism and reform that attracted legions of dedicated workers.[87] "The new politics" seems to be one of those recurring features of American politics that political writers are always rediscovering. The trademark of "the new politics" is intense precinct work, one-to-one conversations with citizens—the same interpersonal style that machines have relied on for generations. As a Democratic organization politician in New York observed: "If the new politics teaches anything, it's that the old politics was pretty good. The McCarthy kids in New Hampshire rang doorbells, made the telephone calls, made the personal contact that people associate with the old-style machine."[88]

Both kinds of "new politics" have at least one thing in common: they tend to be found in elections that draw a great deal of attention and arouse strong emotions. State and local elections and party primaries (except presidential ones) rarely attain much visibility. Candidates for the city council, the state legislature, or the city or state underticket seldom attract much public atten-

---

[87] It is interesting that Stevenson and Goldwater, while very attractive to one strain of party activist, had exceptionally low popular personal appeal for the electorate as a whole. See Donald E. Stokes, "Some Dynamic Elements of Contests for the Presidency," *American Political Science Review,* 60 (March 1966), 19–28. The same problem haunted McGovern also. Candidates with most appeal to elite activists seem to have difficulty in attaining mass popularity.

[88] Quoted in the *New York Times,* 1 June 1970, p. 27.

tion. Even paid media advertising in most such elections is not feasible because the voting jurisdiction for a single candidacy generally includes only a fraction of the reading or viewing audience of the most widely used media. An occasional mayoral or gubernatorial race may get a good deal of media space and arouse popular enthusiasm, but otherwise these elections do not present a high profile in most voters' perspectives. This is particularly true for local elections, which generally are not concurrent with national campaigns, as well as for party primaries and campaigns for any state office except the governorship. These low-salience contests are particularly amenable to the resources typical of machine politics. A New York state senator explained this point bluntly:

> My best captains, in the primary, are the ones who are on the payroll. You can't get the average voter excited about who's going to be an Assemblyman or State Senator. I've got two dozen people who are going to work so much harder, because if I lose, they lose.[89]

In elections of this type, where neither the mass media nor idealistic amateurs are likely to participate, most of the spoils of machine politics are at stake. Because precinct work is effective in inverse relation to the salience of the election,[90] "old-fashioned machines" do not seem too threatened by either form of "the new politics."

To summarize my argument: Because an increasing proportion of urban populations is poor and uneducated, it is not persuasive to argue that growing prosperity and education are diminishing the constituency for machine politics. While governments now assume responsibility for a minimal level of welfare, other trends are not so inhospitable to machine politics. Various kinds of patronage still seem to be in reasonable supply and are as attractive as ever to those people—by no means all poor—who benefit from them. The proliferation of government programs provides more opportunities for the exercise of favoritism. The continuing bureaucratization of modern government gives more scope for the machine's putative function of serving as a link between the citizen and the state.

These trends would seem to have expanded the need for the services the machines supposedly performed for the poor. Yet surviving machines apparently are not performing these functions, and machine politics has not flourished in many cities where the alleged need for these functions is as great.

The potential constituency for political favoritism is not limited to the poor; many kinds of business and professional men can benefit from machine

---

[89] Quoted in the *New York Times,* 17 June 1968, p. 30.

[90] Raymond E. Wolfinger, "The Influence of Precinct Work on Voting Behavior," *Public Opinion Quarterly,* 27 (Fall 1963), 387–98.

politics. They do in some cities but not in others. Again, it appears that the hypothesized conditions for machine politics are found in many places where machines are enfeebled or absent.

Real and imaginary changes in campaign techniques are not inconsistent with machines' capacities.

In short, machines have not withered away because the conditions that supposedly gave rise to them are still present. The problem with this answer is that the conditions are found many places where machines are not.

Some Consequences of Machine Politics

What difference does it make if organization politics predominates, as in New Haven and much of the Northeast, or is virtually nonexistent, as in California? Some very general, tentative, and incomplete answers can be ventured.

With machine politics, the party organizations themselves are interest groups with powerful resources and motivations for influencing various kinds of governmental decisions. These interest groups are almost insignificant in different sorts of party systems.[91] In general, any machine wants to maintain and expand opportunities for the exercise of political influence, and to register its claims in all such instances. Machines are a factor in individual decisions on personnel appointments and the numerous details pursuant to the execution of public policy. On larger questions, they oppose extension of civil service, elimination of judicial patronage, and constitutional changes that centralize formal authority. During the Lee administration the New Haven Democratic organization consistently pressed for favoritism in zoning decisions and urban renewal administration (see Chapter 7), and against the appointment of out-of-town experts (see Chapter 9). In a tacit coalition with the Republican organization it defeated several charter reform proposals (see Chapter 11).

Such interest group activity imposes standards other than merit in personnel matters and introduces political connections as a criterion in making administrative decisions. The machine's appetite for patronage impedes the use of professional talent in government. Skilled professionals are cosmopolitans, moving from city to city as job opportunities become available. Their career patterns are incompatible with the parochial orientations of political machines, which result in pressures for residence requirements for civil servants and other attempts to restrict municipal jobs to city residents. Mayor Lee's ambitious urban renewal and antipoverty programs required a variety of experts in fields ranging from traffic engineering to remedial edu-

91 See V. O. Key, Jr., *Politics, Parties, and Pressure Groups,* 5th ed. (New York: Thomas Y. Crowell Company, 1964), Chap. 13.

cation. Such people are, of course, recruited in a national job market. Yet in entering this market, Lee had to contend with the Democratic organization, one of whose leaders expressed to me the machine politician's prototypical view: "There's not a job in city hall that couldn't be filled by a Democrat who lives right here in New Haven."

A second major consequence of machine politics is to increase each party's potential autonomy with respect to private pressure groups. Where it is available, patronage provides politicians with a good share of the resources used in the political arena. These resources otherwise would have to be raised from private sources. Thus wherever there are political machines—in a ward, city, county, or state—the party in that jurisdiction *can* be less dependent on constituent interest groups because the availability of patronage relieves somewhat the party's need to rely on those groups for money and manpower.[92]

In his study of the party constituencies of congressmen in Cook County, Illinois, Leo M. Snowiss found that in the suburbs, where patronage was scanty, ideologically-inclined Republican businessmen had much more influence over congressional nominations because the politicians were more dependent on their financial contributions. But closer to the city, the politicians could raise money on their own terms and so could afford to pay less attention to the businessmen.[93]

The parallel situation is much more noticeable in the Democratic party, where labor union influence varies in inverse ratio to the prevalence of machine politics. In Detroit, for example, there is little patronage and not much of a party organization, and hence the United Automobile Workers are so influential that they often seem to *be* the party. In Chicago, on the other hand, unions are a rather slight factor in party affairs.[94] The same is true in New Haven. Although 36 percent of our sample of registered voters belonged to unions or had a union member in their immediate family, the labor organizations were not really very important in Democratic politics. The reason for this relative impotence was the Democratic party's ability to raise plenty of money and recruit hundreds of campaign workers by means of its own resources. It had little need for organized labor and therefore could pay less attention to labor's demands than would be prudent if the unions were a larger proportion of the available sinews of political power.

92 This general statement resembles the familiar proposition that interest groups are weaker where parties are stronger, although I doubt that most advocates of "more responsible parties" would welcome attaining stronger party discipline by means of patronage.

93 Leo M. Snowiss, "Congressional Recruitment and Representation," *American Political Science Review,* 60 (September 1966), 627–39.

94 For other examples supporting this generalization, see J. David Greenstone, "Party Pressure on Organized Labor in Three Cities," in *The Electoral Process,* eds. M. Kent Jennings and L. Harmon Zeigler (Englewood Cliffs, N.J.: Prentice-Hall, Inc., 1966), pp. 55–80.

Machines' ability to withstand the claims of major constituent groups varies with the issue context—it is greater in nominations and weaker in substantive issues—and with the cohesiveness of the party, for in a divided party one faction or the other naturally will look for allies outside the "patronage system." The consequences of machine politics for relations between parties and interest groups, then, are twofold: (1) the parties are more able to resist substantive policy demands; and (2) their most specialized function, that of selecting candidates, can more easily be exercised without "outside" interference.

The humble origins of most leading machine politicians, the services that they allegedly render the poor, and the more proletarian quality of their activist constituencies have led some writers to the conclusion that machine politics has been favorable to the interests of the working classes. Is it true that, in addition to being of the people and by the people, it is also for the people? Does machine politics benefit the poor more than other incentive systems found in American city politics? Answers to these questions are found throughout this book. Let me here provide some highly oversimplified general responses.

An ideal type of machine politics system is not concerned with substantive issues as such, but it is very much concerned with "details" of policy, and its concerns here are likely to have an anti–working-class bias. One such bias is found in those areas where local governments have regulatory functions and where administrative discretion is affected by political influence, for example, in housing code enforcement. Much regulation of this kind is designed to help the less well-off, as consumers, by substituting governmental intervention for their lack of market power. Such local regulation is notoriously amenable to political influence, attained chiefly through campaign contributions. The consequence, then, is to benefit those who have the resources to influence government this way, and to disadvantage the intended beneficiaries of the subverted laws. Where money talks, the poor are silent. For this reason it is wise to discount the argument one sometimes hears that corrupt politicians, like Robin Hood, benefit the poor by redistributing income downward.[95] In this connection, it is also wise to remember that local tax systems generally are rather regressive and thus that the poor pay for the "favors" and "humanity" they get from machine politics.

The individual voter's support for the machine is not likely to be rewarded by its leaders' formulation of policy programs. Machines do not pay off their rank-and-file supporters with social policies, nor are they pressed to do so.

[95] See, for example, McKitrick's approving quotation of an observation attributed to David Riesman that with corruption, local politics is "soaked in gravy which we can well afford." McKitrick, "The Study of Corruption," p. 450. Of course, because local taxes are usually regressive, even the direct costs of corruption are not financed by McKitrick's presumably well-to-do reference group.

Whyte explains why: "If a man wants three things—to keep out of jail, to get a job, and to have new play space for his children—he will not ask for them all at once."[96] He is likely, in fact, to ask for them in the order Whyte lists, which means that the availability of personal and divisible benefits will divert voters' attention from pursuit of more general policies of greater long-run value to them. Moreover, such policies are likely to be more harmful to some group's interests, and thus their advocacy is a riskier political strategy.

Paradoxically, this same issue-free quality makes it possible for machine politics to provide the sinews of effective policy innovation when innovative leaders are in control. Machine politics is an incentive system that builds organization without commitments on issues. It presents a skilled leader with the opportunity to meet the maintenance needs of his organizational allies without substantive compromises. If the most important consideration to aldermen is not the content of policy but who gets the jobs and contracts, then an innovative mayor is a good deal less hampered than if he has to negotiate with politicians who care about policies as well as patronage. Dahl has described the advantages of machine politics in the following passage distinguishing between the various clienteles to whom political leaders must appeal:

> The policies that leaders promise to constituents and followings—I shall call them *overt* policies—are not always identical to, or indeed even consistent with, the covert commitments they make to their subleaders. From the point of view of a leader concerned with the task of building his following, it would be ideal if his subleaders were indifferent to his overt policies, for this would give him freedom to develop overt policies exclusively adapted to the desires of constituents and followings. But this kind of complete independence from the desired subleaders is almost impossible for a leader to attain. It could exist only where the flow of rewards for which subleaders give their services did not depend at all on the overt policies of leaders.[97]

More than any other incentive system, machine politics separates the rewards to subleaders and the overt policies that are or can be promised to voters. One of the ironies of American city government is that machine politics provides the strongest resources for innovative mayors, but at the same time, in its weak emphasis on issue appeals, is unlikely to attract such leaders or develop a popular demand for them.

These conclusions about machine politics are very similar to those in the preceding chapter about the characteristic politics of nationality groups. There are, indeed, many affinities between the two political styles, and they are often found together. In both instances constituents are offered similar or compatible benefits: tangible but divisible ones like jobs, and indivisible

---

96 Whyte, *Street Corner Society,* p. 246.

97 Dahl, *Who Governs?,* pp. 98–99 (emphasis in the original).

but intangible ones like recognition. The characteristic political demands of ethnic groups are those which machine politicians are most accustomed to accommodating, which least threaten their tacit alliances, and which present them with similar raw material for maintaining their organizations and negotiating agreements with other politicians. Neither style has been particularly successful in redistributing income or in mobilizing rank-and-file supporters for substantive policy demands.

Do Immigrants and Machines
Go Together?

We come at last to direct examination of a familiar theme which has been closely skirted in much of the previous discussion: relationships between the social character of local populations and the prevalence of machine politics. The juxtaposition in New Haven—and many other cities—of a large ethnic population and pronounced machine politics might seem to lend credence to the popular notion that immigrants and their offspring have a distinctive affinity for the politics of patronage and favoritism. The most influential formulation along these lines is that popular attitudes toward the nature and goals of politics can be subsumed in two conflicting orientations, one typical of ethnic groups, the other held by old Americans. This view was stated in a famous passage by the late Richard Hofstadter:

> Out of the clash between the needs of the immigrants and the sentiments of the natives there emerged two thoroughly different systems of political ethics. ...One, founded upon the indigenous Yankee-Protestant political traditions, and upon middle-class life, assumed and demanded the constant, disinterested activity of the citizen in public affairs, argued that political life ought to be run ... in accordance with general principles and abstract laws apart from and superior to personal needs.... The other system, founded upon the European backgrounds of the immigrants, upon their unfamiliarity with independent political action, their familiarity with hierarchy and authority, and upon the urgent needs that so often grew out of their migration, took for granted that the political life of the individual would arise out of family needs, interpreted political and civic relations chiefly in terms of personal obligations, and placed strong personal loyalties above allegiance to abstract codes of law or morals. It was chiefly upon this system of values that the political life of the immigrant, the boss, and the urban machine was based.[98]

This formulation has been elaborated in a series of publications by Edward C. Banfield and James Q. Wilson. One of the "main lines of analysis" in

[98] Richard Hofstadter, *The Age of Reform* (New York: Alfred A. Knopf, Inc., 1955), pp. 8–9.

their book on American urban politics "emphasizes the fundamental cleavage between the public-regarding, Anglo-Saxon Protestant, middle-class ethos and the private-regarding, lower-class, immigrant ethos."[99] The latter ethos

> is the conception of those people who identify with the ward or neighborhood rather than the city "as a whole," who look to politicians for "help" and "favors," . . . and who are far less interested in the efficiency, impartiality, and honesty of local government than in its readiness to confer material benefits of one sort or another upon them.[100]

Banfield and Wilson attributed a bundle of specific institutional and policy preferences to each ethos. A desire for city managers, nonpartisan ballots, at-large city council elections, civil service, urban renewal, and city planning, as well as willingness to bear a greater property tax burden, were all said to be elements of "public-regardingness," and the opposite set of preferences was attributed to immigrants and their progeny.[101]

It is hardly controversial that different people have different feelings about the goals, institutions, procedures, and policies of local governments, or that some people are more community-minded or evaluate politics in more abstract or universal terms. One of the distinctive features of the ethos theory is that it posits *two coherent ideologies* toward all these things.[102] Banfield and Wilson argue that popular perspectives on these subjects tend to "coalesce into two opposed patterns. These patterns reflect two conceptions of the public interest that are widely held." Thus attitudes are grouped in regular and consistent ways. As Banfield and Wilson put it, "people who are decidedly public-regarding or decidedly private-regarding on one matter tend to be so on all matters."[103] One way to judge the ethos theory is to see whether in fact the attitudes it subsumes are organized into two dichotomous syndromes such that an individual's attitudes toward some elements of the theory can be predicted by knowing what he thinks about other elements. If the theory were valid, one would expect to find an association between, say, support for

99 Banfield and Wilson, *City Politics,* p. 239.

100 *Ibid.,* p. 46.

101 *Ibid.,* pp. 92, 95, 154, 170, 330.

102 The ethos theory seems to exaggerate most Americans' capacity for thinking about political topics in ideological terms. For an impressive demonstration of the scarcity of such coherent, interrelated perspectives, see Philip E. Converse, "The Nature of Belief Systems in Mass Publics," in *Ideology and Discontent,* ed. David E. Apter (New York: The Free Press, 1965), pp. 206–61.

An interpretation emphasizing self-interest rather than "pure" ideological views of government, and an economic rather than an ethnic definition of the pressures for adoption of "public-regarding" institutions, may be found in Hays, "The Politics of Reform in Municipal Government in the Progressive Era."

103 Banfield and Wilson, *City Politics,* pp. 46, 235.

at-large elections and willingness to bear a higher tax burden for purposes that did not benefit the taxpayer.

When it was stated in *City Politics,* a second major feature of the ethos theory seemed to be another dichotomy, between native-stock residents (supplemented by upper-middle-class Jews) and persons of foreign stock: "In all social classes the proportion of voters who are decidedly public-regarding is higher among Protestants than among other ethnic groups." Aside from singling out Poles and Czechs as particularly prone to private-regardingness, Banfield and Wilson did not discuss the likelihood that nationality groups might vary in this respect, nor did they differentiate among various kinds of old Americans.[104] Each of these two broad categories includes a vast and disparate array of social types. "Old Americans" can be Yankee patricians, hillbillies, midwestern dairy farmers, southern sharecroppers, New England fishermen, and so on. People of foreign stock include Jewish schoolteachers, Polish steelworkers, midwestern dairy farmers, southwestern farm laborers, California fishermen, and so on. Banfield and Wilson subsequently recognized the inadequacy of such gross categories. Their revised "theory suggests that certain groups, provisionally defined along lines of income and ethnicity, have conflicting views about the nature and purpose of politics...."[105] More recently they wrote that the public-regarding grouping "would have been better described as 'upper-class' or 'upper-middle-class.' "[106]

Evidence for the ethos theory can best be examined under the two rubrics stated above: (1) Do different hypothesized elements of each ethos actually "coalesce into two opposed patterns," or are these various opinions in fact not found in association with each other in the perspectives of voters? (2) How are these views of politics distributed among different groups?

One might expect that the various institutions and policies said to be part of the public-regarding ethos would be found together in American cities, and that the same would be true of the private-regarding ethos. That is, cities with mayors should also have partisan elections and ward-based councils, and less civil service coverage, urban renewal, and city planning. The opposite pattern should be found in manager cities. In fact, there *is* a limited public-

104 *Ibid.,* p. 235. In a subsequent article, the authors said that they regarded ethnicity rather than income as the key social factor associated with preference for one ethos or the other. See James Q. Wilson and Edward C. Banfield, "Public Regardingness as a Value Premise in Voting Behavior," *American Political Science Review,* 58 (December 1964), 885.

105 Banfield and Wilson, "Communications," *American Political Science Review,* 60 (December 1966), 998–99. Other supporters of the ethos theory still seem to think that this dichotomy is useful and valid. See, for example, Robert L. Lineberry and Edmund P. Fowler, "Reformism and Public Policies in American Cities," *American Political Science Review,* 61 (September 1967), 701–2.

106 James Q. Wilson and Edward C. Banfield, "Political Ethos Revisited," *American Political Science Review,* 65 (December 1971), 1049.

regarding syndrome with respect to some structural features, in that most manager cities do have nonpartisan ballots and at-large councils. They are not, however, any more likely than cities with mayors to have extensive civil service, urban renewal, or city planning. Cities with mayors do not display any structural consistency; they have, in roughly equal proportions, every possible combination of type of ballot and method of electing councilmen.[107]

Surveys of attitudes toward aspects of political ethos reveal a similar lack of association between different dimensions of either ethos; popular attitudes do not fall into two consistent, mutually exclusive patterns. Philip B. Coulter measured inclinations toward public-regardingness and private-regardingness in a sample in Springfield, Massachusetts. Only 36 percent of his respondents were decidedly inclined toward one ethos or the other. The remaining two-thirds of the sample gave a balanced mixture of public- and private-regarding answers. Most of the respondents were clustered not at the extremes of the distribution, but at the midpoint. Moreover, their answers did not form a Guttman scale; knowing a respondent's answer to one question would not help predict his attitude on other items.[108] These findings suggest that Coulter was not measuring two coherent and exhaustive bodies of political belief, but a collection of discrete and randomly interrelated opinions.

The same conclusions seem warranted by Wilson and Banfield's attitude research on a Boston sample. They defined three dimensions of political ethos, each of which had a public-regarding and a private-regarding pole. (These two perspectives were given new names for this study: "unitarist" and "individualist.") For either ethic, the three components were weakly and inconsistently related to each other, which indicates that they did not form parts of two coherent, interrelated political outlooks. Only 12 percent of the sample had the expected combination of either "unitarist" or "individualist" attitudes. Wilson and Banfield concluded that few Boston residents displayed either political ethos.[109]

Relationships between the prevalence of ethnic groups and the strength of private-regardingness seem to be equally uncertain. Cities with larger foreign-stock populations are not more likely to adopt any of the institutions and policies that are said to be manifestations of private-regardingness.[110] A study of contemporary referenda on changes in the form of municipal govern-

107 Wolfinger and Field, "Political Ethos," pp. 312–24. Another study shows that cities with nonpartisan ballots and with the city manager form have slightly *smaller* urban renewal programs. See Michael Aiken and Robert R. Alford, "Community Structure and Innovation: The Case of Urban Renewal," *American Sociological Review,* 35 (August 1970), 658–70.

108 Philip B. Coulter, "Political Ethos Reexamined: A Test with Survey Data" (unpublished paper, University of Massachusetts, 1970).

109 Wilson and Banfield, "Political Ethos Revisited."

110 Wolfinger and Field, "Political Ethos," pp. 317–26.

ment in Pennsylvania cities revealed no relationships between ethnicity and preferences for the status quo—the commission form—or either council-mayor or city manager forms.[111] On the other hand, voting patterns in Cleveland and Chicago bond referenda reveal that foreign-stock voters were less favorable than old-stock Americans and blacks to taxing themselves for the benefit of others, and thus presumably were more private-regarding.[112]

The two attitude studies, by Coulter and by Wilson and Banfield, are equally inconclusive. Coulter reports that only 13 percent of his ethnic respondents were private-regarding, and only a third of the Yankees were public-regarding. He did find that Yankees were more likely than ethnics to be public-regarding, but this relationship vanished when his data were controlled for income. In their Boston attitude study, Wilson and Banfield found that well-to-do Yankees living on Beacon Hill (the only kind they included) were indeed more public-regarding than Irish or Italian respondents. Poles, earlier singled out as exceptionally private-regarding, were found to be somewhat public-regarding (or "unitarist"). Negroes, previously labeled public-regarding, turned out to be rather the opposite.

While these assorted findings do put a considerable dent in the ethos theory, they do not deal directly with the proposition that nationality groups have a characteristic affinity for machine politics and native-stock Americans do not. This belief seems to reflect the undeniable fact that in many places "old-style" organizations draw their voting support mostly from nationality groups, while reform movements are in the hands of Yankees and well-to-do Jews. Boston, Chicago, and New York are three cities where this has been the case for generations; they are also the sites of universities whose faculties have shaped contemporary social scientific thinking about these subjects, as well as the homes of many influential nonacademic writers on urban politics. But are these cities an adequate sample? Are their largely ethnic residents typical of all foreign-stock Americans? Are the embattled, upper-middle-class reformers around Hyde Park, Morningside Heights, and Beacon Hill really typical of old-stock citizens throughout the country?

One point of departure in answering these questions is the history of New England in the days before ethnics gained such influence in the region's political parties. Connecticut's current brand of machine politics is surely less private-regarding than the rampant public dishonesty and tightly centralized control associated with the long reign of the notorious Republican boss J. Henry Roraback, a Yankee relying on a Yankee-manned organization.[113] Rhode Island politics now is indisputably ethnic and allegedly private-regard-

---

111 James W. Clarke, "Environment, Process and Policy: A Reconsideration," *American Political Science Review,* 63 (December 1969), 1177–80.

112 Wilson and Banfield, "Public Regardingness as a Value Premise."

113 Duane Lockard, *New England State Politics* (Princeton: Princeton University Press, 1959), pp. 245–51.

ing. But as Duane Lockard wrote of an earlier era in Rhode Island: "Often boss-ridden and corrupt, the Republican party was the representative of business interests and rural Yankees."[114]

Elsewhere in the country machine politics is often found in places where nationality groups are scarce. The famous "courthouse rings" of many southern states are one example. Indiana politics is, as already described, notably private-regarding, yet only 8 percent of the state's residents are of foreign stock. The remarkable mingling of public business and political party profits in Indiana has "not been an issue in recent campaigns."[115] Indeed, one researcher reports that

> Indiana is the only state studied where the governor and other important state officials described quite frankly and in detail the sources of the campaign funds. They were disarmingly frank because they saw nothing wrong in the techniques employed to raise funds, and neither did the opposing political party nor the press nor, presumably, the citizenry.[116]

Far more interesting than social class differences are regional or subregional variations in the practices of machine politics and in attitudes toward them.[117] Public acceptance of patronage appears to vary a good deal from place to place in patterns that are not explained by differences in population characteristics like education, occupation, ethnicity, and so forth. Although systematic data on this subject are not available, it does seem that in parts of the East and South voters are tolerant of practices that would scandalize most people in, say, the Pacific Coast states or the Upper Midwest. In his account of a patronage squabble in bucolic Centre County, Pennsylvania, Frank Sorauf reported that the county chairman of the Democratic party told the local newspaper about his plans to fire Republican highway workers to make room for deserving Democrats. The whole controversy was debated in the press with no evident self-consciousness by the native-stock residents of Centre County, who seemed disturbed by the idea of *firing* public em-

114 *Ibid.,* p. 175. Also see Steffens, *Autobiography,* pp. 367, 464–69.

115 McNeill, *Democratic Campaign Financing in Indiana, 1964,* p. 39.

116 Fenton, *Midwest Politics,* p. 7.

117 Several studies show major regional or subregional variations in voting behavior or attitudes toward political subjects that cannot be accounted for by varying demographic characteristics. See, for example, Irving Crespi, "The Structural Basis for Right-Wing Conservatism: The Goldwater Case," *Public Opinion Quarterly,* 29 (Winter 1965), 523–43; James W. Prothro and Charles M. Grigg, "Fundamental Principles of Democracy: Bases of Agreement and Disagreement," *Journal of Politics,* 22 (Spring 1960), 276–94; and Raymond E. Wolfinger and Fred I. Greenstein, "Comparing Political Regions: The Case of California," *American Political Science Review,* 63 (March 1969), 74–85. For a general discussion and survey of the literature, see Samuel C. Patterson, "The Political Cultures of the American States," *Journal of Politics,* 30 (February 1968), 187–209.

ployees for partisan reasons, but were not opposed to hiring them on political grounds.[118]

The demographic battle lines of politics in New York or Boston do not seem to be duplicated in parts of the country more removed from the gaze of established social scientists. Machine politics often is found where ethnics are scarce. The converse is also true: immigrants are numerous in many places where public-regarding institutions and styles predominate, such as the large cities of the West Coast—San Francisco (44 percent foreign stock in 1960), Los Angeles (33 percent), and Seattle (31 percent). In fact, these cities are equally or more ethnic than eastern and midwestern cities characterized by machine politics, for example, Chicago (36 percent), Philadelphia (29 percent), and St. Louis (14 percent).

California is a particularly useful contrast to the East Coast. While the state has a cosmopolitan population and an urban, industrial economy, it also displays virtually no signs of machine politics. The governor of California, for example, has about as many patronage jobs at his disposal as the mayor of New Haven. Californians who worked in John F. Kennedy's presidential campaign report the bemusement of Kennedy organizers from the East who came to the state with thoughts of building their campaign organization around public employees. These and other practices that are widely accepted in the East are abhorred on the West Coast. Paying precinct workers is commonplace in eastern cities. But when Jess Unruh, a prominent California Democratic leader, hired some precinct workers in the 1962 election, he was roundly denounced from all points of the political spectrum for importing such a sordid practice. The president of the California Democratic Council said that Unruh's action "smacked of ward politics" and sternly announced "I am firmly convinced that the expansion and development of the use of paid workers is unhealthy for the Democratic party in California."[119]

The reasons for these marked geographical variations in political style are not easily found, but looking for them is a more promising approach to understanding machine politics than the search for functions supposedly rooted in the socioeconomic composition of urban populations.[120]

The last few paragraphs suggest three propositions about relationships between machine politics and socioeconomic conditions that both summarize

[118] Frank J. Sorauf, "Chairman and Superintendent," in *Cases in State and Local Government,* ed. Richard J. Frost (Englewood Cliffs, N.J.: Prentice-Hall, Inc., 1961), pp. 109–19.

[119] *San Francisco Chronicle,* 17 December 1962, p. 10; and *CDC Newsletter,* December 1962.

[120] For an interesting typology of three American political value systems that encompasses the regional differences concerning machine politics discussed here, see Daniel J. Elazar, *American Federalism: A View from the States* (New York: Thomas Y. Crowell Company, 1966).

much of this chapter and suggest questions that must be answered in a satisfactory explanation of machine politics in the United States:

1. Many places with large immigrant populations have never been dominated by machine politics, or were freed of this dominance generations ago.
2. Machine politics continues to flourish where populations are ethnically homogeneous.
3. In other places, such as Pennsylvania and Connecticut, political machines have been just as successful whether their constituents were immigrants or old-stock Americans.

II *the foundation of policy innovation*

5 *the politics*
of urban renewal

Urban renewal is a common and important example of comprehensive, coordinated, innovative policy directed toward solving major city problems. Because the foundations and first steps of New Haven's extraordinary urban renewal program are the principal empirical focus of this book, it is necessary to explain the substantive and political aspects of this policy area. This chapter describes in general terms postwar urban decline, the proposed solution of urban renewal, and the political hazards of this "solution." The chapter has two main purposes: (1) to explain urban renewal so as to make my later account of New Haven programs comprehensible; and (2) to analyze the political difficulties of urban renewal and thus define the dimensions of Mayor Lee's achievements. In dealing with this second purpose my intention is to state criteria for an intellectually satisfactory explanation of a successful urban renewal program. This statement is the rationale for the way this book is organized.

Although this chapter is not devoid of more contemporary data and arguments, it is written essentially from the perspective of the late 1950s, when most of the events described here were conceived. The current blossoming of interest in all sorts of urban subjects may induce in some readers the belief that scholars and officials alike were indifferent to the problems of our central cities until very recently. In fact, writers have been discovering "the urban crisis" since the end of World War II.

By the end of the 1960s it had become common to link "urban" and "black": the problems of the central cities were assumed or asserted to be in large measure problems concerning Negroes, and vice versa. As everyone knows, a large and growing proportion of many urban populations is black, and a number of urban problems are exacerbated by the racial composition of the people involved. Nevertheless, it is important to realize that our cities would be in serious trouble even if all Americans were the same color. The likelihood of mass violence would be a good deal less, but in other respects core city decay would still pose a formidable challenge to analysts and policy makers. This will, I hope, be apparent from the following section. It was also apparent to me during my year in New Haven's city hall. Blacks were not a trivial concern then, but they were far from the most important preoccupation of any high officials. Times have changed in New Haven (and almost everywhere else) in this respect, but the exacerbation of race relations in the past few years should not obscure the nonracial character of the fundamental physical and social problems confronting many cities.

The Problem

Urban renewal is a generic term for government policies designed to improve or maintain a city's physical plant. Although slum clearance is an important part, it is by no means the only aspect of urban renewal, which is a means of modernizing all urban facilities—commercial, transportation, service, and industrial, as well as residential. The basic goal is to make cities viable in the face of trends threatening to weaken their appeal as places in which to work, live, and shop.

Quantitative data about the quality of American housing are no exception to the generalization that statistics can be misleading; but, while not always susceptible of careful and comparative analysis, they do reveal the existence of millions of grossly inadequate housing units. The following passages from a Census Bureau publication express the federal government's current definition of substandard housing:

> Dilapidated housing does not provide safe and adequate shelter. It has...
> defects in sufficient number to require extensive repair or rebuilding.... Examples... include: holes, open cracks or missing materials over a large area of the floors, walls, roof, or other parts of the structure; sagging floors, walls, or roof; damage by storm or fire.
> A housing unit is considered substandard by the Public Housing Administration if it is dilapidated or lacks one or more of the following facilities: flush toilet and bathtub or shower inside the structure for the exclusive use of the occupants, and hot running water.[1]

In 1960, 13 percent of all occupied housing units in New Haven were substandard by these definitions, the same proportion found in all 212 standard metropolitan statistical areas.[2] Unfortunately, a change in the Census Bureau's definitions between 1950 and 1960 makes it impossible to compare the two years to ascertain the trend in housing quality.[3]

[1] U.S. Bureau of the Census, *U.S. Census of Housing: 1960, Special Reports for Local Housing Authorities,* Series HC(S1), No. 22 (Washington, D.C.: U.S. Government Printing Office, 1961), pp. 1–3. Henceforth this will be cited as *New Haven Housing Census.*

[2] *Ibid.,* p. 1; and Housing and Home Finance Agency, *Our Nonwhite Population and Its Housing* (Washington, D.C.: HHFA, 1963), p. 82.

[3] In 1950 the Census Bureau used two categories to classify housing quality, "sound" and "dilapidated," while for 1960 an intermediate category, "deteriorating," was introduced. The Census Bureau says that "although the definition of 'dilapidated' was the same in 1960 as in 1950, it is possible that the change in the categories introduced an

Poor immigrants to cities tend to be concentrated in the most decrepit and least attractive districts. Overcrowding is motivated by housing shortages, tenants' desires to spread the cost of rent, and owners' greed. These conditions depress property values, repel investors, and discourage those remaining homeowners and tenants who can afford other housing. The result is progressive deterioration. Most cities have building and housing codes that prohibit these conditions, but as a general proposition, corruption, official unconcern, shortages of decent low-cost housing, and inadequate personnel and enforcement procedures have made code enforcement an ineffective antislum device.[4]

None of this is new; these conditions have been found in American cities for generations.[5] How can one account for the pronounced postwar growth of concern on this issue, particularly in view of the improvement in housing quality? Doubtless there are many explanations, including growing social consciences, the dawning realization that privately constructed low-income housing was economically impossible, and the obsolescence of many houses built during the first flush of urbanization. The prime reason for concern, however, is that slum housing, its attendant blighting effects, and deterioration of nonresidential property have become a far graver threat to core cities, especially to those cities built before the advent of the automobile, because the suburbs have become an alternative. New Haven's postwar history is typical of many older cities. It lost 16,000 residents from 1940 to 1960 (see note 5, p. 16), while the surrounding towns in its metropolitan area gained 120,000 people, double their prewar population. Most other cities in the region underwent a similar exodus. Of the 29 northeastern cities with 1960 populations of 100,000 or more, 22 lost population between 1950 and 1960.

---

element of difference between the 1960 and 1950 statistics" (*New Haven Housing Census,* p. 3). For this reason it is difficult to assess 1950–60 trends in housing quality, although there seems to be no question that the proportion of substandard dwelling units in cities declined considerably during this decade.

[4] See Henry N. Osgood and A. H. Zwerner, "Rehabilitation and Conservation," *Law and Contemporary Problems,* 25 (Autumn 1960), 719–20.

[5] As Negroes have become the principal urban immigrants, the blighting process has accelerated because of racial discrimination in housing, which limits blacks not just to low-cost housing, but to only a fraction of the accommodations they can afford. This concentrates them in smaller areas and forces up the rents they pay, which in turn leads to further crowding as tenants try to find friends and relatives to share their rooms and rent. White resistance to housing integration, realtors' manipulations ("blockbusting"), and blacks' lower income levels all combine to intensify the slum-making dynamic. In New Haven in 1960, 26 percent of all dwelling units occupied by Negroes were substandard, twice the citywide total (*New Haven Housing Census,* p. 1). Nine percent of the white occupants of substandard housing in New Haven paid $70 or more in monthly rent, compared to 28 percent of the black occupants (*ibid.,* p. 9). In the country's 212 standard metropolitan statistical areas (SMSAS), 36 percent of the housing units occupied by blacks were substandard (*Our Nonwhite Population and Its Housing,* p. 82).

Boston, the worst case, had 104,000 fewer residents in 1960 than a decade earlier.

These figures do not adequately describe the cities' decline, for the people moving to the suburbs were far better off than those remaining behind in the city or newly arriving in it. As early as 1949 the urban–suburban status discrepancy in New Haven was considerable: 55 percent of families in the city had incomes below $3,000, compared to only 37 percent in the rest of the metropolitan area.[6] In the North as a whole, 41 percent of suburban residents and 32 percent of those in center cities had incomes, in 1951, of more than $5,000.[7] These and similar findings are not just reflections of the racial and ethnic differences between the two areas. The authors of *The American Voter* compared *northern, native-born whites* who grew up in a big city but had moved to a smaller community or to the country with those who were raised in the country and presently (in 1956) lived in a metropolis, and found that these two categories stood "at the polar extremes among the array of population groupings with regard to almost every social and economic characteristic."[8] For example, only 18 percent of the first group made less than $4,000 a year, compared to 57 percent of those who moved to a big city from a rural area.[9]

Suburban growth would have had less impact on the cities if the suburbs really were bedroom communities whose inhabitants continued to shop and work in the city. But the emigrants not only sleep in the outlying towns, they increasingly make and spend their money there as well. And they have far more money to spend than the urban immigrants who have replaced them, while needing fewer municipal services. From 1948 to 1954 the volume of retail sales in downtown New Haven decreased 5 percent, while it went up 31 percent in the rest of the metropolitan area.[10] In the 1950s Boston's central business district lost 14,000 jobs and $78 million in assessments.[11]

The causes of this decline are not difficult to discern, for the pattern is common in older cities all over the country.[12] These cities were largely built

6 Source: City of New Haven, *Short Approach Master Plan*, 1955.

7 Source: University of Michigan Survey Research Center data, analyzed in Fred I. Greenstein and Raymond E. Wolfinger, "The Suburbs and Shifting Party Loyalties," *Public Opinion Quarterly*, 22 (Winter 1958–59), 476.

8 Angus Campbell et al., *The American Voter* (New York: John Wiley & Sons, Inc., 1960), p. 460.

9 *Ibid.*, p. 462.

10 U.S. Bureau of the Census, *Census of Business: 1954, Central Business District Statistics,* Bulletin CBD-25—New Haven, Connecticut (Washington, D.C., 1956). The Census data were adjusted for the rise in the cost of living from 1948 to 1954.

11 Walter McQuade, "Boston: What Can A Sick City Do?" *Fortune* (June 1964), 134.

12 Morton Grodzins, "Metropolitan Segregation," *Scientific American,* 197 (October 1957), 40.

before automobiles were commonplace; typically their central business districts (CBDs) are in the oldest sections. In dozens of cities it is difficult to drive to or through the CBD or to park in or near it. By contrast, suburban shopping centers are close to new residential communities and easier to reach. Often, indeed, they are more accessible even from parts of the core city. Their stores are newer and usually more attractive and efficient. The appeal of downtown stores often is also diminished by the distasteful effects of declining adjacent residential areas.

Cities also face stiff competition for industry from outlying areas. Many urban factories are old, multistory structures unsuitable for assembly line techniques and in locations that have no room for expansion. Land is cheaper in the suburbs, the setting is more attractive, and new freeways offer easy access unimpeded by urban traffic and parking tangles.

In short, the universal use of automobiles presents the city with a new set of problems while it simultaneously makes possible an alternative that draws off many of the city's most valuable resources. Slums require more municipal services—police, fire, health, welfare—than other residential areas and contribute less in taxes. Attempts to stop their spread by code enforcement require expenditure of city funds and considerable political courage. As slums expand, adjacent residents move out of town and their taxes are lost to the municipal treasury. Most important, the tax base is weakened as stores lose business. To maintain its services at a level satisfactory to its remaining businesses and residents, the city must impose a higher tax rate on a relatively smaller base. This adds to the cost of living and doing business in the city and leads to a bigger exodus, further weakening the tax base. The alternative is to reduce the level of municipal services, but this too accelerates the processes of degeneration. Thus the effects of urban decay are progressive and mutually reinforcing. These problems were fairly encapsulated before 1945. Since then, they have threatened the continued viability of many cities and commanded attention that the social evils of slums alone could never claim.

Such problems generally cannot be solved by private action. Improvements in the old neighborhood must be sufficiently widespread to create an attractive environment. An isolated new apartment house or store encircled by rundown buildings would be unappealing to prospective customers or tenants. This interdependence effect often discourages individual property owners from investing in improvements: why spend money when the net impact will be small? (Indeed, in this situation, adjoining property owners will be the ones to profit from improvements: they benefit from an incremental increase in the area's appeal, but the owner who does the improving bears the entire cost burden. This cost-to-benefit calculation discourages expenditure by an individual owner.) Tenements and unfashionable stores are often expensive to buy, and thus are not an attractive investment for land developers. Moreover, acquiring an adequate amount of land usually requires assembly of a number of parcels with unwanted but expensive income property on them. A single owner can wreck a development scheme by refusing to sell. Considering other investment opportunities, slum clearance is seldom an attractive proposition for private investors, nor are attempts to replace decaying commercial areas. Moreover, banks and other sources of money often refuse to make real estate loans in rundown neighborhoods.

The difficulties of assembling a worthwhile piece of land are enhanced by parking and traffic problems. New urban stores cannot compete with suburban shopping centers unless easy access and parking are provided. Private interests might build parking facilities (although these often need to be subsidized), but only public action can produce adequate streets and highways.

Urban Renewal

Aside from housing codes, the first major governmental remedy for slums was public housing, funded primarily by the federal government. The Housing Act of 1937 was an attempt to provide sound housing for poor families by making grants to local agencies for housing projects. (There has also been a small amount of state and local public housing.) Led by realtors, business and other conservative interests have always vigorously opposed public housing. In recent years, however, its unpopularity has spread across the political spectrum. The buildings—unattractive, sterile, and inhuman—are said to be administered in similar style.[13] They are expensive to construct and operate, and are so often considered "Negro housing" that in many cities poor whites do not live in them.[14] About 600,000 units of public housing had been built by 1965, and despite the general political disenchantment with the program, many projects had long waiting lists.

Even a wholly successful public housing program would have dealt only with one aspect of the urban dilemma, leaving untouched the middle-class exodus, commercial decay, and other problems. After the war new approaches to the slum problem were discussed. One suggestion was an expansion of the uses of eminent domain. Traditionally this government power to acquire private property had been used to obtain sites for public facilities: housing projects, government buildings, roads, parks, and so forth. A new departure

13 Lawrence M. Friedman, *The Government and Slum Housing* (Chicago: Rand McNally & Co., 1968).

14 Catherine Bauer, "The Dreary Deadlock of Public Housing," in *Democracy in Urban America,* eds. Oliver P. Williams and Charles Press (Chicago: Rand McNally & Co., 1961), p. 484; and Elizabeth Brenner Drew, "The Long Trial of Public Housing," *The Reporter* (17 June 1965), 16–17.

would be to use eminent domain to acquire land for private uses that would be in the public interest. The government would buy land, clear the buildings, and resell the land to private developers whose "re-use" of it would accomplish a socially desirable purpose, such as construction of decent housing. Land with buildings on it costs more than the same land without buildings; thus "redevelopment" would be a prohibitively expensive proposition for local governments without financial support from the federal treasury.

Increasing public concern with housing quality in the postwar years eventuated in the landmark Housing Act of 1949. The two ideas of expanded eminent domain and federal subsidies were expressed in Title I of the act, which established the federal urban renewal program. Title I authorized the use of federal funds to lend local agencies the money needed to plan redevelopment projects and to buy, clear, and resell land. The federal government would pay the local agency a "capital grant" to absorb two-thirds of the loss involved in such a project. Offhand, this looks like a bargain that cities would rush to exploit. A description of the administrative procedures should shake this impression, and a discussion of the political perils of redevelopment will dispel it completely.

Redevelopment is done either by the city government itself or by a local authority with eminent domain and bond-selling powers; this is the local public agency (LPA). The first step in a redevelopment project is LPA submission to the federal Urban Renewal Administration of an application for a survey and planning grant for a particular area, complete with elaborate proof of the area's eligibility for redevelopment.[15] (If a project does not go into the execution phase within a specified number of years, the funds for survey and planning must be repaid to the federal government.) The LPA also requests a capital grant reservation, asking the URA to set aside the amount of money it estimates it will eventually need to cover two-thirds of the loss.

The LPA surveys the project area thoroughly and draws up detailed plans for developing it. These plans are submitted to the URA. When they are approved, the LPA prepares a final project report and forwards it to the URA. The final report includes extremely detailed plans for land acquisition, including appraisals of every parcel; land disposition and use; relocation of project area residents; and financing. When the final project report is ap-

---

[15] When the Department of Housing and Urban Development (HUD) was formed in 1965, it incorporated the existing Housing and Home Finance Agency and its various components, including the URA. I have described the procedures followed by the URA since these are most relevant to the time period covered by our research in New Haven. Similarly, I have limited my description of the program to the same period. Although details of these procedures have been changed and numerous modifications of the program have been introduced, the essential features remain the same, as do the political problems discussed later.

proved, the LPA presents the plan for local approval, which usually involves hearings and formal approval by the municipal legislature. This is a crucial decision-making period and the time when plans are subject to greatest political pressure. The LPA then resubmits the whole package, usually including responses to whatever additional conditions the URA has imposed. It also submits an application for a capital grant, to cover two-thirds of the net project cost (the cost of buying the property less the price received for the cleared land) and a temporary loan, to supply the LPA with ready cash to acquire property. The URA reconsiders the application, perhaps presenting more questions and conditions. Eventually the contract is signed and the project enters the execution stage.

Titles of all property in the project area are searched and another set of appraisals is made and sent to the URA for its approval. The LPA determines, subject to approval by the URA, a price to be paid for each parcel. Negotiations for purchase of the property are then begun. If they are unsuccessful the LPA condemns the property. Prices paid for land are customarily rather high, if only because the LPA wants all the land at the same time and thus must buy in a seller's market. Families in the area are relocated. The federal government pays residential relocation costs up to $100 (raised to $200 in 1959), and moving expenses and compensation for direct property losses by businesses up to $2,000 (raised to $2,500 in 1957 and to $3,000 in 1959). There is no compensation to businesses for loss of income or good will.

The LPA then clears the land and sells or leases it, either by bid or by negotiation. The URA may require bidding, but this is often not a feasible means of land disposition where potential developers may have to spend considerable amounts of money just to investigate the opportunities offered by development schemes. Land is "written down" in price; developers pay less for it than the city did. This is a result of clearance and often also an outright subsidy to attract developers. Usually the city counts on making up its share of the loss in increased tax revenues. The final project report contains detailed plans and standards for re-use. The LPA supervises the developers to insure their compliance with this plan.

The URA must approve all purchase and resale prices. In a number of other ways it maintains surveillance over the project and must consent to deviations from the approved plans. In New Haven, as in many other cities, land disposition agreements with developers must be approved by the Board of Aldermen after a public hearing.

The LPA borrows from the federal government the money it needs to acquire land and pay for some other costs, including legal and administrative services, appraisals and title searching, demolition and site preparation, interest costs, and public capital improvements in the project area. The difference between these expenditures and income from the resale of land is the net project cost. Two-thirds of this is paid by the federal government and one-third by the city. (A later amendment provided an option for a three-quarters/one-quarter financing arrangement.) The LPA is given credit for city capital expenditures in the project area as part of its contribution. These are called a "non-cash" contribution, and offer many opportunities for reducing the local fiscal burden by counting as part of the city's share expenditures which would be made anyway.

Redevelopment is the term used in this book to describe complete clearance of a tract of land, in contrast to *renewal* projects, where demolition is selective and only hopelessly blighted property or buildings which violate the project land use plan are bought and cleared. Owners are encouraged to rehabilitate their property, financing the work by home improvement mortgages insured under Section 220 of the Housing Act of 1954, and codes are strictly enforced. A third approach, *conservation,* is concerned with maintenance of standard conditions in neighborhoods that might otherwise decline. The New Haven urban renewal program includes all these approaches, but projects described in detail later in this book were limited almost entirely to redevelopment.

Since 1949 numerous major changes have been made in federal urban renewal legislation, introducing a variety of innovations, exemptions, and special incentives for accomplishment of particular purposes. In addition, other approaches to the housing problem have been adopted. Most of these amendments came after the period of our research and thus fall outside the scope of this book, but a few changes in the basic forms embodied in the 1949 Act are important to this story. Most of these were adopted in the Housing Act of 1954, which reflected five years of experience with the original legislation. The most important provisions enacted in 1954 were these:

1. Adoption of renewal and conservation as goals of federally-aided projects.
2. "Section 220" mortgage insurance for rehabilitating buildings and constructing new ones in project areas; and "Section 221" mortgage insurance for housing displaced families.
3. A provision that 10 percent of federal funds appropriated for urban renewal could be used in projects that were not predominantly residential before or after redevelopment. This "10 percent exception" was expanded to 20 percent in 1959 and to 30 percent in 1961.
4. A requirement that federal funds for public housing and urban renewal be granted only to cities which had adopted "workable programs" embracing the following elements:
   a. Adequate building and housing codes.
   b. A comprehensive community plan.
   c. Intensive neighborhood analyses.
   d. An effective, clearly defined system of administrative organization for implementation of the workable program.

e. Appropriation of necessary funds for staff and improvements.
f. Relocation assistance and availability of housing for people displaced by projects.
g. Citizen participation in urban renewal.

The workable program requirement was intended to meet a variety of criticisms whose nature is apparent from the items in the program. As a practical matter, adoption of a workable program has required symbolic more than tangible commitments from most cities. The URA did not judge local program submissions very critically, nor did it closely scrutinize the extent —often minimal—of their implementation.[16]

Passage of the Housing Act of 1949 did not lead to a bustle of development action, for cities were very slow to start. The number of projects undertaken increased every year since 1949, except for a dip in the first part of the Eisenhower administration and again in 1959. Through fiscal year 1964 the federal government had authorized $4 billion for urban renewal grants. Half this sum was authorized during the first 12 years of the program; the other half was provided in the first 3 years of the Kennedy administration. Only 26 percent of these funds had been disbursed by June 30, 1964.[17]

Initial progress was so painfully slow that a decade passed before tangible results could be detected. More than two years after passage of the legislation just one project was under way, although more than 200 cities had received capital grant reservations.[18] At the end of 1954, the program's fifth anniversary, 87 projects were in the execution phase and only $146 million was actually obligated in capital grant contracts, although $500 million had been authorized in 1949.[19]

By 1959 the number of projects in the execution phase had risen to 390. Actual disposition of cleared land had begun in 86 of these projects, and had been completed in 51 of them. In other words, ten years after urban renewal had come into being, only 86 projects had reached the stage where construction on cleared land was possible. Just 25 projects had been completed, of which 16 were finished in the tenth year.[20]

---

16 Charles S. Rhyne, "The Workable Program—A Challenge for Community Improvement," *Law and Contemporary Problems,* 25 (Autumn 1960), 591–97.

17 Data on fund disbursement were obtained from the URA.

18 Catherine Bauer, "Redevelopment: A Misfit in the Fifties," in *The Future of Cities and Urban Redevelopment,* ed. Coleman Woodbury (Chicago: University of Chicago Press, 1953), pp. 7–25.

19 Housing and Home Finance Agency, *8th Annual Report* (Washington, D.C.: HHFA, 1955), p. 454.

20 Housing and Home Finance Agency, *13th Annual Report* (Washington, D.C.: HHFA, 1960), pp. 275–76. These figures for project completion have both conservative and generous biases. A project is listed as "completed" when the final federal payment

In 1964, 15 years after the beginning of urban renewal, 107 projects had been completed, 655 were in the execution phase, and 596 were in planning. An additional 295 projects had been terminated locally, either by opposition or by economic failure.[21]

Progress in individual projects was as halting as in the national program as a whole. About a quarter of the 107 projects were completed less than five years after the first planning advance from the URA; half took from five to ten years; and the remainder dragged on more than ten years from the beginning of detailed planning to completion. Most of the completed projects were in cities with populations under 100,000. Ninety-six of the projects in planning in 1964 had been at that stage for more than ten years and had not yet reached the execution phase.[22]

Although urban renewal became considerably more commonplace in the program's second decade, at the beginning of 1964 there were still seven cities with populations in excess of 250,000 that had no project in execution. Twenty-three of 79 cities with populations between 100,000 and 250,000 had no active project, nor did over half of all cities in the 50,000 to 100,000 category.

Urban renewal projects vary enormously in scope. They range in size from 0.4 acre to 2,500 acres, in the number of people displaced from nobody at all to more than 10,000, and in funding from a few thousand dollars to over $100 million. Most projects have rather modest dimensions. Of all the projects in "advanced planning" or execution in 1964, almost a quarter covered less than 10 acres, and almost three quarters were under 50 acres.[23]

These projects were as diverse in character as in size. One of the most important features of urban renewal is its protean quality; it is a highly flexible means of rearranging parts of a city's physical environment. It can be nothing more than a device for taking land to build a playground or parking lot (with a federal subsidy), or it can be the clearance and reconstruction of a central business district. This is a far broader conception of

---

has been made to the LPA and all land disposed of. Thus re-use construction may be substantially finished in a project that is not classified as completed. On the other hand, "completed" projects may not in fact have all construction finished and in use.

These data are limited to urban renewal projects authorized under Title I of the Housing Act of 1949 or amendments to it in the 1954 act. Subsequent legislation authorized a variety of other activities administered by the URA, involving grants and/or loans to LPAs for disaster area reconstruction, demonstration grants, and assorted programs for federal assistance in the preparation of surveys, master plans, community renewal programs, and Model City projects.

[21] Data on project status were obtained from the URA. Project data are for 31 March 1964 and exclude projects in Puerto Rico.

[22] Urban Renewal Administration, *Urban Renewal Project Characteristics, June 30, 1964* (Washington, D.C.: URA, 1964).

[23] These data were compiled from *ibid.*

urban renewal than the familiar idea that the program is to be judged for its direct impact on the housing supply, but it is also much more in accordance with practical experience.

Urban renewal was originally conceived and passed as a technique for expanding and improving the supply of *housing*. It is still generally thought about in these terms, but in fact the program has not increased the supply of housing and clearly has diminished the amount of housing for the poor. For example, the projects completed by mid-1963 involved the demolition of 17,256 dwelling units and the construction of only 10,679. A year later, of 958 projects in execution or advanced planning, almost 700 concerned predominantly blighted residential areas; but the completed project areas would be exclusively or predominantly residential in only 406 projects. A third (by cost) of the planned construction was to be new private housing and another third was for commercial developments; most of the rest was for public uses *other than* low-income housing.[24]

Despite the hopes of its sponsors, urban renewal has been used for a variety of purposes other than improving housing. For example, many hospitals, universities, and other public-serving institutions are hemmed in by slums and in desperate need of room. They can grow by clearing slums or by moving.[25] The latter is usually impossibly expensive and renewal has been used to provide land for such facilities, at the cost of reducing the housing supply. Redevelopment is thus a form of federal subsidy for these institutions, and for their municipal governments if local officials are skilled at manipulating the noncash provisions of the laws. By an amendment to the Housing Act

[24] The data in this paragraph were obtained from the URA. Precise figures on new housing for the projects under way in 1964 were available only for some 577 projects where land had been committed or conveyed to developers. These were expected to provide 138,331 private housing units and 8,124 public housing units.

This is not the whole story about low-cost housing, however. While hardly any public housing is built in redevelopment projects, a considerable (if not adequate) amount is constructed otherwise. A total of 368,227 low-rent public housing units was initiated under the Housing Act of 1949 in the first 15 years after that law was passed. Source: Congressional Quarterly Service, *Housing a Nation* (Washington, D.C.: Congressional Quarterly, Inc., 1966), p. 11.

Many innovations to encourage privately-constructed low-income housing were adopted during the Kennedy and Johnson administrations and may eventually produce a significant increase in the supply of housing for the poor.

[25] A third alternative in these circumstances is more intensive use of available land through high-rise construction. This path is usually more expensive and inconvenient, but has been chosen by institutions like Columbia University that face explosive community resentment of expansion. The question may come down to who is to suffer: the institution through construction costs, or the surrounding residents through displacement. Discerning the public interest in such cases is not easy.

For a description of the University of Chicago's early political involvements in urban renewal motivated by a desire for institutional survival, see Peter H. Rossi and Robert A. Dentler, *The Politics of Urban Renewal* (New York: The Free Press, 1961).

of 1959, improvement by educational institutions in or near project areas can be credited toward the LPA's share of the net project cost as a non-cash contribution. Improvements made as much as five years before approval of a loan and grant contract can be counted for this purpose.

More generally and importantly, urban renewal is a way to carry out a variety of improvements of the physical aspects of urban life: speeding the flow of traffic, providing access for a neighborhood blocked by an archaic embankment (or, alternately, separating residential and industrial areas with a new freeway), designing a shopping district to fit the tastes and capacities of an affluent and mobile population, providing decent housing adjacent to major centers of employment, shopping, and culture, and so on.[26] City planners traditionally have been frustrated because there were no devices to implement their recommendations concerning private property or functions usually performed by private business. Land use patterns were controlled chiefly by the market, constrained by diverse ownership and the profit motive. The principal sanction available to local governments was the negative zoning power. Urban renewal supplements the market as a factor in land use decisions. The second element in Title I—federal financial participation —provides a means of transferring most of the fiscal burden from overtaxed local sources to the ampler federal treasury. Indeed, adroit local officials can use urban renewal to obtain federal subsidies for a variety of conventional municipal facilities, including streets, schools, and parking and recreational facilities, that could not otherwise be afforded. In New Haven, for example, the antiquated street pattern that funneled most cross-town traffic through one five-way intersection was adapted for the twentieth century by an urban renewal project, which also was used to subsidize the city's purchase of land for a new high school.

Probably the most common public motivation for urban renewal has been strengthening core cities' tax bases. Ever since the war the growth of urban problems has been accompanied by a shrinkage of local fiscal capacity to cope with these problems. This trend reached crisis proportions in many cities at the beginning of the 1970s. Proposals for revenue sharing and federal block grants, layoffs of city employees and drastic reductions in programs, and ensuing riots and work stoppages all testify to the importance of maintaining local tax bases—and to a widespread failure to do so.

Urban Renewal as a Political Issue

At first glance Title I seems a bonanza for cities, their businessmen, and their politicians. The cities have their physical plants modernized and their

[26] For a summary description of some attempts to achieve more attractive and gratifying urban environments through urban renewal, see Wolf Von Eckardt, " 'There is No There There,' " *New Republic* (21 September 1963), 17–20.

tax bases strengthened, eyesores are eliminated, local politicians get the credit, and the federal government pays the bill. People who subscribe to this view consider ambitious urban renewal programs federally subsidized political Potemkin Villages, not difficult achievements. As Hugh Douglas Price asked,

> Is the New Haven story a sort of miracle to be attributed to a great man theory of political leadership, or more simply a case of massive outside funds serving as a sort of deus ex machina?...the more emphasis one puts on the important and unusual resource base of federal funds the less weight one need attach to the Mayor's particular talents.[27]

The data in the preceding section on the halting pace of urban renewal leave no room for doubt that this position is wrong, that urban renewal is not a painless, popular program.

One difficulty is the federal government's slow procedures and cumbersome requirements, resulting in elaborate and redundant submissions by LPAs at every step of the process, followed by months-long delays while regional and national federal agencies mull over applications.[28] Moreover, project land competes for investment capital with privately-developed real estate, where legal and political restrictions are far less onerous and financial arrangements more flexible.

Another hazard in renewal projects is litigation. In *Berman* v. *Parker* the United States Supreme Court held that the use of eminent domain for renewal purposes was constitutional, when the proposed re-use had been found by properly constituted authority to be in the public interest.[29] State courts have generally agreed. Nevertheless, those who are adversely affected by an urban renewal project may challenge the project in court, on one ground or another. Hence litigation often further delays and jeopardizes the process.

The weightiest impediments to urban renewal (and, by analogy, to any comprehensive, coordinated change of urban life patterns) are political. Urban renewal presents direct, immediate political hazards; the rewards, on the other hand, generally are problematic, distant, or politically diffuse. The easiest way to explain this is to discuss the various likely sources of opposition and support for redevelopment. Because urban renewal takes so many forms and sizes, generalizing about it is difficult. The following discussion is most germane to projects of some size, involving displacement of old resi-

---

[27] Hugh Douglas Price, review of *Who Governs?*, *Yale Law Journal*, 71 (July 1962), 5319. Similar views are expressed by Norton Long in "Community Decision-Making," *Community Leadership and Decision-Making* (Iowa City: University of Iowa Institute of Public Affairs, 1966), p. 3.

[28] Richard Leach, "The Federal Urban Renewal Program: A Ten-Year Critique," *Law and Contemporary Problems*, 25 (Autumn 1960), 780–81.

[29] 348 U.S. 26 (1954).

dents, destruction of sizable numbers of buildings, and re-uses that include at least some private development.

In very general terms, the political drawback to redevelopment is that people with the most direct, immediate, and specific interest in a project are likely to be its victims. The beneficiaries usually are involved later, after the most difficult political battles have been fought. Often their gain from the project, for example, by living in a new apartment house, is not the sort that leads to political action, in contrast to the parallel involvement of being displaced from one's home. Urban renewal displaces residents and businesses, and alters in drastic and often unforeseeable ways the land use pattern of part of the city. A project's repercussions spread far beyond the project boundaries, touching the interests of many organizations and individuals: businessmen faced with competition from out-of-town firms, churches threatened by dispersion of their parishioners, politicians losing their constituents, and so on. These disruptions impose tangible hardships on definable groups of people at a time when the project's beneficiaries may not even be aware of their future good fortune. The general public, which can be expected to take civic pride in the completed project, as well as fiscal gratification from the strengthened tax base, has first to endure years of dirt and noise and traffic detours.

It is often said that urban renewal will have the backing of locally-oriented businessmen whose prosperity depends on the economic health of the area where they have large fixed capital investments: a utility's equipment, a realtor's contacts and knowledge, a bank's local investment portfolio, a merchant's clientele. These groups arc thought to be quick to discern the advantages to themselves of federally-subsidized attempts to make CBDs competitive with the suburbs and replace close-in slums with shopping centers and high-rent apartments. Perhaps the most conspicuous exponent of this viewpoint is Robert H. Salisbury, who argues that recognition of the city's problems has led to a characteristic contemporary political coalition as a result of reentry into local politics by prominent businessmen.[30]

There is no doubt that urban renewal can be used to deal with the problems of urban decline in ways that are beneficial to local businessmen. These interests account for much of what might be called "latent support" for redevelopment.[31] There is a wide gap, however, between latent opinion that favors a policy in principle, and active, determined political support for

[30] Robert H. Salisbury, "Urban Politics: The New Convergence of Power," *Journal of Politics*, 26 (November 1964), 775–97. Radical critics of urban renewal have attacked it as a means to enrich the business community at the expense of minority groups and the poor. See, for example, Staughton Lynd, "Urban Renewal—For Whom?" *Commentary* (April 1961), 34–45.

[31] See Dahl, who attributes Lee's successful urban renewal program in part to "the wide degree of latent support for redevelopment that already existed in New Haven and needed only to be awakened." Robert A. Dahl, *Who Governs?* (New Haven, Conn.: Yale University Press, 1961), p. 310.

specific measures. As V. O. Key put it, the development of latent opinion

> is limited by the processes that limit the numbers of persons who become aware of a political stimulus. It is limited by the clarity of relevant norms in the minds of those who perceive the stimulus. It is limited by the fact that policy proposals often need to be associated with objective circumstances if latent opinion is to be stirred.[32]

The steps that convert latent support into concrete action ordinarily are the province of politicians, not businessmen. (This is not to say that businessmen cannot act like politicians, but only that they are not likely to.)

The coalition that Salisbury describes can be found in some cities, but usually on a project-by-project basis. Some renewal projects are masterminded, at least in part, by their private beneficiaries; even in such cases, support from politicians is essential.[33] Most projects are the products of leadership by government officials. More commonly, however, businessmen and politicians have failed to play the roles attributed to them by Salisbury, whose ideal type coalition is far from an accurate model for the common run of local politics.

Most businessmen have been hostile or indifferent to the concept of urban renewal. The Chamber of Commerce of the United States strongly opposed adoption of Title I and has consistently maintained that the program is a failure and should be terminated.[34] At the local level business attitudes toward urban renewal vary widely. Businessmen's political opinions, like those of most people, are of greatest consequence in concrete situations—the "objective circumstances" that Key mentions. Businessmen in some cities have supported particular projects. Local chambers of commerce, doubtless influenced by these specific situations, have cooperated in redevelopment projects and even issued statements endorsing the concept of urban renewal.[35] But a local business community seldom has taken the lead in formulating, adopting, and executing an urban renewal program. In Newark, a prototypical example of urban decline, Kaplan found that "the model of alert interests, strongly committed to their goals and prepared to press these goals at every occasion, does not apply to Newark renewal."[36] Local businessmen agreed that the city was decaying, but even after they had reluctantly accepted the

---

[32] V. O. Key, Jr., *Public Opinion and American Democracy* (New York: Alfred A. Knopf, Inc., 1961), p. 280.

[33] See, for example, Rossi and Dentler, *The Politics of Urban Renewal.*

[34] Congressional Quarterly Service, *Housing a Nation*, pp. 6, 25–27; *Washington Post,* 28 February 1965, p. A4.

[35] For such resolutions in Minneapolis and Chicago, see, respectively, *Congressional Record* (daily ed.), 8 June 1964, p. A3079; and *Congressional Record* (daily ed.), 1 June 1964, p. 11833.

[36] Harold Kaplan, *Urban Renewal Politics* (New York: Columbia University Press, 1963), p. 117.

idea of urban renewal, city officials "could not persuade even one local corporation to redevelop a site in Newark or to finance redevelopment by others."[37] They did not believe that Newark's decline could be reversed by redevelopment. Newark eventually had an ambitious urban renewal program, but development of the cleared land was done by out-of-town firms.

Even where local businessmen are not opposed to urban renewal, re-use development may be done partially or wholly by firms from distant places. This is most likely in smaller cities and with more ambitious re-use schemes that require orchestration of a number of kinds of activity. The scope of many new developments, the additional difficulties and delays resulting from involvement with federal officials *and* local politics, the variety of special substantive problems, and the resulting very long building time all make redevelopment contracting a field dominated by big, experienced firms operating on a regional or national scale. These organizations usually lack a network of connections in the city's social and economic life that can be used to build political support for the project. Taking in a local businessman as a partner is only a partial solution to this problem.

Local business is hostile in part because it confuses urban renewal with public housing, long a bete noire to conservatives. In fact, generalized ideological opposition to "spending," "big government," "federal interference," and "socialism" seems to explain many businessmen's attitudes toward redevelopment. Such ideologically-rooted antipathy may be particularly strong in smaller cities, where the prevailing sentiment may be cold even to such requirements of the workable program as building codes and master plans. A local politician in upstate New York remarked, "You would have thought we were importing the NKVD by hiring a building inspector the way people reacted here."[38] In several western cities urban renewal failed because members of the John Birch Society led successful referendum campaigns to repeal building codes, which they characterized as communist techniques to destroy privacy. In at least one of these cities the campaign featured lurid propaganda about the sexual outrages that might ensue if building inspectors were given access to private homes.[39] In 1961 the Phoenix City Council repealed the housing code and then, impelled by a desire to satisfy the URA's requirements in order to obtain federal urban renewal grants, reversed itself. This led to a referendum in which the code was again revoked, in the name of "free enterprise," and over the opposition of what some people would call the city's "power structure."[40]

37 *Ibid.,* p. 24.

38 Quoted in the *New York Times,* 12 July 1965, p. 14. The *Times* reported that this attitude was not uncommon, even in cities losing business to suburban shopping centers.

39 Information about the building code referenda was supplied by officials of the URA.

40 Andrew Kopkind, "Modern Times in Phoenix," *New Republic* (6 November 1965), 15.

The growing number of cities engaged in urban renewal suggests that this kind of ideological hostility is receding. One politician in a small eastern city said, "Change comes hard to this town. I think renewal is a must here, but if you're going to use my name I will say for the record that we have to take our time and go slowly. Off the record, I think we have to go faster."[41]

In addition to general ideological concerns, businessmen often find more specific reasons for opposing redevelopment. Firms in the project area are forced to move with no assurance that they will be able to find new quarters at comparable rents. Since a fairly large number of businesses are removed in a short time from areas where rents are usually very low, they do indeed have to pay more for new accommodations. Retailers dependent on local customers have to move to strange locations where they may have to cultivate a new clientele. Tenants who have made improvements in their old facilities have no legal basis for compensation by the owners for such improvements, for most business leases include "eminent domain clauses" which protect the owner from any such claims by the tenant in the event the property is condemned. Because of the character of areas slated for redevelopment, as well as political considerations that often cause adjustment of project boundaries to exclude larger firms, businesses in project areas tend to be rather small, which further increases the hazards that they are likely to face when displaced.

Reliable data on the impact of urban renewal on displaced businesses are scarce, perhaps understandably so. Most LPAs are reluctant to reveal, or even to collect, useful data on this subject. Until 1962 the URA did not effectively require submission of such information. Thus it is often difficult to measure this particular aspect of the consequences of urban renewal. The executive administrator of the Small Business Administration estimated in 1965 that by 1972 almost 120,000 small businesses would be displaced by redevelopment projects, of which about 30 percent would go out of business as a result.[42]

Outside the project area, adjacent businesses often lose customers because of traffic interference, dust, noise, and assorted other consequences of demolition and construction. Since an aim of many projects is to provide more attractive retail facilities to compete with outlying shopping districts, businessmen outside the area, contemplating competition from the new firms, face this prospect without enthusiasm and in many cases have succeeded in altering or vetoing projects.

41 *New York Times,* 12 July 1965, p. 14.

42 Testimony by Ross D. Davis before the Subcommittee on Intergovernmental Relations, Committee on Government Operations, United States Senate, 1 July 1965. Retail stores, perhaps because of their smaller capitalization and reliance on local clienteles, have a lower survival rate than other types of displaced firms. See Martin Millspaugh, "Problems and Opportunities of Relocation," *Law and Contemporary Problems,* 26 (Winter 1961), 26n.

Almost any project will have an impact on the politically-sensitive areas of traffic and parking. Traffic patterns are altered once while demolition and construction block streets, and again when the new street plan is in operation; and changing the flow of cars may deprive some merchants of customers. Speeding traffic by means of one-way streets and no-standing regulations irritates motorists and angers retailers who want the maximum number of potential customers to drive past their stores. A New Haven official complained that "the merchant's ideal dream is that everybody in town can park at the curb in front of his store all day, for nothing." Regulations interfering with this dream often provoke organized opposition from retail associations. But municipally-operated parking facilities put the city into competition with owners of private lots and garages, thus arousing their opposition.

Property owners in the project area may or may not be a source of serious opposition. If they are slum landlords they are usually vulnerable to strong pressure from city officials because they are likely to be guilty of flagrant violations of the building and housing codes.[43]

It scarcely needs to be said that the residents of project areas are likely to be unhappy about being displaced. Areas inhabited by Negroes pose additional problems, as well as some political opportunities. The opportunities, which seem to be largely a thing of the past in the North, lay in the fact that Negroes typically did not have as much political influence or skill as other groups. Until the flowering of black power in the late 1960s they could more easily be pushed around. By the end of 1964, 62 percent of the families relocated from urban renewal projects were nonwhite.[44] As black militancy increases, it may be *more* difficult to displace Negroes, or it may simply be necessary to pay a higher political price to their leaders in order to do so.

A second, and probably more important, racial consideration is that the displaced Negroes have to go somewhere, and the white neighborhoods into which they move are likely to be populated by the most prejudiced elements in the community. Moving blacks into such districts often produces considerable political repercussions. Such situations can involve loss of political support on both sides of the fence. After a large project in Newark distributed thousands of Negroes to other parts of the city, the mayor lost votes in the next election both from those white areas into which Negroes had moved and from black ghettos expressing their resentment at the displacement.[45]

Black or white, residents of the worst slums usually are not the kind of

---

[43] See Kaplan, *Urban Renewal Politics*, p. 136.

[44] This percentage is based on 138,152 relocated families. The race of another 28,145 displaced families (mostly from New York and presumed to be largely Puerto Rican) was not reported. These data were obtained from the URA.

[45] Kaplan, *Urban Renewal Politics*, p. 160.

people who are able to maintain coherent political opposition to government policy. Even by the footloose norms of American society, they tend to move from place to place frequently. In San Francisco's Western Addition Area 2, the turnover rate of residents was more than 33 percent *a year*.[46] Many slum neighborhoods have a very low level of social integration, like the Washington ghetto described by a community organizer:

> No Girard Street community existed at all. While all these people shared the sidewalks and alleys which surrounded their homes, they did not know each other, trust each other or have any feeling of common purpose.[47]

People who do not know their neighbors, have not lived in one place long enough to form attachments, and have known little from life but disappointment and defeat are not likely to be formidable opponents. Some urban renewal projects, however, have included less deteriorated areas with more stable patterns of residence, family structure, and neighborhood institutions. These areas often put up very stiff resistance to projects in which they are included.

The political structure of project areas may present extra incentives for protest organizers. Where a strong party organization is lacking, where politics is factional and unstructured, it is commonplace for ambitious candidates and would-be candidates (and more currently, would-be "revolutionaries") to try to make political capital by exploitation of grievances. If one grievance is urban renewal plans, such aspiring politicians can mobilize grass-roots opposition. Where politics is loosely organized, there is no leader or set of leaders with whom officials can negotiate and whose decisions are sufficiently authoritative that they are unlikely to be successfully challenged.[48] Since the mid-1960s federally funded legal assistance programs have provided leadership for many neighborhood campaigns against renewal projects.

Emphasis on the role of federal financing in urban renewal obscures the fact that local communities pay a third or a quarter of the net project cost. While those LPAs most adroit at milking the federal treasury manage to claim credit for many improvements that might have been built regardless of urban renewal, such expenditures still represent a drain on the local revenue base. In New Haven, where some writers think urban renewal has been without cost to local taxpayers, local cash expenditures for the projects under way in 1964 amounted to $3,377,000. Local non-cash expenditures (capital items which were credited toward the city's one-third share of the net project cost) exceeded $18 million. It is likely that many of these items

[46] Source: letter to the author from M. Justin Herman, executive director of the San Francisco Redevelopment Agency.

[47] Quoted in the *Washington Post,* 20 April 1965, p. A19.

[48] Kaplan, *Urban Renewal Politics,* pp. 136–39.

would not have been undertaken in the absence of urban renewal. In view of these tangible money costs, it should not be surprising that difficulties in financing the local share of the project cost were an important factor, if not the single one, in local termination of 46 projects.[49]

Urban renewal is also likely to impinge directly on the interests of politicians. Population shifts worry local leaders who see safe wards and precincts wiped out as their constituents are scattered across the city, often upsetting the political balance in their new neighborhoods as well. Resentment is particularly likely when appeals to ethnic solidarity are important. The political tastes of new project area residents, who are usually well-to-do, may not be compatible with the old local leaders' styles.

The jobs and contracts generated by urban renewal provide additional patronage, but its use for political purposes is limited by various legal and practical considerations. For one thing, officials whose salaries are paid from federal funds are covered by the Hatch Act, and thus barred from partisan political activity. Such jobs can be used to reward politically deserving party workers, but then further political participation by the jobholder is somewhat risky. Urban renewal requires highly skilled and energetic professional officials to deal with both federal requirements and local opponents of any project, as well as to overcome the mountainous obstacles seemingly inherent in the urban renewal process. Hiring for most positions is therefore best done in the national professional marketplace rather than local party clubhouses. Some jobs are relatively undemanding and can be filled politically; this was the case in New Haven with the managers of acquired but temporarily uncleared property, for example. By the same token, such services as title searching and property acquisition negotiation could be treated as patronage. In New Haven, negotiators' fees for part of one project amounted to $54,000 and were paid to a number of politically deserving people. But most jobs and most contracts were not placed politically, for they were too important to the program and required too much skill and energy to be used as patronage.

Even one project requires a good deal of policy coordination. Applications to the URA, land disposition agreements, and budgets all have to be approved by the municipal legislature, whose members may well have constituencies indifferent or hostile to the LPA's plans. In addition to the LPA, those agencies concerned with city planning, traffic, parking, code enforcement, and budgeting must work together. Municipal governments typically are congeries of semisovereign agencies, each with its own patrons and re-

---

[49] Data on the causes of local termination were obtained from the URA in 1964. The data should be interpreted with caution, for they are based on the assessments of regional and national URA officials and by their nature contain some element of subjective judgment. The end of a project was often attributed to more than one factor. A total of 368 causes was involved in the 295 terminated projects.

sources.[50] Even where the city charter prescribes centralized decision making, in "strong mayor" cities, political realities vitiate formal rules; where governments are formally decentralized, fragmentation is written into the constitution. Similar problems make trouble even when projects are underway. In Buffalo, for example, a 161-acre project was stalled for three years after all buildings were demolished because of a deadlock between the Republican mayor and his Democratic council over which developer to hire.[51] The URA found that "problems of coordination among local governmental bodies" were a principal factor in the abortion of 26 projects.

The opposing party or faction can mobilize people adversely affected by a project and exploit their grievances for campaign material against the municipal administration. From a political standpoint one great disadvantage of urban renewal is that a project's inconveniences are apparent long before the compensating rewards are visible. For the general public, the completed project may be a convincing argument that the expense and dislocation are a small price to pay for a new neighborhood, enjoyment of new facilities, and civic pride at replacement of blighted areas. The drawback is that it takes many years to achieve these good things; in the meantime, the opposition has the better exhibits. Promises from city hall about the bright new future are likely to be taken with a grain of salt, for such talk is a staple item in the publicity flow in every city in the country. Any mayor contemplating a redevelopment project will have to run for reelection at least once before the project achieves tangible results other than displaced families and rubble; the payoff is far in the future, but the risks are closer at hand. Of the 295 locally terminated projects, governmental or community opposition was an important factor in 130 cases.

In light of this recital of problems, it is hardly surprising that so many American cities have made only timid beginnings at urban renewal, and that in 1964 almost three times as many projects had been abandoned as completed. Clearly projects do not result easily from the availability of federal dollars. The quickening pace of project initiation and completion does show, however, that urban renewal is becoming somewhat less difficult as administrative techniques have been refined, a corps of experienced local and federal officials has grown, and political feasibility has been demonstrated.

Despite the formidable list of "latent opponents" of urban renewal, it seemed to some observers in the early 1960s that an even more imposing coalition of "latent support" could be found in many cities; it was this prototype that Salisbury termed "The New Convergence of Power." The principal components of this coalition were thought to include the mayor,

[50] The best description of fragmented municipal government remains Wallace S. Sayre and Herbert Kaufman, *Governing New York City* (New York: Russell Sage Foundation, 1960).

[51] *Wall Street Journal*, 28 January 1964, p. 16.

downtown commercial and financial interests, the local press, and assorted liberals. For the reasons given above, I think it unwise to assume that a city's commercial leaders will necessarily support redevelopment: sometimes they will and sometimes they will not; the talents and goals of the city's political officials probably will have as much to do with this as anything else. (Other interests than businessmen may demand urban renewal, but in fact they seldom have done so. Their relation to urban renewal is like that of businessmen: determined on a project-by-project basis, and responsive to the leadership of elected politicians and professional officials.) In the absence of a ready-made constituency for urban renewal, politicians will not rush to embrace it. The most important thing to be said about urban renewal as a political issue is that it is tactically *unnecessary* for almost all mayors. Politicians who make it their issue are not bowing to necessity but are venturing onto a long and risky path.

Salisbury argued that the interests in the new coalition not only want urban renewal, but have the political power to get it. In particular, he said that big-city mayors did not have to worry about general public opinion and reelection, that incumbency and their new-found business support would carry them through the vicissitudes of electoral politics. As examples of well-entrenched mayors he mentioned Raymond R. Tucker of St. Louis, Richard J. Daley of Chicago, and Robert F. Wagner of New York. Daley seems to be almost invulnerable, but the same could hardly be said about the other two. Within a year of the publication of Salisbury's article, Tucker had been denied renomination by a challenger campaigning against his redevelopment projects, while Wagner announced he would not run again after polls showed that John V. Lindsay was far more popular. (After one tumultuous term, Lindsay was denied renomination in the Republican primary and won an uphill battle for reelection with 42 percent of the vote.)

The contemporary electoral careers of other big-city mayors are equally strong evidence against Salisbury's proposition; not only is political survival difficult, but support by the local business community and press seems almost randomly related to success. In Los Angeles in 1961 Samuel Yorty unseated the incumbent mayor, who was supported by the allegedly omnipotent *Los Angeles Times* and most of the city's business leaders. Eight years later Yorty, hardly a mayor in the Salisbury mold, upset a challenger and won a third term over the opposition of the *Times*. Also in 1961, a young and obscure man named Jerome P. Cavanagh defeated the incumbent mayor of Detroit, who enjoyed the support of not only the press and business community, but the United Auto Workers as well. Cavanagh soon enough attracted the favor of all three, but nevertheless he found being mayor so onerous that he retired in 1969. Such individual cases could be recounted at length to demonstrate that mayors—of big cities and little ones—have a remarkably low survival rate. A majority of American mayors serve less than five years in office. This is a point of considerable theoretical importance, to which I will return in the final chapter. At this stage, it will suffice to say that mayors have to worry about public opinion and all too often fail to deal with it well enough to stay in office.

In describing the political perils of urban renewal I have tried to show what obstacles must be overcome to have a successful program. By the same token, this description covers the points that might be considered in an adequate explanation of such a program. One can think of three categories of people whose direct or indirect support must be secured: the electorate, political officials and bureaucrats, and specialized local publics, particularly businessmen. An ambitious mayor must be able to do the following: (1) win electoral support to buy time for projects to come to fruition; (2) get approval of appointments, budgets, and plans from the municipal legislature, and control the decisions of relevant municipal regulatory bodies and line agencies; and (3) attract enough business backing to neutralize the opposition of businessmen who are adversely affected by redevelopment.

These tasks are interrelated, of course. An unpopular mayor is unlikely to command much support from other politicians. A mayor who cannot coordinate municipal agencies so as to deliver on his policy commitments will be less able to make alliances with special publics. Attaining these goals requires control of political nominations, a campaign organization, and the ability to appeal to both general and special publics.

Why should any mayor bother with urban renewal any more than he has to? As it is seldom politically necessary, what would induce a mayor to undertake an ambitious program in this risky field? This is a very difficult question to answer about Richard Lee, as it would be about any politician. I have tried to deal with this question in the following chapter, which is concerned with Lee's political career and with the strategies he employed to win electoral support for his administration. Chapter 7 deals with problems of policy coordination among fragmented governmental bodies. Chapter 8 describes Lee's manipulation of the "urban renewal public" and some general aspects of business participation in politics. Together, Chapters 6 through 8 describe the development of the political foundation for urban renewal in New Haven.

6 Lee and his administration

This chapter gives an overview of Richard Lee's mayoral career. Because one way to characterize a man or a period is by contrast, I introduce my narrative of the Lee administration with a description of Lee's predecessor, who responded to similar conditions in very different ways. One purpose of this chapter is to provide enough information about the Lee administration to make the following more specialized chapters comprehensible. A second purpose is to describe the political ambitions that led Lee to his urban renewal program and the strategies that made it possible to execute the first stages of that program. A third purpose is to illustrate generalizations in the previous chapter with data from New Haven.

The Celentano Administration

During the Depression and war, from 1932 through 1945, the Democratic administration of John W. Murphy occupied New Haven's city hall. A machine politician in the classic style, Murphy was business agent for an American Federation of Labor cigarmakers local. His principal policy goal seems to have been economy in government; reportedly, he roamed about city hall turning off lights. His winning platform in the 1931 election included a promise to restore the city's credit rating, then at a low ebb. Although a depression might not be considered the best time for a deflationary fiscal policy, Murphy pursued it determinedly and successfully, reducing the city's bonded indebtedness from $19 million to $6.3 million.[1]

Murphy's parsimony hit the public schools particularly hard. Although New Haven had many dilapidated school buildings dating as far back as the Civil War, Murphy, intent on a debtless city, did nothing to replace them, refusing even to use federal Public Works Administration funds for school construction or renovation. Not a single school building was constructed in New Haven from 1929 to 1947. The school system, starved for funds in

[1] Murphy has been called the unsung hero of the city's urban renewal program, for his policies left most of New Haven's statutory bonding allowance unused and earned it an AAA rating from Moody's bond-rating service. In 1957 only 3 of the 23 largest cities in the country had such a rating; see Seymour Freedgood, "New Strength in City Hall," *Fortune* (November 1957), 159.

other respects as well, consistently was near the bottom in regional rankings on expenditures per pupil.[2] One consequence of Murphy's policies was a 36 percent rise in private school enrollment from 1931 to 1941.[3] This increase at a time when money was scarce reveals the fading appeal of the city's public schools.

Murphy kept a tight lid on municipal expenses in every other respect as well. From 1940 to 1946 the budget remained fixed between $9.7 and $9.8 million. The mayor's natural frugality was reinforced by the local press. Murphy reportedly spent part of every Friday afternoon in John Day Jackson's office, listening to the conservative publisher's views on public affairs and judgments of what was good and bad for New Haven.

While Murphy's parsimony earned him Jackson's support, it also brought about his downfall in the 1945 election. Parents who were most concerned about education could escape the effects of the mayor's budgets by sending their children to private school—if they could afford it—but the teachers and other educational employees had no way out. They suffered particularly under wartime inflation, as Murphy refused their requests for salary increases. With the approach of peace Murphy could point neither to domestic nor to foreign crises as justifications for not improving the schools and other rundown features of local government. The teachers again asked for a raise and were told that their demands would be considered when all the city's bonded indebtedness was paid off. This was the last straw for the teachers, who were quick to respond to the assurance given by William C. Celentano, the Republican mayoralty candidate in 1945, that he would be more generous toward the schools.

Like most of his political associates and rivals, Celentano was a self-made man. His father ran a fruit stand. Celentano quit school after the ninth grade to help his brother through medical school and eventually earned his high school diploma at night. He became an undertaker, opened his own funeral parlor, and quickly attained prominence in his profession. He was elected president of his state trade association in 1931 and later was head of a national morticians' organization. Celentano's political career paralleled his professional rise. His business, of course, was an excellent way to make a wide circle of acquaintances and earn the gratitude of thousands of people. Ethnic solidarity seems to be an important consideration in the undertaking

[2] *New Haven's Schools: An Investment in Your Future* (New Haven Board of Education, 1947), p. 23; and Connecticut Public Expenditure Council, *Local Public School Expenses and State Aid in Connecticut* (Hartford, Conn.: Connecticut Public Expenditure Council, 1946).

[3] For the sources, see Robert A. Dahl, *Who Governs?* (New Haven, Conn.: Yale University Press, 1961), p. 143.

business and morticians have often been "natural" political leaders in ethnic neighborhoods.[4]

All his adult life Celentano had wanted to be mayor of New Haven. He was scarcely in his twenties before he was chairman of his ward committee, and he was elected alderman before he was thirty. He served twelve years on the Board of Aldermen, including several terms as Republican leader. As the first Italian mayoral candidate, he gave Murphy a close call in the 1939 election. He had to wait six years for a second chance at city hall, however. But by 1945 Celentano had the support of another rising star in the Republican party, a lawyer named George DiCenzo, whose career is also instructive about the ways of urban politics in the mid-twentieth century.

Unlike Celentano and his contemporaries in the Democratic party, DiCenzo had the advantages of a college education. After graduating from the University of Maryland Law School, he returned to his home town in the late 1920s to practice law. Uncertain about which party to join, he was persuaded by a friend to become a Republican and campaigned energetically in the 1927 election. In the following months, as Al Smith's presidential candidacy gained, some of DiCenzo's new Republican friends began to make much of Smith's Catholicism and the great political handicap that it posed. DiCenzo, a practicing Catholic himself, was nettled by these comments and began to express his feelings on various public occasions. (Reflecting on these events 30 years later, DiCenzo felt that his reaction was somewhat naïve.) Local Democrats soon heard about his views and invited him to participate in the Smith campaign. DiCenzo was something of a valuable political property in New Haven: not only could he deliver campaign speeches in Italian, but he was one of a handful of Italian professional men. He was even more active for the Democrats in 1928 than he had been as a Republican the year before, becoming head of an Al Smith club and even running successfully as a Democratic candidate for justice of the peace.

After the election, but before DiCenzo could be sworn in to the office he had won, he was again approached by the friend who had recruited him for the Republicans. His friend argued that as a young Italian attorney hoping to gain influence in the court system, DiCenzo would be better off as a Republican; court personnel were appointed by the governor, who was likely to be a Republican for the indefinite future. Impressed by this argument, DiCenzo declined to take the oath of office for the post to which he had been elected on the Democratic ticket and quickly plunged into Republican organization politics.

[4] On the political role of undertakers in Italo-American communities, see William F. Whyte, *Street Corner Society,* enl. ed. (Chicago: University of Chicago Press, 1955), pp. 201–2; and Samuel Lubell, *The Future of American Politics* (Garden City, N.Y.: Doubleday & Company, Inc., 1956), p. 225.

His state senatorial district was controlled by the surviving Ullman brother and his allies; two of the other three New Haven districts were held by local representatives of the Ullmans' enemy J. Henry Roraback, the legendary Republican boss of Connecticut in the 1920s and '30s.[5] DiCenzo allied himself with the Roraback faction and set out to wrest control of his district from the Ullman forces, by gathering a following in each ward of a dozen or so supporters who would work hard to register voters on the Republican primary list, which qualified them to vote in the obscure elections that chose ward committeemen. Through his alliance with Roraback, DiCenzo gained some influence in the courts and could offer as inducements for political support concessions like lighter sentences for bootleggers. Moreover, Italians were moving into the district, and DiCenzo, the president of several nationality organizations, exploited these connections to the hilt.

DiCenzo took control of his senatorial district in 1941 and became a man to be reckoned with. He began to build his influence in other neighborhoods, particularly those with heavy Italian concentrations, where he signed up many new voters; he soon had the makings of a citywide organization. The prime Republican leader in New Haven, however, was Frank Lynch, who had become head of the local Roraback forces after the latter's suicide in 1937. Lynch, who served as state finance commissioner in the administration of Governor John Lodge in the early 1950s, was the "regular" Republican leader in New Haven during our study.

In 1941 DiCenzo had rejected Celentano's request for his support for another mayoral nomination, arguing that with Italy fighting at Germany's side, Italian candidates would not be well received. Two years later the Republicans came within 2,700 votes of beating Murphy with a Yankee candidate, Angus Fraser, who wanted the nomination again in 1945. So did Celentano, and now, with Italy on the side of the Allies and the war in Europe over, DiCenzo agreed that the time was ripe. But Lynch and his associates preferred Fraser, perhaps because Republican chances looked so good that Celentano was not needed at the head of the ticket. Indeed, they may have felt that Celentano's popularity and alliance with DiCenzo would make him less dependent on their support, perhaps even a threat to their primacy. In any event, Celentano did not accept the leadership's rebuff as he had in 1941 and 1943. He and DiCenzo launched an intense struggle for the votes of delegates to the nominating convention, venturing from DiCenzo's stronghold on "the Hill" into Lynch territory. The two Italian leaders won. At the "customary meeting at the Taft Hotel" the night before the convention, they confronted Lynch with their delegate majority and secured his agreement not to contest Celentano's nomination.

[5] For a brief description of Roraback's career, see Duane Lockard, *New England State Politics* (Princeton, N.J.: Princeton University Press, 1959), pp. 245–51.

The political situation was favorable to the Republicans. Fourteen years of Democratic rule had produced a low level of municipal services and shabby public facilities. Top city officials were complacent and for the most part not very competent. Campaigning mostly on the school issue, Celentano attacked Murphy's record and promised new buildings and equipment, higher salaries, and an end to political considerations in personnel decisions. For years civic organizations had expressed alarm at dirty, unsafe, and dilapidated schools, obsolete textbooks, cramped playgrounds, and low teachers' salaries. DiCenzo mobilized some of these groups behind the Republican ticket. Approaching the leaders of the Teachers' League, and exploiting their hopes of promotion, DiCenzo organized the teachers into a strong pro-Celentano bloc.[6] The Teachers' League circulated a leaflet, signed by many of its members, claiming that Murphy did "not believe in progress... [his] only policy, therefore, is one of economy." Similar grievances and promises brought Celentano the support of the school janitors union and of other city employees and their organizations, all encouraged and mobilized by DiCenzo.

What with his ancestry and the condition of the schools, Celentano forged a coalition of municipal employees, Yankees, middle-class voters concerned about education, and Italians (largely working-class) eager to see one of their own in city hall. With the issue so clearly drawn as economy versus profligacy, the Jackson newspapers supported Murphy, but Yankee businessmen contributed, almost automatically, to the Republican campaign fund. Celentano defeated Murphy by 6,145 votes.

Celentano took office at the head of a faction, not a party. His nomination had been achieved over Lynch's opposition and his election owed little to Lynch's efforts. Once in power Celentano had to decide what to do about his rival, who controlled most ward organizations and still dispensed state patronage and the Republican share of probate court appointments. Lynch had the better connections in the state Republican organization. He had been the man to see about jobs and favors in the past and, in the expectations of many Republicans, would continue to be in the future. With all these resources, Lynch could maintain his organizational position and did not need to make peace with Celentano and DiCenzo. Celentano's control of city hall, with its patronage, contracts, municipal services, and coercive powers, probably put him in a stronger position for an intraparty struggle with Lynch *if* he were inclined to spend the time and energy required to make use of these resources. Had he done so successfully, he or DiCenzo doubtless would have replaced Lynch as the man in New Haven with whom

---

6 The head of the Teachers' League was a Republican, but most teachers were Irish Democrats. Celentano and DiCenzo worked with the teachers, not the administrators, who remained loyal to the regime that had promoted them, while the teachers, less indebted to Murphy, could be won away by promises of higher pay.

other Connecticut Republicans had to deal. But driving Lynch from the field would have required a great deal of time and trouble. Celentano decided to get along with Lynch rather than fight him for control of the wards. In so doing he failed to heed Machiavelli's advice that "men must either be caressed or else annihilated; they will revenge themselves for small injuries, but cannot do so for great ones; the injury therefore that we do to a man must be such that we need not fear his vengeance."[7]

Once Celentano made this fateful decision, he faced the consequences Machiavelli predicted, for he could not escape strengthening Lynch. Celentano had not named his party's slate of aldermanic candidates and Lynch was able to use his control of the local share of state patronage, particularly his control of the City Court, to prevent the mayor from having a working majority on the Board of Aldermen. Since the Democrats usually were united in opposition, Celentano had to bargain with the Lynch faction to get many of his proposals passed. Every concession made to Lynch—typically on appointments or contracts—enhanced his position in the party. On the other hand, Lynch had no governmental responsibility and so did not have to fashion policies that required Celentano's acquiescence; thus the flow of concessions went primarily in one direction. Celentano's popularity and incumbency protected him from possible denial of renomination, but they did not insure the success of his policies. His influence within his party therefore was severely limited.

The new mayor ran into difficulty with the aldermen from the beginning of his first term, when they failed to elect his chosen candidates for majority leader and president of the Board. A year or two later, while the Republicans still had a majority on the board, the aldermen refused to approve Celentano's budget until it was amended to provide satisfactory salary increases for policemen and firemen. Celentano's troubles with his legislature increased after 1949, when the Democrats gained control.

Actually, the Republican split was not as great a limitation as it might have been with a more adventurous mayor, for there were not so many things that Celentano wanted to do. He had wanted to be mayor for a long time and very much enjoyed the job, but apparently his ambitions for higher office were mild. His political strategy seemed to be cautious and unenterprising, based on "recognition," jobs for his supporters, compliance with those interest group demands that did not arouse significant opposition or require

---

[7] Machiavelli's maxim would seem to be good advice only where a politician has some possibility of controlling his rival's sources of support, perhaps in city politics but certainly not in most state legislatures and national politics. This is one of the reasons for the various formal and informal manifestations of courtesy in legislators' relations with each other: typically any member cannot have much influence on his colleagues' chances of reelection and so must learn to live with them.

major political effort, and staying on the good side of the newspapers. The mayor was seldom given to bold ventures; he did not seem to feel that the returns from innovation would outweigh the risks of opposition from some affected interest or from the *Register*. It was claimed that, like Murphy, he visited John Day Jackson for weekly consultations. Others have scoffed at this, but few deny that he was anything but solicitous of Jackson's concern for economy in government. Celentano spent only a few hours a day at city hall and devoted the rest of his time to his business interests. The calculus of rewards favored sitting tight except when popular demands for action were strong enough to suggest that inaction would be politically costly. As we will see, such demands were unlikely. In the absence of ideological preferences, public pressure, or an ambition which he tried to serve by spectacular achievement, Celentano had no real reason to interfere in the activities of many city agencies except to control spending and be sure that no serious violence was done to his popularity. In contrast to his successor, he left such agencies as the Board of Zoning Appeals alone. For these reasons Celentano's regime was similar to his predecessor's in its decentralization and lack of innovative spirit.

These observations apply also to the school system, once Celentano kept his promises—public and private—in that area. He built three elementary schools and closed several unsafe nineteenth century buildings. Teachers' salaries were increased, although by 1954 the range was only $2,800 to $5,000. He appointed a number of distinguished citizens to a Citizens Advisory Committee on Schools and commissioned a comprehensive study of the school system. This project resulted in a voluminous report recommending many drastic changes, including a massive building program. The administration largely ignored its proposals. Celentano also rewarded some of the teachers who had campaigned actively for him. One was made principal of one of the city's two academic high schools, another became principal of a junior high school. Both men still held these positions in the early 1960s. As a group, the teachers resumed their customary passive role in local politics. Two kinds of politics continued to be relevant to promotions and assignments: party influence and factional relationships within the Department of Education. These represented individual alignments, however, not group action.

Celentano's response to the city's economic decline was consistent with his performance in other fields. New Haven's stagnation had been apparent for decades. As early as the 1930s many local businessmen had come to believe that it was a dying and defeatist city. The most conspicuous results of this feeling, however, seem to have been intermittent exhortation. In 1941 a municipal City Plan Department was formed and the well-known firm of Maurice E. H. Rotival and Associates was hired to prepare a master plan for the city.[8] A year later this document was completed and duly approved by the Board of Aldermen, and then, in the finest traditions of city planning, forgotten.

In the early postwar years some downtown businessmen began to worry about competition from suburban shopping centers. At the time an adequate remedy seemed to be more parking facilities in the central business district. The scarcity of open land made it difficult for private business to meet this need. The cost and difficulty of acquiring built-on sites for parking lots or garages required a public authority with the right of eminent domain and the power to issue bonds to finance the development of parking facilities and, perhaps, subsidize their operation. The Chamber of Commerce advocated formation of such an authority, a step requiring state legislation. Some members of the Chamber arranged to have the necessary bill introduced in the General Assembly. After discussing the problem with Celentano, they felt that he agreed with them. But when a state legislative committee held hearings on the subject, DiCenzo, representing the mayor, astonished both the authority's champions and the committee by testifying that the city administration would go along with the proposal only if it were approved by New Haven voters at a referendum. The legislature carried out the administration's wishes and scheduled an election for the fall of 1951.

The businessmen who initiated the campaign for the parking authority found it difficult to persuade their fellow merchants to support them, although it clearly was in their interests to do so. The Chamber of Commerce conducted an extensive canvassing and promotional campaign for the authority, which was vehemently opposed by the *Register*. On the Sunday before the election Celentano wrote a front-page article for the *Register* listing the arguments for and against the measure. It passed by a ratio of more than three to one.

Once established, the Parking Authority did little. It was unable to secure the support of many downtown businessmen for a comprehensive program. A few merchants realized the central business district's increasing vulnerability to suburban competition, but they could mobilize neither city hall nor most of their colleagues. The administration anticipated more dangers than rewards from any attempts at meaningful action and remained aloof. One vigorous business champion of government action in this field complained that "businessmen wanted leadership and Celentano would not give it." This complaint could be made with equal justice of the downtown business com-

---

[8] Rotival himself was a flamboyant and influential man, accustomed to thinking on a broad scale. Among his more impressive achievements were the extensive modern rebuilding of Caracas and an ambitious regional plan for Madagascar. Rotival had held visiting appointments at Yale and his organization had a branch office in New Haven.

munity, which did not try to organize political strength to reverse Celentano's policy of abstention.

Much the same pattern was followed with urban renewal. Early in 1950 a Democratic alderman thought of forming a redevelopment agency to take advantage of the Housing Act of 1949. The Democratic leader on the Board of Aldermen discussed the proposal privately with Celentano. (The Democrats had an 18–15 majority on the Board, not enough to override a mayoral veto.) Celentano was reluctant to start on such an unknown course, but also realized that if he did nothing he would be attacked by the Democrats. He agreed not to veto the proposal if it were sponsored by a Republican. This was acceptable to the Democrats and the resolution passed. The mayor and the Democrats then agreed on the five members to be appointed to the new agency. The Democrats who raised the issue seemed motivated in some degree by a desire to do something about the city's problems, but also, and probably more importantly, they saw an opportunity to embarrass Celentano for not pushing redevelopment and to make the Democratic party look more progressive and active.

Once established and staffed, it was natural that the Redevelopment Agency should look for something to do. The City Plan Department and Rotival, at last provided with a means of executing the advice they had been giving for years, urged that the agency start with the city's worst slum, the Oak Street section. A federal survey and planning grant was obtained for Oak Street, but then nothing much happened. There is no indication that Celentano impeded the Redevelopment Agency's progress, but he did not press for action, either. For one thing, doing so would have required a level of active direction and advocacy that very likely would have exceeded his allocation of time to his mayoral duties. Although Oak Street seemed the most politically suitable starting point for urban renewal, opposition might well come from displaced businessmen, adjoining merchants fearful of competition from new stores, and residents of the neighborhoods into which the displaced residents would move. The Democrats could be expected to make capital of any shortcomings in the plan or its execution. Most important of all, the newspapers were expected to oppose redevelopment in principle, because it would require public spending. On the other side of the ledger, Celentano and his advisers could not discern powerful community interests that might be mobilized to support such a project; they did not consider New Haven "ready for redevelopment." New Haven was not a good town for middle class reformers. The banks, utilities, and manufacturers would be apathetic, leaving the project without business support. Although there was some demand for action from do-gooders, downtown merchants, and the Chamber of Commerce, it was neither vigorous nor widespread. In retrospect, some Republican politicians and businessmen reconsidered the city's readiness and thought that the mayor was afraid to offend the *Register*'s owner. But at the time there was little pressure for progress and redevelopment languished.

As the years went by, more plans and programs appeared. The Chamber of Commerce presented its "Ten-Point Program," which in fact was based on a previous City Plan Department document. More of its members were worried about the city's problems and wanted to "do something about them," but none of them seemed to know what that something might be. They expressed their worries and wishes to the mayor. A former president of the Chamber of Commerce described the situation to us:

> Celentano agreed a hundred per cent with the idea, but nothing happened until Mayor Lee took over.... The whole board of the Chamber was in back of it. I guess there are about 25 on that board, and all—modestly—leading citizens. But this Chamber program that we visualized for a long time was too big for the Chamber and too big for the city administration; I mean it had to be a collection of city leaders to put this thing over.

Looking back at that period after several years' experience with the Lee administration, some of the businessmen concerned expressed doubts about Celentano's willingness or ability to cope with the problems involved, which they saw as largely technical and administrative: "It was too big for him to handle. The magnitude of the problems required a real effort, and I think that the prior administration wasn't prepared to do that." But at the time these businessmen who were worried about the city's future neither rallied their associates nor put much pressure on Celentano, to whom they continued to give campaign contributions and electoral support. Within a few years many of them would give their contributions and support to Celentano's very different Democratic successor.

Richard C. Lee

Lee was born in 1916 to poor parents who lived in a cold-water flat in a near-slum neighborhood. Lee's father died when he was in high school. His mother seems to have been the dominant parent; her belief in the virtues of diligence and neatness are reflected in her son's personal and political style. In addition to working on weekends and after school he found time for a variety of other activities, including service as an altar boy. The Depression and his family's poverty kept Lee from attending college and he worked in a grocery store after graduating from high school. His cheerful industry favorably impressed many customers, one of whom introduced him to the managing editor of the *Journal-Courier* when he was 18. Lee was offered a job as a reporter after falsely claiming that he was a good typist. That night he borrowed a typewriter and practiced on it until morning, when he reported for work at the newspaper. He covered mainly the police and city hall beats, where his energy and curiosity gained him a wide circle of acquaintances and the beginning of a vast knowledge of local affairs.

Living in a poor Irish ward where politics was a popular spectator and participant sport, Lee was working for the Democratic organization before he reached voting age. In 1939 the passage of the Hatch Act forced Lee's Democratic alderman to choose between his political career and a $3,600 job as a WPA official. Jobs were scarce and the ward soon needed a new alderman. Lee was an articulate, presentable young man with a strategic job and a bright future. His ward chairlady got him the nomination, which was tantamount to election. Lee asked to be assigned as the aldermanic member of the City Plan Commission, a body that until then had been doubly futile: its plans were ignored and it lacked funds to hire a professional staff. In 1941 Lee helped remedy the latter deficiency with the formation of a City Plan Department. He was also instrumental in appropriating money to hire Rotival, the city's long-term private planning consultant.

The year he became an alderman Lee went to work for the Chamber of Commerce doing promotional activity that brought him into contact with the city's retailers.[9] By then he had joined dozens of local organizations and helped to found new ones, including a Junior Chamber of Commerce and a celebrated summer series of popular music concerts in Yale Bowl. He became president and secretary of the Junior Chamber and achieved a good deal of visibility as master of ceremonies for the concerts.

In 1942 Lee was drafted into the infantry. A series of illnesses, including his first ulcer, broke his health; by the time the army gave him a medical discharge, Lee weighed 106 pounds. Back home and without his job, he was asked by Yale University to run its wartime news digest. He accepted reluctantly, worried that his working-class origins and lack of a college education would be humiliating handicaps in a world of cultured Yankee patricians. Lee's boss at Yale was Carl Lohmann, the secretary of the university and for many years an important force there, a socially prominent, independently wealthy man of impressive erudition. He recognized Lee's intelligence, energy, and ambition and virtually made him his protégé, helping and encouraging his adjustment to Yale.

Under Lohmann's guidance and friendship the job at Yale became a tremendously important experience for Lee, tantamount to the education he had missed. The superficial manifestations of this socialization were apparent:

---

[9] Lee's three-year stint as a public relations man for the Chamber of Commerce may be the basis for Floyd Hunter's characterization of him as a "businessman." See Hunter's review of *Who Governs?* in *Administrative Science Quarterly*, 6 (March 1962), 518, 519.

Lee soon had an Ivy League wardrobe; he is one of the few non-Yale graduates to belong to Mory's, the famous eating club; and he was made a fellow of one of Yale's residential colleges. More basically, he became familiar with and sympathetic to liberal upper-middle-class values and ways of looking at the world. Many of his policies and strategies as mayor seemed influenced by his knowledge of the world of ideas and his acceptance of the enlightened values he encountered at Yale. He even had a well-developed taste in architecture and often nagged businessmen to think about aesthetics when planning new buildings. Many of Lee's broader political goals may represent not only his acceptance of Yale values, but also a desire to demonstrate to his former associates there that, without their education and social advantages, he could achieve successes that even they would admire and respect: achievements by their standards, not just by the criteria of the organization politicians and Main Street businessmen in whose world he had lived prior to 1943.[10]

Lee clearly was proud of his continued associations with Yale, his friendships with its late president, A. Whitney Griswold, and other university figures, and the honorary degree which he received in 1961. He was not, however, a snob about these things. He had a touch of disdain for the "impracticality" of "longhairs." Like most New Haven politicians, he had more than a touch of prejudice against Yankees, who were often stereotyped locally as debilitated and mean-spirited. Moreover, Lee's emotional attachments to Yale did not deter him from exploiting town–gown hostilities to drive a very hard bargain in various negotiations over the years.

It should not be thought that Yale changed Lee from a regular party man into a "reformer." He was skilled at organization politics and I have no reason to believe that he intrinsically disapproved of it. Indeed, I remember his satisfied comment when an agreement for a new development in a renewal project had finally been signed and a parade of contract-seekers began to call on him: "Now for the practical side of redevelopment." Lee was perfectly comfortable with patronage, but he did not, like conventional machine politicians, value it for its own sake, or merely to maintain his own party position. While his decisions about patronage recognized the maintenance needs of the Democratic organization (and were generally made in concert with Golden and Barbieri), Lee also used his patronage resources in pursuit of policy goals that were more congenial to liberals than to ward bosses. (His administration has been called "New Frontier policies on a *Last Hurrah* foundation.") Working with the Democratic machine, Lee also

10 Robert Moses has attributed much of Al Smith's ambition and enlightened political policies to his desire to "show" Yankees that he was as admirable as any of their political leaders. See Moses, "La Guardia, a Salute and a Memoir," *New York Times Magazine* (8 September 1957), 18.

built up a more personal organization that was increasingly important in the last years of his administration when he and Barbieri became enemies.

At times Lee went out of his way to display his belief in causes that intellectuals cherish and machine politicians avoid. He was an outspoken critic of the late Senator Joseph R. McCarthy, even before hostile audiences. He resisted attempts by Catholic organizations to restrict the exhibition of motion pictures of which the Church disapproved, and he conspicuously and gratuitously denounced a manifestation of intolerance in a nearby city that received nationwide attention.[11]

In short, while Lee had always been a liberal, energetic, and ambitious man, one might guess that his ten years at Yale widened his intellectual vistas and established different standards of achievement: "It took me a long time to get to be mayor and when I finally made it, I made up my mind that I wasn't going to be an ordinary mayor."

Lee's association with Yale had some less profound and more direct political consequences. On the negative side, it made him vulnerable to suspicions of being soft on Yale, a serious charge in view of the university's local unpopularity. Lee leaned over backward to compensate for this problem. On the positive side, Lee's many friendships at Yale could be exploited in a variety of ways. For example, he helped local political figures or their children gain admission to Yale, thus incurring useful obligations. Once he helped an unsuccessful black Yale graduate student gain admission to Yale Law School. The student had been an energetic Republican leader in the local black community. He switched parties after being admitted to law school and almost immediately began to repay Lee's favor by defending the mayor against attack from black Republicans who had been his associates a few months earlier.

The year after he went to work for the university Lee took over the Yale News Bureau and proceeded to do an outstanding job of public relations. Typical of his diligence and energy was a survey of all department chairmen to find out what interesting research was under way. Using the responses as

---

[11] The head of a Veterans of Foreign Wars post in Norwalk, Connecticut had urged citizens to report indications of "subversive" behavior by their neighbors to the VFW. The widespread critical attention which this proposal attracted caused the antisubversive campaign to wither away. Some examples of this attention: Bernard DeVoto, "Norwalk and Points West," *Harper's Magazine* (April 1954), 10–12; George W. Groh, "Norwalk, NATO and the VFW: What's All the Hollering," *The Reporter* (16 March 1954), 28–30; and James Rorty, "Thirty Days that Shook Norwalk," *Commentary* (April 1954), 330–36.

Ten years later Governor George C. Wallace of Alabama accepted an invitation from the Yale Political Union to speak at the university. Embroiled in a reelection campaign in which Negro votes were crucial, Lee denounced the students for the invitation and said that Wallace was "officially unwelcome" in New Haven. Wallace declined the invitation and bested Lee by inviting him to speak in Alabama on any subject he chose.

leads, Lee spent six months interviewing professors on their current projects and used their information for a judiciously timed barrage of news releases that kept Yale's name in the mass media. His greatest single coup was getting Griswold on the covers of *Time* and *Newsweek* in the same week.

Lee's three jobs—at the *Journal-Courier,* the Chamber of Commerce, and Yale—taught him a great deal about the substance and style of many different worlds. They helped him make hundreds of acquaintances who formed the foundation of a pervasive intelligence network which made him by far the best-informed man in New Haven. (Like most prominent politicians, Lee was brought information by many people who hoped to earn his goodwill with their tidbits of news.) Having worked for the Jackson newspapers, he could partially offset their owner's political hostility through his many friends on the papers.

Lee's First Mayoralty Campaigns

Murphy lost most of his political influence after his defeat in 1945. The mantle of organization leadership fell somewhat insecurely on the shoulders of John Golden, Murphy's Director of Public Works. His experience, contacts, and position as Murphy's chief lieutenant gave Golden the presumption of preeminence, but with neither city nor state patronage at his disposal, he had difficulty keeping challengers in line: "These new younger men began to try the crown on for size and they liked the feel of it, and started to put in primaries against Golden." As early as 1946 there were factional intraparty fights in which Lee, a promising alderman but hardly a titan, threw in his lot with Golden. For the next several years Golden had his hands full defending his leadership from various rivals, of whom the most important was B. Fred Damiani, a state senator who controlled one of the city's four state senatorial districts from his home base in the twelfth ward. The Democrats ran an obscure Italian dentist for mayor in 1947, reportedly because Golden wanted to prove that Italian ancestry was not enough to beat Celentano and that, therefore, "recognition" of Italians was not the pathway to success. In 1949 Golden picked the 33-year-old Lee for the nomination, which was sought also by two veteran Irish politicians. Lee's opponents and their supporters hoped to overthrow Golden by defeating his mayoralty candidate. A bitter struggle ensued in primary elections to choose each ward's delegates to the Town Committee, which would nominate the party's candidate. Golden and Lee won in 27 of the city's 33 wards. This outcome was a result not only of Golden's organizational strength, but of Lee's public relations talents, popularity, and consequent appeal as the man with the best chance of beating Celentano. (Lee's formidable ability to use the mass media was a great source of strength in intraparty relationships.)

Lee conducted a vigorous campaign against Celentano, emphasizing planning for a modern city. He lost by 712 votes out of 70,000. A few days after the election Lee learned that one of his supporters in charge of collecting absentee ballots from precinct workers had gotten drunk on election day and forgotten to turn in his ballots—which numbered more than 700. Lee's later passion for making sure of every detail and avoiding surprises and spontaneity may well have been intensified by the poignant moment when he looked down at the ballots that would have made him mayor.

The local Democratic party was still badly split; "no one was talking to anyone else." In 1950 Golden, with Lee's help, conducted a series of primary campaigns that stripped Damiani of all party offices except his chairmanship of the twelfth ward. The election of Chester Bowles as governor of Connecticut that year further consolidated Golden's position by giving him some patronage to dispense. Lee's good showing in 1949 and Golden's continued sponsorship gained him the nomination again in 1951. This time Lee's tactics were rougher; the campaign was bitter and personal. Lee charged Celentano with corruption, pointing out that a trucking firm in which he was a partner had been hired by the Department of Education. Lee also made a great commotion about assessments, publicizing the fact that the opulent residence of a Republican contractor was assessed at less than $5,000. The local newspapers claimed that the Democrats' advertisements were libelous and refused to publish them. At the height of the campaign Lee suffered an attack of ulcers that incapacitated him for several days. Again some Democratic leaders did not support their candidate. The first tally of the returns showed Celentano the winner by 36 votes. Lee charged irregularities in the counting and demanded a recount, which was conducted ward by ward. When only a few wards had been recanvassed Celentano's margin was cut to two votes and both sides were threatening suits for various violations of the election laws. It was apparent that a continuation of the recount might reverse the original outcome, but equally apparent that it would result in a series of legal actions that might seriously embarrass both parties. Acting on the principle that "you always have to think about the next election," Lee abandoned the contest and Celentano was declared the winner by a plurality of two.

When the time for nominations came around in 1953 there was some possibility that Lee's record of failure would count against him. But a "spontaneous petition by 5,000 independent voters" asking him to run again averted this risk. Nominated for the third time, Lee reverted to his earlier, more positive campaign strategy. New Haven was an old city, he said, with an honorable past but a clouded future unless bold action were taken to modernize it. Celentano was asleep to these needs, a part-time mayor too timid to lead the drastic campaign necessary to solve the city's deficiencies: slums, traffic jams, inadequate parking, rundown community facilities. These problems were too immense and complicated to be dealt with by government alone. Lee proposed to mobilize the whole community in a citizens action committee to work with his administration in making and executing imaginative, comprehensive plans.

Some of Lee's Yale friends, interested in politics and attracted by his liberal views, had helped him in previous campaigns. Adlai Stevenson's candidacy in 1952 had stimulated enthusiastic, widespread political participation by intellectuals in New Haven, as it did elsewhere. Lee's active work with Volunteers for Stevenson gave him an additional point of contact with many people in the Yale community. His persuasiveness, ability, and platform made his candidacy a natural outlet for Volunteers who were interested in continuing active political participation. Building on this base, Lee organized "Independents for Lee." It was headed by two friends, Chester Kerr, secretary of the Yale University Press (and now the director), and Eugene V. Rostow, then a prominent professor, soon to be dean of the Yale Law School, and, later, Undersecretary of State for Political Affairs. This group enlisted the services of many people, largely from Yale, who ordinarily paid scant attention to local politics. It waged a vigorous campaign for middle-class votes on the basis of Lee's promises of a rejuvenated approach to the city's problems. Independents for Lee was important to him. It was a vehicle for the political expression of people who, because of their very different backgrounds and attitudes toward public affairs, were uncongenial to the regular party workers. It was a means of appealing to independent voters. And, because it was an effective vote-getting organization, it gave Lee a counterweight to the party machine. (Lee formed a similar organization in each of his subsequent reelection campaigns, but called it "Citizens for Lee" because Republicans had pointed out that most of the leading "Independents" were registered Democrats. By 1957 Citizens for Lee was financed almost entirely by Lee's own campaign funds rather than by contributions from the people whose names were associated with it. As I said earlier, this organization was much less important to Lee once he was in office.)

Such tactics struck at Celentano's weaknesses, for his administration was in much the same torpid state that Murphy's had been eight years before. Public services were clearly inadequate in many respects. Various citizen groups, including one chaired by Rostow, were again expressing dissatisfaction with the schools. In spite of his fear of the *Register,* Celentano had found it necessary to make four increases in the tax rate totaling eight mills; in addition the city's bonded indebtedness had increased by 150 percent. Except for three new elementary schools, it was hard to see what had been accomplished. Lee's confident, brassy energy contrasted favorably with Celentano's easygoing manner. It seemed to many voters that the administration had lost whatever vigor it originally may have possessed.

Stung by Lee's criticism of his inaction on downtown problems, Celentano made a serious blunder. He suggested that one solution to the city's traffic problems would be to turn the central Green into a parking lot. This spacious open area faces Yale on two sides and the central business district on the other two. Three churches with roots deep in New Haven's past are there, along with the bones of the earliest settlers. The Green is in the care of the "Proprietors of the Common and Undivided Lands," a group of descendants of the oldest Yankees, and thus undoubtedly would never have become a parking lot. But many New Haven residents who were not Yankees also considered the proposal to use the Green for such such a purpose almost sacrilegious.

Lee took 52 percent of the vote in the 1953 election, winning by a margin of almost 3,600; the Democrats won 24 of the 33 seats on the Board of Aldermen. Although Celentano retained or even slightly increased his Italian support, taking the wards with the biggest proportion of Italians by as much as four to one, Lee gained votes almost everywhere else, from the upper-class eighteenth ward to the Irish districts where he was raised. His victory can be attributed to the increased effectiveness of the Democratic organization because of its new-found unity, the growing inanition of the Celentano Administration, and, capitalizing on these shortcomings, the successful appeal made by Independents for Lee to middle-class voters.

The Political Foundation for Urban Renewal

Lee's ambition was to rise high in the world, above and beyond the New Haven city hall. He hoped to go from there to the governor's mansion or the Senate; some of his friends thought that perhaps his ultimate ambition was to be vice president. He planned to accomplish this by making an extraordinary record as mayor of New Haven. By carrying out his campaign promises he would not only be doing what he believed, but helping his own career. On taking office, he planned to honor his pledge to do something about the city's increasing obsolescence, but he did not then realize how important urban renewal would be either to New Haven or to his political future. Initially, he "just did everything," trying to make an impact in many fields of government. All the while he was seeking a policy area that would become the major focus of his resources and his ambition, the first call on his energies, and the trademark of his reputation. He thought for a time that this might be the schools, which were certainly in need of attention. But his initial successes in urban renewal demonstrated its feasibility and suggested to Lee the great gains that a real plunge would produce. Although his massive commitment to redevelopment evolved gradually, one important milestone was his two-to-one victory in the 1955 election, just after announcement of his first redevelopment project; and the second was his parallel triumph two years later, following revelation of a second project. Subsequently, his urban renewal program was a case of reinforcing and diversifying (for example, in antipoverty efforts) in the area of his proven success.

At the outset redevelopment's delayed payoff was a serious political problem, for no project could bear fruit before Lee would have to run for reelection. He could not rely on such projects to make a record of performance in office, and thus he needed to do things that would yield quick returns during the gestation period of his major planning schemes and would ameliorate some of their disadvantages—increased expenditures and short-run inconvenience. Furthermore, he knew that his ability to sell particular redevelopment policies to his party would be in large measure a function of his popularity. Lee solved these problems very successfully, in general by communicating to the electorate his passion for efficiency and his willingness to bring a fresh approach to municipal government, and in particular by executing numerous intrinsically desirable minor projects which were presented as parts of the administration's comprehensive plans for civic betterment.

Lee took office with a bang. From the day of his inauguration a flow of press releases signaled the vigor and imagination he brought to the city's problems. He announced that, unlike Celentano, he would be a full-time mayor. For a time Lee seemed to be reorganizing everything. His reform of the city hall telephone system symbolizes his later effect in weightier fields. Before 1954 there were more than 100 separate listings for municipal departments in the telephone book. Lee installed a central switchboard with one number for all city agencies. He publicized numerous organizational changes designed to improve administrative efficiency and increase his control of governmental operations. Among other reforms an IBM data processing system would record all traffic violations and thus prevent ticket fixing—or so it was claimed. As it turned out, the new system had the even happier consequence of centralizing the ticket-fixing process.

A professional public administrator was hired to advise on reforming the city's fiscal policies. In the previous administration budget surpluses had been applied to the next year's operating expenses. Lee established a capital improvement fund with a $273,000 surplus from the 1953 budget and continued to use this method as a significant source of capital funds. One use of the new fund was to pay for many small items which previously had been financed by bonding. This practice had reached the depth of floating a bond issue to pay for painting some city buildings. It had long been the practice of municipal departments to obtain appropriations for salaries on the assumption that all staff positions would be filled throughout the year. This never happened, of course, and the resulting surpluses were then spent for other purposes during the last quarter. Lee put a stop to this and thereby saved several hundred thousand dollars, which he then used for the new positions required by his ambitious plans.

By these and many other actions Lee simultaneously improved administrative efficiency, reallocated funds for his programs, and warned the municipal bureaucracy that he would exercise much closer control than had Celentano. He implicitly and explicitly served notice on other political actors that he would be more vigilant, determined, energetic, and ambitious than his predecessor.

The new administration's biggest initial splash was in recreation. Lee seized on real needs, in an area dear to the hearts of all parents and sports fans, to build an impressive record with relatively small expenditures, financed largely from the new capital improvement fund. In 1954 every city athletic field was rehabilitated; in most cases this was the first attention in many years, except perfunctory maintenance. Four abandoned schools in poor neighborhoods were demolished and their sites used for badly needed playgrounds. By 1957, 21 new playgrounds and athletic fields had been built and 10 others rehabilitated. An extensive athletic center was constructed around the high school football stadium and numerous other facilities were added, mainly on land reclaimed from an adjoining swamp. A new clubhouse was built on the municipal golf course. Esoteric sportsmen were courted with a flycasting pool and a clubhouse for devotees of Scottish lawn bowling. A new animal shelter was built. On a Saturday afternoon television program featuring Lee with dogs and cats available for adoption, more than 1,700 animals were given away.

The construction sites of these and other city projects were graced with billboards reading "An Awakened New Haven Builds for its Future." Each new facility was opened with well-attended ceremonies at which Lee held out the image of a shining new city. Every new playground was described as part of this great development program, a product of a vigorous city administration supported by an aroused citizenry. These numerous small projects—cheap, appealing, and easy to build—were samples of the more ambitious undertakings to follow. The new playgrounds, the animal shelter, slum clearance, and a new downtown were all presented as parts of the effort to make New Haven a better city. Together with Lee's fiscal and organizational reforms, these low-cost, low-risk projects were a learning experience for the new administration. More important, they helped to create a climate of opinion that would be receptive when Lee turned to more ambitious, costly, risky enterprises. They also conveyed a sense of Lee's determination and helped convince dubious special publics like businessmen that he was forceful, able, and interested in "practical" issues like efficiency and economy.

In addition to making Lee's development program attractive and real, his recreational achievements gave him a reputation as a great friend of children. During his first years in office Lee visited an average of two schools a week, talking with every teacher and class. He estimated that by 1957 he had been in each classroom in the city at least twice. He became a great favorite with New Haven children; invariably they flocked around him whenever he stopped in a neighborhood.[12] Respondents to opinion surveys mentioned Lee's interest in children as one of his most important and appealing traits.

Lee also was determined to provide new symbolic gratifications for each of the city's ethnic groups. The crucial Italians, for instance, got a Columbus Day parade to parallel the annual St. Patrick's Day parade, together with a new coat of gilt and floodlights for the statue of Columbus. Lee professed to be baffled, however, by the problem of what to do for the not-very-numerous local Germans, rejecting a municipal beer garden as inappropriate.

During the initial years of his administration Lee also made progress on his urban renewal program, although without at first winning much popularity or making much substantive impact. In 1954 he created a Department of Traffic and Parking, hired a professional traffic engineer, and, most important, followed his advice in the matter of one-way streets and parking restrictions despite the anguished complaints of many merchants and motorists. Several municipal parking lots were opened, downtown and near Yale, to be operated by the Parking Authority. A more ambitious facility was begun: the country's first municipally-owned pigeonhole garage, located at the edge of the central shopping district. The City Plan Department and the Redevelopment Agency were greatly enlarged, and appropriations for them and for Maurice Rotival were multiplied until within a few years the city was spending $250,000 annually for these three activities.[13] Another long-term project was revision of the city charter to make the government more efficient and responsible. The mayor appointed a bipartisan commission of prominent citizens to recommend a draft charter which was eventually approved by the Board of Aldermen and put on the ballot for decision at the 1955 election. Lee's promise to create a Citizens Action Commission within 60 days of taking office had been a prominent feature of his successful campaign. But he had

---

[12] For further evidence of Lee's popularity with school children, see Fred I. Greenstein, *Children and Politics* (New Haven, Conn.: Yale University Press, 1965), pp. 62–63n. Almost every child in Greenstein's sample of New Haven students could identify the mayor, but only 40 percent of a sample of children in East Haven could identify the chief executive of that city.

[13] In 1959 the budget for these agencies, the Department of Traffic and Parking, and the Office of the Development Administrator totaled $371,065, compared to $50,723 in 1953, before the latter two agencies were founded. In 1958 New Haven spent much more for city planning than any other American city with a population less than 250,000. Source: Orin F. Nolting and David S. Arnold, eds., *The Municipal Year Book 1959* (Chicago: International City Managers Association, 1959), pp. 292–93.

great difficulty persuading men of sufficiently high caliber to serve on such a body and nine months passed before the CAC held its first meeting. (The CAC is described in detail in Chapter 8.)

Lee gave wide publicity to his administration's vastly intensified interest in planning and development, but at first there were few tangible results of all the activity and the city had grown far too familiar with grandiose claims. The first major achievement was the decision of the Connecticut Highway Department, announced in the fall of 1954, to build the Oak Street Connector, a throughway to carry and distribute traffic from the Connecticut Turnpike (Interstate Route 95) past the central business district. (The Connecticut Turnpike is a massive freeway across the length of Connecticut, from New York to Rhode Island. It runs just north of Long Island Sound and skirts the western shore of New Haven Harbor. The Turnpike was completed in the late 1950s.) This was a signal victory for Lee, for the state had intended to dump Turnpike traffic at the edge of the central business district, which would have made a monumental daily traffic jam and accelerated the city's commercial decline. The ten-lane Connector would occupy a strip more than 300 feet wide and a mile long. Its western end would adjoin the Oak Street Project Area and complete the job of clearing it. And, best of all, the State of Connecticut would pay for it.

Simultaneous with the news of the Connector, the city announced that work on the Oak Street Redevelopment Project was progressing; final plans and then federal approval would soon be forthcoming. By the summer of 1955 a tentative plan was made public: an enormous office building, modern apartments, and various auxiliary facilities would replace the tenements and loft factories of Oak Street. But this was still only a blueprint, the federal government had not yet approved the plans, and, all in all, few people thought that anything was likely to happen. Then, just two weeks before the 1955 election, Lee announced the great news: the Urban Renewal Administration had approved the final project report and would give New Haven a grant of $2,536,000 and a loan of $4,114,000 to carry out the plans. At last, it seemed, it was possible to do something about the city's slums.

A few weeks before approval of the Oak Street application there had been a more spectacular development. Lee revealed that the city's high schools woulld be sold to Yale for $3 million. This money and state grants would pay for two new schools to be built on unused city land, thus giving New Haven new high schools at virtually no cost.[14] The city's entire high school plant consisted of several dilapidated, overcrowded buildings on a six-acre lot squeezed between a cemetery and parts of the Yale campus. Inadequate in every respect, the high schools had been the object of sporadic, futile com-

---

[14] This claim was based on little more than the mayor's wishful estimate of the costs involved. In fact, the new schools cost the city somewhat in excess of $2 million.

plaints for decades. The Board of Education had tentative plans for one new school some time around 1960, but when Lee took office there were no firm intentions of doing anything. Selling the high schools suddenly became a live possibility when Lee and Griswold were together for another purpose. Lee cannot remember for sure who first advanced the idea, but thinks it was he. The sale met Yale's desperate need for building room and provided the money the city needed for new high schools. In spite of the obvious mutual benefits, such a transaction, although in the wind for 20 years, had never before been seriously attempted.

The Oak Street Project was a tortuous, unfamiliar proceeding, with many a possible slip between the grand plan and any tangible results. But the high school sale was a real estate transaction. Because it was easily understood, it had a greater impact on the public than the redevelopment announcement. Once the Board of Aldermen approved the deal—and any doubts on this score were quickly removed—the replacement of the old schools by new ones would be inevitable. This transaction became the prime issue of the 1955 mayoralty campaign and left a heritage of hostility and suspicion that seriously affected the eventual progress of the Oak Street Project and other future relations between Yale and the Lee administration.

Haunted by fears that New Haven voters would consider him unduly sympathetic to his old employer, their favorite bete noire, Lee tended to make inordinately high demands on the university so as to dispel any suspicions of favoritism. (See Chapter 9 for one example of his behavior.) In fact, however, Yale was extraordinarily indulgent to the city on the high schools—and on most other issues as well. The neutral appraisal of the high schools was considerably under $3 million. Lee told Griswold that the sale posed difficult political problems and suggested that a price of $3 million would "look better" than the proposed $2.7 million. Griswold felt that community goodwill was worth the extra money and agreed to Lee's price. Yale paid for the property years before it took delivery and so, while occupying the buildings rent-free, the city collected approximately $150,000 in interest on the money before it was spent for construction of the new schools. Delay caused by protracted bargaining with the Park Board over the land to be used as building sites for the new schools, and the year spent in preparing one site, prevented the city from meeting the deadline for turning the old buildings over to Yale. But the university gave the city a year of grace, saving Lee from a very embarrassing predicament. Finally, although the buildings had been sold complete with furnishings, Yale let the city carry off whatever it wanted. In spite of this record of extraordinary generosity, many New Haven residents were convinced that Yale swindled the city. Lee exploited this popular sentiment to extract concessions from the university, which seems to have been motivated by a desire to maintain good town–gown relations. It is difficult to escape the conclusion, however, that Lee found the Yale administrators to be easy marks.

Lee Establishes Himself

Celentano was expected to attempt to regain his office in 1955. He waited until September and then, much to his party's surprise, announced that he would not run. Frank Lynch and his associates began an urgent search for a candidate, only to find the most likely choices reluctant to challenge Lee. After half a dozen refusals they succeeded in bestowing the dubious honor on Philip Mancini, Jr., a 33-year-old lawyer.

The Republican candidate had an uphill fight from the start. With the election of Abraham Ribicoff as governor in 1954, New Haven Democrats had gained control of more patronage, thereby eliminating their opponents' major remaining source of organizational strength. The numerous achievements of his first 18 months in office had boosted Lee's popularity considerably; adding to this image were the series of dramatic announcements in the weeks before the election: the high school sale, federal approval of the Oak Street plan, and the pigeonhole garage opening just before election day. Lee's campaign was based on the progress he had made to date and his promise of greater things to come. His various pieces of sensational news helped compensate for a series of ulcer attacks that incapacitated him for months in the summer and fall of 1955, drastically curtailed his campaigning, and led to an operation in which much of his intestinal tract was removed.

The biggest campaign issue was the sale of the high schools, which Mancini called a flagrant betrayal of the city's interests in an attempt to exploit the resentment of the proletarian, ethnic electorate for a tax-exempt, upper-class, Yankee institution. This tactic found a receptive audience; four years later the sale of the high schools was by far the most frequently mentioned reason given by survey respondents for disliking Lee. Mancini probably lost votes in middle-class wards by his attacks on the university and suggestions that "Little Boy Blue" Lee was its stooge. Lee encouraged this reaction by a clever maneuver. Shortly before the election a friendly printer brought him a copy of a campaign leaflet which the Republicans had ordered. It showed Lee playing quarterback in a football game and looking up in the stands to a figure wearing a mortarboard with the question, "What do I do now?" The mayor promptly ordered several thousand copies for his own use and, while Mancini's workers were distributing the leaflet throughout the Italian parts of town, members of the Democratic organization were doing the same in the middle-class neighborhoods.

Lee crushed Mancini on election day, winning 65 percent of the vote and all but two wards. His share of the middle-class vote was greater than in the city as a whole and he won 71 percent of the vote in the elite eighteenth ward. Lee's winning percentage was the highest any mayoralty candidate had earned in more than a century and greater than any received in New Haven by any national or state candidate. A proposed new city charter failed of adoption because it was not approved by a sufficient proportion of the voters. The major factor in this outcome was the opposition of both party organizations.

The 1955 election was a watershed for Lee. The great electoral strength revealed by his two-to-one margin was a potent counterbalance to the organization's vote-getting power and thus strengthened his intraparty position enormously. This vote also showed Lee the potential political appeal of urban renewal, and, as much as anything else, led to his subsequent concentration on this issue, in which he used his increased power to initiate a truly impressive program and protect it from the organization's patronage and favoritism demands.

The pace of the redevelopment program quickened after the election. In the next few months the final formalities of approval for the Oak Street Project were completed and the city began to acquire property in the area. During the summer it signed a contract to sell five acres of Oak Street land to the telephone company for construction of a huge office building. The following spring the apartment house land was sold. Demolition in the project area began in February 1957; by the election that fall the area was almost wholly cleared and some construction work was under way. Meanwhile Lee was taking the first specific steps toward an extraordinary expansion of the city's urban renewal program. Within nine months after the 1955 election the city obtained three more survey and planning grants, a total of $398,590, for projects involving redevelopment or renewal of 624 acres. A few months later another project entered the planning stage. Throughout 1956 new ventures were undertaken. After lobbying the necessary authorization through the state legislature, the city and the CAC jointly turned 21 acres of swampy surplus park land into a commercial development for businesses displaced by the Oak Street Project. Construction started on a new nursing wing to replace part of Springside Home, a shamefully decrepit municipal facility for the aged; a federal grant covered 30 percent of the cost. Work began on a building to house the city's vehicles and equipment, replacing a structure dating from the era of horse-drawn wagons. The Dixwell Neighborhood Program was inaugurated to provide after-school activities in the crowded black section. Construction began on the new high schools, street paving continued at a rate several times greater than in the past, and new and rehabilitated recreational facilities continued to appear.

In June 1957 Lee revealed federal approval of the Church Street Project, a vast and daring scheme to demolish much of the central business district and build there a new hotel, office building, department stores, dozens of modern shops, and a huge parking garage. Linked to a freeway network through the Oak Street Connector, the new development would lure shoppers back from the suburbs and make New Haven a major commercial center again. The federal government would contribute a grant of $13,275,000 and a loan of $25,750,000. This was the second largest redevelopment project in the country, and the only one that proposed destruction of a major part of a city's downtown area. The immense dimensions and risks of this proposal brought Lee nationwide publicity. *Time* gave him extensive and favorable coverage; that fall he was the hero of an article in *Harper's Magazine* and next spring received similar treatment from *Life* and the *Saturday Evening Post*.[15]

The Church Street Project insured that redevelopment would be the dominant topic in the 1957 campaign, a bad sign for the opposition, which could not compete with Lee on this issue. The search for a mayoral candidate was not made easier by most Republican leaders' belief that Lee was invincible in 1957, nor by a suggestion from a well-known businessman that, since Lee was so popular and effective, the Republicans also should nominate him. Celentano was still the first choice of most Republican leaders, but he again declined. Finally the party settled on Mrs. Edith Valet Cook, a socially prominent widow with a long and distinguished record in civic affairs, currently serving in the state legislature. Party leaders felt that the novelty of a female candidate might attract a few votes.

A third candidate in the race was the "Independent Democrat" Samuel Malkan. A veteran Democratic politician and state legislator, Malkan had fallen out with his party, reportedly because his patronage hopes were disappointed when Lee first took office. Difficulties with his nominating petitions had kept him from running in 1955. In addition to Malkan, the Independent Democratic slate featured half a dozen aldermanic candidates. Malkan was not taken seriously and had very little money to spend.

The mayor had been so successful in selling the city on the virtues of redevelopment that it was unwise for any candidate to oppose his program and very difficult to ignore it. In the familiar fashion of a candidate whose opponent is identified with a popular program, Mrs. Cook could only endorse redevelopment, claim that "its roots began in a Republican administration,"[16] and promise to do it better by eliminating the haste, secrecy, and high-handedness characterizing Lee's handling of the issue. But she inevitably

---

15 *Time* (24 June 1957), 28–29; Jeanne R. Lowe, "Lee of New Haven and his Political Jackpot," *Harper's Magazine* (October 1957); *Life* (22 March 1958), 87–90; and Joe Alex Morris, "He is Saving a 'Dead' City," *The Saturday Evening Post* (19 April 1958).

16 Quoted in the *New Haven Evening Register*, 26 June 1957, p. 1.

found herself on the defensive, complaining that the mayor was "not telling the truth when he has claimed that I and the Republican Party are opposed to redevelopment and that we would stop all progress if we were elected."[17]

For the most part Lee ignored his opponent, leaving the job of attacking her to the cochairmen of the 1957 Citizens for Lee, two ladies who were not only neighbors of Mrs. Cook but virtually her sociological mirror images. He emphasized the examples of "four years of progress" that were evident in all parts of the city: the new schools, the playgrounds, and street paving. He also benefited from several adroitly timed events: the nursing wing of Springside Home was dedicated in late September and three weeks later he officiated at similar ceremonies for the Central Services Building for city equipment. Construction began on the telephone company's $15 million Oak Street office building. These and other developments were given prominent coverage by the *Register*, which also had several extensive picture spreads and feature stories on the "Changing Face of New Haven." The *Register* continued to be hostile to Lee, but it could hardly ignore major changes in New Haven, particularly when they were so gratifying to local patriotism. Thus the paper's vehement criticism of Lee was accompanied by lavish coverage of his works. The radio and television stations gave him continual friendly or neutral coverage. Lee had three television programs a week, hundreds of spot ads on television and radio, several brochures, numerous newspaper advertisements, lavish receptions, and personal appearances by various celebrities.[18]

The result was another landslide. Lee took 65 percent of the vote to 29 percent for Mrs. Cook and 6 percent for Malkan. As expected, Mrs. Cook bettered Mancini's showing in the middle- and upper-class neighborhoods, but she fared worse in the Italian wards, presumably because of her sex and social status, as well as her apparent lack of enthusiasm for her membership in the Catholic Church. As in 1955, those elements of the Republican organization controlled by DiCenzo and Celentano did not appear to make a vigorous effort in her behalf. The Republicans also lost one of their two seats on the Board of Aldermen.

In his first two terms Lee had prepared the foundation for his long-term political trademark—urban renewal—and buttressed his fledgling program with popular support attracted by a variety of easy and inexpensive accomplishments. In the summer and fall of 1957 his public image began to pass

17 Quoted in the *New Haven Journal-Courier,* 27 October 1957, p. 1.

18 In addition to his frankly electioneering television programs, financed by the Democratic party, Lee also appeared in several series in which, as mayor, he "reported" to his constituents or answered "their" questions, with the time donated by the local station. The chairman of the Republican Town Committee repeatedly asked for equal time, but the station consistently refused on the grounds that Lee's appearances were a public service.

from this first stage to a second one in which his career and prestige were more clearly staked on urban renewal, as the program began to display tangible results.[19] By the end of 1957 urban renewal dominated public perceptions both of Lee and of the political "agenda" in New Haven, that is, the principal problems confronting the community.[20] In September 1957 Lee's earlier accomplishments were still in the forefront of public consciousness: the most frequently mentioned admirable features of his regime were, in order, new playgrounds, slum clearance, schools (especially the new high schools), and street paving. Selling the high schools to Yale "too cheaply" was his most unpopular action; in fact, there was more criticism than praise for this transaction. Two years later it was still the most unpopular thing he had done, although it was mentioned spontaneously by only 5 percent of the sample. Up through 1957 schools and playgrounds were the most frequently mentioned of Lee's accomplishments, but by 1959, when asked to name things Lee had done which they liked, 46 percent mentioned redevelopment, compared to 27 percent who mentioned other subjects. (Only 3 percent offered redevelopment as something he had done which they disliked.) In 1959 the three most important problems facing New Haven were judged to be redevelopment (mentioned by 38 percent of the respondents), traffic and parking (27 percent), and housing (12 percent). I know of no comparable data from other cities and so cannot document the extent to which Lee was responsible for the salience of urban renewal in local political perspectives, but contrasting these findings with the frequency with which other issues were mentioned will help put the above data in context. The next three most frequently mentioned problems facing New Haven were unemployment (8 percent), crime and juvenile delinquency (8 percent), and—in a hostile sense —Negroes (6 percent). Four percent of the respondents said that racial discrimination was a problem.

Both the mayor and his principal program were very popular. When asked to describe Lee, 78 percent of our summer survey sample provided only favorable answers, 7 percent were unfavorable, and 10 percent were both. Lee was seen as aggressive, active, and effective. In an earlier Harris survey two respondents mentioned his achievements for every one who attributed their votes to his personality or personal qualities. Only a sixth of our sample

[19] In many cities the mayor takes pains to represent himself as independent of the urban renewal agency, a policy that minimizes the possible political backlash from urban renewal, but also reduces his ability to reap the benefits or use his power and prestige to help the program. This was the case in Chicago, where the city administration did not identify itself with the Hyde Park Project. See Peter H. Rossi and Robert A. Dentler, *The Politics of Urban Renewal* (New York: The Free Press, 1961), p. 251.

[20] Beginning in 1955 Lee hired Louis Harris and Associates to survey public opinion in New Haven every six months or so. Unless otherwise indicated, these Harris surveys are the source of the public opinion data presented in the text.

said that he had done nothing that they particularly liked, and three-fifths could think of nothing that they especially disliked. Fifty-nine percent thought that redevelopment was good for New Haven, a third could see both good and bad things about it, and just 6 percent thought it was bad for the city. Slum clearance was the common reason given for liking redevelopment; there was no widespread recognition of its impact on traffic, parking, the tax base, and retail trade. The latter considerations were the principal justifications for the program, but Lee made no real effort to explain this to the general public (although he did to such specialized audiences as the CAC), nor did the local press.

Lee's popularity and achievements, culminating in his 1957 victory, not only strengthened his hand in New Haven but seemed to bring him closer to higher office. A Senate seat would be up for election in 1958. The incumbent Republican, William Purtell, had been narrowly elected in the 1952 Eisenhower landslide and was not considered a formidable candidate. The year 1958 was widely (and correctly) considered a "Democratic year," not least in Connecticut, where the entire Democratic slate would benefit from the popular Governor Ribicoff at the head of the ticket. Mrs. Cook had given Lee some anxious moments by demanding that he declare his intentions: would he commit New Haven to enormous redevelopment undertakings and then skip off to Washington? Lee genuinely did not know the answer and managed to avoid being pinned down during the campaign.

Lee's landslide reelection increased speculation about his plans. It was generally assumed that he would be the strongest candidate for the Democratic nomination; unlike ex-Governor Chester Bowles and ex-Congressman Thomas Dodd, he was acceptable to all factions of the party. Most local Democratic organizations in Connecticut were similar to New Haven's in the incentives and perspectives of their members. Governor Ribicoff and state chairman John Bailey had considerable organizational strength through the resources available to the state government and alliances with local leaders.[21] But because both Dodd and Bowles had such deep roots in the party, Ribicoff and Bailey were reluctant to take too bold a position.

By 1957 Lee had built a strong coalition of local supporters around his massive urban renewal program and had committed the city to unprecedented measures, notably the drastic Church Street Project to demolish a good part of the central business district. A number of people in New Haven exerted strong pressure on him not to desert them. Roger L. Stevens, the man who was to build a new downtown New Haven, also insisted that Lee remain and see his commitments through. He may have indicated that if Lee left town, he would withdraw from the project, which would have been a serious

---

[21] For a description of the Connecticut Democratic party, see Lockard, *New England State Politics,* Chaps. 9, 10.

embarrassment to Lee's senatorial campaign. Lee was still keenly interested in the nomination and after his reelection campaign investigated senatorial life in Washington sufficiently to satisfy himself that he could be as happy in the Senate as in the governor's mansion, which had been his first higher goal. In January 1958 Louis Harris conducted a survey for Lee in various Connecticut cities to see how well he and the other likely Democratic candidates would run against Senator Purtell.

Lee thought that Dodd, who had run unsuccessfully for the other Senate seat in 1956, had committed himself to supporting Lee for the 1958 Senate race. The mayor also believed that Ribicoff and Bailey would give him their support for the senatorial nomination if he requested it, but he was unwilling to put himself in their debt by doing so. In February 1958 he announced that his commitment to the success of the New Haven redevelopment program precluded running for another office. Lee did not abandon hope for the Senate, however, and he seems to have modified his earlier reluctance to be obligated to Ribicoff and Bailey. The latter urged the mayor to run, but Lee refused to enter the race without a statement from Bailey and Ribicoff that his candidacy was essential to maintain party unity. The mayor's motives are obscure. Perhaps he shrank from a fight with Bowles and Dodd; perhaps he felt he needed a statement of his indispensability to calm his allies in New Haven; perhaps here, as in New Haven, he found it difficult to tolerate uncertainty. In any event, Lee coyly nudged the door open a bit in the spring of 1958, hoping for a draft that never came. As matters worked out, he never again had such a good chance to leave New Haven.

Lee's Political Style

My five months in Lee's office began early in 1958, his fifth year as mayor. By this time he had mastered the office and established the personal and political style that characterized his administration. While my observations of the personal qualities displayed in his official conduct are in no sense an explanation either of his success or of the directions his administration followed, they may help to put my account of these larger subjects in a more complete perspective.

In public Lee was a forceful, unpolished, and effective speaker, with a rough, heavy voice and few inhibitions about sentimental appeals ranging from the pathos of poverty to his experiences as an altar boy. He averaged four speeches a week and also had a weekly television program, with time donated by the local station, to answer "viewers'" questions about local government. In the classic urban political style he appeared at every social, fraternal, and civic function he could manage, as well as floods, fires, and other natural or human disasters. He read the obituary columns faithfully, wrote letters of condolence whenever he had the slightest connection with any of the principals, and attended two or three wakes a *day* on his way home from work. He made sure that his frequent drives through the city would not go unnoticed by using an enormous late-model Cadillac as his official limousine, and then carefully showed how he had a heart despite the cares of office by making a habit of giving children a ride home from school. Many survey respondents alluded to these episodes as proof of Lee's interest in children.

Perhaps because he found it hard to forget his own lack of a college education, Lee was very much concerned with doing things with style and taste. He is a neat and modish dresser. The mayor's office, which he found a clutter of autographed photographs and ceremonial shovels, was skillfully remodeled to match any executive suite. These and similar manifestations were by no means mere expressions of grandiosity or frustration, however, for they helped to further a public impression that the government of the City of New Haven was an august institution which should be entrusted to a man capable of meeting its grave responsibilities. The mayor's salary, which was $10,000 in 1953, was $18,000 by 1960.[22] Lee gave himself a $3,000 raise in the election year of 1957 and at the same time made handsome increases in the salaries of his top executives, whose relatively high rates of pay testified not only to the importance of municipal service but also to Lee's desire to attract competent men.

In private Lee was quick, abrupt, restless, and totally preoccupied with his job and his plans; he seemed to have no small talk. Driving around the city in his limousine, he frequently called his office by radio to be sure that nothing had happened that he should know about; and he had the same habit when on vacation. His outstanding characteristics as mayor were daring in his choice of goals combined with persuasiveness and a propensity for planning every detail. As one might expect of a man who had had two years to brood about an election lost by two votes, he liked to be certain that every contingency had been anticipated. But this characteristic seemed to have deeper roots, to grow out of an overwhelming need to be in control of everything, a dislike of loose ends, and a fear of being vulnerable through failure to anticipate and deal with all conceivable possibilities. Politicians typically like to know what is going on in their constituency, but Lee's curiosity was extraordinary, and continually fed by an extensive network of friends, acquaintances, and officials.

Lee was an excellent administrator, able to attract highly talented officials (see Chapter 9), delegate authority to them, and keep them working well

---

[22] In 1959 the average salary for mayors of cities with populations from 100,000 to 250,000 was $12,187. Source: *Municipal Year Book 1959*, p. 155.

together at a high pitch of activity. Nevertheless, he had a remarkably fussy concern for details, particularly visual ones. His restless roaming around the city produced a flood of memoranda like the following, the first addressed to a city official, the second to the Dean of the Art and Architecture School at Yale:[23]

Dear Tom:

The landscaping at Conte [school] stinks. I told you to put Merion Blue in the specs for the lawn. It looks like plain Rye to me. Take care of this.

Dear Gib:

My apologies for bothering you. Please look at the west wall of your building at York and Chapel [streets] across from Paul Rudolph's new monument. The drapes are dirty, untidy, and pulled awry—a completely magnificent structure with very poor housekeeping.

Lee's fear of the unexpected was manifested particularly in his dislike of encounters with the public or his political opponents in circumstances not wholly under his control. Despite his frequent public speeches, his rhetorical skill, and his ability to judge the mood and interests of audiences, Lee invariably was nervous before speaking in public, so much so that he customarily wore old suits for such occasions because he sweated so heavily that his jackets had to be sent to the cleaners afterward. He observed that any politician who consented to debate his opponent was foolish; he had done so himself once with Celentano and had vomited before the debate.

Lee's aversions to spontaneity and loose ends, both stemming perhaps from his fears of vulnerability, seem ill-suited to legislative as opposed to executive political roles. Legislators make general decisions and seldom can usefully pursue details. Spontaneous give-and-take is, of course, their principal means of communication with their peers, both in committee meetings and in floor debate. Thus some of the personality characteristics that helped make Lee such a superlative mayor might not have been conducive to a successful career in Congress.

In other respects Lee displayed the qualities that various writers have attributed to politicians. Writing about political leaders whom he had known, Rexford G. Tugwell observed that

politicians are, in fact, notoriously cold-blooded and unsentimental, though the reverse kind of impression is sought to be projected in all that affects their strictly political function. They almost never act in ways unrelated to the fur-

---

[23] Quoted in Allan R. Talbot, *The Mayor's Game* (New York: Praeger Publishers, Inc., 1970), p. 149.

therance of their careers, and this furnishes one point of reference of which
their biographers can be sure.[24]

Harold D. Lasswell has suggested one reason for this: "The power oriented
person is not given to quick and unpremeditated responses. His egocentricity
is too great so that he takes a detached and objective position toward the
bonds of sentiment."[25] Another possible explanation is the emotional drain
to which politicians are subjected. They are forever being asked for favors,
even by passersby, and must endure many interactions motivated by a desire
for contact with a celebrity, yet they are constrained to respond pleasantly to
all members of the public; they must soon grow tired and wary of all unanticipated casual encounters. Moreover, since politicians progress in part by
manipulating people in and through interpersonal situations, they are less
likely to enjoy affective relations with people, for to be so personally involved
with individuals one is using must be very punishing. Thus an important
qualification for political life is the ability to engage in numerous personal
relationships without involvement.[26]

No one should be shocked to read that "egocentricity" and "cold-blooded-
ness" are commonplace among politicians. Men whose careers are based on
appealing for popular approval must spend a lot of time calculating how
best to present themselves to the public, just as men whose careers are based
on selling newspapers must think about what the public wants to read and
how their paper appears to its readers. This self-absorption may not be an
attractive personal quality, but it seems inescapable in candidates for major
public office.

Elective officials who want to pursue a serious political career must of
necessity worry about how they will fare in the next election. (This is less
true for holders of safe legislative seats and for incumbents in part-time,
nonpartisan local government posts.)[27] This concern is probably greatest for
an ambitious man in Lee's position: his office is partisan and he could count
on determined Republican opposition every two years. New Haven was not
so big a city that its mayor automatically would be a prominent figure in
state and national politics. Lee could not become senator or governor simply
by being the mayor of New Haven. He was too scrupulous to be a dema-

24 Rexford G. Tugwell, *The Art of Politics* (Garden City, N.Y.: Doubleday &
Company, Inc., 1958), p. 106.

25 Harold D. Lasswell, "The Selective Effect of Personality on Political Participation,"
in *Studies in the Scope and Method of "The Authoritarian Personality,"* eds. Richard
Christie and Marie Jahoda (New York: The Free Press, 1954), p. 206.

26 Dahl has made a similar suggestion. See *Who Governs?,* p. 298. Lee, incidentally,
liked to refer to himself as an "expert in group dynamics."

27 See pp. 395–404 for a further discussion of careers for incumbents in various
political offices.

gogue; lacked the looks, money, and style to be a personality candidate; and was unlikely to become the protégé of a more powerful leader who could deliver a desirable nomination to him. Thus if he wanted to rise in the political world he would have to be a famous mayor who did many wonderful things. Politics being what it is, whatever else his accomplishments were, they would have to be popular, which meant (by the logic of politicians, if not of voting behavior specialists) that Lee's success as mayor would be judged by the size of his electoral majorities.

This subject was seldom far from Lee's thoughts. He really did not have to worry about being voted out of office, but if he won reelection by less than a landslide, his political prospects dimmed. A decline in his majority would have had other important undesirable consequences: (1) Because of the party column ballot, his vote was directly reflected in the vote for Democratic aldermanic candidates. The higher his margin, the fewer Republican aldermen and thus the smaller the chances of opposition on the Board of Aldermen. (The Democrats held all but one or two aldermanic seats during the period of our study.) (2) Lee's popularity was an important source of his strength vis-à-vis the Democratic organization. His big majorities made it clear that he could not be successfully challenged in a primary, that he helped carry lesser candidates to victory and ensured Democratic control of city hall, and thus that it would be mutually advantageous for Lee and the party regulars to get along together[28] (3) Because Lee's majorities were interpreted as testimonials to the popularity of his policies, they discouraged potential opponents from attacking those policies. At times even the victims of urban renewal were so overawed by popular approval for the mayor that they hesitated to attack him (see Chapter 10). Thus Lee's electoral success helped him achieve his policies and his policies generally helped him win votes.

The Nonpartisan Republicans

By 1957 Lee had plenty of campaign money. His popularity, Democratic unity, and the construction boom produced by his policies brought in increased contributions from the traditional sources of political funds. Beyond this, Lee received a good deal of financial help from his new business allies, more "nonpolitical" men whom he had brought to local politics through the Citizens Action Commission (see Chapter 8). In 1957 the Democrats officially

[28] Lee's intraparty position doubtless was enhanced by New Haven's vigorous party competition, which made it more important to have a popular mayoral candidate. In uncompetitive cities party leaders probably are more powerful with respect to elected officials, because there is less need for an appealing candidate in the general election, while primaries are more easily controlled by machines.

reported contributions in excess of $75,000, more than double the Republicans' receipts. Republican leaders were distressed at their diminishing financial support from the business community and tended to think of the CAC as little more than a front for city hall.

In addition to facing the supremely popular opposition candidate and the alienation of the business community's affections, the Republicans were still plagued by the schism that had begun with Celentano's nomination. The essentially issueless nature of ethnic politics, which had contributed so much to the maintenance of the party's strength in New Haven, was also a vulnerability during the Lee administration, for the mayor weakened the party by exacerbating the Celentano–Lynch split and subverting some Republican leaders with rewards their own party could not provide. When Celentano was mayor his enemies within the party had been sustained by patronage from other jurisdictions; an uneasy and partial alliance between the two factions was maintained by their common desire to enjoy the benefits of municipal office. Celentano's influence within his party declined once he left office. His most important source of power, his popularity with the voters, was relevant only if his name were on the ballot, and Celentano did not choose to run against Lee. He retained some organizational power, chiefly through DiCenzo's influence in one of the city's four state senatorial districts, but for the most part the party machinery was in the hands of the Lynch forces, which controlled county, probate, and federal patronage. These rewards were puny compared to the gargantuan bounty available in city and state government, but they gave the Lynch faction resources which Celentano and DiCenzo lacked. Celentano could have had the mayoralty nomination in the elections subsequent to his defeat, but otherwise Lynch and his associates were dominant within the party.

Republican disunity helped the Democrats, of course, but the Celentano-DiCenzo faction was in danger of withering away. Perceiving the danger of opposition unity, Lee consistently encouraged the split by helping Celentano in ways that partially compensated for his loss of patronage. Lee retained a number of his predecessor's political appointees on various boards and placed some city insurance orders through Celentano's supporters. He also refrained from criticizing his predecessor. These maneuvers were trifling compared to the new administration's very cordial relations with DiCenzo. Among other things, DiCenzo was the attorney for a group of displaced merchants who built College Plaza, a $750,000 retail and office development in the Oak Street Project. In this capacity he carried the burden of negotiation with the Redevelopment Agency, hardly a role for a man who was *persona non grata* at city hall. (In the summer of 1957 DiCenzo's daughter, a college student, worked for the City Plan Department, which did not consider her a security risk.) Lee chose DiCenzo to be chairman of his hand-picked Charter Revision Commission in 1958 (see Chapter 11). In 1959 the Connecticut judicial system was reorganized and forty circuit judges, twenty from each party, were appointed by Democratic Governor Ribicoff with the advice of local party organizations. DiCenzo was the only New Haven Republican appointed to one of these $15,000-a-year positions. He certainly was not recommended by the local Republican organization; his appointment probably was due chiefly to Lee's influence.[29]

For at least a few years after his defeat Celentano was thought to want to run again for his old office when Lee moved on. Therefore it was not in his interest for another Republican mayoralty candidate to make an impressive showing. Each year the Lynch forces picked the Republican nominee and each year DiCenzo, Celentano, and their followers were less than enthusiastic campaign supporters. Celentano declined to raise money for Mrs. Cook, who ended her campaign with a deficit in excess of $10,000. DiCenzo gave the Democrats advice that year, and he and Celentano reportedly discouraged many Italians from voting or told them to vote for Lee. Ten years later, with Lee still in city hall, Celentano's hopes of replacing him faded and the relations between the two men warmed. In the mid-1960s, Lee appointed Celentano chairman of the city's new Equal Opportunities Commission. Lee reached similar understandings with other Republicans, giving them jobs, appointing them to boards, or granting other favors.

Progress and Disappointments

In June 1958 the mayor announced federal approval of a third major urban renewal scheme, the Wooster Square Project. The eastern half of the 235-acre project area consisted of rundown factories mixed with tenements; it would be cleared and developed as an industrial park separated from the rest of the area by a state-built freeway running from the Connecticut Turnpike to Hartford and points north. The somewhat better neighborhood west of the freeway would be rehabilitated, with spot clearance of factories and hopelessly rundown houses. In this section the city would build a new fire department headquarters and a combined school and community center, and sell some cleared land for private commercial and residential development. The federal grant would be $10 million and the loan $14,152,000. Private investment was estimated at $9 million. Furthermore, the city would take advantage of a recently-passed state law to get a state grant for half of its one-third share of the net project cost.

The Wooster Square Project had been stalled in the planning stage for some time while the city tried to use it to solve a hidden crisis. Early in 1957 Lee learned from a friend that Sargent and Company, a local hardware

[29] (Bridgeport) *Sunday Herald*, 10 May 1959, p. NH-4.

manufacturing firm with 1,200 employees and a $5 million annual payroll, was planning to move out of town. Lee thought this would be a bad blow to his redevelopment program and persuaded the Sargent board of directors to wait while he tried to find a solution to their problems—chiefly an obsolete plant—that would keep the firm in New Haven. The apparent solution was quickly found in the Wooster Square Project, which abutted the Sargent plant. It was thought that the project boundary could be extended to include Sargent's, whose buildings would be bought and cleared; the firm would buy filled land next to the Connecticut Turnpike for a modern plant. The Wooster Square final project report, then almost completed, was drastically revised to make this change. Taking the Sargent buildings would require imposing a higher standard of structural quality on other factory buildings in the project area; to be consistent, if Sargent's was cleared, some other buildings that had not previously been scheduled for demolition would have to be demolished also. The amended final project report was submitted and for some months the city and the URA fought over the inclusion of Sargent's. In April 1958 this change was finally rejected.

Lee gave the bad news to the Sargent management, then told them of another possible solution pending before the state legislature: an industrial redevelopment bill that would authorize state grants to cities to cover half the cost of clearing obsolete industrial properties. Lee urged them to express their intense interest in the bill to state legislators with whom they had connections. They were most reluctant to do so, however, fearing too great involvement in "politics." Indeed, Lee usually had great difficulty persuading businessmen to lend public support, by lobbying or testifying before legislative committees, to measures that would benefit them directly.

The eventual passage of this bill cleared the way for the 348-acre Long Wharf Project, announced just six weeks after the disclosure of Wooster Square. Long Wharf was not really a redevelopment project; it was primarily aimed at reclamation of filled land on both sides of the Connecticut Turnpike along the western shore of the harbor. But the project's boundaries reached up to the head of the harbor to include the Sargent plant, which was bought for $2.8 million. Sargent then put up a one-story $4 million plant on a 30-acre site in the Long Wharf Project area. In addition to several other industrial sites and various recreational and cultural facilities, including a repertory theatre, the Long Wharf Project also included a new, merchant-owned food distribution center to replace the unsanitary and dilapidated old market scheduled to be torn down by the Church Street Project.

In 1959 Lee's administration was troubled by scandal. Property tax assessments on about 125 residences were reduced after the legal deadline for entering such changes, and among the beneficiaries were several relatives of Arthur T. Barbieri, the city's Director of Public Works and chairman of the Democratic Town Committee. The amounts of money involved were small, but since about 10,000 property owners had their assessments increased in 1959, there was a large and attentive audience for these pecadillos. After an investigation several members of the assessor's office were released and the politics-ridden agency was reorganized. At Lee's request Barbieri resigned as Director of Public Works, but stayed on as Town Chairman.

The mayor was also embarrassed by delays in the Church Street Project; although several blocks in the center of the city were cleared, no construction had begun and the land was being used as parking lots. The Republican mayoralty candidate in 1959 was James Valenti, a well-known junior high school principal. He cut Lee's share of the vote from 65 to 62 percent and contributed to electing six Republicans to the Board of Aldermen, all from wards with heavy concentrations of Italians.

In the first six years of his regime Lee had been able to avoid any increase in the tax rate, which remained at 35.5 mills while those of comparable Connecticut cities went up considerably. Because a rate increase affects all property owners equally and so would be a unifying focus of common resentment, Lee preferred to meet his budgetary requirements by reassessment.[30] Because it is selective and depends to a considerable degree on the discretion of the assessor, reassessment can be used to distribute the tax burden in the light of political friendships and enmities.[31] This discretionary feature, however, involved a considerable political risk in that it might serve the interests of influential individuals rather than the administration as a whole and so expose the mayor to accusations of corruption—as in 1959. By 1960 Lee had exhausted the political benefits of cheap programs in fields like recreation and could squeeze no more money out of fiscal and administrative reforms that exploited overlooked resources. His 1961 budget was 60 percent higher than the budget he had submitted when he first took office and he had to raise the tax rate by more than 10 percent. (By 1964 the rate was

[30] In this period Lee's budgets increased at a slightly *lower* rate than Celentano's had, but by 1966 the rate of growth had increased. For the most part the city's principal antispending organization, the business-supported New Haven Taxpayers' Research Council, maintained a wary silence on Lee's programs. The TRC's active and knowledgeable executive director was, to say the least, suspicious of Lee, but his hostility was balanced by the mayor's close relations with various business concerns that were well represented on the TRC's board of directors. (See Chapter 8 for a description of Lee's relations with the business community and Chapter 11 for further discussion of the TRC.) The newspapers historically were the leading watchdog of the local treasury, and Lee was often characterized in their editorial columns as an irresponsible spendthrift with questionable motives.

[31] The most pervasive bias in assessments was in favor of modestly priced residences, which were taxed at a considerably smaller percentage of their market value than the houses of the rich, multiple dwellings, or business property. The latter category was by far the most severely taxed of any kind of real property. For the data and a discussion of this bias, see Dahl, *Who Governs?*, pp. 79–81.

up to 44.75 mills, and by the end of Lee's administration it had jumped to 70.85 mills.) Early in the 1960s Lee also tried to remove some of the political sting from tax assessment by calling in an outside firm for a complete re-assessment of all property in the city.

Early in 1961 a second hammer blow fell on the mayor's popularity. Roger Stevens, the Church Street Project developer, virtually ran out of money and construction on the project came to a standstill. The cleared land at the center of the city had been a big parking lot for more than two years. That fall Lee came within 4,000 votes of defeat at the hands of Henry H. Townshend, Jr., a wealthy and attractive descendant of one of the city's old families; ten Republicans were elected to the Board of Aldermen.

This was the nadir of Lee's electoral fortunes, however. In 1962 there was tangible progress on the Church Street Project, which seemed finally to be on its way. The 1963 election showed that Lee was out of the woods; he beat Townshend by 11,000 votes. By this time the city's growing black population and the national heightening of racial tensions had made race relations a salient issue in New Haven. A sweeping plan to end de facto segregation in the city's schools was put into effect in 1964, over the heated protests of a citizens group.[32] The leader of this organization was the Republican mayoralty candidate in 1965. Lee defeated him by a two-to-one ratio and in the process captured every ward and every aldermanic seat. Lee did almost as well against another challenger two years later in his last reelection campaign.

The Lee Administration in Retrospect

As I said in the first chapter, this book is not an evaluation of Lee's policies. Some of his programs were begun, and most of his accomplishments realized, after the period I studied. But as a major premise of this book is that Lee achieved a great deal as mayor of New Haven, it is useful to describe briefly what he did do and what additional problems he encountered in the 1960s.

By the last years of his administration Lee had succeeded in reversing the commercial decline of downtown New Haven. The core elements of the Church Street Project were completed and doing a flourishing business: two new department stores, a 19-story hotel, a shopping mall, a 14-story office building, and a 1,300-car garage fed directly by the Oak Street Connector, which led to a regional freeway network that carried automobile traffic into the heart of the city. Under construction across the street were the inter-

---

[32] For an intimate account of these events, see William Lee Miller, *The Fifteenth Ward and the Great Society* (Boston: Houghton Mifflin Company, 1966). By 1970, 27 percent of the city's population was black.

national headquarters of the Knights of Columbus and a municipal coliseum and convention center. A short distance away the city's third new high school, named after Lee, had been completed. Half a dozen other urban renewal projects provided many new factory and wholesale buildings, several secondary retail centers, office buildings, housing for all income groups, and assorted municipal facilities. More than 2,000 acres in New Haven were under renewal. Although New Haven was the eighty-first largest city in the country in 1960, it consistently had the fifth or sixth largest urban renewal program during most of the 1960s. On a per capita basis, it has had by far the largest effort of any city. In 1966, for example, its program amounted to $790.25 per capita, compared to a mean of $53.51 for all cities.[33] By the end of 1969 New Haven had spent $50 million of local funds and $87 million from the federal treasury, and had obligated $44 million more in federal money. Over $150 million in private construction was completed or underway.

Urban renewal greatly strengthened the tax base, enhancing the city's ability to finance municipal programs. The new developments provided thousands of jobs close to low-income residential neighborhoods, thus avoiding the vast distances between employment and home that so often afflict ghetto dwellers.

Lee's interest in architecture and in doing things in a first-class way combined in his persistent pressure on officials, politicians, and private builders to hire noted architects. The results are striking and represent a serious effort by the administration to improve the visual quality of the urban environment. The new New Haven is not to everyone's taste. Some observers consider the city an architectural showcase; others judge it an "area of urban cataclysm."[34]

[33] The size of urban renewal programs is measured by federal capital grants for all projects in the execution phase or with a loan and grant contract approved but not formally executed. The figures for 1966, based on a similar measure, are from Robert R. Alford and Michael Aiken, "Community Structure and Mobilization: The Case of Urban Renewal" (unpublished paper, University of Wisconsin).

[34] The author of this verdict, the noted Yale art historian Vincent Scully, is perhaps the best-known unfriendly critic of the aesthetic aspects of New Haven redevelopment. In the restrained rhetoric that seems typical of his discipline, Scully called the Knights of Columbus headquarters a "jackbooted sentinel of corporate power." This building, Lee High School, and the coliseum were all designed by Kevin Roche, John Dinkeloo, and Associates, the firm founded by the late Eero Saarinen. To Scully these buildings "develop a quality at once cruelly inhuman and trivial...[and] share a kind of paramilitary dandyism." Saarinen's firm "continues to sense and to embody the most deeply seated, perhaps unconscious, aspirations of its political and corporate clients." See Vincent Scully, *American Architecture and Urbanism* (New York: Praeger Publishers, Inc., 1969), pp. 204, 249, 200.

Scully also condemned the city planning concepts executed in New Haven—the trouble with the Church Street Project is that "the suburb is brought into the city" (p. 247)—but did not explain why this is to be deplored.

By 1969 more than 6,300 housing units had been destroyed by urban renewal and freeways. The latter were built by the state but, under strong city pressure, in concert with redevelopment projects. About 7,000 households (families and single individuals), or a total of more than 25,000 people, were displaced to make way for the new construction or for rigorous enforcement of the housing code. This process began in the late 1950s and for some years the city had an exemplary relocation program but did little to provide more low-income housing. The consequences of this neglect were mitigated by several considerations. Sixteen percent of the displaced households moved out of town.[35] New Haven lost 12,400 residents from 1950 to 1960 and another 14,341 from 1960 to 1970. This trend, common in older cities, reduced the demand for housing and expanded the supply available to poor people.[36]

At the beginning of the 1960s the city began at last to do something about housing the poor. Lee paid more attention to the Housing Authority and named as its chairman Herbert Kaufman, a well-known Yale expert on municipal politics. The Lee administration had inherited 2,200 units of conventional public housing and was reluctant for both political and policy reasons to build more. Instead, it took advantage of several new federal aid programs in a diversified and imaginative approach. Because a major fraction of the poor are old, the administration concluded that public housing designed expressly for the elderly would serve a need and also be less alarming to fearful neighbors. A program of federally-subsidized projects for the elderly produced 584 new housing units by 1969, with 120 more units on the way. The city also developed a "Rent Certificate" program: it leased conventional private housing and then subleased it to poor families for 23 percent of their income, the same rate as public housing. In 1969 there were about 300 Rent Certificate families scattered around the city. In its "turnkey" program the Housing Authority encouraged private construction of housing which it then bought and leased to poor families at subsidized rates.

Federally-subsidized "221 (d)(3)" moderate-income cooperatives and

---

[35] Fifty-five percent of the displaced households were white. Six percent had been displaced twice and a handful of unlucky families had been moved three or more times. About 1,500 business firms were displaced, of which a fifth had gone out of business.

This discussion of the Lee administration's record in urban renewal and publicly-assisted housing is based largely on information obtained from the New Haven Redevelopment Agency in 1972. The data cover activities completed or actually underway at the end of 1969, when Lee left office, and thus exclude many completed projects that were in advanced planning during his regime. I am grateful to William T. Donohue, Executive Director of the New Haven Redevelopment Agency, for his help, and to David Jay Weber, who ably sought out the information I needed.

[36] Housing vacated by the middle classes historically has been the principal source of improved housing for the poor. One consequence of the exodus to the suburbs, then, was to expand the supply of core city housing available to the poor.

rental housing units were built in renewal projects by sponsors as diverse as labor unions, the Junior Chamber of Commerce, and the Jewish Community Council. The rents ranged up to $115 for a three-bedroom apartment; monthly carrying charges went to $125 for a four-bedroom apartment (both figures included utilities). The administration helped arrange a revolving loan fund to provide the $325 down payment for the coops, and the Housing Authority used federal funds to subsidize monthly payments for very poor families. By 1969, 729 of these units had been built, and an equal number were under construction. These projects were scattered through the city in small packets, while subsidized poor families were dispersed through the projects. The goal was to reduce the visibility of public housing and the accompanying stigma, and to avoid concentrations of very poor, potentially disruptive families. In addition to these programs, the city also was responsible for rehabilitating 8,337 private housing units, at a cost of over $15 million.

All in all, by 1969 the Lee administration was responsible for 2,600 new publicly-assisted housing units for people of modest incomes. In addition, almost 1,000 more luxurious private apartments were built or under construction. The net result of Lee's programs was an increase in the amount and quality of the city's housing supply. In 1950, with a population of 164,443, New Haven had 47,385 housing units, of which 11 percent were overcrowded and 14 percent lacked adequate plumbing. Twenty years later the city had 137,707 residents and 48,893 housing units, of which 7 percent were overcrowded and 3.5 percent lacked adequate plumbing.

As the city's urban renewal program progressed, its redevelopment officials learned a good deal about the conditions of urban poverty and some of them became convinced of a need for innovative policies far beyond what any government was attempting. In the middle and late 1950s the city tried unsuccessfully to interest the Ford Foundation in funding various sorts of programs to help the poor. At the beginning of the 1960s a redevelopment official named Howard Hallman led a group that wrote a detailed and ambitious proposal for a comprehensive attack on poverty. Lee had not given these efforts much attention or priority, but when the Ford Foundation showed signs of serious interest in the Hallman plan, the mayor began to participate actively in the negotiations.

In 1962 the foundation gave a three-year, $2.5 million grant to a specially created agency called Community Progress, Inc., to carry out the ideas in the Hallman proposal. Ostensibly an independent, quasi-private organization, in fact CPI worked closely with city hall. Its first director was Mitchell Sviridoff, the president of the Connecticut Labor Council, a member of the CAC and the New Haven Board of Education, and a friend and political ally of Lee's. (Sviridoff left New Haven in 1966 for a similar position in New York City and then became vice president for national affairs of the Ford Foundation.)

Sviridoff recruited the same kind of ambitious, energetic, imaginative, and intelligent people who had conducted New Haven urban renewal. CPI pioneered some of the major ideas later embodied in the federal antipoverty program, including Neighborhood Legal Offices, the Job Corps for training unemployed youths, and the Head Start program to provide prekindergarten schooling for ghetto children. Schools in seven neighborhoods were opened for training programs and community use from 12 to 16 hours a day all year. In four Neighborhood Employment Centers the unemployed were counseled, tested, and referred to on-the-job training programs conducted by CPI in cooperation with local employers. After the passage of the Economic Opportunity Act of 1965, CPI became New Haven's agency for the national poverty program and also began tapping the federal treasury. From 1962 to 1966 CPI spent $16.3 million; in 1967 alone it had an income of $6,131,000 and a staff of more than 300. In 1965 CPI spent approximately $7,700 for every local family with an income under $4,000. Of the 35 education and employment programs recommended by the Kerner Commission to reduce the causes of urban unrest, 26 were already in operation in New Haven.[37] In the war on poverty New Haven was "a national showcase to which people make pilgrimages to see how it is done."[38]

By the end of the 1950s the city already had attained the same position in urban renewal and Lee and his enormously talented first development administrator, Edward J. Logue, exerted considerable influence on the national scene. In 1957, when the Eisenhower administration proposed drastic cuts in urban renewal appropriations, Logue organized a delegation of mayors who, with Lee as their spokesman, met with the president and persuaded him to restore the funds. New Haven officials also had close relationships with legislative committee members and staffs in Hartford and Washington, and helped write urban renewal legislation in both places. At various conclaves Lee touted the civic and political virtues of redevelopment. He became chairman of the urban renewal committee of the American Municipal Association, with Logue as committee secretary. New Haven officials gained positions of leadership in the National Association of Housing and Redevelopment Officials and other such organizations. In 1959 Lee was made chairman of the newly-formed Advisory Committee on Suburban and Urban Problems of the Democratic Advisory Council, again with Logue as secretary. The following year he organized a conference on urban problems as part of

---

[37] This description of CPI is taken from Russell D. Murphy, *Political Entrepreneurs and Urban Poverty* (Lexington, Mass.: D. C. Heath and Company, 1971). The data for 1967 are from Fred Powledge, *Model City* (New York: Simon & Schuster, Inc., 1970), p. 84.

[38] *New York Times,* 14 June 1966.

John Kennedy's presidential campaign. In 1963 Lee was president of the United States Conference of Mayors.

Lee's fame continued to spread in the 1960s. His renewal program transformed New Haven's geography and showed the way to other cities. (According to the New Haven Redevelopment Agency, 242 magazine articles and eight books had been written about the city's urban renewal by the late 1960s.)[39] Robert C. Weaver, the first Secretary of Housing and Urban Development, said, "I think New Haven is coming closest to our dream of a slumless city." An official from New York City, after touring New Haven, concluded, "It is like a dream. Everything is done with so much style."[40]

The men in New Haven who were responsible for the city's preeminence in renewal and antipoverty programs were very proud of their accomplishments, but they were also more reserved than outsiders. Logue, who had gone on to a similar position in Boston, said that "New Haven is only relatively the best city." Lee said, "For everything we've done, there are five things we haven't done, or five things we've failed at. If New Haven is a model city, then God help urban America."[41] Lee was right about his administration's accomplishments: they were impressive in absolute terms and monumental in comparison with other American cities, but there were still many areas of governmental activity to which his attention had been scanty or belated. This is inevitable. All politicians have priorities. If nothing else, their time and energy do not permit all-out attacks on all problems simultaneously. Even those areas that do have first priority may present such intractable problems as to defy complete or speedy solutions. After sixteen years of Lee's regime New Haven still had slums where babies were bitten by rats and contracted lead poisoning; the schools were more impressive physically than academically; the police were not notably competent or unbiased.

Of all the unsolved problems, the ones with the greatest political weight were the related issues of race relations and "community participation." Lee had been an active liberal on racial issues long before the rise of the civil rights movement in the early 1960s. He began various programs aimed specifically at black neighborhoods and took a strong line against prejudice in redevelopment housing. In 1958, when the two new high schools were completed, some distance from each other, Lee decided that the boundary line for their attendance districts should run two blocks from one of the schools to equalize the proportion of Negroes attending each school. This

[39] Powledge, *Model City*, p. 25.

[40] Both quotes are from the *New York Times*, 7 September 1965.

[41] These quotes are in *Time* (1 September 1967), 9. Lee often said this, both privately and publicly.

decision was not publicized and when it became known, the reason for it was not disclosed.[42] CPI's beneficiaries were, of course, disproportionately black, and it had substantial numbers of black officials. In addition to his liberal policies, Lee used his patronage to build organizational support in black neighborhoods. Black machine politicians were his allies in factional struggles with the regular Democratic organization.

As his behavior on the high school boundaries illustrates, Lee preferred not to display his racial policies too openly,[43] because he felt that the white majority in New Haven was anti-Negro. When the Board of Education (comprised of his appointees and policy allies) adopted a busing plan in 1964, Lee steadfastly refused to comment throughout the ensuing bitter controversy, leaving the Board of Education to deal with its critics alone— and successfully. Two years later Lee explained his position in a not unpersuasive rationalization:

> A man in public life can't possibly take on every issue as a major personal issue. He has to pick his battles and choose his struggles and select his wars. You have to postpone a lot of your battles until your army is ready. And you'll find sometimes that when your army is ready, the battles don't need to be fought.[44]

Lee had always been secretive about policy development in all fields until he was ready to disclose fully worked out plans. (See Chapter 10 for a discussion of this "submarine" policy and the drawbacks of open planning in urban renewal.) This method was antithetical to the notion that public policy should be formulated in cooperation with the affected citizens, and it was increasingly at odds with the growing black assertiveness of the mid-1960s. As black spokesmen emerged in New Haven, they were given responsible jobs by the city or CPI, which included them in the policy formation process but silenced them as critics of the administration. Thus the black community suffered a continuing drain of leadership and a drastic weakening of its moderate organizational strength.

Lee's secretive and rather paternalistic style had been defended years earlier by one of his lieutenants in a terse statement of Edmund Burke's philosophy: "Two years is a hell of a short time and if people don't like it,

---

[42] The local NAACP chapter, then headed by a black Republican politician, bitterly denounced the decision on the grounds that it had not been consulted.

[43] One spectacular exception to this policy occurred in 1960, when Lee advised a black audience to stage sit-ins during the evening rush hour in order to impede affluent commuters driving home to the suburbs and force them to see conditions in the ghettoes. This speech, which Lee quickly regretted, was a brief front-page sensation in many newspapers.

[44] Quoted in Bernard Asbell, "Dick Lee Discovers How Much Is Not Enough," *New York Times Magazine* (3 September 1967), 41. Lee was in poor health during this controversy and was hospitalized three times in 1964.

they can throw us out." But electoral politics was not a promising remedy for black militants in New Haven. They could not overcome the mayor's popularity and the Democratic organization to defeat Lee in the primary. In 1965, when the Republican mayoralty candidate ran a backlash campaign, it made no sense at all to field a black independent candidate to draw votes away from Lee. Fred Harris, the most prominent black militant leader, tried his hand at electoral politics as an independent candidate for the state legislature and won less than 5 percent of the vote.[45]

In these circumstances militants found few promising avenues of political action. For years various groups of discontented citizens had asked unsuccessfully for an equal voice in planning and executing policy in renewal, antipoverty, and school programs. By 1967 there was considerable tension on this issue between the administration and an assortment of largely radical community groups. Late that spring the group headed by Fred Harris demanded money from CPI for its independent summer program, and Harris readily told reporters that "this is not a nonviolent organization."[46] After the windows in some of CPI's neighborhood offices were broken, Lee gave Harris a grant of $32,000.

By this time, if not before, Lee had come to believe that New Haven could erupt in racial rioting any summer. In 1967 he refused to be out of town overnight during the riot season. One night that August a white lunchroom proprietor shot a Puerto Rican who allegedly had threatened him with a knife, setting off a riot that went on for three nights. The rioters, mostly black teenagers, threw rocks at windows and passing cars, set fires, and looted. No one was seriously hurt, no policeman fired a shot. (Lee ordered them not to use their guns), and property damage was under $1 million.

The riot has been a political Rorschach test for critics of the Lee administration. To Vincent Scully, who dislikes the aesthetics of New Haven redevelopment, the riot expressed popular distaste for the use of space in the city's plans for one deteriorating black neighborhood.[47] To Fred Powledge, who is pessimistic about liberal democracy, the riot signaled the failure not only of Lee's policies, but of "every other city in the nation," or even of "America."[48] The youths who burned and looted during those three August nights can hardly have been aware of the symbolic burdens they carried.

In the long run a less portentous interpretation may seem more valid; the riot may have been what one disinterested observer called it: "a teenage

[45] Powledge, *Model City,* pp. 153–54. Powledge, an apologist for confrontation politics who takes a dim view of elections as legitimizing devices for politicians, conceded that "there is no record that the black or otherwise oppressed voters of New Haven mounted any kind of a sustained effort to impress Lee with their voting power" (p. 326).

[46] Asbell, "Dick Lee Discovers How Much Is Not Enough," p. 41.

[47] Scully, *American Architecture and Urbanism,* p. 251.

[48] Powledge, *Model City,* pp. 93, 313–16.

tantrum."[49] To pronounce a "failure" any policy that is followed by violence or evidence of discontent betrays a naïve view of the causes of violence or a dangerously authoritarian view of democratic politics. Violence is more likely in times of social change and improvement,[50] and disagreement is least evident in tyrannies.

Despite his fame and accomplishments, Lee's career did not progress beyond New Haven's city hall. No further opportunities for higher elective office became available after he passed up his chance for the Senate in 1958. When Governor Ribicoff joined President Kennedy's Cabinet in 1961 he was succeeded by his lieutenant governor, John Dempsey, who occupied the governor's mansion until 1971. The other Senate seat was open in 1962, but Ribicoff's claim for the nomination could not be denied. Any thoughts Lee might have had of "putting in a primary" against Senator Dodd in 1964 were frustrated when his ally, President Kennedy, was replaced in the White House by Dodd's friend Lyndon Johnson.

Lee was considered for various important positions in the executive branch in the early 1960s, including—if only briefly—director of the Office of Economic Opportunity. But his prospects were badly hurt by a widespread belief in Washington that he had terminal cancer. For a time Lee himself believed that he was dying.[51] Even when these fears were dispelled, however, he remained in New Haven. A year or two later, Lee declined to be considered for an assistant secretaryship in the new Department of Housing and Urban Development.[52]

In June 1969 Lee announced that he would not be a candidate for mayor that fall. He had run for the office ten times before and had been mayor for 16 years. In the last years of his administration Lee was often in poor health and seemed dissipirited at times. He was increasingly at odds with the regular Democratic organization, by then largely under the control of Arthur Barbieri, the Town Chairman. Barbieri picked Lee's successor as Democratic candidate, and mayor, a veteran alderman named Bartholomew F. Guida. Lee was not invited to Guida's inauguration.

Lee had hopes of winning the senatorial or gubernatorial nomination in 1970, but they did not materialize and he was not a serious contender by the time of the Democratic convention. Instead, he was given a fellowship by Yale, thus gaining not only an income but an office, secretarial help, and other perquisites. He has continued to receive fellowships from Yale and also teaches undergraduate courses based on his experiences.

49 Asbell, "Dick Lee Discovers How Much Is Not Enough," p. 42.

50 Hugh Davis Graham and Ted Robert Gurr, eds. *The History of Violence in America: A Report to the National Commission on the Causes and Prevention of Violence* (New York: Bantam Books, Inc., 1969), Chaps. 17–19.

51 Talbot, *The Mayor's Game,* p. 194n.

52 Miller, *The Fifteenth Ward and the Great Society,* p. 275n.

7 policy coordination

Division of formal and informal power is an abiding feature of every level of American government, and methods of overcoming this fragmentation preoccupy both politicians and political scientists. Regardless of their formal structural arrangements, almost all city governments have multiple centers of power. Municipal legislatures independent of the chief executive are the most common and important example of divided governmental authority, but even within the executive branch mayors typically share authority with a variety of appointed boards and commissions. The weakness of decisive central authority impedes innovation except in times of crisis or massive consensus; new policies must be approved by a series of units in the decision-making structure, while a single veto is enough to maintain the status quo. Implementation of programs that require coordination among various public agencies is also difficult, as each agency is likely to have its own bases of power in the electorate and thus its own administrative autonomy.

Although New Haven, by virtue of its elected mayor, has a chief executive with his own political franchise, the charter makes him a "weak mayor," required to share authority with a variety of separate or quasi-separate appointed boards and commissions as well as with the Board of Aldermen. More than 90 percent of all municipal employees are formally responsible to their respective governing boards, not to the mayor. As a practical matter, however, the city government was seldom as decentralized as this suggests. The mayor appointed most board members, the budget was one form of central control, and party leaders' interest in patronage also restrained board decisions. Nevertheless, the charter and the political culture together produced a system with many possible degrees of fragmentation from one mayor to the next. Before Lee's election it seems that the city usually *did* have a weak mayor; many municipal agencies operated without much central control except over patronage, contracts, and budgetary limits. It was expected that an agency would make its political contributions chiefly by patronage, not through public response to its policies. The mayor's appointive powers seldom were used to enforce policy coordination, perhaps because of a feeling that attempts to do so were politically unnecessary and would offend party leaders and the clienteles of the various agencies. Thus there was a good deal of delegated or uncontested independence within city hall, with unavoidable points of difference settled by bargaining.[1]

Lee disliked this state of affairs for several reasons. He could not carry out impressive policies in any area without exceeding the control that his predecessors had exercised over the city government. As urban renewal became the focus of his energies, the need for centralization of power increased. It grew yet again when the requirements for a really adequate renewal program became clear. Because Lee was concerned that scandals in his administration might abort his higher ambitions, he took pains to protect himself from this danger.

Finally, and perhaps equally important, Lee's personality needs reinforced his perception of his political requirements. A meticulous and impatient man, he wanted to know about and control what was going on; disorder and inefficiency were intrinsically abhorrent to him. Restless, inquisitive, and compulsive, he roamed the city in his big black Cadillac, noting offensive conditions and demanding fast remedial action.

In the years after his election Lee imposed a considerable degree of hierarchical control on many formally independent organs of local government, making them instruments in the development and execution of his policies. This was done without structural change in the city charter, by making use of resources available to the mayoralty. As we will see later, the mayor's attempts to formalize his de facto centralization by amending the charter were opposed by the Democratic organization and ended in total defeat. In this chapter I will describe in detail Lee's acquisition of control over two government agencies not formally subordinate to him, the Board of Aldermen and the Board of Zoning Appeals, and then touch briefly on his dealings with several other boards. These cases illustrate the prerequisities and costs of different methods of policy coordination. They also demonstrate the deficiencies of the well-known argument that political machines commonly have the "function" of coordinating policy in formally decentralized municipalities, a point discussed at some length at the end of the chapter.

The Eclipse of the Board of Aldermen

The Board of Aldermen is the legislature of the City of New Haven. According to the city charter it "shall, with the approval of the mayor or over his veto, as hereinbefore provided, exercise all of the powers conferred upon said city, except as otherwise provided."[2] In Celentano's day the board performed

---

[1] For a fuller description of this period, see, in addition to pp. 161–66 above, Robert A. Dahl, *Who Governs?* (New Haven, Conn.: Yale University Press, 1961), Chap. 16.

[2] *Charter of the City of New Haven, Connecticut,* September 1952, sec. 38.

these functions with considerably more independence than it displayed after 1953. Then it was a genuinely independent agency, susceptible to the mayor's influence but by no means subservient to him. The mayor had to bargain with the aldermen for what he wanted; other political forces acted on the board and sometimes were stronger than the mayor. In fairness to Celentano, it should not be forgotten than he never enjoyed the lopsided aldermanic majorities that were a fixed feature of Lee's regime, and that he was plagued throughout his administration by the split with Lynch. On the other hand, it appears that he was seldom, if ever, vigorous in using available sanctions to discipline Republican aldermen.

This state of affairs could not continue if Lee were to realize his goals of major innovation. He had no need for the board's active participation in developing and administering his programs. Its members had no vital technical skill to contribute to policy formulation, nor was it necessary to build a political base. But the board did have to approve the budget and pass various ordinances, and federal urban renewal provisions required local legislative assent at innumerable points in any project. The New Haven aldermen came to perform this function with great regularity, dutifully ratifying redevelopment measures as they were brought before the board.[3] When the board considered the key land disposition agreement in the Church Street Project, "not a word was raised pro or con" as it approved sale of the city's commercial heart to an out-of-town developer for $4,307,246.[4]

For many years the aldermen treated Lee's legislative requests on redevelopment as too sacred to touch, although their personal opinions on the issue often differed from this official reverence. On May 17, 1962, several years after our research ended, the Board of Aldermen for the first time in seven years "failed to give its automatic approval to a redevelopment proposal."[5] The issue was a minor one, concerning disposal of a small parcel of land in the Church Street Project. The circumstances are instructive, however. The 1961 election, marking the low point of Lee's electoral popularity, gave the Republicans 10 of the 33 aldermanic seats. The land disposition agreement was clouded by confusion about the city's title to the land. Ten aldermen, seven of them Democrats, did not attend the meeting. The seven Republicans present, joined by a perennial Democratic dissident, Salvatore Ferraiuolo, picked up three more votes, and, aided by one abstention, stalled the agreement on a tie vote. This decision was reversed at the next board meeting and

---

[3] The board did refuse to create the post of Development Administrator for Logue in 1954, but Lee accomplished the same result by executive order (see Chapter 9). An apparent aldermanic veto, described in Chapter 10, was inspired by the mayor.

[4] *New Haven Evening Register*, 8 July 1958, p. 1.

[5] *Ibid.*, 18 May 1962, p. 1. Although the issue was trivial, the board's recalcitrance was so newsworthy that the action was prominently reported on the front page of the *Register*.

for the next several years New Haven's aldermen resumed their habitual deference to the administration's renewal program.

While redevelopment seemed to occupy a particularly high niche in aldermanic perceptions of administration programs, Lee did not fail to get what he wanted from the board in other areas. Budgets commonly provide a prime opportunity for legislatures to frustrate executive desires. Each fall the Board of Aldermen approved the city's budget for the coming year, first hearing testimony at an open hearing and then considering the document in closed meetings. Under Lee's management the latter deliberation was so perfunctory that the board's resolution approving the budget often was written before the meeting at which the decision was formally made. One alderman remarked to us about this procedure that "in my short time [on the board] no one has even *thought* of not accepting the budget." Another alderman described the board's budget-making role:

> The aldermanic hearing on the budget is a formality. . . . We aldermen sit as a troop in the front of the public hearing room. . . and listen to a long and varied string of testifiers, and then we enact the budget as it was presented to us.[6]

With this degree of legislative submergence, New Haven had something of a de facto parliamentary form of government. The mechanics of executive–legislative relations were simple. The Board of Aldermen ordinarily met at night on the first Monday of every month. On Monday morning the mayor invited the Democratic aldermen to his office. Usually the meeting was attended by the president of the Board, the majority leader, and two or three others. Barbieri and one or two high city officials were also customarily present. Lee discussed each item on the evening's agenda in which he was interested, stated his position, and explained it or asked one of his aides to do so. This was not a planning session but an occasion for the mayor to tell the aldermen what he wanted. Only rarely did he devote time to persuasion. Free discussion was likely only when the administration did not have a position on an agenda item.

That night, some time before the scheduled time for the formal meeting, the Democratic members caucused, heard the mayor's wishes, and discussed any measures on which he had withheld his views. The actual meeting of the board then began, usually before a very sparse crowd. As one alderman admitted, "our public sessions are mumbly and unimpressive."[7] There was seldom any debate, as all decisions were made in caucus or, usually, in the mayor's office. Speeches were made "for the record" and for the newspapers, which gave them scant play.

---

6 William Lee Miller, *The Fifteenth Ward and the Great Society* (Boston: Houghton Mifflin Company, 1966), p. 31.

7 *Ibid.*, p. 48.

Explanation of the board's subordination to Lee begins with the character of the aldermen themselves. For the most part, they were not very formidable persons. It was not much of an honor for an ambitious man to be one of 33 municipal legislators. Aldermen were not paid and typically devoted only a small amount of time to their duties. A good part of this time was spent in dealing with constituent problems: a city job, installation of a traffic light, a tax abatement, administrative complications with a municipal department. The alderman called the right office, or obtained the right forms and helped to fill them out. For the most part these duties attracted either people of small talents and limited ambition, those to whom politics is an avocation, or ambitious young men beginning their political careers.

Most aldermen were attorneys (but not in the city's major law firms), white-collar workers, minor executives, city employees, or small businessmen. The motivations of many New Haven aldermen are captured in this remark by "Shrebnick," a city councilman in the very similar northeastern city studied by Rufus Browning: "I felt there was no better way [than going into politics] to meet more people and benefit others, and to get more business for myself." Shrebnick's gratifications from political activity are also pertinent to New Haven aldermen (and to New Haven politics):

> I'll be frank with you, I enjoy some sense of power, of being able to do favors for people, of the pride of my family when I am able to do things for people. Even parking tags (but only for family or very close friends), or I can fix a summons for anyone. I get pleasure out of the recognition. A couple of weeks ago, my sister-in-law was here, and we walked up Main from Broad to First, and she was amazed, I stopped and said hello to maybe 50 people in that short stretch, people I feel I can say I know well. I know so many people.[8]

Largely because of the slight significance of any single alderman, the impediments to ticket splitting presented by Connecticut voting machines, and the city's strong political organizations, only a very unusual aldermanic candidate could make an electoral appeal in his own right. Candidates' votes are almost wholly dependent on the showing of the citywide ticket, that is, on the popularity of the respective mayoralty candidates. Of the 66 aldermanic contests in 1955 and 1957 there were only 7 instances where a candidate's vote was more than four percentage points different from the vote received in his ward by his party's mayoralty candidate; in every case the aldermanic candidate trailed.[9] The absence of independent political appeal was both a cause and an effect of the board's humble public image. While

---

[8] Rufus P. Browning, "Businessmen in Politics: Motivation and Circumstance in the Rise to Power" (unpublished doctoral dissertation, Yale University, 1960), pp. 121, 123.

[9] I am indebted to Bruce R. Russett for these data and for much of the information on benefits received by aldermen from the city.

almost every respondent in our summer survey knew who the mayor was, only 24 percent could name their alderman, two-thirds could not, and 10 percent gave the wrong name.

The average alderman's political and personal position helps explain the immediate reason for the board's responsiveness to Lee's aggressive drive for power, for men of greater stature would have been less amenable to his influence, less cowed by his sanctions, and less gratified by his indulgences. But the fact is that most aldermen were dependent for their livelihood, wholly or in part, on the good wishes of the mayor. In 1958 eleven aldermen were full-time employees of the city or the court system, and three others had close relatives so employed. Five more aldermen did business with the city or worked for concerns which did; at least two of these considered the city their best customer.[10] Thus nineteen aldermen were vulnerable to the mayor's ability to influence their central economic interests or those of close relatives. Four more aldermen received appreciable sums of money as compensation for part-time service on municipal boards or as party registrars; another had a relative receiving such benefits, which in most cases amounted to about $500 a year. Five additional members were appointed to the board by Lee to fill vacancies. Thus twenty-nine of the thirty-three aldermen were under considerable obligation to the mayor for past or present favors.

Any aldermen who were attorneys could profit in a number of ways from political favoritism. They could, for instance, be given legal work by the Judge of Probate, a friend and ally of Lee's. They and other aldermen who sold goods and services might also enjoy business from friends and associates of the mayor, city contractors, or merely people who wanted to demonstrate their solidarity with the Democratic party. While people in the latter categories would usually be attuned to local political mores and seldom need prompting, a hint from city hall could help maintain party discipline. Those aldermen or their relatives who were engaged in businesses affected by police powers, such as parking regulations and health inspections, were vulnerable to pressure from city hall. Lee could control or at least veto nominations for a number of higher political offices. One alderman was nominated for a safe Democratic state senate seat in 1958. Another, the majority leader, was appointed to a $15,000-a-year judgeship on the recommendation of the local Democratic organization.

In concert with the Democratic organization, Lee could deny renomination in many wards; he did this with irreconcilably dissident aldermen. For many years B. Fred Damiani's twelfth ward was an exception. In 1959, when Damiani opposed Lee in the Democratic primary, the Democratic organization narrowly failed in an all-out effort to eliminate Ferraiuolo, the twelfth

---

10 One of these was an officer of a firm that was paid $4,000 to $5,000 annually for printing the aldermanic journal, despite a charter provision prohibiting such transactions. This arrangement was terminated in 1960.

ward alderman, in the primary. A few years later Lee, Barbieri, and Golden succeeded in disposing of Ferraiuolo and, apparently, most of Damiani's remaining political influence. There are reports that the organization made unsuccessful attempts to deny renomination to another Democratic alderman who was intermittently hostile to Lee's programs. This maverick was, however, vulnerable to city hall pressure on other fronts.

During our study the most conspicuous purge victim was Nathan Portnoy, a veteran Democratic alderman. In the course of a libel trial (in which the defendant, who had made a number of spectacular charges against various personages in the Democratic organization, was represented by Damiani) the public learned that Portnoy, employed by the Public Works Department as an "inspector of excavations," also held down a full-time job as a pants presser at the Johnny-on-the-Spot Drive-In Cleaners in nearby Hamden. Portnoy had been in and out of various city jobs in preceding years and his pressing career doubtless was known at city hall. Lee fired him after the public revelation. It is probable that Portnoy would have quietly been given another city job after the next municipal election, but he felt that he had been treated unfairly and began to oppose administration measures on the Board of Aldermen. His ward committee nominated another candidate for his seat in the impending election. Portnoy contested this choice in a primary, which he lost by a wide margin.

Another, less dramatic episode concerned a maverick Democratic alderman who made trouble for administration proposals. Shortly after one display of independence, small retail establishments run by two of his relatives were virtually encircled by "No Parking" signs, thus making deliveries and customer access far more difficult. The alderman asked Lee for help with this problem, not knowing that Lee was responsible. The mayor removed the signs, gaining not only the alderman's political support but also his gratitude.

As is usually the case when a leader has such drastic sanctions available and makes clear his determination to use them, it was seldom necessary to do so, or even to threaten to. It was generally assumed that the organization would reward its friends and punish its enemies. Often the promise existed only as a vague expectation that at some indeterminate future time one would be better off by virtue of the organization's favor and worse off for its displeasure. Only occasionally, then, was it necessary to remind dissidents what power the mayor could command, or even, as in Portnoy's case, to demonstrate it.

Organization leaders also exploited individual personality weaknesses in exerting pressure on the Board of Aldermen. In 1958 an alderman with no business vulnerabilities or higher political aspirations was opposed to an important administration proposal. He was a rather timid man heavily dependent on the approval of his friends. Party leaders urged many of his friends to appeal to him to change his vote on grounds of friendship, party loyalty, and gratitude. He was reminded that Lee originally had appointed him to the board, and that his campaign manager had paid most of the last campaign printing bill, purportedly out of his own pocket. The alderman capitulated.

There are other reasons why an alderman might respond to direction from the mayor's office. Charles Blitzer, a member of the Yale Department of Political Science in the 1950s and early 1960s, was an alderman for several terms. Blitzer enjoyed his membership on the board and thus had reason to be grateful to Lee for his original nomination and for subsequent support against hostile party leaders in his ward. Blitzer was able, by virtue of his good relations with Lee, to gain adoption of several measures that were important to him and otherwise would have been overlooked. On one such occasion, he joined with another alderman to get a fourfold increase in the appropriation for purchase of books for school libraries. Another time, he secured Lee's vigorous intervention to bring about needed improvements in the Legal Aid office. These examples illustrate a more general point: if an alderman wanted to pass any bills of his own he had to cooperate with the administration, otherwise Lee could block action through his influence over the majority of the board. This power further reduced the possibility that an alderman might build an independent political appeal, since he could not deliver the goods to his constituents without the approval of the administration.

A single alderman, or a small group, had little power against the majority. Even delay and obstruction were costly. The board's rules prescribed that before a measure was approved it must lie over until the next meeting. This delay could be avoided by unanimous consent. A maverick could refuse to give his consent, but this could be countered by calling a special meeting a day later, rather than waiting a month for the next regular meeting. A few such incidents would gain the dissident little but the dislike of his colleagues. This is not to say that aldermen were afraid to refuse unanimous consent, for they did so with administration measures; but the device did not give mavericks much effective nuisance value. While unanimous consent was usually reserved for minor or noncontroversial items, it sometimes was used for measures of the greatest importance. In August 1958 the Wooster Square Project was approved under unanimous consent, without debate, although the lone Republican alderman's ward was in the project area.

The tremendous Democratic majorities on the Board of Aldermen (31 to 2 in 1956–57 and 32 to 1 in 1958–59) during our study reduced the influence of dissidents, since even a dozen defections would not have shifted effective control. This suggests that large legislative majorities may not have the potential for disunity suggested by some political scientists. According to their line of argument, when the majority party has many more seats than its opposition, it tends to become undisciplined because there is no spur of danger.[11] With a small margin, on the other hand, every vote is crucial and the majority must stick together. The New Haven case suggests an opposite relationship between party balance and majority party unity: when legislative parties are evenly matched, one or a few potential defectors have a good deal of bargaining power, because it takes only a few vote changes to affect the outcome. But when one party has a huge majority, a legislator has less to gain by switching, as his vote will not be decisive. The administration's temporary setback in 1962 illustrates this point, for it came when just four Democrats defected. In earlier years, four votes lost would have made no difference.

Lee ordinarily was direct in telling the aldermen what to do and did not shrink from bluntly reminding obdurate aldermen that they were on the payroll or otherwise vulnerable to his displeasure. Needless to say, this behavior was far from ingratiating. But aldermanic resentment was mitigated by several considerations. Lee was a winner and when he carried a ward, so did the Democratic aldermanic candidate. Lee's popularity insured that the spoils available from city hall would go to Democrats. As long as unity prevailed in the Democratic organization, the best route to a share in these rewards was party regularity. While Lee exercised strict control over many aldermanic policy decisions, he did not deny aldermen their patronage. Since this was more important to most aldermen than substantive questions of public policy, their subordination to the mayor did not deprive them of their prime incentives to political activity. This was not the case with the Board of Zoning Appeals, which presented a different kind of policy coordination problem. The contrast between the two cases illustrates some important generalizations about policy coordination.

The Board of Zoning Appeals

Like most communities, New Haven has an ordinance that divides the city into a number of zones and specifies standards for each of these zones with respect to the size and type of buildings and the uses to which they may be put. Requests for variances, that is, for exceptions to these rules, are made to a Board of Zoning Appeals whose five members are appointed by the mayor to one-year terms. As scores of such requests are made annually, the granting or refusal of variances soon comes to have an important impact on the city. The board's decisions may stifle healthy economic growth or permit the development of blighting influences, such as garages in residential blocks or factories in shopping districts, that depress the quality of residential and

11 This "law of economy" is discussed at length by E. E. Schattschneider, *Party Government* (New York: Holt, Rinehart and Winston, Inc., 1942), pp. 85–96. For further criticism of this "law," see pp. 353–55.

commercial districts. The latter extreme has been approached almost every-where in the United States, for zoning ordinances customarily are adminis-tered with great tolerance for exceptions.[12]

Until the late 1950s this was the situation in New Haven, but then the mayor and his urban renewal officials changed the familiar pattern. At first they tried to impose strong hierarchical control on the Board of Zoning Appeals, as they had done with the aldermen. When this proved unsatis-factory, Lee made a complete change in the composition and procedures of the board to bring it into conformity with the city's overall urban renewal program. This is a particularly well-defined example of increased policy coordination—what Dahl calls the shift from spheres of influence to an executive-centered coalition.[13] It also illustrates the clash of values between machine and program-oriented politicians as well as the impact that new programs can have on interagency relations.

The New Haven Board of Zoning Appeals would have been ill-equipped for its important role even in a political culture where machine politics was less prevalent. It had no staff of any kind to furnish information on the many complicated questions presented to it, nor did the City Plan Department give its opinions to the board. This lack of expert information was compounded by the absence of clear standards in the original zoning ordinance enacted in 1926. (As we will see, appointment to the board of persons familiar with construction and real estate was hardly a solution to the problem.)

These drawbacks would not have been insuperable to a board dedicated to the preservation of neighborhood standards. The basic trouble with the BZA was its members and the political style they represented. In the scheme of things in New Haven politics the board was a source of patronage and the other rewards that come from inside political connections. As Dahl delicately put it, "Some of the members were thought to rest their decisions on considerations other than the regulations themselves."[14] The nature of such considerations is suggested by the occupations of the board's five members during the first years of Lee's administration: official of a car-penters' union, attorney often representing real estate interests, treasurer of a cement and construction company, president of a lumber brokerage firm, and proprietor of a plumbing, heating, and air conditioning supply house. At least one member had been a concealed party at interest in a case before the board. Most BZA members were active in organization politics and were generally thought to be receptive to intercession by party leaders and other persons with political influence.

[12] See Edward J. Logue, "Urban Ruin—or Urban Renewal?" *New York Times Magazine* (9 November 1958); and Quintin Johnstone, "The Federal Urban Renewal Program," *The University of Chicago Law Review,* 25 (Winter 1958), 340.

[13] Dahl, *Who Governs?,* Chaps. 16, 17.

[14] "Revolution in New Haven," paper delivered at the Yale Alumni Seminar, New Haven, June 1959, p. 12.

The BZA often granted variances that were at cross purposes with the urban renewal program and that city planners considered harmful to the public interest. For the first years of Lee's regime this was not important to him and may not even have been clearly realized. By themselves, members of the City Plan Department had relatively little influence with the mayor, while the BZA was a useful source of rewards to party activists.

In 1955 Logue took charge of all aspects of the city's urban renewal program. For the first time there was central scrutiny of local public actions affecting New Haven's physical environment by a powerful official in whom the mayor had great confidence. As redevelopment got well underway Logue became increasingly aware of the importance of zoning and came to realize that changes in the BZA's policies were needed. If not, other neighborhoods would decline as fast as the old slums were cleared and rebuilt. Logue persuaded the mayor of the importance of zoning variances. Lee's enormous majorities in 1955 and 1957, attributed in large measure to redevelopment, had convinced him of the issue's political appeal. This popularity and Lee's skill in exploiting the powers of his office had enabled him to expand and consolidate his power in his party. Thus he had both the assurance and the means to challenge a source of organization spoils. He authorized Logue to bring the City Plan Department's opinions on each case to the attention of the BZA and passed the word to the board to heed Logue's orders.

The BZA soon came to resent this dictation. Logue's often peremptory manner in demanding compliance was made all the more awkward by the actual procedure at a BZA hearing. Often a request for a variance would be presented, favorable testimony would be given, and then, in the absence of any citizen opposition, the City Plan Department counsel and zoning officer, Clyde O. Fisher, would read a technically-phrased letter from Logue recommending denial. The members of the board felt humiliated by this naked assertion of their subordination to Logue. Not unnaturally, the people requesting variances also objected to the new policy. Reports of their dissatisfaction reached the newspapers in the first part of 1958. In March of that year attorneys in several pending cases issued a statement objecting to "interference" in BZA proceedings by Logue and the City Plan Department. (It should be noted that there was no specific legal basis for Logue's intervention, a fact which Lee used as an excuse when pressed to oppose requests to which the planners had no objection.)

A "Memorandum of Policy" was issued to reply to this criticism, establish the City Plan Department's role, and salve the feelings of board members. This document ostensibly was a product of the BZA itself, but its tone and origin may be judged by this paragraph:

> This Board is proud to be a part of this magnificent effort for making our City a better place in which to live and work, and the Board wishes by this

memorandum to outline the policy it will pursue in meeting its responsibility under the Workable Program.

The policy, in brief, was to "accord great weight" to the views of the City Plan Department. In return for this commitment, Lee agreed that Fisher would read his letters in the board's executive session rather than in public and that Logue's influence would be exercised more discreetly to spare the feelings of BZA members by minimizing public evidence of their loss of independence.

Lee applied to the members of the BZA the same combination of deprivations and rewards which was so effective with the Board of Aldermen. (As we will see, these proved inadequate, largely because to follow Lee's orders was to sacrifice most advantages of membership on the board. But until this situation became clear to the board members, they were, no matter how sulky and reluctant, responsive to Lee's direction.) In the first place, the mayor appointed the BZA. One of the most active and forceful members, who frequently served as acting chairman, did a good deal of business with the city and city contractors. He also aspired to public office and in 1958 was elected to the state legislature. The other most active member was the secretary of the board. An attorney and an alderman, he also was thought to have political ambitions which the mayor could block.

Coercion and procedural palliatives did not solve the board members' basic grievance: they had become nothing more than a rubber stamp for Logue. This was not only humiliating, it also deprived them of the opportunities for personal and political advantage that had been such an attractive aspect of BZA membership in earlier times. And, of course, it meant that it was no longer such an honor to be on the board.

The rebellious BZA found support in the Democratic organization. There were several intertwined reasons for machine opposition to the substitution of "doctrinaire planning preachments"[15] for the older criteria of inside connections. The new policy removed a source of privilege and therefore reduced the stock of rewards available as incentives to political participation. John Golden in particular was a channel of requests for variances. If these favors could no longer be done, he would lose one way of accruing the obligations ("piling up good will") that were such an important source of his political strength. Logue's influence encroached on organization prerogatives; old customs were being flouted by "out-of-town experts," the traditional bugaboo of machine politicians. Thus party leaders with no personal ulterior motives feared that the organization would be weakened and a dangerous precedent

---

[15] The phrase is from the *New Haven Sunday Register,* 8 February 1959, p. 14. The *Register* was critical of Lee's attempts to control the BZA and did not explain the issues involved.

set. In addition, those politicians who could contemplate past or future profits because of their access to the BZA had more compelling regrets.

At this stage of his administration Lee and the party leaders had worked out a satisfactory modus vivendi which in effect recognized two spheres of influence, a policy sphere and a patronage sphere. The policy sphere included those issue areas where Lee wanted to make his mark; urban renewal in all its ramifications accounted for most of it. Here Lee would make decisions about personnel, contracts, and the implementation of policy in accordance with the needs of the program. The organization's interests in patronage and favors would be heeded only if they did not impede performance. In this sphere Lee was supreme and Golden and Barbieri played relatively minor parts. In the patronage sphere, on the other hand, the three men consulted as equals. Here the prime explicit criterion was maintaining a strong Democratic organization. Each of the three also tried to use patronage—both from the city and from other sources—to maintain his organizational position vis-à-vis the other two. There was occasional skirmishing along the borders of the spheres but no all-out warfare. Even when the interests of the three leaders were directly opposed, as in the charter revision campaign in 1958, they took pains to keep their disagreement at the lowest possible level, so as to avoid prejudicing their long-run alliance.[16]

The problem posed by the BZA was that Lee wanted to move it from the machine's orbit to his policy sphere. Legally he could appoint anyone he chose to the BZA. As a practical matter, because he did not want to provoke the organization unnecessarily, he could not ignore the maintenance needs and vested interests of its other leaders. If he could demonstrate that the party would not suffer by the BZA's departure from the patronage sphere, he would remove the major rationalization for the pursuit of private gain in the granting of variances. He could not do this by claiming that his policy as such would pay off at the polls, for it was clear that the issue in general terms was not very gripping; few votes would be attracted by a policy of denying requests for "nonconforming uses." On the other hand, there might be a short-run, personal appeal in opposition to a particular variance by neighbors who feared that it would reduce the pleasure or profit of their property. In order to strengthen his hand in relation to the party, in the spring of 1958 Lee often encouraged or instigated neighborhood opposition to requests for variances, usually by instructing the pertinent alderman to

[16] In the latter years of the Lee administration Barbieri supplanted Golden as the preeminent Democratic machine politician in New Haven and an open split developed between him and Lee. Barbieri was allied to Senator Dodd, the local congressman, Robert Giaimo, and Edward L. Marcus, a veteran New Haven politician who was majority leader of the state senate. Golden and Lee were politically friendly with Senator Ribicoff and John M. Bailey, the Connecticut party leader who was Democratic National Chairman during the Kennedy and Johnson administrations.

agitate against the proposal. The aroused neighbors were thus a potential source of political trouble who should not be antagonized.[17] In addition to balancing the demands of the politically connected, neighborhood opposition was also a convenient excuse for Lee. When asked to help obtain a variance, he would reply that his hands were tied as long as the neighbors and alderman were so adamant, as their opposition made it politically impossible for him to intervene on the opposite side. In one such case he blandly suggested that his caller try to persuade his neighbors to change their minds.

From the beginning of Logue's intervention in the fall of 1957, the BZA had not denied requests to which the City Plan Department was opposed but had tabled them. By the spring of 1958 more than a dozen such cases were pending and the issue had approached a key point of decision. That June, Lee, Fisher, Barbieri, and one member of the BZA met to resolve the situation. The BZA member complained heatedly that the board's independence was threatened by city hall. Lee responded that he was doing his best to fight slums and could not afford any "Sherman Adams cases" in his administration. After detailed technical and political discussion of each of the cases, the quartet then toured the city in Lee's limousine, inspecting each of the properties in question. Most of the requests for variances were denied.

When the board resumed operations that fall its members' resentment of Logue increased. Their hostility passed the threshold of tolerance in the case of a request to convert to office use a house in a fashionable neighborhood where many other large residences already had been converted. The City Plan Department opposed the request and a number of adjoining residents filed a petition taking the same position. One of the interesting marginal features of the case was the prominence of many of the petitioners, who included the dean of Yale College (Logue's father-in-law), a former president of Yale, the ranking partner in one of the city's two most eminent law firms, a number of descendants of original settlers, and William Howard Taft III.

BZA members felt that a variance would only be consistent with the "natural" change in the area. They were finding their service on the board unrewarding and were not considered good candidates for reappointment in January. Following an acrimonious session with Logue, the board, somewhat in the spirit of a defiant farewell gesture, granted the variance. The secretary of the board resigned almost immediately, followed during January by the other four members, who chose this method of departure rather than accept Lee's refusal to reappoint them, by then a foregone conclusion. Subsequently

[17] The administration encouraged the formation of neighborhood associations as vehicles for advocating planning standards. One such group was the Roman-Edgehill Taxpayers' Association, composed of more than 150 property owners in the city's most elegant neighborhood. Logue, who lived in the area, played an important role in building the group and shaping its activities, which were directed toward protecting the area's residences from conversion to more profitable and destructive nonresidental uses.

some of the petitioning neighbors tried unsuccessfully to challenge the vari
ance in the courts.

Lee had tried to control the BZA by threatening to discipline its members
if they did not comply with his wishes. This approach, so successful with
the aldermen, did not work with the BZA, perhaps because acceding to the
mayor's instructions would prevent attainment of the rewards that had made
appointment to the BZA so attractive. The possibility of not being reap-
pointed was not much of a threat in these circumstances: if the price was
following the City Plan Department's recommendations, staying on the board
had little appeal to the incumbents.

After the mass resignation Lee changed tactics. He removed the BZA
from the patronage sphere by appointing to it people with no organization
connections. The new members were motivated by their policy goals, not
by hopes of spoils or party influence. They were in basic agreement with
Lee's program and thus likely to be receptive to the city planners' advice. As
the *Register* put it, each of the new appointees was "a recognized leader in
the fields of manufacturing, business, education and public service."[18] None
was in real estate, construction, or building materials. Their occupations: a
vice president at Winchester, headmaster of a private school, manager of the
local office of the Connecticut State Employment Service, an executive of a
major trucking firm, and president of an automobile dealership. Almost
certainly Lee or Logue had sounded out each new member beforehand.

The new board soon announced its intention to refer all petitions to
relevant municipal departments and to rely on city agencies for guidance.
Petitions were to include much more information. The City Plan Department
drafted a comprehensive new zoning ordinance including more stringent
criteria. While the new members were not so amenable or vulnerable to the
persuasive methods Lee had used on their predecessors, apparently he could
exert influence over them. In one early case the City Plan Department approved a petition to permit construction of a grocery store in a declining
residential section. The neighbors protested vigorously, Lee apparently
changed his mind, and the BZA did not grant a variance. It seems likely that
the BZA gave in to an appeal from the mayor not to jeopardize its long-range
goals by overlooking political considerations.

Our active data gathering came to an end in 1959 and so I do not know
what happened subsequently to the BZA, whether it became an essentially
independent body, an appendage of the administration, or reverted to its
old role as a source of spoils for the organization. Its reform in the winter
of 1958 was dictated by the substantive needs of the program to which
Lee had committed his administration and was brought about through
Logue's insistence. The reform unquestionably hurt Lee in the short run by

[18] *New Haven Evening Register,* 6 February 1959, p. 1.

incurring the hostility of some party stalwarts, including Golden, who was very distressed by Lee's action. The reform of the BZA was part of the political price Lee had to pay to get along with his redevelopment experts and maintain consistency in the program on which he had staked his career and hopes of fame and political advancement.

Other Boards

The Board of Finance is generally supposed to be the most important appointed body in the New Haven government. It consists of the mayor, one alderman, six members appointed by the mayor, and the controller, also a mayoral appointee. The board meets weekly. Except for the mayor and controller, its members were paid $25 per meeting at the time of our study. It prepares city budget estimates for final approval by the Board of Aldermen (which can cut but not increase items), recommends a tax rate for aldermanic ratification (the aldermen can raise but not lower the proposed tax rate), allocates each municipal agency's share of the budget, approves transfers of funds within departments, passes on the creation of major new official positions, and in other ways supervises the city's financial affairs.

Most of the members of the Board of Finance were businessmen,[19] and the board had a pronounced conservative cast. It often cut the Department of Education's budget requests and turned a distinctly cold eye on many social welfare measures. At least once, when Lee was not present, it stalled an administration request in the ordinarily sacrosanct field of redevelopment. In some local circles the board was regarded as the conservative watchdog of the treasury. Lee encouraged this reputation by retaining most of Celentano's appointees.

The Board of Finance had a remarkably cheering effect on those readers of *Who Governs?* who were dedicated to the proposition that all American cities are dominated by tiny groups of businessmen. The board's composition and penurious orientation led them to the happy discovery that here was the *real* source of power in New Haven, the ultimate hidden hand that manipulated Lee, Logue, and other superficially influential persons.[20] That Lee retained board members from the previous administration was, of course, conclusive evidence for this interpretation: mayors come and go, but behind the circus of partisan politics the power elite remains.

As a matter of fact, Lee never failed to win board approval for items that

---

[19] In 1950–55, 58 percent of the appointed members of the Board of Finance were business executives and 24 percent more were small independent businessmen.

[20] See, for example, Floyd Hunter, review of *Who Governs?*, *Administrative Science Quarterly,* 6 (March 1962), 519.

were central to his political plans and were known to reflect his wishes as opposed to the aspirations of particular municipal agencies. Requests from the Board of Education for a school psychologist might be reduced or denied. This did not happen to plans for financing the new high schools, creating new positions in the enormous urban renewal establishment, or funding redevelopment measures. The board's major exercises of independent influence were in politicially marginal areas where Lee was indifferent and did not express his preferences.

The board's reputation was useful to the mayor in dealing with supporters whose proposals he considered politically ill-advised or substantively peripheral. One important Lee ally, who often was frustrated by the board's stinginess toward the schools, felt that it had a balancing function:

> Maybe he needs this kind of counterplay. I mean, the kind of people he's put on the Board of Education are the kind of people that are stamped with the stamp of free spender, which they're not, but they're the kind of people that say "We need more money on it."...The kind of people he put on welfare, too, who if you get a quick association in people's minds, it's the stereotype of the free spender. So, he needs a counterpressure. You can't be surrounded, I suppose.

In addition to being a center of conservative influence within the administration and an excuse to liberal allies, the Board of Finance had a reputation for parsimony that was a guarantee of sober deliberation on government spending.[21] In Lee's opinion the role it played in passing his fiscal policies was a source of reassurance to people who worried about "spending." One group that was not impressed was the chief antispending lobby in New Haven, the business-supported Taxpayers Research Council, which called the Board of Finance useless and recommended its abolition.

Lee got what he wanted from the board not only because he was extraordinarily persuasive but because, once again, he controlled and was willing to use sanctions and rewards to which board members were vulnerable. In 1957–58 several of them were associated with business firms that dealt with the city, and another had reason to be very grateful to Lee for decisions that were beneficial to his business interests. Two of the six appointed members

---

[21] Toleration—if not cultivation—of opposing viewpoints for the sake of tactical flexibility and a broader base of support is a familiar practice of chief executives. For example, during the early days of the New Deal President Roosevelt kept the conservative Lewis Douglas as his Director of the Budget for such reasons. See Arthur M. Schlesinger, Jr., *The Coming of the New Deal* (Boston: Houghton Mifflin Company, 1959), pp. 289–90. Roosevelt frequently used this tactic; see Richard F. Fenno, Jr., "The Presidential Coalition: The Case of Jesse Jones," in *Readings in American Political Behavior,* 2nd ed., ed. Raymond E. Wolfinger (Englewood Cliffs, N.J.: Prentice-Hall, Inc., 1970), pp. 125–37.

were men in modest circumstances for whom the $25 stipend was an important source of extra income. I attended one brief meeting at which the board dealt with two or three routine matters and adjourned. Several members arrived just then and the mayor, who presided, obligingly reopened the meeting so the latecomers could be reported present and thus qualify to collect their $25 stipends.

Lee extended his control over a number of boards and commissions, making these formally independent bodies elements in an essentially hierarchical decision-making system.[22] Many boards retained their customary autonomy, generally because their jurisdictions were outside Lee's priority issue areas. Most of these remained in the patronage sphere. Some boards, such as those concerned with welfare or the library, had little patronage value and were usually manned by public-spirited citizens with no particular political aspirations. Lee needed to control two sorts of boards: (1) those whose formal purviews included most issue areas and whose assent was necessary for almost any major innovation, such as the Board of Aldermen; and (2) those boards whose limited jurisdictions were within his high-priority issue areas, such as the Board of Zoning Appeals. Thus he achieved both *intrapolicy* and *interpolicy* coordination.

The inherent demands of office did not bring Lee to these extensions of mayoral power. His reach for control over the government was a result of his long-run political strategy. Having decided to make his political mark as mayor of great achievements, Lee found that he had to make some sacrifices—for instance, in the goodwill of the Democratic organization—to bring about the accomplishments on which his hopes for political success were based. The immediate bases of this greater coordination were patronage and Lee's power of appointment. These resources were available to his predecessor, who for the most part did not seem motivated to use the mayoralty as vigorously as Lee did. In addition, Lee's series of impressive electoral victories fortified his intraparty position and made it more difficult for disgruntled Democrats who might have contemplated challenging him.

Methods of Policy Coordination

The foregoing cases illustrate two methods of coordination: (1) exercising sanctions over members of formally autonomous bodies; and (2) appointing to such groups people who share the administration's policy goals. The first method was used successfully on the Board of Aldermen and unsuccessfully

---

[22] One exception to this centralized control was the Board of Park Commissioners, which inflicted a serious defeat on Lee by refusing to part with the park land the Board of Education wanted for the two new high schools that were built after sale of the old schools to Yale. See Dahl, *Who Governs?*, pp. 207–8.

on the Board of Zoning Appeals, whereupon the second method was employed, with at least initially satisfactory results. These events suggest several general propositions about policy coordination.

Lee controlled the Board of Aldermen because he had a good deal of influence on the economic fortunes of most of its members. These sanctions were *extraneous* to the substance of the various measures on which the board did his bidding. Most aldermen did not care deeply about these policies. To put it another way, acceding to Lee's wishes did not so completely subvert the attractiveness of service on the Board of Aldermen that its members chose to resist because going along with him would have meant foregoing those rewards that had led them to become aldermen in the first place. The opposite was true for the old BZA. Given the kinds of people appointed to the BZA, the principal attraction of membership would be vitiated by following the mayor's lead rather than other claims. The aldermen could go along with the mayor without sacrificing their prime political goals, while the old BZA could not have. Therefore the mayor's coercive powers were inadequate to the task of controlling the BZA, short of replacing its membership with people less interested in patronage and more concerned with policy.

The alternative method, appointing men who agreed with the administration's substantive goals, had the advantage of making coercion and rewards largely unnecessary in dealing with the BZA. It had, however, one weakness which, while it was not manifest during our study of New Haven, had the potential for future embarrassment. As many politicians know, the trouble with people who become one's allies because of a shared desire for a policy goal is that their desires for that goal are not always modified either by a balanced view of all the politician's purposes nor by a sense of tactical restraint in their particular area. Such enthusiasts are likely to put more emphasis on attaining the substantive ends they have in common with their political sponsors, while the latter commonly subordinate any policy goals to the prime end of maximizing votes. When the two goals conflict, the politician often may have no way to coerce the enthusiast and must rely on his powers of persuasion or his ability to avoid taking a stand. Lee followed the latter tactic during the furor engendered by his Board of Education's busing decision in 1964. Programmatic allies in official positions usually can embarrass their sponsor by resigning en masse, and can use this power as a resource in bargaining for more substantive progress.

The Democratic party organization plays an ambiguous role in this account of Lee's efforts to achieve policy coordination: it was both the principal mechanism that Lee used to extend his control and the principal source of resistance to his doing so. The first role conforms to the conventional wisdom in the social sciences, while the second is more consistent with the facts of local government.

In Chapter 4 I discussed some aspects of the functionalist proposition linking machine politics and informal coordination. I argued that this formulation confuses incentive systems and centralization of power, and does not even attempt to confront the problem of explaining why, if machine politics is "necessary" to coordinate policy, there are so many cities without significant machines. I expressed doubt that machine politics *resulted from* a need to centralize formally fragmented government agencies and that machines survive because they continue to serve this function. Here I want to discuss a somewhat different question: irrespective of the causes of machine politics, do machines in fact ordinarily serve as an important means of policy coordination? If they do, and machine politics is indeed declining, then it will be reasonable to concur with the judgment of scholars like Edward C. Banfield and James Q. Wilson that weakening classic machines reduces the effective power that city governments muster to deal with urban problems.[23] On the other hand, if machines are not commonly mechanisms for policy coordination, then their demise—real or imaginary—can be contemplated without fears that the result will be executive weakness in city hall.

The best-known and best-described contemporary city with a very strong political machine is Chicago, where the Democratic organization, currently headed by Mayor Richard Daley, has controlled city hall for many years. Banfield's *Political Influence* gives a sophisticated and detailed description of Chicago politics, with particular emphasis on the problems of policy coordination.[24] Chicago is a strong case for testing the functionalist proposition, as its Democratic organization's power is unsurpassed in any other major American city. Banfield dwells on (1) the "extreme formal decentralization of authority which is so striking a feature of the Chicago political system"; (2) how "formal decentralization is somehow overcome by informal centralization"; and (3) the fact that "by far the most important mechanism through which this is done is the political party or machine."[25]

When Banfield gets down to cases, however, it appears that the coordinating function of the Democratic machine is exercised in a rather limited fashion as the last stage in certain kinds of disputes.

> Civic controversies in Chicago are not generated by the efforts of politicians to win votes, by differences of ideology or group interest, or by behind-the-scenes efforts of a power elite. They arise, instead, out of the maintenance and enhancement needs of large formal organizations. The heads of an organization

---

23 Edward C. Banfield and James Q. Wilson, *City Politics* (Cambridge, Mass.: Harvard University Press and The M.I.T. Press, 1963), pp. 125–27. The proposition that machines are coordinating devices seems inconsistent with Banfield and Wilson's definition of "private-regardingness" as parochial, in contrast to the comprehensive, citywide view taken by exponents of "public-regardingness" (*ibid.,* p. 46).

24 Edward C. Banfield, *Political Influence* (New York: The Free Press, 1961).

25 *Ibid.,* pp. 307, 237.

see some advantage to be gained by changing the situation. They propose changes. Other large organizations are threatened. They oppose, and a civic controversy takes place.[26]

The parties in these disputes may be public agencies, but they are more likely to be private bodies: a newspaper, labor union, business firm, or civic organization. By the time the argument comes before a political head (usually but not always the mayor, for some issues involve the county government), he does little more than preside over an agreement which reflects the balance of power among the contenders:

> The political head, therefore, neither fights for a program of his own making nor endeavors to find a "solution" to the conflicts that are brought before him. Instead, he waits for the community to agree upon a project. When agreement is reached, or when the process of controversy has gone as far as it can, he ratifies the agreement and carries it into effect.[27]

The formidable Chicago machine "overcomes formal decentralization" in good measure by facilitating the administration of agreements between largely private interest groups that rely on *their own* political resources in the bargaining that precedes agreement.

Daley has to respond to the demands of his role as leader of the political organization, and is also the mayor and therefore the director of the municipal bureaucracy and the symbolic head of the city government and steward of public affairs in Chicago. To a considerable degree it is the latter roles that draw him into the controversies. Irrespective of the role, however, he is a reluctant "coordinator." He acts only when he must, on the initiative of others. Banfield attributed this mayoral reticence to "the Chicago view" that "a policy ought to be framed by the interests affected, not by the political head or his agents."[28] It also seems to reflect Daley's long-run strategic calculations:

> In a profile of Mayor Daley, Keith Wheeler wrote that the Mayor laughed and giggled when it was suggested to him that had never, in his whole life, committed himself to anything whatever until he absolutely had to. "That's a pretty good way to be, don't you think?" Wheeler quoted Daley as saying. "Pretty good way to run any business."[29]

The Democratic organization in Chicago unquestionably is more amply endowed with political resources than any other actor or likely coalition of

---

26 *Ibid.*, p. 263.
27 *Ibid.*, p. 253; see also pp. 271–72.
28 *Ibid.*, p. 270.
29 *Ibid.*, p. 346.

actors in that city. More than other institutions, it has the ability to coordinate public policy, but it is not at all clear that it also has the will to do so. *Why should it?* The organization's resources, while numerous, are not unlimited, and the first claims on them are to maintain the organization's influence in the Democratic party in the city of Chicago and the state of Illinois.[30] The organization's first priority then is winning primary elections in Chicago. Policy coordination is not considered important for this purpose. Even more programmatic politicians might agree with this assessment, and because the machine considers issues to be obstacles rather than opportunities, it is not surprising that substantive matters are inconspicuous in its electoral appeals.[31]

As in the case of the New Haven Board of Zoning Appeals, imposing central control over municipal agencies chokes off the flow of favors that nourish the organization. Thus policy coordination *weakens* the machine, whose "maintenance and enhancement needs" lead it away from centralization of any political processes except those concerned with nominations and patronage. In the absence of irresistible demands from outside the machine, its leaders impede rather than aid attempts at concerting policy decisions, for these would hurt the organization with no corresponding gain to it.

In Chicago the organization's power is used reluctantly and as a last resort for coordination, and then in the service of civic tranquillity rather than innovation. Can the same be said about cities where machine politics flourishes but no organization has the cohesion and control found in Chicago? In these cities the case against the functionalist proposition is even stronger, for here a machine's interests are best served by maintaining fragmentation. Machine politicians typically are not concerned with substantive policies. They are not as likely to be held responsible for public affairs as Mayor Daley is. The rewards that sustain their organizations represent, in many instances, deviations from uniform enforcement of the laws. Therefore they generally resist attempts to extend central control over the discrete agencies of local government.

Numerous books and articles about various cities demonstrate the truth of these propositions. One of the most detailed of these is Wallace S. Sayre and Herbert Kaufman's thoroughgoing study of New York, which, like Banfield's book on Chicago, is particularly concerned with problems of coordination and control.[32] In New York, "numerous, separate centers of power are the dominant phenomena of the city's politics and government."[33] The mayor "is the central focus of responsibility and accountability for all

---

30 *Ibid.,* p. 245.

31 *Ibid.,* p. 259; and James Q. Wilson, *Negro Politics* (New York: The Free Press, 1960), p. 117.

32 Wallace S. Sayre and Herbert Kaufman, *Governing New York City* (New York: Russell Sage Foundation, 1961).

33 *Ibid.,* p. 699.

that occurs in the city,"[34] but he is neither successful in achieving coordination nor persistent in trying to do so.[35] A far cry from Chicago, "the parties are aggregations of segments rather than organic entities. They are decentralized and fragmented and undisciplined, but they achieve sufficient unity of purpose and action and leadership to identify them as organizations."[36] Party leaders have most influence on nominations and appointments. Their involvement on substantive matters is "most concerned with discrete aspects of policy and its application rather than on its range and content."[37]

The leaders' involvement in the substance of public policy is a result of local constituency demands and is undertaken to maintain the network of obligations that motivate their organizations. These interventions typically tend to subvert centralization, not further it:

> The party leaders are for the most part neutral toward the policy questions involved and try to get what is asked simply to satisfy the petitioners and render them beholden. Most of the time, the petitioners are not seeking to make or change policy; rather, *they want exemptions from the policies and procedures in force.*[38]

Decentralization maintains the party politicians' power to secure exceptions to general policies and for this reason the organizations have blocked centralization of the many governmental functions performed by the borough offices. The most common way for the party leaders to retaliate against the mayor was to block the legislation he wanted. Being less conspicuous, council members were more dependent on their party organization for renomination and tended to side against the mayor's attempts at centralization. In striving to exert control over the city's sprawling officialdom, the mayor also faced a common element of political reality: many appointed officials were more loyal to the party organization that sponsored them than to their nominal superior. Thus "patronage tended to fragment the executive branch as much as did election of administrative officers."[39] Because party leaders were more

---

34 *Ibid.*, p. 657.

35 *Ibid.*, pp. 676–79, 715.

36 *Ibid.*, p. 455.

37 *Ibid.*, p. 452.

38 *Ibid.*, p. 457 (emphasis added) ; see also pp. 464–65.

39 Herbert Kaufman, "Emerging Conflicts in the Doctrines of Public Administration," *American Political Science Review,* 50 (December 1956), 1068. Kaufman intended this remark generally, as part of his argument that "the patronage system strengthened party leaders and legislators more than it did executives" (*ibid.*, p. 1068). He is one of the few political scientists to express doubts about the unifying effects of patronage. Another is Frank J. Sorauf, who argued that patronage was not helpful in attaining policy coordination because it often did not benefit those interests that wanted coordination. See his "Patronage and Party," *Midwestern Journal of Political Science,* 3 (May 1959), 123–24.

interested in patronage than policy and retained great influence in the appointive process, the weight of the party organizations was more often felt
on the side of fragmentation than coordination.

The New York pattern appears to be fairly common, particularly in the
distinction between machine politicians and those actors concerned with
public policy. Harold Kaplan reported that

> in Newark, as in many other cities, there is a gap between the electoral system
> and the policy-making system. The former focuses on the filling of elective and
> appointive positions; the latter focuses on broad issues and the substance of
> policy.[40]

There was a similar dichotomy in St. Louis between the mayor's office,
interested in broad policy questions and appealing chiefly to downtown businesses and the more civic-minded members of the middle classes, and the
aldermen and county office holders, sustained by patronage, concerned with
innumerable minor problems, and appealing to the working classes. The
latter faction, incidentally, "exhibits a sharp antipathy to any suggestion of
increased tax rates," while the former is "more sympathetic to the needs
for more tax revenue."[41] Despite these different interests, the two groupings
need and can get along with each other:

> The group focused on the mayor is not interested in patronage. . . . By the same
> token, the county office group and many of its electoral supporters are pro-
> foundly indifferent to most matters of public policy. Aldermanic courtesy does
> create conflict, since the granting of individual favors. . . often runs counter to
> broader policy concerns. . . . Nevertheless, there are many areas of policy and
> of patronage where each element of the party is content to let the other element
> control. Each group needs the other. The county office people need the financial
> support for their precinct workers which the mayor-led group contributes to
> the party. The mayoral group needs the support of the delivery wards to get
> many of its policy goals put into effect.[42]

There was a similar division of political actors in New Haven, where one
set of officials and private citizens was involved with party matters and an
almost wholly different group dealt with, say, urban renewal. There were
some important differences between the two cities, however: (1) New
Haven's mayor, with a foot rooted firmly in each camp, maintained adequate

[40] Harold Kaplan, *Urban Renewal Politics* (New York: Columbia University Press,
1963), p. 182.

[41] Robert H. Salisbury, "St. Louis Politics: Relationships Among Interests, Parties
and Government Structure," in *Democracy in Urban America*, eds. Oliver P. Williams
and Charles Press (Chicago: Rand McNally & Co., 1961), p. 398.

[42] *Ibid.*, p. 403.

unity between these different forces and, for all practical purposes, united them without recourse to serious compromise. His popular success, persuasiveness, and skill at reconciling differences kept both groups sufficiently content. (2) The "policy constituency" was not a "natural" part of the ordinary New Haven political scene, but a somewhat artificial creation of Mayor Lee's. Its chances of surviving his departure are a fairly open question.

To summarize this argument, patronage-based party organizations are not likely to volunteer themselves as policy coordinating mechanisms. (1) They are principally concerned with nominations, elections, appointments, and contracts. (2) By and large, their typical political strategies do not rely on policy appeals. (3) Securing exceptions to general rules is a major incentive for such organizations (as well as a source of income for their leaders), yet an important aspect of centralized administration is that rules must be enforced equitably. (4) Otherwise, involvement in substantive policy brings trouble for organizations of this type.

When machines are employed as integrative devices, it is not to assure their own survival, but because other political elements—most likely policy-oriented officials—impose this role on them or extract it from them in return for concessions. The difficulties of using them this way are suggested by the case of the New Haven Board of Zoning Appeals; the advantages, by the New Heven Board of Aldermen. Machines can best be used to coordinate policy when their members are not interested in the policy and therefore make no claims to be consulted about it, and can be more readily controlled because their reward—patronage—can easily be manipulated.

8 businessmen in politics
and the
Citizens Action Commission

The Democratic organization's compliance was essential to a successful urban renewal program, but it was not an adequate base of support. The program required widespread approval and the explicit agreement of special publics who were not ordinarily involved in local party politics. Lee needed devices to achieve these ends and to sustain his popularity during the difficult years when dislocation and destruction would be the only results of redevelopment. For this purpose the coercive powers that brought the organs of municipal government into line were largely irrelevant. To win extra-governmental support for redevelopment Lee drew on the informal, unused resources of his office to create new institutions and involve new groups in his administration's policies. The New Haven Citizens Action Commission, Inc., is the prime example of this tactic.[1]

The CAC was designed to sell redevelopment to those groups that remained fairly aloof from local politics—professional men, middle-class do-gooders, liberals, and, most important, big businessmen—and to use their membership to lend an aura of prestige, nonpartisanship, and business community support to redevelopment. According to one of its annual reports, "the CAC and its Action Committees are in the best sense 'grass roots' organizations which include a cross section of community life with all its rich and varied character." Lee described it more accurately, if less lyrically:

> We've got the...biggest set of muscles in New Haven on the top CAC....
> They're muscular because they control wealth...because they control industries,
> represent banks. They're muscular because they represent the intellectual por-
> tions of the community...because they're articulate, because they're respect-
> able, because of their financial power, and because of the accumulation of
> prestige which they have built up over the years as individuals in all kinds of
> causes, whether United Fund, Red Cross, or whatever.

These "muscles" were not used on the city administration, whatever other uses they were put to. The CAC was a manufactured pressure group that increased support for Lee's policies without in any significant way extending or sharing influence over them. The CAC is worth detailed examination not only because it was an elaborate and successful charade of citizen participa-

---

[1] Except where noted, this chapter describes the CAC as of 1959, before its reorganization.

tion in decision making, but because it played other roles in the city's reconstruction. It also is a convenient vehicle for discussing some aspects of business participation in politics and for examining some relationships between self-interest and political participation.

The Reluctant Businessmen

Accepting his third mayoral nomination in 1953, Lee outlined the problems facing the city and proclaimed that their solution required that "we must take the public of New Haven into partnership with the city government." He promised to form a citizens action commission within 60 days. This proved to be impossible and nine months passed before the mayor could announce the appointment of an executive committee for the CAC. (The term *CAC* was commonly given both to the entire membership, numbering over 400, and to the smaller and more important group consisting of the chairman, vice-chairman, members-at-large, and action committee chairmen. I will call the latter body the "executive committee" whenever ambiguity is possible.)

Recruiting prominent businessmen was the central problem in creating the CAC. Business support was essential for the execution of redevelopment, which required private interests willing and able to buy cleared land, obtain financing, and in many other ways work with the local business community. Any project would be vulnerable to political attacks that it was "unbusinesslike" unless it had substantial business endorsement. On the other hand, no organization like the Chamber of Commerce, that represented only business interests, would fill this need, if only because such a narrowly based group would be sure to arouse suspicions of exploitation. A new group would have to be organized to embody business backing in a communitywide framework.

Lee felt that the chairman would have to be a businessman of outstanding reputation and that forming the CAC began with the chairman. His first recruiting effort was discouraging:

> After I was elected I selected a guy I thought would be a good CAC chairman. I took him out to lunch...at Mory's.... I asked for his help in setting up the CAC. He's a very prominent citizen, one of the biggest men in the city, and he told me that: (a) he did not believe that all of these things were possible; (b) he did not believe that even if they were possible that I would pull them off because I was too young and too idealistic and too inexperienced; (c) that while he was my friend he had not voted for me and had contributed to my opponent; and (d) that he was too old to get tagged with a project that was so ethereal as to be doomed before it got off the ground. Well, he left me dejected; this was a hell of an attitude to be confronted with....[2]

---

[2] After Lee's reelection in 1955 this man sent him a note recanting his previous views and congratulating him on his redevelopment program. A $500 contribution was enclosed.

Lee met with the same reception elsewhere:

> People had been shooting off their mouths for years in this town, many [predict-ing] a great and rosy future, and then doing nothing about it. So there was no great interest in this attempt to inculcate or instill a new spirit in the city and wherever I went I was met with this sort of passive resistance to me because I was a young squirt. I was 37 years old. I was a Democrat and I hadn't had any particular business experience.

At bottom, however, this reluctance had little to do with Lee. It appears to have been rooted in businessmen's aversion to conflict, their lack of interest in welfare policies, divergences of interest in the business community, and class and ethnic differences between businessmen and politicians. Although their importance varies a good deal from issue to issue and city to city, these considerations are not limited to New Haven. For example, Kent Jennings reported limits on business power in Atlanta:

> [The Chamber of Commerce is] undoubtedly the single most influential inter-est group in the community. In order to maintain its cohesion and its essentially conservative character, the Chamber seldom takes public stands on the very controversial issues in the community.[3]

In other words, one source of the Chamber's influence was its cohesion, but one prerequisite of that cohesion was avoidance of political involvement when its members might not agree with each other, or with significant other ele-ments in the community. For example, Jennings reports that there was scarcely any participation by Atlanta's economic leaders in a highly con-troversial $87 million bond issue election held during his study of the city.[4]

Harold Kaplan, studying urban renewal politics in Newark, a city that resembles New Haven more than Atlanta does, found that businessmen there eschewed controversy for reasons of taste rather than tactics:

> The model of alert interests, strongly committed to their goals and prepared to press these goals at every occasion, does not apply to Newark renewal.... The civic leaders and their spokesmen generally found political conflict highly dis-tasteful and sought harmony on almost any terms.[5]

Another motivation for avoidance of controversy is purely commercial: businessmen hate to lose customers and so tend to keep from saying things that might offend people.

[3] M. Kent Jennings, *Community Influentials: The Elites of Atlanta* (New York: The Free Press, 1964), p. 146.

[4] *Ibid.,* pp. 83–84.

[5] Harold Kaplan, *Urban Renewal Politics* (New York: Columbia University Press, 1964), p. 177.

Political participation is not equally likely to mean controversy everywhere, which might explain variations in business political involvement. I have the impression that business and businessmen are more respected in the South than in the Northeast. This may be a result of traditional southern paternalism, and perhaps as well of the more current passion for industrialization and economic growth there. Whatever the reasons, the more deference paid to businessmen's opinions, the more unlikely that their ventures into politics will be greeted with disagreement.

Some local governmental forms encourage controversy. The most obvious example is partisan elections, which add an extra conflictual dimension to local politics because they insure the continued existence of a built-in, organized opposition to the party in power. When city hall is in the hands of Democrats, then, apart from any other configuration of interests, the local Republicans will be alert for opportunities to attack and embarrass the administration, will look for political allies among presently or potentially disgruntled groups, and will be able to mobilize a significant portion of the electorate in the next election simply by invoking the party symbol. The minority party will be likely to oppose whatever the administration does: "the business of the opposition is to oppose." The partisan ballot thus makes an independent contribution to controversy. Where it is used, many businessmen may be more reluctant to enter the political arena except in ad hoc negotiations to achieve immediate, individual, and particular interests. The regional distribution of partisan and nonpartisan local electoral systems encourages business participation in the South and discourages it in the Northeast. Sixty-one percent of northeastern cities over 50,000 population have partisan local elections, compared to 19 percent in the South.[6]

A third factor with considerable regional variation also seems relevant to businessmen's willingness to become generally involved in local politics. The more highly developed are the politically specialized elements in a city, that is, the more powerful the local political organizations, the more hesitant businessmen (and everyone else) will be to participate in civic and governmental affairs.[7] There are several reasons for this. (1) Strong organizations have command of major political resources and so are not dependent on

[6] Two-thirds of midwestern cities use the nonpartisan ballot, while the West is almost wholly nonpartisan. For a discussion of the interrelationships among region, demographic factors, and municipal governmental forms, see Raymond E. Wolfinger and John Osgood Field, "Political Ethos and the Structure of City Government," *American Political Science Review,* 60 (June 1966), 306–26.

[7] This discussion does not apply to political involvement by men in politically sensitive businesses like construction, real estate, building materials, insurance, liquor, and so forth. Immediate economic considerations are likely to lead to participation by at least a significant fraction of people in such "political businesses." Indeed, their level of participation in local politics may be *higher* in machine politics cities, since favoritism in contracting and regulatory activities is an important part of the resources sustaining political organizations in such places.

businessmen (or unions, for that matter) for contributions and campaign workers. (2) By the same token, these bases of power enable them to withstand electoral challenges from other elements. (3) Where such organizations flourish, government officials are more likely to be professional politicians, skilled in negotiation and conflict, and hence more formidable adversaries.[8] (4) Businessmen want to avoid—either for moral or for public relations reasons—the possibility of being tainted with the corruption that is often associated with machine politics. (5) In the Northeast most big businessmen will be Yankees and most politicians ethnics; hence social differences, if not outright prejudice, will impede collaboration between the two elements. Where the Yankees have been deprived of their former political eminence by mobilized ethnics, their exclusion allows them to be moralistic about patronage, corruption, and other bad habits that the ethnics picked up from their native-stock predecessors. (6) And, of course, the businessmen are mostly Republicans and the politicians mostly Democrats. As *Fortune* concluded:

> Far too frequently they [businessmen] also have a strong distaste for politics and politicians—distaste that can be particularly strong when the politicians happen to be Democrats. . . .
>
> Big corporations have been making a great point of community participation —some have put vice presidents in charge of such activities—but big executives are more loath than anyone to mess in anything that smacks of politics, and their community-relations effort is apt to be on the innocuous level of open-house days at the plant, children's tours, and free use of the company's baseball diamond.[9]

The consequence of all this is that in many northeastern cities there is considerable distance between the worlds of big business and local machine

---

[8] Big businessmen in Newark were unfamiliar with political bargaining, averse to controversy, and hence no match for the city officials with whom they negotiated: "The civic leaders and their staffs shared a strong reluctance to be drawn into City Hall politics and also a fear that the politicos would try to make the [civic] committees part of their personal political organizations." Kaplan, *Urban Renewal Politics*, p. 72, and also Chap. 4.

Private civic groups in Newark could not raise enough money to hire staff members with the ability to deal on even terms with municipal officials (p. 112). In very large cities, however, the scope and division of labor in economic and civic life may reach a point where both economic organizations and business-supported civic groups can support professional staffs able to bargain with politicians and government officials. This seems to be the situation in Chicago, where such organizations provide many items on the agenda of political controversy. Edward C. Banfield argues that this is a result of the search for justification and expansion by these organizations' professional staffs. See his *Political Influence* (New York: The Free Press, 1961), esp. p. 263.

[9] William H. Whyte, Jr., in *The Expanding Metropolis*, Doubleday Anchor ed., ed. The Editors of Fortune (New York: Doubleday & Company, Inc., 1958), pp. xvii, xviii.

politics. Before the CAC brought them together, few, if any, of New Haven's business leaders had known John Golden. This may not be unusual. Although David Lawrence had been chairman of the Allegheny County (Pittsburgh) Democratic party since 1920, it was not until the late 1940s that he met Richard K. Mellon, the head of that family's extensive interests in Pittsburgh (and elsewhere).[10]

It was hardly surprising that Yankee Republican New Haven businessmen were reluctant to become involved with ethnic Democratic politicians in support of an untried and drastic solution to problems whose scope and gravity most of them had not acknowledged. Redevelopment offered innumerable opportunities for shady practices. It would certainly disturb the lives and business interests of thousands of people. This would lead the local Republican politicians to make an issue of redevelopment, while Lee could be expected to exploit it for selfish purposes. As businessmen saw it, they were being asked to embroil themselves in political controversy and perhaps in corruption to help a "socialistic" program conducted by a liberal politician. And for what? Most of them were fairly indifferent to slums. They saw no connection between redevelopment and parking and traffic deficiencies in the central business district. In any event, these problems hurt only the retailers, not the rest of the business community.[11] Urban renewal was a complicated, untried, bureaucratically complicated interference with free enterprise. An unsuccessful project would leave blocks of rubble in the middle of the city and million-dollar deficits in the city treasury. Lee was a Democrat with no business experience. Were he and his New Dealers and ward heelers likely to succeed?

Lee worked hard to sell his program, seizing every opportunity to speak before audiences of businessmen and to expand his enormous circle of acquaintances at lunches, dinners, and other gatherings. His emphatic, unpolished speaking style and rather brusque manner were unlikely to sustain stereotypes that he was an impractical dreamer, but for months he made little progress. At least three more prominent business and civic leaders refused invitations to head the CAC.

From a social scientist's viewpoint the most interesting thing about this is the way it reverses the customary picture of politics: groups make demands on the government and politicians respond to those groups whose support is

10 Frank Hawkins, "Lawrence of Pittsburgh: Boss of the Mellon Patch," *Harper's Magazine* (August 1956), 58.

11 A survey of more than 2,200 business executives conducted at the end of the 1950s indicated that utility and retail executives were far more concerned about urban decline than other businessmen, although only a third of them thought that the problem was "serious" or "critical." There was little active involvement in attempts to deal with the exodus from cities by *any* category of firms. See George Sternlieb, "Is Business Abandoning the Big City?" *Harvard Business Review*, 39 (January/February 1961), 6–14.

best calculated to keep them in office. Here the mayor was pointing to needs and offering programs to do something about them, trying to arouse businessmen's interest in ways that they could benefit from proposed policies, and the businessmen failed to respond. This indifference seems not to have been peculiar to New Haven; indifference to the profit possibilities represented by urban renewal was widespread among American businessmen.[12]

Innovation Through the Pork Barrel

Two developments in 1954 began to improve Lee's reputation among businessmen. His fiscal and administrative reforms convinced many of them that he was practical and efficient, not a boodler or dreamer. Lee publicized his economies as widely as possible, losing few opportunities to remind businessmen that he had saved almost a million dollars by more competent management. While the mayor's standing improved, redevelopment was still no more appealing to the business community. For months Lee had been "preaching human values" to businessmen. His stories about the miseries of the slums had little impact, nor was he able to convince them of the relationships between traffic, parking, slums, zoning, and downtown commercial stagnation.

He changed his tactics and appealed to businessmen in hard-cash terms rather than trying to change their value structures. He began to emphasize the immediate pocketbook costs of slums, using the moribund Oak Street Project as an example: the present Oak Street area cost the city $200,000 a year and contributed only half that amount in taxes; other taxpayers subsidized the area, "a deficit area not just in human values, but in dollars and cents as well." Tax income from the neighborhood was declining every year, just as the cost of maintaining it was going up. If the project were completed, the area would pay four times as much in taxes as it would then cost for city services. But if the project died, Oak Street would spread blight to adjacent blocks, hastening the decline of the city's obsolescent central shopping district and thereby weakening the tax base while increasing demands for higher taxes.

The mayor pointed to the traffic that packed the city's eighteenth century streets and overflowed its inadequate parking facilities. Shoppers shunned the central business district because they could not park. There was little new commercial or residential construction in New Haven; as Logue indiscreetly remarked in a speech, it was a dying city. As we have seen, a few businessmen had made feeble, partial efforts to remedy some of these problems, and

12 See Stephen G. Thompson, "Urban Renewal and the Ambivalent Businessmen," *Architectural Forum* (June 1959), 147–49; and "The Businessmen's Stake in Urban Renewal," *Architectural Forum* (November 1959), 146–47.

others had been dimly aware of them. Lee not only reminded the *entire* business community of its danger from these trends, he showed them a path toward salvation, a path which his economy record and increasingly evident personal competence made appear less and less unrealistic.

Beyond the general argument that redevelopment would strengthen the tax base and remove the fiscal burden of "deficit areas," which touched all businessmen's interests, Lee pointed out more specialized benefits. The banks grew with their community through local investment, principally in real estate; economic stagnation threatened the value of these holdings. Public utilities had an obvious and salient interest in local economic growth, the major source of increasing demand for their products. Merchants would profit from redevelopment through improved parking and traffic facilities that would help them meet suburban competition. Finally, any given redevelopment project would affect the fortunes of individual firms by virtue of its location and the opportunities and threats that it might offer.

Lee constantly told his audiences that the federal government would pay two-thirds of the cost. This argument appealed to a persistent complaint in Connecticut: the imbalance between the federal taxes paid by its residents and the amount of federal spending in the state. Median personal income in Connecticut is the highest in the country, thus it makes a healthy contribution to the federal treasury. Because it lacks military bases, farms, reclamation projects, or other opportunities for federal public works, Connecticut commonly ranks near the bottom of all states in federal expenditures. Therefore, it usually pays about two dollars in taxes for every dollar received in federal grants. The *Register* often mentioned this low tax/benefit ratio and many Connecticut residents feel short-changed by it.[13]

One of Lee's favorite rhetorical devices was to say that the federal government should spend as much per capita on urban problems as it did for aid to farmers. This was a shrewd, double-edged argument. On the one hand, it was a visionary liberal claim that cited lavish agricultural subsidies as a justification for similar generosity toward the nation's declining cities. On the other hand, it reminded urban businessmen that redevelopment was one way to redress the unfavorable balance of payments and so recover for local spending some of the taxes that previously had gone disproportionately to other parts of the country. Lee began to win business support for the idea of urban renewal in New Haven. Such approval clearly was not the result of ideological conversion, as this comment by a prominent business member of the CAC illustrates:

---

[13] Data on the tax/benefit ratio are from the Tax Foundation, Inc. The *Register* used figures like this to argue against urban renewal, implying that every additional dollar of federal aid for local purposes would necessitate the payment of two additional dollars in taxes!

Too much money has gone into the federal government to be disbursed at the capricious whim of a politician.... But the way I look at [it] is if taxes are going to remain high and there is going to be a socialist program in the United States...if personal income taxes cannot be reduced, why there's only one thing to do and that is to devise ways and means so that we can share in it.... I'm not interested in building a highway through Montana or anything like that or a TVA down South, and I'd like to see some of those dollars come back into Connecticut so that we can enjoy some more benefits.

What Lee managed to do was to give urban renewal a pork barrel image for many local residents. This suggests some important but generally overlooked features of federal grant policy. One consequence of grants-in-aid is separation of the revenue and spending functions, thus removing any direct and proportionate link between expenditure (by the locality) and taxation (by the national government). A city's residents do not pay more taxes because of the federal funds obtained by their local public agencies. Therefore, if a proposal is made for a project that will be funded by the federal treasury, they are far less likely to object that it will increase their taxes. (Federal grants often require some local matching funds, but these usually are dwarfed by the federal contribution.) Such objections are a major impediment to innovation, and politicians' anticipations of taxpayer revolts probably play an even greater role in stifling progress. In the national perspective, federal grants are, of course, paid for by the taxpayers, but in any particular place taxes do not reflect federal grants received. Indeed, the availability of federal funds often motivates local officials to wangle as much money as they can. A favorite argument of the local proponents of a federally funded project is that inaction will lead to "loss" of federal aid. (This seems to be a particularly common appeal to spur on local approval of highway construction.) Thus grants-in-aid are an incentive for each locality to maximize its share of the rewards, as the local share of the costs is largely fixed.[14]

The federal urban renewal program is not a good example of this dynamic because of its numerous unpopular aspects. Less complicated grant-in-aid programs such as federal support for airports, highways, and hospitals illustrate local eagerness to obtain "free" outside money. Here, as elsewhere, individual short-run calculations are more important motives than collective long-run ones. In many policy areas the net demand for federal aid reflects the sum of the disaggregated benefits far more than the aggregated costs. The political advantage of outside aid, then, is that it has little effect on local

---

[14] On the other hand, because successful applications for categorical grants usually require bureaucratic sophistication, and because there are so many different grant programs, this system requires a level of industry and ingenuity that may be beyond the capacity of many cities. Revenue sharing at least does not place a premium on grantsmanship. Intentionally or not, it will have a leveling effect.

tax burdens; or, if it comes as matching grants, its effect is disproportionate to the amount received.

Federal support for local projects is in the form of "categorical grants," that is, contributions from funds that are authorized and appropriated for a particular purpose, and disbursed for specified projects or programs. Categorical grants are made under hundreds of different programs. For all practical purposes, there are seldom limits on the amount of money that any locality can receive under any given program. Receipt of a grant for a given project does not reduce a city's chances of funding for other projects in the same program, nor for grants in other programs. Local grantsmanship is not a zero-sum game in which a successful application reduces the chances of other claimants in the community. There is minimal local rivalry for federal money from champions of different projects; obtaining aid for a new hospital does not affect the chances for a housing grant, and so on.

These aspects of the present grant-in-aid system seem to be unrecognized by proponents of the currently fashionable notion of "block grants" or "revenue sharing," which presents a sum of money to each state and locality to be spent as it chooses. Revenue sharing will inhibit innovation because each city has a fixed amount of money to be apportioned among contending interests. Because any allocation from the grant would reduce the funds available to other potential or actual claimants, revenue sharing will turn all such contenders against each other. One result may be to raise the barriers to *any* given proposal, for the advocates of other uses for the money will not want to see their chances diminished by a reduction in the size of the pie.

A second consequence of revenue sharing may be a sharp increase in group conflict because a gain for any faction would be a loss for others. Revenue sharing does not seem to be a step toward racial harmony. A precursor of this conflict can be seen in the quarreling among different minority groups for higher shares of the fixed local allocations to Model Cities and antipoverty agencies.[15]

The amount of each locality's share under revenue sharing is determined by a formula that does not permit variation from city to city. This rigidity could not accommodate varying levels of citizen demand or political leadership. Revenue sharing will provide neither the incentives nor the opportunities for ambitious politicians like Lee and innovative professional officials like

[15] In Theodore Lowi's well-known issue typology, "distributive policies" are "made without regard to limited resources" and do not pit groups against each other: "The indulged and the deprived, the loser and the recipient, need never come into direct confrontation." "Redistributive policies," on the other hand, do create a zero-sum game with winners and losers confronting each other. See Theodore J. Lowi, "Distribution, Regulation, Redistribution: The Functions of Government," in *Readings in American Political Behavior,* 2nd ed., ed. Raymond E. Wolfinger (Englewood Cliffs, N.J.: Prentice-Hall, Inc., 1970), pp. 245, 246. A change from categorical grants to revenue sharing would be a change from distributive to redistributive policies.

Logue. Because the amount of money received by a city is fixed, new programs lacking developed local clienteles stand a smaller chance of funding. Categorical grants help compensate for local political weakness by providing money that does not represent a deprivation of groups that are more capable of getting what they want at city hall. Thus federal power helps offset local weakness in winning a share of public money.

Categorical grants also strengthen the hands of municipal officials who want to enforce locally unpopular rules. The most obvious example here is opposition to racial discrimination. At present officials trying to enforce federal rules have a strong argument: "The government in Washington is forcing us to do it; if we don't they will cut the money off." In principle, revenue sharing would work the same way. As a practical matter, it is difficult to see how a block grant would be reduced to penalize rules violations in a particular program when the distinguishing feature of revenue sharing is that the federal grant is not earmarked.

A national urban policy should reflect these considerations by avoiding ceilings on aid to cities and continuing and increasing the separation between taxing and spending constituencies. This would provide the greatest incentives to local action by removing the constraint of worry about higher taxes, and would minimize the likelihood of group conflict for fixed resources by removing the fear that success for one claim would hurt any other group's chances.

This discussion of the local impact of federal grant policy was written in 1970, two years before the Nixon Administration's revenue sharing plan was enacted. Unhappily, initial experience with the new program confirms my propositions about the divisive and anti-innovative consequences of revenue sharing. As municipal governments learned how much federal money they would receive, many scheduled hearings on how to spend the funds. These affairs dramatized the dog-eat-dog response to revenue sharing. Because the supply of money was fixed, each proposal was a threat to every other one and the level of discussion quickly became appropriately impassioned. The first of these rancorous affairs in San Francisco seemed "like a horde of greedy relatives at the reading of the will of a rich uncle." Faced with the prospect of continuing conflict, local politicians are taking the easy way out by advocating safe, consensual, unenterprising uses for the new federal money. The most obvious solution is tax reduction, which seems to be the favorite policy nationwide, followed in popularity by such uncontroversial purposes as capital improvements.[16] If these practices continue, revenue sharing will have a chilling effect on municipal innovation unless the level of federal categorical grants remains unaffected, which is a very shaky assumption.

[16] The description of the hearing is quoted in the *San Francisco Chronicle,* 20 February 1973. The best source on cities' early spending decisions is a survey by the Subcommittee on Intergovernmental Relations of the United States Senate, reported in a column by Joseph Kraft in the *San Francisco Chronicle,* 20 February 1973.

A Balanced Ticket on the CAC

Lee had been working closely with officials of the Chamber of Commerce, who wanted to form a committee under Chamber sponsorship to make its ambitious "Ten-Point Program" come true. It was unlikely that such a committee would accomplish much (one city official said of the Chamber that "their specialty is hot air"), but it could wreck the CAC by taking the field first. Lee persuaded the Chamber's leaders to join forces with him. This entailed not only picking a chairman, but also establishing the subjects to be considered by the CAC. After considerable negotiating the Chamber agreed to broadening the proposed CAC's purview to include noncommercial fields like recreation, and in turn Lee conceded that it would not take up education, a field which the Chamber wanted to avoid. (Lee formed a separate organization for education and merged it with the CAC a few years later.) Lee, Logue, and Chamber leaders drew up a list of possible chairmen of the CAC and a committee was formed to recruit one of these men.

Early in his search for a chairman Lee had asked A. Whitney Griswold, then the president of Yale, to be a vice chairman of the CAC. He assured Griswold that his participation would be mainly symbolic and that he would never have to preside or otherwise assume the responsibilities of chairman, or even attend meetings regularly. Griswold had been president only a short time and wanted to improve the university's rather distant relations with city hall and thereby modify the community's traditional animosity toward Yale. Moreover, strengthening the tax base through redevelopment might help relieve pressure to amend the university's tax-exempt status. Griswold became convinced that Lee was serious about using the CAC to improve New Haven and agreed to serve provided that the chairman be a man in whom he had confidence.

The Chamber had directed Lee's attention to one of its former presidents, Carl G. Freese. The president of the Connecticut Savings Bank, Freese, a Republican, had been active in civic affairs for many years and had a wide reputation for integrity and intelligence. Making use of Griswold's tentative acceptance and of the banks' dependence on the economic health of the core city, Lee persuaded Freese to accept. The tide now turned. Freese's presence at the head of the CAC was a guarantee to businessmen that it would be a nonpartisan, high-level body. With the curse of politics removed, the CAC could credibly be defined as the right sort of civic group and recruitment became much easier. Redevelopment could be seen as the sort of thing that businessmen understood and were skilled at: buying and managing property, arranging financing, selling and developing real estate. Freese, Lee, Logue, the Chamber's executive vice president, and one or two other businessmen worked together to convince other leading businessmen to join the CAC.

Recruiting ethnic representatives, labor leaders, and liberals was easy. Urban renewal could more easily be sold to them and they were, by and large, Democrats and strong Lee supporters already. Like the businessmen, few of them had exerted any significant pressure for redevelopment before Lee formulated and presented his initial plans. Asked about labor interest in redevelopment, one union leader answered:

> At the local level it doesn't rank as a major issue except in New Haven where somebody like Dick Lee has sparked the issue. But in the absence of that kind of local leadership, no matter how great the need, there isn't as much concern with it at the local level as there should be.

Lee's appointments to the executive committee were designed to involve every major element in the city in his urban renewal program. The following description of its membership in 1957 suggests a good deal about the CAC's functions. The group's composition had remained substantially the same since its formation in September 1954, except for a change in chairmen; Freese was replaced by Lucius S. Rowe, the president of the Southern New England Telephone Company. Rowe had agreed to head the CAC once his firm's negotiations to buy land in the Oak Street Project were completed. When Freese had a serious heart attack late in 1956, Rowe was already on the executive committee and stepped into the top position. Freese had placed his prestige and services rather unreservedly at the call of the administration. Rowe was more active, and also more assertive. He used his company's talent and facilities in his CAC work and also played an important part in redevelopment politics.

In 1957 there were seventeen members of the executive committee, not counting the chairmen of the five "action committees," who were *ex officio* members: eleven businessmen, two Yale officials, two labor leaders, one lawyer, and John Golden. Griswold was still one of two vice chairmen; the other was a manufacturer esteemed by businessmen for his equable disposition and money-raising talents. There were two other industrialists: A. C. Gilbert, Jr., president of the A. C. Gilbert Company and of the Manufacturers' Association of Greater New Haven; and James A. Walsh, Sr., chairman of the board of the Armstrong Rubber Company. Walsh's firm was not located in the city, nor did he live there. But he was thought by many to be "the biggest businessman in the area," and was appointed on this basis and his position as head of one of the country's major tire companies. He was also prominent in Republican politics in the adjacent town of West Haven. Like Walsh, several other CAC businessmen who lived in outlying towns were active in local politics there. But with the exceptions mentioned below, none of those who lived in New Haven itself played an active part in party politics, and several of them expressed revulsion at what they conceived to be the common run of city politics.[17]

Public utilities were represented by Rowe; George Alpert, president of the New York, New Haven and Hartford Railroad; William C. Bell, president of the United Illuminating Company, the local power company; and James W. Hook, chairman of the board of the same firm. Alpert had taken the seat of Patrick McGinnis, his predecessor as president of the New Haven. He rarely attended meetings and often sent a representative. The New Haven helped obtain legislation the city wanted by lobbying at the state capitol. Hook probably was the most prestigious businessman in New Haven until his death in late 1957 at the age of 74. In his long career he had restored several firms to economic health, played a prominent part in the National Association of Manufacturers and the Republican party, and been asked by party leaders to run for governor. He also maintained a busy round of civic activities, having been chairman of the Board of Trustees of the University of Connecticut. In the 1920s and '30s he had pressed fruitlessly for action to solve New Haven's traffic and parking problems. For the CAC his most important credentials were his reputation for integrity, judgment, vision, intelligence, and courage.

The president of the Chamber of Commerce was always a member of the CAC. In 1957 this post was held by a senior vice president of the city's largest bank. The other banker member was Frank O'Brion, president of a smaller bank and chairman of the Redevelopment Agency.

Two businessmen were appointed for reasons other than their standing in the business community. Unlike the other business members, they were both Catholics. One was William J. Falsey, a senior partner and municipal finance expert in the city's largest stock brokerage firm. Falsey was also a member of the Board of Finance and an active, conservative Democrat. The second "political" businessman was Joseph R. Mariani, president of the Mariani Construction Company, the builder of the Oak Street Connector. He was also associated with the Democratic organization and was a close political ally of Lee's. He represented Italians.

The other ethnic representative was Louis Sachs, senior partner in the law firm of Sachs, Sachs, Giaimo, and Sachs.[18] Sachs also had had a long and

---

[17] The tendency for businessmen to participate in local politics where they live rather than where they work seems to be nationwide. See Sternlieb, "Is Business Abandoning the Big City?" Only 12 percent of Sternlieb's respondents were active in local politics in the city where they worked, compared to 27 percent who participated where they lived.

[18] In the mid-1950s the partners in this firm were Sachs and his two sons, one of whom was campaign manager for Robert Giaimo in his unsuccessful congressional race in 1956. Subsequently Giaimo was made a partner in the firm and in 1958, again with Arthur Sachs as his manager, was elected to Congress in the Ribicoff landslide. He has

intimate relationship with the Democratic party and was then serving as a state Workmen's Compensation Commissioner. Although there were other Jews on the CAC, Sachs was there explicitly to represent the city's large and diverse Jewish community, in which he had been active for generations and was highly respected: "Louis Sachs would have the support of the Oak Street Jews and the Woodbridge Country Club Jews."[19]

There were two labor representatives, both of whom lived in New Haven: Joseph M. Rourke, former head of the Connecticut Federation of Labor and then secretary-treasurer of the merged state AFL-CIO; and Mitchell Sviridoff, president of the same group and former president of the Connecticut CIO. Both were able men with records of activity in a variety of civic works as well as the Democratic party. Rourke was elected to the state House of Representatives in 1958, while Sviridoff was a Lee appointee to the Board of Education. Naming both of them to the CAC had the advantage of avoiding any trouble from splits between the two wings of the labor movement. Neither Rourke nor Sviridoff seemed uneasy about the alliance between Lee and so many local businessmen. Both professed complete confidence in the mayor's dedication to the public interest and to liberal policies. They seemed to know Lee better than the CAC businessmen and to be more at ease with him, and he with them.

The other Yale member beside Griswold was Eugene V. Rostow, then dean of the law school. A well-known liberal, Rostow had been active in civic and political life in New Haven, his home town. He was considered a very effective participant in committee meetings and was appointed to be an advocate for Lee's policies.

Chamber of Commerce leaders objected strenuously to Golden's appointment, partly because of a somewhat vague feeling that he was a sinister figure, partly because it made the group more "political." But Lee insisted:

> Dick felt...that if Golden were not in it, he would be agin it; that it was very important for Dick in his rather bold, new venture of trying to create a nonpartisan, broadly based, strongly business-supported approach to all of these things, not to cut off the Democratic organization from his rear and he felt that with Golden as national committeeman and as the leader of the organization in

---

been reelected since then and appears to be fairly secure, barring an overwhelming Republican victory similar to the one that unseated his predecessor. An ally of Barbieri in the party split in the late 1960s, Giaimo publicly criticized Lee's renewal and antipoverty programs.

[19] Much more than other local ethnic groups, New Haven's Jews appear to have an integrated and elaborate communal life. See Charles Reznikoff, "New Haven: The Jewish Community," *Commentary* (November 1947), 465–77. Shopkeepers in the areas most likely to be redeveloped were almost wholly Jewish and Lee was concerned to avoid wholesale Jewish opposition when these businessmen were displaced.

New Haven on the inside from the beginning that problem would be pretty well ameliorated or wouldn't seriously present itself.

After the first few meetings the CAC businessmen changed their opinion of Golden and came to appreciate his judgment and shrewdness. Lee also invited Golden's opposite number, Frank Lynch. The Republican leader equivocated and then declined. This was not an important disadvantage, however, since nine of the seventeen members of the executive committee were Republicans, although none was active in the party in New Haven.

Eight of the seventeen members of the executive committee lived outside New Haven. Most of the committee members had moved to the area from other parts of the country. Few of them came from wealthy families. Griswold was the only one who was invited to the annual Cotillion.

In most cases the executives' standing in the business community seemed to be based on their personal qualities at least as much as on the size of their firms. The businessmen interviewed in the course of our research emphasized judgment, competence, integrity, and other personal attributes when offering explanations for their colleagues' prestige. These were the most important factors in appointments to the CAC. The personal character of business community standing seems to be the case elsewhere. Kaplan reports that in Newark "there is little correlation between the size of a firm and the influence it wields over" the economic development committee established by prominent businessmen.[20] In Chicago, "the influence of these 'civic leaders' derives from the trust that others have in their judgment and in their disinterestedness. If they get their way, it is likely to be...'by main force of being right' and not by promising rewards or threatening penalties."[21]

Certain institutional considerations also influenced the selection of businessmen. Perhaps the most important one is indicated by the heavy representation of the utilities. Our business respondents believed that the telephone company and the power company were far more influential with businessmen than any other firms. Usually they were unable to give very articulate or convincing reasons for this (or for almost any other generalization) except the observation that utilities are usually very cooperative in any community endeavor. In this situation, of course, a reputation for power was almost as good as the real thing, since the purpose of the CAC was to give Lee's program the most convincing endorsement.

Every major economic and ethnic group in New Haven was represented on the CAC, with the exception of Negroes.[22] This was largely because the

[20] Kaplan, *Urban Renewal Politics,* p. 110.

[21] Banfield, *Political Influence,* pp. 282–83.

[22] Reviewing *Who Governs?* in *Commentary* (May 1962, p. 455), Lewis Coser expressed concern at Dahl's failure to discuss the political role of real estate men in

most likely black candidate—indeed, at that time the only black candidate—already had been appointed Corporation Counsel.[23]

"Action committee" members tended to be people whose professions or avocations were germane to the scope of their respective committees: merchants predominated on the Central Business District committee, social workers on the Human Values committee, and so on. Each committee's manifest assignment was the study of one or two major problems. All members of the CAC were named by the mayor and action committee members were also approved by the executive committee. For the most part these appointees' opinions did not conflict seriously with the administration's major orientations. One chairman described how he chose members of his committee:

> I felt that every committee that was set up should have a very large membership including everybody that anyone could think of that would be remotely helpful or influential or be interested. . . . So we ended up with a very large committee— I would say there must be about 60 or 70 or 80 or perhaps more members who have never been called on to do anything yet and who were invited to join on the ground that their help would be infrequently called on.

This chairman's vague impression of the size of his committee leads one to suspect that he had not given much thought to mobilizing it for action.

By 1957 the total membership of the CAC, including the executive committee, was 432. As Lee had planned, they did not duplicate the Democratic organization. Only 16 were on our list of 497 political "subleaders," people active in the nomination process in either party, and 4 of the 16 were Republicans. The CAC consisted not only of different people, but of people in very different parts of society than members of the political organizations, and thus extended Lee's basis of support. A comparison of the ethnic characteristics of everyone in the CAC and in the political "subleadership" group can be made by examining their names. Almost half of the organization members were Irish or Italian, but only 22 percent of the CAC were.

New Haven. The absence of realtors on the CAC suggests that their treatment in *Who Governs?* was realistic: local real estate interests were not an important factor in urban renewal politics in New Haven. Because the city's open land had been exhausted and its population stable (or declining) for more than 40 years, real estate trading and development were at a minimal level of activity. There were no big operators in the city and, taken as a whole, real estate was not the major business that it is in, say, California.

[23] This was George Crawford, a Yale Law School graduate, one of the founding members of the National Association for the Advancement of Colored People, a prominent expert on municipal law, and a Republican. Crawford retired from his city post in 1961 at the age of 84, was practicing law as late as 1965, and died in 1972.

The CAC had somewhat more Jews than the political organizations, and considerably more Yankees.

Interviews with samples of about one-quarter of the entire CAC and political organization members gave us information on their social status. The party workers' incomes and occupations were remarkably similar to those of the electorate as a whole. The CAC, on the other hand, consisted primarily of people in the upper reaches of society. It included 26 of the 105 members of the economic elite who lived in the New Haven area, and 23 members of the social elite. A third of the CAC membership were in one of the high-prestige professions (mostly doctors and lawyers) or were high-ranking executives, compared to 12 percent of the party subleaders and 5 percent of the electorate. More than half of the CAC made over $10,000 a year, compared to 12 percent of the political subleaders and 6 percent of the registered voters. At the other end of the scale, only 7 percent of the CAC were clerical, sales, or blue-collar workers, occupations that accounted for 60 percent of the electorate and 42 percent of the party activists. Six percent of the CAC members had annual incomes of less than $5,000, while two-fifths of the party workers and almost half of the registered voters fell into this category. These data, summarized in Table 8-1, show the vast disparities in social background between the CAC on the one hand and the city's political activists and registered voters on the other. The large elite representation on the CAC is in part a result of its scarcity in the party organizations.

The CAC's paid staff consisted of an executive director and his secretary. During the period covered by this account the director was H. Gordon Sweet, a socially prominent member of an old New Haven family. Unlike all but one of his executive committee members, Sweet was invited to the Cotillion. His office was down the hall from Logue's and for all practical purposes he was part of the redevelopment chain of command.

When the CAC was founded, Lee and several charter members approached the New Haven Foundation, a local charitable organization, for financial assistance. Falsey, an important official of the foundation, was helpful in these negotiations. The foundation had just received a sizable bequest and was willing to assign part of it to the CAC, which was tax-exempt. The Internal Revenue Service questioned this immunity in 1958 and announced a review of the CAC's status. By then the CAC had succeeded in acquiring other sources of support. At a fund-raising dinner in 1959 local industries contributed $16,000, contractors and architects $6,500, and labor unions $2,000. Despite the eminent businessmen on the CAC, Golden was chosen to solicit funds from the contractors and architects—a revealing indication of relationships in this branch of business and politics. There was some dissatisfaction with the $6,500 contribution in view of the construction boom that redevelopment had stimulated.

TABLE 8-1. Demographic characteristics of CAC members, party sub-leaders, and registered voters

	CAC Members	Party Subleaders[a]	Registered Voters
Occupation[b]			
Major professionals, higher executives, etc.	32%	12%	5%
Managers, administrators, small businessmen	46	24	20
Clerks, wage earners	7	42	60
No answer	15	22	15
	100%	100%	100%
N	115	120	525
Income[b]			
Above $10,000	54%	12%	6%
$5,000–$10,000	30	34	39
Below $5,000	6	39	47
No answer	10	15	8
	100%	100%	100%
N	115	120	525
Ethnicity[c]			
Irish	10%	16%	11%
Italian	12	36	31
Jewish	23	13	15
Other[d]	55	36	43
	100%	101%	100%
N	432	497	525

[a] Includes all partisan local office holders, officials of both parties at the city, ward, and state senatorial district levels, and delegates to the municipal nominating conventions (the Town Committee, in the case of the Democrats, who did not have a separate nominating convention).

[b] Determined from a sample of the CAC and subleader membership who were personally interview.

[c] Determined by examination of names and personal knowledge for the CAC and subleaders, and from questionnaire responses for the voters.

[d] In the CAC the "others" were mostly Yankees, with a sprinkling of Negroes, Poles, and other groups. The Yankees were far less numerous among the subleaders and voters.

The formation and membership of the CAC were announced at a luncheon at the socially prestigious Lawn Club attended by 250 people. The main visual attraction was a dramatic exhibit by the Rotival organization depicting New Haven as it would look after completion of urban renewal. That winter Lee induced Patrick McGinnis, then the president of the New Haven Railroad, to treat 75 politicians and CAC members to a trip in his private railroad car to inspect renewal activities in Philadelphia. The administration took pains to insure that the journey would be convivial. One of the travelers later remarked: "The trip would have been a success if we'd never gotten off the train."

The executive committee began to meet monthly in the mayor's office to discuss matters presented to it by the administration. Every month or two there was a CAC luncheon, with an out-of-town speaker. The mayor usually spoke at these affairs, to which all CAC members were invited and which rarely were attended by less than a hundred people. The action committees also gave lunches from time to time for the benefit of their members. The CAC issued a handsome annual report. Occasional newsletters, announcements, and bulletins on special subjects were sent to members. Reports and statements by CAC officials were publicized in the mass media. In 1961 the CAC had a one-hour documentary movie on New Haven redevelopment produced by the local television station and sponsored by the city's biggest bank, which also made copies of the tape available for showing by local groups. CAC representatives invariably testified at public hearings on relevant subjects. The CAC conducted guided tours for the numerous delegations that came to New Haven to inspect the redevelopment program. It also had a major share in organizing several conferences on redevelopment.

The Lawn Club and the private railroad car symbolize the prestige which the administration tried to confer on the CAC. Public ceremonies—to mark the start or finish of a major undertaking, or on other occasions—invariably featured head-table appearances and speeches by CAC figures. City officials were careful to include flattering references to the CAC in their own public utterances. They succeeded in establishing it as a very important organization.

The Role of the CAC

What part did the CAC play in New Haven's redevelopment program? There is no doubt about the action committees. They were, to quote CAC leaders, "a con game" and "window dressing," little more than a mailing list and a set of letterhead names. Here is a description from one chairman of how his committee operated:

> There are so many people involved [as members of an action committee], it becomes a question whether you can ever get a whole committee together and keep them interested enough in the project to make it worthwhile for them to come. They might come the first time, but if they didn't get anything out of it, they wouldn't come the next time. So we prefer to make progress by working with a small group. Then, when we do have a report to make or a project to launch, what we're apt to do then is have a luncheon meeting…and then make sure that all these people on the committee at least come to the luncheon and

bring other people too. . . . We can say, this is what's been going on . . . a chance to give you a little publicity, have a luncheon meeting and have them hear about it, why we hope they'll go back and talk to their friends, business or socially, why, they'll tell people what's going on.

It is difficult to decide which is more remarkable: the continuing acquiescence in this state of affairs by hundreds of action committee members, or the failure of Lee's political opponents to exploit the situation. In 1958 a downtown merchant furiously resigned from the Central Business District, Traffic and Parking Committee following an unsuccessful attempt to get satisfaction from the mayor's office on his complaint about a parking ticket. He told the newspapers:

I get news releases and fancy brochures and every so often I am invited to a luncheon where we are told what has been decided. I assume I was asked to join the parking committee to contribute my viewpoint as a merchant, but no one has ever tried to find out what my viewpoint is.[24]

One danger to amity in the action committees was the possibility that committee members would become overenthusiastic about their particular area and urge action in excess of the administration's policy. This happened in the middle 1950s when the chairman of the Industrial and Harbor Development Committee encountered firm administration opposition to his proposals for deepening the harbor. Lee and Logue felt that this was economically unfeasible and would divert public attention from programs with higher priorities. After a brief, acrimonious controversy the chairman and one or two other frustrated enthusiasts resigned. Reportedly the mayor once asked an action committee member not to take action on a desire to involve the Human Values Committee in a campaign against racial discrimination in housing.[25]

What about the executive committee, self-described as a "citizen-cabinet for the purposes of the New Haven program"? Some of its members said frankly that it was "little more than a rubber stamp." Others maintained that it played an important role in making policy: "We contribute our experience." But when pressed, they replied like this respondent:

I've often felt that the group as a group is inadequate in the sense that we don't really initiate anything as far as I can recall. . . . We discuss what has

[24] Quoted in the *New Haven Journal-Courier*, 22 February 1958, p. 1. Perhaps because it appeared that the merchant's resignation was due to his pique at being unable to fix a parking ticket, this event drew little public attention and had no visible repercussions.

[25] Reading this sentence in a previous draft, Lee said that he could not remember the event.

been developed by the...Redevelopment Agency or the City Planning Commission.... The Mayor or somebody from one of these groups presents it to us and we discuss it, we analyze it, we modify some of it, we change—

Could you give me an example of some cases where you modified or changed any proposal?

Well, I don't think that I can give you an example of anything where I can say that the commission actually changed a proposal.

You can't?

No, I say actually changed. I don't recall any.

The administration controlled the agenda at executive committee meetings, which were spent discussing the problems the mayor introduced and approving the measures he proposed. Typically, Lee drew attention to an area where local governmental action was desirable. The CAC discussed the problem and then asked the mayor to develop plans to meet it. Concurrently, the mayor presented "draft" plans to the CAC for comments and approval, which was always forthcoming, just as the recommended lines of approach to a problem were the ones that the administration wanted to pursue. From 1954 through 1959 there were 48 meetings of the executive committee. In all this time only one objection (see pp. 262–63) to an administration proposal was voiced at these gatherings. At all other levels of the CAC the city also controlled what subjects were discussed and what recommendations were made. The controversy over deepening the harbor is the only case I know of where an element of the CAC initiated a policy proposal independent of the administration. The fate of this proposal indicates what was wanted from the CAC. Finally, the executive director was in charge of preparing such CAC materials as newsletters and annual reports. His work was approved and often planned by Lee and Logue.

One should not conclude from all this that the CAC contributed little to the success of redevelopment in New Haven. Policies must not only be made but executed; while the CAC played no part in the first process, it was very important in the second. One of its members made this point nicely:

Who do you see as the people on the CAC who are primarily responsible or influential in making these decisions?

Well, I think that the question indicates to me an error on your part...in that it implies the CAC in fact had anything to do with the decision. I think it would be more accurate to say the CAC is a stroke of brilliant policy on the part of the regular municipal administration to set up an organization which has as its basic function getting so many people in the swim...that once they were sold, their area of influence in the aggregate would be so large that you can get a substantial portion of the thinking public behind all these projects.

As this indicates, one function of the CAC was to sell city policies to the elements represented on it, particularly leading business and professional men. By virtue of their selection and agreement to serve, the executive committee members were in sympathy with Lee's policy goals and somewhat precommitted to the general outlines of his policies. The monthly meetings were an ideal medium for inducing assent to specific programs. The plans themselves were good merchandise, thoroughly worked out by an extraordinarily competent and publicity-conscious staff. Lee and Logue were skilled persuaders, adept at interesting, dramatic presentations. In the closed meetings in the mayor's impressive office listeners were encouraged to feel that they were privileged to hear confidential plans because of their special status as community leaders chosen to help save New Haven. In this ideal setting Lee and his staff could make their case without the harassment, counterargument, space limitations, and competition for attention that would plague any attempt to explain complicated plans in public. The complexity of redevelopment made radio or television impractical media for presenting major proposals, while the local newspapers were unlikely to be sympathetic.

The CAC was a means of selling not only the city's plans but its officials as well. The monthly meetings were a showcase for the talents of Lee and his chief lieutenants, helping to build confidence that big enterprises could be entrusted to city hall, that if the mayor demolished large and valuable tracts of real estate he could be counted on to put the pieces together again. Every CAC member whom we interviewed, in explaining the success of redevelopment in New Haven, dwelt on the theme of official competence. They were enormously impressed by the technical ability, judgment, and executive skill of the redevelopment officials, as well as by Lee's leadership:

> Being a Republican myself, I don't like to talk that way, but basically I think that Lee has vision and he has power and drive and he has youth. And the whole thing combined has made this thing come to be a reality rather than just a vision, it seems to me.

Once convinced, the well-briefed CAC members were a channel of communication to their friends and colleagues. There were two publics for this interpersonal propaganda, or two kinds of response. One public was the electorate, which responded by voting and expressions of opinion. The CAC was an efficient mechanism for "retailing" by word of mouth. The other set of publics was those groups whose support was necessary for the success of particular measures. Although redevelopment uses compulsory methods (such as eminent domain) to stimulate free market processes, it cannot succeed unless facilitating private decisions are made. The CAC was a means of encouraging such decisions. Its members were often sought out for explanations of specific problems relevant to their professional concerns. After the announcement of the Oak Street Project several businessmen expressed to Hook their fears about the project's effect on underground utility lines. His reassurances carried added weight because of his position as chairman of the board of the power company. Whenever a major undertaking was first made public, CAC members typically did missionary work for it among their friends and business associates.

The executive committee members' high prestige not only made them effective opinion leaders, but helped confer legitimacy on the administration's policies. Businessmen's views carried special weight on policies dealing with land values, business opportunities, costs, profits, and efficient management, that is, with redevelopment. Just as, in some circumstances, governmental actions acquire legitimacy from the democratic ritual, so, in other circumstances, they may do so from their apparent "businesslike" character, attested by their approval by businessmen. In this sense it may be useful to talk of a "business community." When their involvement in an issue is not central, many people who are impressed by the values and goals of private business may conceive of a local community of businessmen and be guided by what they think its opinions are on issues that seem relevant to business. On the other hand, when an issue becomes more salient and particular to an individual, or outside the province of business, then this vague reference group would become less relevant.

The line between prestige and pressure is sometimes difficult to find. When the chairman of the CAC wrote to John Day Jackson about his editorial policies on redevelopment and specifically associated half a dozen eminent local businessmen with his complaint, was he telling the publisher that powerful men viewed his actions with disfavor or merely using their names as a prestige endorsement for Lee's program?[26] One businessman who was considering a public protest against the CAC described his second thoughts to an interviewer:

> Then I stopped and analyzed the situation. Who were the big guns on the CAC? Frank O'Brion, president of my bank and a good customer. Lucius Rowe, president of the telephone company and a good customer.

After these reflections the businessman decided to keep his objections to himself.

Representing every segment of the community, the CAC was also a body of hostages for Lee. As Freese put it, "If anyone throws a rock at the program, they're bound to hit one of their own." In the CAC's heyday in the late 1950s, Republican politicians were reluctant to criticize Lee's redevelopment program. The salience of the program made it easy for him to construe

---

[26] Because of his monopoly of the local newspapers, Jackson was not vulnerable to coercion by advertisers. Indeed, his power over advertisers was thought to be greater than theirs over him.

general attacks on his performance as attacks on redevelopment, which in turn could be characterized as reflections on the formidable array of personages lined up in its support. The Republicans' best chance was to criticize the mayor's execution of the program, but of course it was difficult to call it "unbusinesslike" when so many prominent businessmen endorsed it. Nor were the Republicans in a good position to make political capital of the big-business emphasis on the CAC. The only public criticism on this point came from the "Independent Democratic" mayoralty candidate in 1957, Samuel Malkan, who characterized the CAC as "made up for the most part of non-residents who get into their Cadillacs at 5 o'clock and drive to their houses" in the suburbs.[27]

The Lee administration convinced the people and press that the CAC was a viable force in the city's civic life. Journalistic accounts of New Haven's urban renewal program stressed "extraordinary citizen participation." Many national organizations gave the CAC awards and citations. One of the most notable of these was an "All-America City" award presented to New Haven in January 1959, after the annual contest sponsored by the National Municipal League and *Look* magazine. The city was honored "in recognition of progress achieved through intelligent citizen action." Cities are not invited to enter this contest; they must apply. It was typical of the Lee administration that receipt of the award was the occasion for a four-page memorandum listing dozens of publicity measures to exploit the happy event. Many of these, such as shoulder patches for policemen, were adopted.

Once the CAC gained acceptance it was the principal mechanism for registering "community support" when such evidence was required, as in dealing with the state and federal government. (One item in the "workable program" required of all cities receiving federal urban renewal grants was evidence of "citizen participation.") CAC businessmen were excellent witnesses before congressional committees because their support of urban renewal was thought to be more impressive to conservative legislators than similar remarks from a Democratic politician. There were many audiences that regarded businessmen as peculiarly prestigious, and Lee made full use of his allies in this regard, although he usually found it difficult to persuade businessmen to testify in Washington or to make similarly official or "political" appearances. It was, of course, very difficult for anyone outside New Haven to assert that the CAC was anything less than what it claimed to be. Lee's use of the CAC to exhibit what "the people of New Haven" thought also had the advantage of insuring that "the people" spoke with one voice.

In some respects the CAC was a source of useful practical suggestions. Its members commanded a variety of talent and expertise, much of it relevant to one phase or another of redevelopment. On several occasions CAC members

27 Quoted in the Bridgeport *Sunday Herald,* 27 October 1957, p. NH-3.

contributed their services or those of their subordinates toward the solution of particular problems. Legal advice contributed through the CAC was important in drafting a bill which, passed in amended form by the Connecticut General Assembly, authorized formation of a public authority to develop swamp land within the confines of New Haven and several contiguous towns to the north.

The most important example of direct CAC participation in local affairs was the transformation of 21 acres of marshy surplus land into a light industrial park for businessmen displaced by the Oak Street Project. The CAC executive director, H. Gordon Sweet, directed this effort and made considerable use of technical aid donated by CAC members, under the overall control of municipal redevelopment officials.

The CAC also provided certain peripheral returns to Lee, most obviously as a source of patronage completely under his control and thus not subject to the wishes of the Democratic organization. Printing and other services were contracted for on a political basis. Since the CAC had the reputation of being a blue ribbon group its action committees were ideal for giving recognition to party workers. Appointment to one of these groups, composed largely of upper-middle-class people, conferred a good measure of prestige, unaccompanied by power. Because there was no fixed limit to these bodies' membership, any single appointment did not disappoint another deserving worker. This consideration was limited, of course, by the need to avoid cheapening action committee membership. Nevertheless, the CAC was a useful source of extra patronage.

The CAC was intended to connect the administration to existing interaction patterns in the business community, to exploit those patterns and expand them to include city officials and, incidentally, prominent nonbusiness leaders. The CAC unquestionably accomplished this, but even after more than three years, the quality of knowledge and acquaintanceship among its members was often astonishingly low. Our interviews with CAC members revealed that many of them did not know the names of various prominent figures in the city's public and business life. Some of this ignorance doubtless reflected the gulfs between New Haven's business, political, and academic worlds. Thus the president of one large industrial firm, an active participant in many business and civic associations and a critic of businessmen who shrank from such endeavors, did not recognize the name of Frank Lynch, who had been the local Republican leader for 20 years. By the same token few of the businessmen on the CAC had known Golden before the CAC brought them together. Griswold, who attended nearly every meeting, told Dahl and Polsby of his gratifying associations with colleagues on the CAC and said that he often had a fond image of them all sitting together around the conference table in the mayor's office. But except for friends he had made before the CAC was founded, Griswold was unable to identify a single member of the executive committee. A number of members confused Mitchell Sviridoff, the statewide labor leader whom they saw at least once a month, with his brother Harry, a realtor who worked part-time for the Redevelopment Agency.

More surprising was the remarkable ignorance and lack of familiarity among the business and professional members of the CAC. A prominent attorney, senior partner in one of the city's two leading firms, could not remember Frank O'Brion's name, although both men attended the monthly meetings. Other businessmen had similar blind spots in their knowledge of leading personalities in civic and business life. These were not the rule but they recurred often enough to indicate that even in this stable and compact city of 150,000 people, the quality and quantity of interactions among "the elite" were far slighter than one might expect.

It seems likely that this ignorance was not confined to the problem of who was who. We gathered no data on the knowledge about local affairs possessed by any of our collections of elite respondents, nor do the interviews reveal this information. But I was impressed by an episode I witnessed in the mayor's office one afternoon, and think that it probably was not atypical. The president of a local bank had come in to discuss a problem with Lee. As he was leaving, he remarked on the enormous wall map displaying various redevelopment and highway projects. The mayor began to describe some of these: Route 91, an eight-lane freeway that would replace slums and form a barrier between a new industrial park on one side and a restored residential neighborhood on the other; a project to renew another large slice of the central business district; and so on. None of these various schemes was a secret; some of them in fact were well under way. Yet the banker scarcely knew the boundaries and ultimate purpose of the Oak Street Project, and had only the sketchiest and most inaccurate knowledge of most of the other developments. His bank, of course, should have been vitally concerned with changing land uses and values, investment opportunities, and other aspects of the local business scene. He may have been a uniquely ill-informed businessman. On the other hand, he may not be too unusual.

These various types of civic ignorance have several implications. For one thing, the value of organizations like the CAC is evident: where the normal processes of information and association are so deficient, both the need to "educate" important people and the opportunity to do so can be exploited by clever politicians. Second, various scholarly assumptions about the character of community life may stand in need of revision. For example, assumptions about the cohesiveness of the rich, which have taken a beating on other grounds, may also be deficient in that the rich do not even know each other. Third, a variety of research methods which assume that respondents know what they are talking about when asked to generalize may not produce results in which a prudent person would have confidence. Thus one drawback to asking prominent citizens to name the most powerful people in their city is that these informants might not be too good at remembering names—a failing that most of us can appreciate.[28]

The CAC as a Political Coalition

Lee had several levels of business support. Many businessmen approved his redevelopment program without knowing a great deal about detailed policies. A few, mainly those on the CAC, played a very active role in bringing projects to fruition and were an important element in the redevelopment coalition. Most of these activists, plus some other businessmen, extended their participation from support of Lee's policies to support of Lee the candidate. Almost all the businessmen on the CAC were Republicans and several of them were active in the party in their respective suburban communities. Yet without exception they were Lee's fervent supporters in municipal elections and some declared that they would be equally enthusiastic if he were to run for senator or governor. Many of them made campaign contributions up to $500.

Beginning in 1955 CAC members solicited contributions for Lee from their fellow businessmen, most of whom had been apathetic about municipal politics or had contributed reflexively to the Republicans before 1955 or 1957. (These supporters wanted their help to be inconspicuous, and several of them declined to be chairman of Citizens for Lee in 1955.) By 1957 Lee felt sufficiently confident of his appeal to the business community to mail letters requesting contributions to virtually every bank and utility director in New Haven. In that year he and the Democratic party took in over $75,000 in contributions, while the Republicans collected approximately $31,000 and reported a deficit of $12,000 on official expenditures of $43,000. They listed only six contributions of over $250, while the Democrats had dozens.

The CAC businessmen we interviewed agreed that the local Republican party was indifferently led and apparently incapable of providing leadership. They did not express high opinions of Celentano's abilities either. They were also scornful and contemptuous of the local newspapers. Even the most conservative ones scorned Jackson's views, which many of them attributed to an excessive concern with his taxes. They had no faith in the newspapers and felt that Jackson's preoccupation with economy had weakened his influence in the community since Lee's inauguration. One prominent and conservative

---

[28] I have discussed elsewhere the likelihood that such informants would be inadequate sources of generalizations on politics. See "Reputation and Reality in the Study of 'Community Power,'" *American Sociological Review*, 25 (October 1960), 636–44; and "A Plea for a Decent Burial," *ibid.*, 27 (December 1962), 841–47.

manufacturer said of the elderly Jackson, "I think he's one of the most undesirable elements in our whole community," and thought that the publisher's views on government spending were

> just a bug he has. He just feels the tax rate should be half what it is; we just spend money on a lot of useless things...my gosh, when he starts attacking putting up skating rinks for the kids and things like that, he's going too far.[29]

As the focus of Lee's program shifted from the downtown projects to residential rehabilitation, and then to the poverty program and other problems less interesting to most businessmen, how much of their support remained? Some lost interest, but others stayed. Some were "converted" by their exposure to city hall; some came to realize that the different aspects of a comprehensive renewal program should not or could not be separated, that poverty, unemployment, slums, and downtown prosperity are related. Moreover, the more socially-oriented turn which Lee's policies took in the 1960s benefited from the generalized aura of sanctity which the CAC helped to provide for redevelopment, as well as from his personal prestige. Public perceptions were not so acute as to make fine distinctions between the various elements in his public image.

The Public Utilities and Redevelopment

At the innermost circle of Lee's alliance with business was the Southern New England Telephone Company, which worked very closely with his administration for several years in the late 1950s. The telephone company first became deeply involved in urban renewal when it helped guarantee the success of the Oak Street Project by agreeing to buy a sizable parcel of land there. The firm's president, Lucius Rowe, became chairman of the CAC in 1956. He devoted considerable time to his CAC duties and was helpful to city hall in a variety of ways. If the CAC was a body of general character witnesses for Lee's program, the telephone company was a more specific guarantor. Some businessmen were impressed by the company's eminence.

[29] Republican politicians thought that, despite Jackson's attitudes, the local newspapers were biased in favor of Lee, that his many friends at the papers consistently managed to present him and his activities in a favorable light. This was certainly not my impression, nor that of Lee and his associates. While Lee did have connections on the two papers, he felt that the press was an enemy to be manipulated and neutralized, not an ally. The papers did not explain the underlying issues and purposes of urban renewal, zoning reform, and other controversial policies; and they pounced eagerly when one of Lee's programs seemed to be in trouble.

Some believed, mainly as an article of faith, that it was more powerful than other firms and hence not to be defied without risk. Rowe was an effective adviser, representative, and intermediary.[30] His help was particularly effective with potential opponents of administration measures in the business world or people still dubious of city officials "who never met a payroll." (In 1959 one distinguished banker, discussing his major reservation about Lee, said, "I don't think Dick has ever had any real business training.") When the occasion seemed to call for implicit threats, the telephone company's economic influence could be invoked either with individual firms or in the deliberations of business groups.

The telephone company's help was most important in winning agreement with redevelopment among local businessmen, but it was not limited to this role. Undoubtedly Rowe and perhaps other executives made campaign contributions. The company's publicity department helped produce campaign material in at least the 1957 mayoralty election. Its publicity director, Raymond A. Loring, who called himself the "dean of the public relations community" in New Haven, coordinated Lee's campaign publicity in 1957 and was a close and prestigious adviser to the mayor on other occasions.

Why was the telephone company (and, to a lesser extent, the power company) so helpful to Lee? Why would Rowe, a Republican, give so much support to policies associated with liberal Democrats? Part of the explanation lies in Rowe's character: he is an aggressive, energetic, determined man. Although reluctant to take the chairmanship, once he did, he was fully committed to it. Moreover, he was convinced that Lee's program was good both for New Haven and for his firm.

Public utilities customarily are more involved than most businesses in community activities, as welll as in politics.[31] They are regulated by the government and receive certain privileges from it. By state law telephone companies in Connecticut were exempted from paying local taxes on their "personal property," their equipment. Instead, they made payments to the state. Street paving and other housekeeping operations that might disturb their lines bring utilities into routine contact with city hall. Being interested in securing the best treatment, they seek cordial relations with politicians and try to maintain a friendly climate of public opinion. Furthermore, utilities are concerned with the local market to which their operations are confined. Their monopoly position and the absence of unsatisfied demand means that they can expand chiefly through population growth and industrial or

[30] Lee often used his labor leader allies as ambassadors when the city had labor trouble.

[31] The utilities' involvement in local public affairs contrasts with the almost complete inactivity of executives from Winchester, the biggest employer in town. Winchester's guns and ammunition were sold all over the world, not just in New Haven, and as merely one branch of a larger corporation, it had fewer local ties.

commercial development. The telephone and power companies followed a policy of encouraging their executives to participate in civic activities.

Urban renewal, which would bring business development and hence greater use of electricity and telephones, promised great opportunities to the utilities. Once the telephone company decided to buy land in Oak Street, it had an additional specific reason for supporting that project. Urban renewal would also pose problems, for any extensive rearrangement of the city's physical plant had many ramifications for utility lines. Thus there were good reasons for the utilities not only to support urban renewal, but to maximize their influence over project execution. Lee may have mentioned these considerations to utility officials; perhaps they needed no reminders of their opportunities and vulnerabilities and decided spontaneously to participate so as to protect their interests.

One important example of the utilities' interest in friendly relations with city hall concerned the problem of underground utility cables, which are usually laid under streets and must be relocated when street patterns are changed, as in the Church Street Project. State law required that utilities be compensated for the entire cost of moving conduits disrupted by highway construction but said nothing about the effects of redevelopment. The utility companies asked the city for compensation. After some debate within the administration on the legal basis of this claim, the city negotiated an agreement with the utilities to pay them half the cost of relocation as a project cost, of which two-thirds would be paid by the federal government. Federal officials refused to approve this arrangement, on the grounds that the city was not legally obligated to make such compensation. The utilities then had a bill introduced in the state legislature requiring compensation for public utilities for half the cost of relocating underground lines displaced by redevelopment. Local public agencies throughout the state considered New Haven the leader in urban renewal and consequently many of them asked the city's officials for their opinion of the proposed legislation. The reply was always that it seemed a fair and reasonable provision. The utilities' measure was passed in 1959. By that time the cost of utility conduit relocation in the Church Street Project was estimated at $400,000. The new law saved the utilities half of that, and the federal government paid two-thirds of the city's one-half share.

City hall and the two utilities collaborated in plans to develop the Quinnipiac Valley, a 13-square-mile expanse of intermittently soggy meadows stretching from the tip of New Haven northward through three adjoining towns. A bill authorizing establishment of a Quinnipiac Valley Development Corporation (QVDC) was suggested by the city, drafted with the help of power company executives, and passed with some amendments by the state legislature. The three smaller towns in the QVDC tended to be jealous and suspicious of their high-powered neighbor, but since New Haven had so much more expertise, it took responsibility for the lion's share of the staff work. In turn, much of the work was done by industrial development experts in the power company. The benefits to the two utilities of developing the Quinnipiac Valley were obvious, but they could not have formed and participated in the QVDC directly. It was one of the fruits of their collaboration with the Lee administration.

Although the administration's close relations with the telephone company were familiar to the politically knowledgeable, it was difficult for any of Lee's major opponents to attack him on this score. At that time there was no significant radical activity in New Haven; indeed, Lee was at the leftward end of the spectrum. By the time a radical opposition arose the telephone company had terminated its active alliance with the mayor. The newspapers were much too respectful of big business to cast aspersions. The Republicans, of course, were in a similar dilemma. Michael DePalma, the only Republican alderman to survive the 1957 election, hinted during the campaign that the telephone company had received favored treatment from the city, but did not supply specifics. To the best of my knowledge this was the only public criticism of the entente during its existence.

The Curse of Politics and the Decline of the CAC

In a nonpartisan way, businessmen...had done much to support the city renewal movement, but they did not like hobnobbing with politicians or taking sides, and until only a few years ago it was still regarded as somewhat disreputable for a businessman to get very close to City Hall.[32]

There was little explicit political color to the CAC, whose members mostly regarded it as a wholly nonpartisan organization. Executive committee members, particularly the businessmen, told us approvingly how free of political motivations the mayor's calculations were. In 1958, however, Lee brought the CAC much too close to city hall and caused it to take sides in an open partisan conflict. Even worse, the CAC found itself on the losing side.

The issue was Lee's attempt to revise the city charter. At the October 1958 meeting of the executive committee, two or three weeks before the proposed new charter would be voted on by the electorate, Lee suggested that the group discuss the new charter freely and consider whether it should take a position on it. He then made a long speech in favor of an "adequate instrument" of government. After a lengthy discussion, a motion that the CAC support the new charter passed unanimously. It was decided to send

---

[32] The Editors of Fortune, *The Expanding Metropolis*, p. xviii.

a statement on the CAC's position on the charter to all members of the executive committee for their comments and criticisms. A few days later the CAC's endorsement was released to the public with this statement:

> The Citizens Action Commission is not concerned with political issues; it is a non-partisan group whose chief interest is in the continued progress of the New Haven community through urban renewal. Believing that this progress depends on adoption of the proposed Charter, the Citizens Action Commission, in its concern for the welfare of a community in which we all have a vital stake, has adopted the following Resolution and calls upon Citizens Action Commission and other non-partisan groups in the City to join in supporting this position.

The announcement was sent to all the 400-plus CAC members, as well as to the newspapers. The CAC's action was reported in a very short news item on page 5 of the *Register*.[33] It had no perceptible impact on the electorate, which rejected the charter proposal by a two-to-one ratio.

The New Haven Republican party had been vehemently opposed to charter revision, terming it a flagrant attempt by the Democrats to give themselves an unfair advantage. A few weeks after the election Henry DeVita, chairman of the Republican Town Committee, issued a statement claiming (correctly) that the CAC's endorsement had been made without the support of most of its several hundred members, who had not even been notified that the issue was being considered. Several members of the executive committee said publicly that they had not known about the endorsement and were opposed to "involving the CAC in politics." After a brief flurry of public statements the controversy flickered down, leaving no evident damage to the CAC's reputation.

Several of the organization's leading members, including its chairman, were profoundly disturbed by the affair. It was one thing for a member of the executive committee to make a discreet campaign contribution and another to seem to be part of a political front group. A number of ordinary CAC members also expressed their displeasure. Some CAC leaders evidently began to feel that they had been too responsive to the mayor for some time, and not just on the charter issue. The tone of CAC meetings changed in 1959; arguments and anxiety replaced the old jolly amity. It is impossible to know whether this development represented embarrassment at the public controversy or an awakening to the ways in which the CAC had been manipulated.[34] In any event, Rowe evidently felt that he had been used. About this time Sweet left his position as executive director to become an official of the Redevelopment Agency. Having appointed a committee to recommend a

---

[33] *New Haven Evening Register,* 30 October 1958.

[34] Some of the dissension on the CAC may have reflected general nervousness at delays in the Church Street Project. See pp. 340–43.

reorganization of the CAC, Rowe also resigned. He soon ceased to play an important part in urban renewal or to have a close relationship with the mayor.

The reorganization, announced in 1959, brought a number of structural changes to the CAC. It also revealed that the organization intended to be more independent of the city administration. The new executive director was chosen by a committee of CAC members. The executive committee became a board of directors. Henceforth directors would be elected by all CAC members at the annual meeting, not appointed by the mayor. There were no longer so many important personages on the board. The CAC was not as close to city hall, nor did it take on new roles. In 1960 it received about $13,000 in contributions from industries and other such sources, compared to $33,000 in 1959. This loss in income was not compensated and left the CAC with a 1960 deficit of more than $11,000.

By the early 1960s the CAC's image was badly tarnished: "It had served Lee's purposes in urban renewal but in serving them it had lessened its credibility and effectiveness." Its "political currency had been debased" and its plausibility as an independent political force was greatly diminished.[35] The CAC lingered on through the decade and finally went out of existence in 1969. I do not know what functions, if any, the CAC served after 1958. Despite its inglorious end, it played a crucial role in the early days of the city's redevelopment program and helped to produce a continuing favorable orientation toward urban renewal.

The CAC as a Ruling Elite

In *Who Governs?* Dahl interpreted the facts about the CAC in much the same fashion that I have here, but some of his critics have drawn very different conclusions: rather than being Lee's creature, the CAC represented his masters; rather than being so powerful (and persuasive) that the CAC always agreed with him, Lee was so weak that he proposed to it nothing but policies congenial to its big-business members. Perhaps the best-known statement of this view is in Peter Bachrach and Morton S. Baratz's "Two Faces of Power":

> That the CAC did not initiate or veto actual proposals by the mayor was to Dahl evidence enough that the CAC was virtually powerless; it might as plausibly be evidence that the CAC was (in itself or in what it represented) so powerful that Lee ventured nothing it would find worth quarreling with.

[35] These quotations and the characterization of the CAC's slipping reputation are from Russell D. Murphy, *Political Entrepreneurs and Urban Poverty* (Lexington, Mass.: D. C. Heath Company, 1971), p. 39.

How...can a judgment be made as to the relative influence of Mayor Lee and the CAC without knowing (through prior study of the political and social views of all concerned) the proposals that Lee did *not* make because he anticipated that they would provoke strenuous opposition, and, perhaps, sanctions on the part of the CAC?[36]

One assumption here, of course, is that the CAC was acting as an "executive committee of the bourgeoisie" to look after the interests of the upper class, which is assumed to be united. But the business members of the CAC were not quite a representative sample of the economic elite, for they shared certain traits that were not universal among the city's businessmen: they were favorably inclined toward the mayor or his goals and willing to be identified with his administration. Thus personal or political enemies like John Day Jackson were not members (indeed, they were not asked), nor were men like the anonymous executives who ran the Winchester plant.

This argument also overlooks the extent to which Lee persuaded the CAC members: first, to join the organization at all; and second, to support particular proposals. As we have seen, it took him nine months to find a chairman, for he had great difficulty convincing a suitable candidate that massive redevelopment was feasible and that he could carry out such a program. Before his election urban renewal had languished in New Haven, as in almost all cities. Most big businessmen were indifferent to the problems and dubious about redevelopment as a solution. Thus if Lee were the creature of the CAC, instead of the other way around, it is difficult to explain why he had so much trouble starting it and why he persevered until he had succeeded in finding a chairman. Do politicians usually insist on forging the chains that bind them?

Having induced CAC members to make a general commitment to his program, Lee repeatedly persuaded them to endorse his specific plans and help secure community acceptance for them. The CAC could not be taken wholly for granted, particularly when details of a proposal might affect their interests. Lee was very sensitive to what the CAC would accept and often spent months laying the groundwork for a scheme like the Church Street Project that might well have been condemned if it had been suddenly presented.

The importance of this painstaking preparation is suggested by the only conflict between the administration and the CAC in the first four years of the CAC's existence. During the summer and fall of 1957 one of the principal features of the Church Street Project was a new department store to be built by the R. H. Macy Company. Macy officials were afraid that this site, three blocks from the Green, was somewhat distant from the center of the city's

[36] Peter Bachrach and Morton S. Baratz, "The Two Faces of Power," *American Political Science Review*, 56 (December 1962), 952 (emphasis in the original).

commercial life. They insisted that one of the intervening streets be closed for a block, thus creating an impression of greater proximity to the rest of the central business district. The matter had not been decided finally and had been kept confidential, but the city had considered the step to the extent of showing the closing of George Street on some maps.

When the executive director of the Revelopment Agency, H. Ralph Taylor, briefed the CAC at its November 1957 meeting, he inadvertently took with him a map that showed George Street closed. This did not escape William Bell, the president of the power company, whose offices were at the corner where George Street would end. Bell protested vehemently, as did Lucius Rowe. The two men reminded the mayor that their firms were the city's biggest taxpayers. Other members joined in. Rowe then caustically invited Taylor to attend future meetings to discuss any other surprises which the city might have in store. The next month he and Bell complained that the minutes of the previous meeting, which as usual were written under Logue's direction, did not accurately reflect the discussion on George Street. Bell added that although the city's proposals had previously been unopposed, the situation was now definitely changing. At his insistence an "extension to the minutes" was prepared to describe the previous month's proceedings more accurately.

After the November controversy the city made further studies of the problem. But the conflict between Lee and his closest big business allies ended when Macy withdrew from the project for the time being. Since it had been the only source of pressure for the closing, there was no reason for the administration to press the point. Commenting on the incident afterward, Lee said that he would have given in to Bell and Rowe. I think it likely that their reaction was due in large measure to the shock of seeing plans, in the apparent state of finality represented by a map, about which they had not been "consulted" and for which they had not been prepared. Whenever these niceties were followed, agreement was always forthcoming.

The evidence about the CAC presented here applies not just to its business members, but to all the other segments of the community represented on its executive committee. If Bachrach and Baratz's criterion is to be applied evenly, one must conclude that not only businessmen, but also labor unions, Jews, Italians, or various other interests were really so powerful that Lee proposed nothing that they would oppose.[37]

It would be more fruitful to consider not the innumerable things that Lee *might* have proposed and accomplished, but rather what actually did happen in New Haven, and how it came about. The municipal government did carry out an unprecedentedly large urban renewal program. The primary cause of

[37] For a discussion of this and other deficiencies in the line of thought represented by Bachrach and Baratz's article, see my "Nondecisions and the Study of Local Politics," *American Political Science Review,* 65 (December 1971), 1063–80.

these events was the mayor. Devotees of the belief that businessmen control politics everywhere in America might argue that the New Haven urban renewal program was a product of the local business community's domination, exercised so covertly that Dahl, Polsby, and I (who were looking for it) could not detect it. But this proposition has to carry the sizable burden of an assumption that New Haven's businessmen are unique, for their city's urban renewal program has not been approached in magnitude anywhere else in the country. It is easy to show that Lee was an unusual mayor. It would be neither easy nor plausible to make this argument about the New Haven business community.

III achievement and frustration in policy innovation

9 *the beginnings of urban renewal*

In 1955, as it had been for generations past, the Oak Street district was New Haven's worst slum. A decade later it was the site of a huge office building, three high-rise apartment houses, office and retail developments, and the tag-end of a ten-lane freeway that linked central New Haven with the city's metropolitan area. The clearance and reconstruction of Oak Street was the city's first urban renewal project. It was a source of experience for redevelopment officials, a proving ground for new techniques in everything from public relations to interagency coordination, a lesson in the political rewards and hazards of redevelopment, and a demonstration to the city's voters, business community, and Democratic machine that the Lee administration was committed to and competent at urban renewal. These subjects have been discussed sequentially in previous chapters; here they are blended and given substance in a description of the first years of the Oak Street Project.

The Early History of the Oak Street Project

The Oak Street area had been the first home in New Haven for many immigrants. Irishmen, Germans, and Italians had lingered in its short, narrow streets and crowded tenements before moving on. Many Russian and Polish Jews who fled pogroms from 1890 to 1910 settled there; for a generation or more they were the largest bloc in the neighborhood. Negroes were the most recent and least transient newcomers to settle around Oak Street. By the 1950s the area was half black.

Oak Street had never been a particularly pleasant place to live. By the turn of the century it was a slum and deterioration continued as the years passed. Its black residents, more permanently handicapped than the earlier arrivals, could not as easily find homes elsewhere in the city. This drove rents up and led to worse overcrowding, since families paying exorbitant prices for housing could make ends meet only by sharing their quarters. As many as 11 people lived in two rooms. Only 29 of the 694 dwelling units in the Oak Street Project area were occupied by their owners. Thus neither the market nor their own comfort induced property owners to maintain their aging tenements. Thirty-nine percent of the dwelling units were dilapidated or lacked running water; 86 percent of all the buildings used for residential

267

purposes were substandard.[1] When these tenements were pulled down, the rubble emitted a fecal stench until it was hauled away. The neighborhood boasted one of the city's two public baths as well as a number of dubious saloons, and a heavy concentration of prostitutes, derelicts, and petty gambling houses. Not unexpectedly, Oak Street received a disproportionate amount of attention from the police, fire, health, and welfare departments.

Oak Street's central location heightened its blighting impact on the rest of the city. The area ran south and west from the edge of the central business district to the sprawling complex formed by the Grace-New Haven Hospital and the Yale Medical School. Oak Street was such an effective barrier between this area and the rest of Yale to the north that nurses and female graduate students rarely ventured from one part of the university to the other after sundown. A tangle of narrow, twisting streets interrupted road patterns to the north and south, funneling northbound traffic through a congested intersection at Congress Square, where a number of other streets met.

The Oak Street area had been an obvious disgrace for generations. In 1907 the mayor named a committee of prominent citizens to consider planning for the city's future. The committee in turn commissioned Cass Gilbert, an architect, and Frederick Law Olmstead, the famous landscape planner, to study the city's needs. The Gilbert-Olmstead Report, issued in 1910, was a comprehensive master plan. One of its recommendations was that the Oak Street slums be cleared. Similar recommendations were made over the years. In 1941 the first of Maurice Rotival's master plans called for wholesale demolition on Oak Street. None of these proposals included plans for financing, and nothing was done.

As we have seen, dealing with Oak Street was the first task of the New Haven Redevelopment Agency when it was established in 1950. The first chairman of the Agency was Myres McDougal, a strong-willed Yale professor of international law. The other voting members were Harry Barnett, manager of a large downtown clothing store; John Ingmanson, a manufacturer; Frank O'Brion, president of the Tradesmen's National Bank; and Matthew Ruoppolo, business agent of a teamsters union local. The executive director, appointed in part through McDougal's good offices, was Samuel Spielvogel, a former assistant professor of city planning at Yale.

Mayor Celentano did not involve himself much in redevelopment. It seems likely that he was dubious about the political merits and feasibility of the issue, but there is no indication that he impeded the Redevelopment Agency. Spielvogel, whose prior experience was in making plans rather than executing them, reportedly tended to be overawed by the difficulties posed by federal procedures and requirements. Members of the Agency could not assume a

---

[1] These and other unattributed data on the project area are from the New Haven Redevelopment Agency. The right-of-way for the Oak Street Connector, which was in similar condition, is not included in these figures.

leadership role, nor did any of them have the political skills required to take charge of the program. Early in 1952 the Agency obtained a survey and planning grant of $78,734 for Oak Street. Spielvogel then turned to the task of completing the final project report. He was still at it in 1954 when Lee replaced Celentano. Oak Street seemed no closer to clearance than it had been when the Agency was founded more than three years earlier. But during this period another series of events had brought a threat to New Haven; their eventual solution opened the door to widespread renewal of the central city.

The Oak Street Connector

Before the war there were long-range plans for a great toll road across Connecticut from New York to the Rhode Island border. In 1941 Rotival's first master plan for New Haven had recommended routing this turnpike along the west side of the harbor, whence a connecting road would carry traffic to the central business district. By the end of the decade the state's plans for the Connecticut Turnpike were well advanced. It would run along the harbor's edge, but there would be no connecting road to the central business district (CBD). Instead, New Haven traffic would join the turnpike by several roads in the Wooster Square area, at the head of the harbor, in a mixed residential, commercial, and industrial district more than a mile from the CBD. More than 30,000 cars daily would stream through a concentrated area whose network of narrow streets was already congested and inadequate for existing traffic. Internal traffic patterns and access to the CBD would be ruined, while it would be almost impossible to enter or leave the turnpike in New Haven. Furthermore, from this point another freeway—now called Interstate Route 91—would run north to Hartford. This road, to be built a few years later, would be routed just to the west of Wooster Square itself. This alignment would cut the square off from the CBD, destroy many good houses, isolate the remaining ones, and eliminate the square as an integrating neighborhood focus. In 1951 Norris Andrews, the New Haven City Plan Director, submitted to the state an alternate proposal, calling for a road connecting the turnpike with the CBD and relocation of Route 91 half a mile to the east, where it would separate Wooster Square from an expanding blighted industrial area rather than squeeze the two together. The state rejected this plan.

Such controversy was and is all too common; disputes about routing have characterized relations between municipal governments and state highway agencies for decades. The highway engineers thought primarily of their specialty: devising the most feasible means to move automobiles rapidly and cheaply across the state; they were uninterested in conflicting goals advanced by men unfamiliar with traffic problems. In addition to this discrepancy of purposes, the Connecticut Highway Department had had many disappointing experiences in making agreements with city governments. Partly because of rapid turnover resulting from the two-year term, municipal officials had a distressing tendency to ignore commitments made by their predecessors. Consequently, the highway department had become accustomed to making plans that did not rely on municipal cooperation.[2]

As the highway department was unwilling to change its plans, the city's only hope was to present detailed proposals showing the technical feasibility of its alternative routes and thus, by talking their language, force the engineers to respond. This required a high level of expertise, but New Haven had no traffic engineer. Andrews recommended that the city hire a traffic expert to deal with the state's engineers and help formulate a plan to deal with its parking, traffic, and redevelopment requirements. At the end of 1952 the city retained Lloyd B. Reid to work with Rotival on a "Short Approach Master Plan." While this document was being prepared, Andrews, Reid, and Rotival urged George A. Hill, the state highway commissioner, to change the alignment of Route 91, build a turnpike interchange near Waterside Park at the head of the harbor, and construct a "connector" from that point to the CBD to carry and distribute the turnpike's traffic load.

Coming to realize the threat posed by the state's plans, some New Haven citizens began to complain. Celentano encouraged this and himself protested, but the effect of these activities was dissipated by their scattered and uncoordinated character. Then in the summer of 1953 Celentano met with his fellow Republican, Governor John Lodge. From all indications, this was the mayor's first attempt to use his political connections on the issue. Up to this point the controversy had been conducted largely by bureaucrats and consultants, with little publicity or involvement by politicians.

Shortly after the November election in which Lee beat Celentano, Highway Commissioner Hill wrote Celentano a letter conceding part of the city's demands. He agreed to build a spur from the turnpike at the Waterside Interchange to State Street, south of the easternmost edge of the CBD, and was "further willing to consider extending it as far west as is deemed necessary if this department as a State agency is to provide reasonable traffic service to the central area of the city."[3] At the time it was deemed necessary to go only that far and no farther. This was the situation when Lee became mayor at the beginning of 1954.

The new plan was only a step in the right direction, not a real solution to the city's problem with the turnpike. An estimated 34,000 cars would descend daily to a single intersection a few blocks from the heart of the

---

2 I have found useful information on the origins of the Oak Street Connector in Daniel Dake, "City and Highway Planning Cooperation in Urban Expressway Development" (unpublished master's thesis in city planning, Yale University, 1961).

3 Quoted in *ibid.,* p. 105.

CBD.[4] Rather than providing an easy route to downtown New Haven, this spur would have the opposite effect, making automobile travel there an even more frustrating experience. The CBD, already choking on more cars than it could handle, would decline at a faster rate.

After he took office Lee launched a campaign to extend the spur at least far enough to the west to carry Turnpike traffic to the CBD and distribute it at several points instead of dumping it in one intersection. In addition to solving the traffic problems posed by the Connecticut Turnpike, this "connector" would also contribute to the Oak Street Project, as it would cut a wide swath along the project area's southern boundary.

The highway engineers repeated that their only concern was expediting statewide road travel; they were not interested in slum clearance, declining business districts, or New Haven's internal traffic problems. They were traffic engineers, not city planners. They were particularly opposed to constructing ahead of schedule a road little more than a mile long that would cost at least $10 million. Furthermore, the Southern New England Telephone Company was planning to construct an office building in the path of the proposed connector, and the state certainly would not take a brand-new major structure. The right-of-way would have to be along a different route. Finally, the highway department refused both to acknowledge the city's predictions of traffic congestion and to undertake the additional detailed studies of future traffic patterns—origins, destinations, and so on—that would be needed to prove the city's case.[5]

Lee argued his case persistently in many meetings with Commissioner Hill. He also rallied other sources of pressure, encouraging the New Haven Chamber of Commerce to protest and prodding the local delegation in the state legislature. The mayor approached the telephone company, explained the problem its plans posed, and offered to buy the land it had already acquired or trade it for a site in the Oak Street Project area. The company agreed not to build in the path of the connector, but did not finally accept any of the city's offers for its land there.

The agreement cleared the way for further negotiations with Commissioner Hill. Lee held one trump card in his dealings with the highway department: the New Haven interchange of the turnpike was scheduled to be built on municipal property. Lee declined to negotiate on this issue until the question of the Connector was settled. In October 1954 the city gave its new traffic projections to the state. After nine months of Lee's bargaining, pleading, and threatening, Hill agreed to extend the Connector eight blocks, to a point west of the CBD.

---

[4] This estimate turned out to be something of an exaggeration. In 1966, 22,000 cars entered New Haven daily on the Connector. Source: *Yale Alumni Magazine* (May 1966), 21.

[5] Dake, "City and Highway Planning."

As a result of these negotiations the Connector was considerably wider than the city had originally contemplated, and two blocks had to be added to the Oak Street Project area to replace the land taken by the freeway. Lee also acceded to the state's demand that College Street, a major road that ended north of the Connector, be extended over it on a bridge. This would provide a direct means of access between the Hill section and the rest of town, avoiding the Congress Square bottleneck. The city would also extend Church Street southward over the Connector, thus directly connecting Yale and the central business district with the railroad station. Municipal agencies would relocate families and businesses displaced by the Connector, a most unusual commitment by the city to take care of the consequences of the state's public works project. The city would also undertake to prevent new construction in the path of eventual westward extension of the Connector. Lee also promised that the Connector would not be an isolated good work but part of an integrated program of improvements demonstrating that New Haven would do things on its own as well as asking the state for help. In short, the city would continue with the Oak Street Project. These terms were embodied in a formal agreement signed in February 1955, which also contained a proviso that the agreement would be void if the city did not sign a contract with the federal government for Oak Street by January 1956.[6]

The Connector proved to be a very expensive road, costing more than $15 million, a 50 percent increase over the original estimate. By the time construction actually began, a Democrat, Abraham Ribicoff, had been elected governor. Two construction contracts were let for the Connector, each for half of the road. Lee's ally Joseph Mariani won the first. Later, when bids for the second contract were opened, a contractor associated with the Republican party was declared the winner. Then the state announced that a mistake had been made in adding up the subtotals in the Mariani bid and that when this error was corrected, Mariani's became the lowest offer. The contract was awarded to him, over the outraged protests of the original winner. (Some years later Mariani was the first person killed in a traffic accident on the Connector.)

Construction began in July 1957 and was sufficiently advanced by October 1959 to permit opening in time for election day. The ceremonies were very elaborate. Governor Ribicoff officiated at the head of a lengthy motorcade that proceeded to a pavilion where refreshments were served to several hundred guests, mostly members of the CAC. The effect of the pomp and circumstance was marred when Ribicoff noticed that there were no guard rails on the Connector. Having made a national reputation on campaigns for highway safety, he saw his duty clearly and ordered the Connector closed until the rails could be installed.

The series of agreements on the Connector were the keys to the Oak Street

6 Dake's thesis was a helpful source for much of the material in this paragraph.

Project. The Connector was a means of clearing 14 acres of slums without major expense or administrative work by the city. It also made the project more attractive for re-use by providing convenient transportation facilities. This feature was even more important for the Church Street Project, as we shall see in Chapter 10.

The Redevelopment Establishment

While the problem of the Connector was being solved, Lee turned his attention to the Oak Street Project itself and was not encouraged by what he found. No consideration had been given to specific re-use possibilities when the land was cleared. Even worse, the rate of progress in completing the final project report was so slow that the city faced the possibility of having to refund part of its survey and planning grant. As things were going, it was doubtful that the project would ever reach the action stage.

Since Celentano had left the Redevelopment Agency pretty much alone and Lee had been busy elsewhere, the primary responsibility for this state of affairs fell on the Agency itself, or rather, on its executive director, Samuel Spielvogel. People familiar with his performance stereotyped him as a planner rather than a man of action. It appeared that to Spielvogel two considerations were uppermost: the interminable complications of dealing with the federal government and the gulf of knowledge between professional planners and laymen. He responded to pressure for action by dwelling on obstacles and depicting arcane mysteries which had to be mastered before success could be assured. In any event, this pressure had not been very strong and Spielvogel's concern about federal red tape had discouraged advocates of a more affirmative posture. Spielvogel and Norris Andrews did not get along and it appeared that the Redevelopment Agency and the City Plan Department were not working together smoothly.

Lee asked Logue, then his executive secretary, to attend Redevelopment Agency meetings as a trouble-shooter. Logue carried out this task bluntly. Spielvogel resented his participation and, at an Agency meeting, challenged Logue's and Lee's authority, arguing that the Agency was not subject to the mayor's executive powers. Lee supported Logue and demanded that the Agency fire Spielvogel. Evidently Agency members had been harboring mounting doubts, for they acquiesced. Soon thereafter McDougal also resigned. O'Brion was persuaded to accept the chairmanship and Frederick W. Waterman, Jr., a steel wholesaler, was appointed to the vacant seat.

Logue became acting executive director of the Agency and in February Lee issued an executive order creating the position of Development Administrator, naming Logue to it, and directing all city department heads to follow his instructions in matters concerning urban renewal. In his new job Logue was responsible for the city's urban renewal program, and then some. He was in charge not only of the Redevelopment Agency, but also of the City Plan Department, the newly-created Department of Traffic and Parking, the Bureau of Environmental Sanitation, and the Building Department. He was authorized to represent the city in all negotiations involving urban renewal. As the full dimensions of the problem were revealed and new functions (such as control of zoning) and agencies became necessary, they were added to Logue's domain by order of the mayor, without changing constitutional jurisdictions. The position of Development Administrator never was written into the charter and could have been abolished by the mayor at any time. The effectiveness of the office depended on Lee's power and his willingness to use it. The result was a very successful administrative arrangement. Logue also was Lee's most important policy adviser and all-purpose lieutenant (for example, he prepared the city's capital budget), and often was called on when Lee needed a trouble-shooter or emissary.

Although Logue had had no particular experience in redevelopment, he was a spectacular success in his new job. A native of Philadelphia, he had attended Yale College and Yale Law School. In law school he had organized Yale's maintenance and service workers in their first union. In 1948, shortly after receiving his law degree, he went to work for Chester Bowles when Bowles was elected governor of Connecticut. Defeated for reelection after two tumultuous years in which he seemed to be trying to reform every aspect of Connecticut life, Bowles was appointed ambassador to India and took Logue with him. This period ended two years later with President Eisenhower's election and by September of 1953 Logue was back in New Haven with thoughts of building a law practice. Almost immediately he became involved in Lee's first successful campaign and then went to city hall with the new mayor.

Next to Lee, Logue was the key to New Haven's urban renewal successes. He is a remarkably able man, ambitious, moved by visions of a better city, and conscious of the need for pursuing visionary goals with a hard eye on techniques and possibilities. His work load was awesome even by the exhausting standards of major political officials; the only time he worked a conventional eight-hour day was during an attack of pneumonia. He was a skilled administrator and leader, unthreatened by strong and talented associates. He was so fiercely committed to his work that when his chief lieutenant announced plans to leave New Haven, Logue called him a "traitor to the program" and scarcely talked to him for the remainder of his stay. An imaginative and eloquent man, Logue could display great charm. He could also be abrasive, giving some observers the impression that he gloried in denunciations, threats, and ultimatums. At a public hearing where a speaker passionately opposed the Church Street Project, Logue, facing the audience, silently mouthed, "you son of a bitch." When a Republican politician said that there were "too many chiefs and not enough Indians in the redevelopment program," Logue appeared at a public hearing with a colorful sign reading "Big

Chief" and induced his assistant to wear a similar "Little Chief" sign. Another major figure in New Haven politics told us, "Ed Logue is a very close personal friend of mine and I like him a great deal; and if I didn't like him I'd hate him."

Logue was now directly in charge, but he lacked an effective professional redevelopment staff. After six months of searching and bargaining he hired as executive director of the Redevelopment Agency a career administrator whose talents approached his own: H. Ralph Taylor, director of the Somerville, Massachusetts Redevelopment Authority and a former federal housing official. Taylor, who held bachelor's and master's degrees from Harvard, was not only a remarkably able man but an experienced professional redevelopment official as well, highly regarded in the federal government and local public agencies around the country.

Within a year Logue and Taylor recruited four more unusually competent men to form the basic team for planning and executing redevelopment projects. Taylor's assistant and successor was L. Thomas Appleby, another experienced housing and redevelopment official and the son of Paul Appleby, the well-known writer on public administration and undersecretary of agriculture during the New Deal. The Redevelopment Agency counsel was Harold Grabino, a young New Yorker and a graduate of Yale Law School. Two men who joined the staff as junior officials were Charles I. Shannon and Robert Hazen.

These six had a good deal in common: none was from New Haven; all were in their twenties or thirties; all came from middle-class families and had attended elite colleges or universities; all had postgraduate degrees (Logue and Grabino were lawyers while the others had master's degrees in public administration); all had cosmopolitan, nationally oriented career expectations.[7] Logue was an apostate Catholic, Taylor and Grabino were Jews, the others were Protestants of one type or another. A familiar and revealing joke in city hall: Lee, when criticized for the absence of Italians on the redevelopment staff, would respond, "What about Grabino?"

---

[7] In 1960 Logue became redevelopment coordinator in Boston, where he commanded a salary 50 percent higher than that of any other public official in Massachusetts. In 1967 he was an unsuccessful candidate for mayor of Boston. At the time of writing he was president of the New York Urban Development Corporation. In 1959 Taylor left New Haven for a job with James Scheuer, a prominent real estate developer (and now a congressman from New York), and from 1966 to 1969 was an assistant secretary of Housing and Urban Development. Appleby succeeded Logue as development administrator in New Haven, was executive director of the District of Columbia Redevelopment Agency, and then president of the United Nations Development Corporation. Grabino succeeded Appleby in New Haven, then was an attorney for the R. H. Macy Company and practiced law in New York. Shannon became executive director of the New Haven Redevelopment Agency and then deputy director of the metropolitan Miami redevelopment department. Hazen followed Logue to Boston and eventually became an urban renewal official in New York City.

None of the six had any significant background in city planning, nor were they especially sympathetic to this discipline. They were part of the new profession of urban renewal officials, a very different breed from planners: much more self-consciously pragmatic and accustomed to negotiation rather than subordination in their dealings with politicians and businessmen. They regarded themselves as something of an elite group, much in the same style as paratroopers or law professors. Although the City Plan Department grew enormously under Logue's regime, it had a curiously subordinate place. Logue and Taylor liked to do a good deal of general planning themselves and often turned to the Rotival organization, which maintained an office on the fourth floor of their building, for technical help.

New Haven quickly acquired remarkably large staffs in all departments concerned with urban renewal. In 1956, for example, its budget for redevelopment and planning was $250,000, while Hartford's was only $30,000. The budget allocation for all departments under Logue's jurisdiction grew sevenfold from 1953 to 1959. Salary levels were very high by municipal government standards.

The members of the Redevelopment Agency—the five voting members described earlier plus five nonvoting, ex officio members—played no significant role in setting goals and defining the outlines of policy. Occasionally they brought about changes in some features of specific plans referred by the staff for their approval. For example, during the 1957 mayoralty campaign Taylor presented for their assent a land sale agreement that did not require a down payment. Lee's opponent that year had called them "unbusinesslike" and, perhaps out of sensitivity to these attacks, they insisted that the buyer be required to make a down payment. They did not, however, impede or basically alter any plans. Through the end of our study all votes taken by the Agency were unanimous: "The Agency is like a gentlemen's club. They [the voting members] want everything unanimous and they get everything unanimous. They will bend over backwards to avoid seeming to infringe on the claimed prerogatives of any member." Their principal political functions were similar to the CAC's: they legitimated the administration's policies and were a sounding board for its proposals.

All but one of the voting members during our study were Republicans, but none had been active in party politics. Their alliance with the Lee administration was based on policy judgments that overrode their party identification. Both parties cited the Agency's partisan composition. To the Republicans it was evidence that redevelopment began with Celentano and was merely exploited by Lee, a latecomer who reaped the benefits of his predecessor's groundwork. Lee and his associates mentioned the point to more limited audiences, chiefly businessmen, as an illustration of their policies' soundness. None of the Agency members had significant vested interests in any redevelopment project or in other areas susceptible to city hall manipulation.[8] They cooperated with Lee, Logue, and Taylor because they agreed with their proposals and admired their skill in achieving them. Like other private citizens concerned with Lee's urban renewal program, they were not prepared to take the lead in developing and executing policy, but they were willing to support a politician who looked as if he could.

The voting members were not active partners, but allies to be kept informed and happy. The major exception to this generalization was Frank O'Brion, the chairman, who had a somewhat bigger part to play than presiding over ratification of the administration's proposals. As the first among equals, O'Brion was the Agency's representative in various kinds of discussions, and thus embodied its sounding board and character witness functions. In playing this role, O'Brion was able to exert some influence as an adviser; on some occasions when he differed with Logue, Lee accepted his views. A childless widower, O'Brion's major avocation was his redevelopment work, which he found enjoyable and exciting. He spent a good deal of time selling the city's program and assisting in negotiations with businessmen.

Urban Renewal and Machine Politics

A high level of technical competence was essential to success in urban renewal, a new field with no proven methods where the course of events was seldom smooth. Unexpected obstacles were common and could be solved only by skill and energy. The federal government's procedures were complicated. The Urban Renewal Administration demanded voluminous documentation and then was prone to follow each local submission with additional queries. Any project was likely to arouse opposition which would challenge plans before public opinion, if not in court. In meeting these challenges it was helpful to have better technicians than the opposition could command. Expertise was also useful in guarding against mistakes which might be exploited by the opposition party. Private developers would be more willing to invest in a project if they thought it would be competently managed, and the CAC's high opinion of the redevelopment staff was a factor in its support of the program.

But Lee was also allied to the Democratic organization. One of the party leaders stated a different recruiting principle: "There's not a job in city hall that couldn't be filled by a Democrat who lives right here in New Haven."

---

8 One Agency member asked that friends of his be given legal work such as title searching. Another member was overruled by the mayor when he attempted to exclude a competitor's establishment from a new development.

The mayor was not unsympathetic to these claims on "the practical side of redevelopment," but as urban renewal became his administration's trademark, his chances of achieving national prominence and higher office were increasingly dependent on its success. His practice was to use redevelopment jobs and contracts as patronage whenever he could do so without risking harm to his program. This meant hiring party stalwarts for tasks that were not difficult or crucial, and rejecting many job candidates whose abilities were not equal to their political connections. Since political influence was not necessarily a mark of incompetence, however, such potential employees sometimes were hired conditionally and then kept on if they performed adequately.

Routine work often was contracted for politically: title searching, appraisals, and the like. This could be lucrative; one Democratic attorney made several thousand dollars by title searching on the Oak Street Project alone. Insurance was placed on a similar basis. Negotiating for the acquisition of property was a well-rewarded service, yielding more than $50,000 in fees in the key four blocks of the Church Street Project. This job was usually done by experienced realtors, sometimes chosen politically. Aside from these concessions, the municipal agencies concerned with urban renewal were able to hire qualified people rather than take the organization's candidates. For instance, Logue successfully resisted pressures to hire the brother of an associate of Golden's. There was a good deal of grass-roots organization grumbling because all the key jobs in redevelopment were filled by men from out of town. One Democratic ward chairman said of Logue, "Lee shouldn't hire a carpetbagger even if he is a good and capable man." Republican politicians charged that Lee's reliance on "strangers" in his renewal program was an insult to New Haven, implying that the community lacked talent.[9] These complaints were more public than those from the Democrats, but far less important.

Redevelopment officials were somewhat reluctant to rely on the staff support of politically appointed city departments, whose members they considered generally inferior in ability, dedication, and energy. Not wanting to trust the Board of Assessors, the Agency had a hand in assessing property in project areas. Rather than using the Corporation Counsel's office, the Agency had in Grabino its own very competent legal officer. When the Church Street Project was threatened by litigation, the Agency retained one of the city's two prominent law firms. Many party regulars resented Lee's giving this plum, which resulted in fees of more than $100,000, to a Republican firm instead of spreading it around among more "deserving" lawyers. To a considerable extent the Redevelopment Agency was bureaucratically self-sufficient. Instead of working through other city agencies, it performed their functions itself insofar as they pertained to urban renewal, or contracted out

9 *New Haven Evening Register*, 23 October 1964.

for the work. This freed the program from inertia and bureaucratic self-interest and made it easier to avoid the party organization's claims in regard to patronage. It also, of course, made the Agency itself a bureaucratic empire; in the late 1960s it had grown to 250 employees.

The practice of following political criteria in "harmless" areas extended also to the Agency's relations with developers and to the city's own building activities in redevelopment projects. The city could not easily dictate a developer's choice of architects, but it had a freer hand in this respect with municipal construction. As was mentioned earlier, a desire for distinction led Lee and Logue to look beyond local architects. The resulting political problem was solved by designating a local man as a "consulting architect," usually for one-twelfth of the total fee. These consultantships were often dispensed as patronage, and Barbieri had a hand in some of the decisions. In some cases Lee suggested subcontractors to firms developing project land. He also helped his political allies take advantage of other opportunities offered by redevelopment. These cases usually fell under the classic justification for patronage: "If two guys can do the job equally well, and one of them is a friend of yours. . . ."

Political connections were involved not only in buying goods and services, but also in requests for special treatment from city agencies, as in allowing an occupant more time before requiring him to move. For the most part, however, party influence was unavailing when it conflicted with technical demands or program political considerations. Golden was the customary channel of communication for requests for special favors, and the regularity and truculence with which Logue denied his requests contributed to the antipathy that developed between the two men.

When Lee did take political factors into consideration in dispensing the resources generated by redevelopment, he often did so in ways that increased his personal organizational strength. Each project involved a great deal of construction (not to mention demolition), with all the ancillary demands of this industry for building materials, bonds, insurance, and the like.[10] Lee was in a strategic position to recommend particular sources of any of these items, and he exploited his advantage so as to expand his network of obligations, to make men beholden to him rather than to Golden or Barbieri. Thus, even when redevelopment was used to create organizational strength, the results often were not to the liking of the mayor's intraparty rivals.

---

10 This construction boom was a source of influence in other issue areas as well. In the spring of 1958 a strike by construction workers threatened to delay completion of the new high schools beyond the opening of the fall term. This caused the mayor some concern, and he tried to settle the strike. At the final negotiating session, held in his office, Lee reminded the contractors of the amount of construction in redevelopment projects and intimated that his inclination to think well of them in connection with these lucrative contracts might be related to their willingness to settle the strike.

With the exception of those people who profited from jobs or contracts, the urban renewal program probably was a source of irritation to the regular Democratic organization. Barbieri thought that the city did too much too quickly, but nevertheless went along with Lee's efforts to keep the Board of Aldermen obedient. By the fall of 1960, when the Church Street Project was in serious difficulties, Barbieri did not bother to conceal his pleasure. He and many other organization figures would have been less than human if they had not resented the sacrosanct position occupied by urban renewal. This priority was sometimes asserted in ways that must have been aggravating. One day, for example, the Board of Aldermen took under consideration, with decidedly benign feelings, a request from New Haven bar owners for an ordinance prohibiting the opening of a new bar within 1,500 feet of an established one. When Lee told the president of the Board that this measure would pose serious difficulties for the Church Street Project, the alderman earnestly professed his devotion to the mayor's program: "Gee, Dick, I sure wouldn't want to do anything that would hurt redevelopment." The proposal was passed after being amended to exclude the central business district.

While Lee was the target for some of the Democratic organization's displeasure, much of it was directed at his staff. Logue in particular was a lightning rod for these sentiments, both as the head of the program and because of his often brusque manner. Some hostility doubtless also came from the conflict in style and ambition between young, cosmopolitan, Ivy League, career-oriented renewal officials and older, less educated, parochial machine politicians. The effect of these disparities was exacerbated by the imposition in the name of redevelopment of hierarchical controls guided by technical criteria, as well as the determined purity of the redevelopers in the face of organization requests for a "more reasonable attitude." It should not be thought that Logue, Taylor, and their assistants were politically innocent or insensitive, for they were far from it. But their views of political necessity were oriented to the programs for which they were responsible, not to the maintenance needs of the Democratic machine.

On balance, then, urban renewal was a mixed blessing for most party regulars. The organization and its leaders were denied much patronage, were often rebuffed when asking special consideration, and suffered some losses of traditional areas of favoritism, such as the Board of Zoning Appeals. In compensation, it benefited in some measure from those aspects of redevelopment that could be conducted politically without serious harm to the program. Moreover, urban renewal was a winning issue which enhanced the party's chances of retaining control of city hall. The organization had something to contribute to redevelopment as well as demands to make. It was part of the coalition that put Lee in office and gave him a Democratic legislature. It paid for expenses that could not be financed by public funds, for example, publicity films. It was also the mechanism through which the mayor exerted control over governmental bodies that were not formally under his authority. Such extensions of mayoral power were not congenial to the organization, as we have seen. Lee reaped his harvest of resentment in the 1958 charter revision campaign (see Chapter 11).

Publicity Techniques for a Hostile Press

The city's two immediate problems in the Oak Street Project were finding developers for the land to be cleared and completing the final project report for submission to the URA. The telephone company, after dropping its plans to build in the path of the Connector, had been looking at sites out of town as well as in outlying sections of New Haven. But without too much ado, it agreed to buy a block in the Oak Street Project area for $578,000. Both parties to the sale agreed that this was a low price. The tax assessment for the land was $60,000 higher than the sale price, which made company officials "very happy." Two considerations influenced the price: the city was very anxious to unload the land and so get the project under way;[11] and tax collections would soon cover the city's share of the subsidy to the phone company. As the sale of the high schools to Yale indicated, political opponents could always muster a plausible attack on such transactions because of the difficulty of making a compelling public case about the fairness of a given price. Yet the telephone company was evidently a less tempting scapegoat than Yale, for no Republicans criticized the deal. On the other hand, many would have attacked the mayor if the project had not moved forward.

For some time Lee and Logue had been discussing with Yale a plan to erect high-rise apartment buildings on Blocks A, B, and C. This deal was never closed, but Yale's willingness to buy the three blocks assured the project's success by providing a market for almost all of the remaining land.

In March 1955 Logue outlined to URA officials the city's proposals for the project. New Haven would request a loan of $4,114,000 and a grant of $2,536,000. It would contribute $600,000 in cash and about $670,000 in non-cash grants-in-aid, expenditures for improvements that were in the project area or could be credited to it. This included almost $50,000 for street paving, over $200,000 for two ancient schools which would be demolished, and $400,000 for a new school. Since many of its pupils might come from the project area, a portion of the construction expense could be counted as a project cost. The manipulation of municipal capital improvements to take maximum advantage of non-cash grants-in-aid approached the level of a fine

[11] Such writedowns are not uncommon in private developments, where the first parcels may be sold as loss leaders. See "After the Cabots—Jerry Blakely," *Fortune* (November 1960), 178.

art in New Haven.[12] This practice made redevelopment cheaper for the city and thus easier to accept.

The URA officials informally approved the city's tentative plans. The next hurdle was completion of the final project report. This became a high-priority task, because Lee, facing his first reelection campaign, wanted formal federal approval and a loan and grant commitment before November. Lacking administrative experience, Logue and his assistant were unequal to the job of completing the federal forms quickly. Taylor's August arrival was in the nick of time. In addition to his other qualifications, he had brought a Somerville redevelopment project to the action phase, a rare accomplishment in those days. Working day and night, he had only one mission: completion of the application in time for federal approval before the election.

The application was submitted to the URA early in the fall. Its speedy favorable consideration was powerfully encouraged by Senator Prescott Bush, a Republican but a good friend of New Haven redevelopment. A member of the Banking and Currency Committee, under whose jurisdiction urban renewal fell, Bush was well placed to be helpful, particularly during the Eisenhower administration. His involvement in the program dated at least from the city's first dealings with Yale. Bush was a member of the Yale Corporation and the university was very interested in the project's success. Some of his local supporters were members of the CAC. Redevelopment gave Bush opportunities for publicity in New Haven, an interest that Lee exploited. Lee also eschewed opportunities to make partisan attacks on the Eisenhower administration and the Republican party when the federal government made unfavorable decisions about the city's requests, such as its unsuccessful attempt to include the Sargent plant in the Wooster Square Project. The mayor and his staff took pains to impress and flatter Bush, often preparing elaborate presentations for use at luncheons at Mory's, the famous Yale club that was one of Lee's favorite places for promotional events.

Late in October the URA approved the final project report. A week before the election, Lee and Bush announced the news at a joint press conference in the mayor's office. For reasons which will be discussed in Chapter 10, New Haven officials preferred to keep all information about a project confidential except when they had to secure formal local approval. Too much had been said in public about the Oak Street Project to permit this kind of secrecy. Some people felt that this was not such a disadvantage, however, given the American municipal tradition of unfulfilled grandiose plans: "No one really thought that anything would actually happen."

---

[12] The Redevelopment Agency made a practice of gerrymandering project boundaries to include adjacent but extraneous areas where scheduled improvements could be credited to its contribution to the net project cost. The ultimate use of this device was in the Dixwell Project, a 250-acre scheme for the black neighborhood northwest of Yale. The project boundaries included the site of the old high schools, on which Yale built two new residential colleges. The city received credit for Yale's improvements.

Public visibility made Lee and Logue very concerned about the *Register's* attitude, particularly in view of the imminent election. To be sure, other channels of communication were available. The three radio stations and one television station were at least neutral and often friendly and would sell Lee time during the campaign or make it available free as a public service in other seasons. In spite of these media and such other channels of communication as the CAC, the Democratic organization, and public speeches, the administration considered the newspapers the public's prime sources of information and its gravest publicity problem:

> Posit a situation where the *Register* is against the Oak Street Project no matter what and it's got [a great deal of space devoted to this opposition]. Pretty soon, Bill Celentano and other guys say, "Jesus, this is the way for me to get on the front page and stay on it," and in a town, believe me, this is elementary politics. There's no quicker way to make spokesmen than to indicate to them that they can get on the front page day after day.

The inherent advantages of printed media were particularly important for a complicated subject like a redevelopment project. When our sample of registered voters was asked the sources of their information about redevelopment, 52 percent mentioned the newspapers and only 7 percent said they learned about renewal mainly from radio or television.

John Day Jackson was considered Lee's personal enemy, and unquestionably was opposed to urban renewal. But the mayor was far from impotent in this situation. His years of experience on one of Jackson's newspapers gave him not only a wide circle of friends on the local papers but intimate familiarity with their practical operating habits. As a public relations man, his job had been to get maximum favorable press coverage, and he had been very good at his job. He used the importance of his office, the newsworthiness of what any mayor says and does, to publicize his name and activities. The *Register* seemed to try to edit him out of news stories, while Lee assiduously intruded his name at every opportunity. One recurring occasion for publicity was the ceremony with which retail establishments customarily open new stores, and the mayor was frequently asked to cut the ribbon. Local journalism being what it is, these events often were reported with a story and a picture.

Although the two newspapers were owned by the same man, there was some competitive spirit between their respective staffs, so that often an item prominently featured by the morning paper would be relegated to the back pages by the afternoon *Register*. This rivalry could be exploited by releasing unfavorable news in time for the *Journal-Courier*, which had a circulation of about 25,000, compared to the *Register's* 100,000. Such an item would lose much of the bloom of currency by the time the *Register* used it, and the

Register's vastly greater readership would see it in a more obscure position, if at all.

The themes of redevelopment propaganda were as shrewdly chosen as the techniques; practicality was emphasized along with social welfare values. The ratio of realistic to idealistic appeals varied with the audience, but Lee never failed to claim that Oak Street was "good business." He supported this with the familiar comparisons of the area's low tax payments and high level of public services before redevelopment and the reversal of this ratio that the project would accomplish. He painted out that this would be achieved at a minimal cost to the city, which would get a $25 million addition to the Grand List of all taxable real estate for a cash outlay of $600,000. Lee had made a practice of describing any public improvement as part of his redevelopment program, thus building popularity for the term. Any public construction, from a corner playground to the telephone company building, was heralded by the same slogan: "An Awakened New Haven Builds for Its Future." Having begun a rash of quick and inexpensive projects in his first months in office, Lee had a number of tangible exhibits testifying to the practicality of "redevelopment."

A crucial time for each project was the two successive hearings required after federal approval of part one of the final project report, before formal local approval. The administration treated these as major events to be planned down to the last detail. They featured favorable testimony from every conceivable municipal department as well as all segments of the community. It was not uncommon for two professional-level staff members to spend several months preparing such a hearing, mainly by writing the testimony for dozens of witnesses. This meticulous care reflected Lee's consuming desire to avoid surprises by arranging the script for all public appearances. A stage-managed hearing, featuring favorable testimony from dozens of witnesses, was designed to overawe possible opposition by displaying solid community support, as well as to make the most convincing arguments for the project. The preparation also suited Logue's preoccupation with making an airtight case in anticipation of future litigation. The adminstration usually tried to pack these meetings with Democratic workers (patronage employees), who were encouraged to come early with their friends and families and take all the seats. The formal purpose of the hearings was to provide the Redevelopment Agency and then the Board of Aldermen with the information needed to make an intelligent decision on the subject. Their decisions, of course, were foregone conclusions.

The Redevelopment Agency hearing on the Oak Street Project opened with a detailed description of the project by redevelopment officials. Then a parade of city department heads began. In his dress uniform the chief of police testified to the area's high crime level. The fire chief reported that the rate of calls from the area was six times greater than from the rest of the city.

A judge said it had the highest level of prostitution. The health department described the distressing amount of disease there. The building inspector spoke of the dilapidation of many buildings, and so on. Next the citizens began to troop up to the stand. Representatives of numerous associations: CAC, Chamber of Commerce, unions, private charities, real estate. They all had nothing but bad words for the area and good words for the project. There was no opposition. That same month the Board of Aldermen gave its approval. In February the loan and grant contract was signed. After years of delay and months of frenzied activity the Oak Street Project had entered the action stage. The problem then was to insure that the manner of the project's execution would offer no vulnerabilities to political attack.

There was only one active opponent of the project, the owner of some apartment buildings located between it and Yale. He told the Redevelopment Agency that he would not oppose the project if there were few small apartments among the proposed new buildings. On being disregarded by the city, he asked hostile questions at a subsequent public hearing and tried to organize downtown merchants against the project. He inspired an antiproject resolution that was passed by the Chamber of Commerce, but the city, which maintained very good relations with the Chamber, secured its repeal.

By the end of 1955 there was little doubt that the idea of clearing the Oak Street area was generally approved in New Haven. The obviously appalling state of the neighborhood gave the project a great deal of popularity. The area had been an eyesore for so long that it was considered a wonderful thing just to be rid of it. In early 1957 the project was approved by 71 percent of the sample in a Harris survey, while only 6 percent disapproved. The main reasons given for liking the project were that it would get rid of slums and provide good housing. Lee nurtured these sentiments by indefatigably publicizing every step of the project and never failing to remind his audiences of the horrors of the old Oak Street. He did his best to make redevelopment the city's trademark and the main focus of public attention. Instead of being presented with keys to the city, distinguished visitors watched tenements being demolished in their honor.[13]

Two publicity efforts will illustrate the variety of the administration's continuing attempts to keep urban renewal in the public eye. As might be expected, the Oak Street area was a haven for rats. Public health officials planned an all-out effort to dispose of them after the area was evacuated, lest the rats move to new homes when demolition began. Instead of killing them quietly, Lee prepared a graphic press release pointing out that the old slums had been so bad that an extraordinary liquidation campaign was neces-

---

[13] This contrasts with many other cities where urban renewal projects are obscurely advertised and the mayors seem to avoid close identification with them, by letting subordinate officials make public announcements.

sary to save the rest of the city from an onslaught of rats departing the crumbling tenements. The release spared no details: the size of the Oak Street rat population, the diseases they carried, the poisons that would be used, and so on. The life and death of the Oak Street rats became a cause célèbre, a front page story. It was a very successful way of dramatizing slum conditions and what Lee was doing about them.

The other publicity device was elaborate briefings on New Haven redevelopment for most of the city's cab drivers, who then were each awarded the title of "civic ambassador." As a result of hearing a diatribe on the city's redevelopment program while being driven home from the train station one night, Logue thought of exploiting the fact that cab drivers talk to a great many people, particularly visitors who are not likely to know much about the city. Taxi executives proved amenable to the idea of having their drivers briefed, particularly under circumstances that emphasized their putative role in informing strangers about the city. It was announced that the mayor and his lieutenants, in response to a request from the president of a taxi company, would conduct two orientation sessions. These events were prominently reported in the *Register*. Subsequently, similar briefings were given to many New Haven barbers and beauticians.

The announcement that the taxi briefing was someone else's request was typical of the Lee administration. On the one hand, the mayor wanted to glorify his role. But he was aware of the danger of developing a reputation as a dictatorial figure, and, even more important, he wanted to celebrate the extent of "citizen participation" and to give many people a feeling of playing a part in his programs. The CAC was the prize example of this pretended self-effacement, but the pattern appeared elsewhere, as with the cab drivers.

Relocation

It is likely that few tenants and landlords in the Oak Street area expected that the project would actually come to pass; there had been many plans, much talk, and little action. The shock of realization that came with acquisition negotiations and displacement notices might have politically nasty repercussions, which required careful thought about the handling of the property owners, businessmen, and residents. About 4,000 people lived in the area of the project and the Connector. The Housing Act of 1949 required the local public agency to help residents of redevelopment areas find suitable housing elsewhere and authorized payment of moving expenses out of federal funds of up to $100 per family. The State of Connecticut did not take responsibility for resettling people displaced by road construction and the city ordinarily would not have been obligated to do so. But few lay persons distinguished between the project and the Connector and in any event city officials would have thought it unwise to abandon people uprooted by the latter while helping people within the project area. Thus the agreement with the highway department committing the city to relocate everyone was very much in the administration's interests. People displaced by the Connector did not receive relocation payments, however, for they were not eligible for federal aid and the state did not authorize such payments at that time.

Residential relocation posed two serious problems. One was providing satisfactory housing to replace the destroyed tenements. Second, Oak Street had an unsavory reputation that could have led to considerable apprehension by the displaced families' new neighbors. Both problems were of course heightened because half of those forced to move were black.

A Residential Relocation Office was established. Formally a branch of the New Haven Housing Authority, the office was in fact part of the redevelopment establishment. It was headed by Alvin Mermin, a professional social worker who performed his difficult assignment with enormous enthusiasm, imagination, and skill. The smoothness of this mass population shift was due in no small measure to the dedication and ingenuity of Mermin and his staff.[14]

Successful relocation was also greatly eased by two "natural" population trends. The city's loss of more than 12,000 residents from 1950 to 1960 left a good deal of housing available to the uprooted families. The 1960 Census showed 2,302 vacant housing units in New Haven, of which 1,430 were available for rent. Black immigration and dispersion obscured the fact that relocation greatly increased the black population of neighborhoods that had been largely white. Oak Street families were not shifted to one or two concentrated ghettoes, but were distributed fairly widely over the city's low- and medium-cost areas. Approximately 75 percent of them moved to private rental housing, 10 percent bought homes, and the rest, largely Negroes, moved to public housing. Almost all of those who bought houses and many who rented moved to better neighborhoods or at least better houses. This improvement in housing conditions was experienced by all racial and status groups in the project area.[15] The administration was reticent about its achievements in residential relocation, not through modesty but for fear of opposition to its share in introducing Negroes into largely white neighborhoods.

The four synagogues and two churches in the project area were a potential source of serious trouble; Hartford's first redevelopment project was stalled

[14] After directing residential relocation in New Haven for ten years, Mermin quit and wrote a book about the subject. This personal and enthusiastic narrative provides many examples of its author's qualities. See Alvin A. Mermin, *Relocating Families: The New Haven Experience 1950 to 1966* (Washington, D.C.: National Association of Housing and Redevelopment Officials, 1970).

[15] Sources of information for these statements include Mermin's book and a study of a sample of 314 families from the Oak Street Project area: Frank West, "Housing and Mobility" (New Haven, Conn.: Yale University, Department of City Planning, 1957).

for several years by the opposition of a Catholic church scheduled for demolition. New Haven redevelopers not only were anxious to avoid a repetition of this experience, but were wary of the advantages that religious institutions enjoy in public controversies. Not the least of these are the intangible "spiritual values" which can readily be invoked to rationalize ecclesiastical hostility to the prospect of scattered parishioners and diminished influence.

The Redevelopment Agency had some advantages in its cautious approach to the synagogues and churches in Oak Street. All the buildings were very old, while the congregations had already dispersed over the metropolitan area as a consequence of their prosperity and acculturation. Thus the buildings were not prizes to be lost. A different location might actually make the institution accessible to more worshipers and proceeds from sale of the old building would go a long way toward financing a replacement in a better location. The agency encouraged this outlook by offering generous prices to all six institutions, some of which were hard bargainers. (It is, after all, very difficult to set a "fair market value" on a synagogue.) The city was also most lenient about demolition schedules in these cases. One synagogue stood until 1960, years after the surrounding structures had been cleared, while a new edifice was built in the affluent suburb of Woodbridge.

There were more than 150 business concerns in the project area and an equal number in the Connector right-of-way. None was of great size and only one or two were major enterprises. Unlike residential relocation, there was no federal requirement that the city help displaced businessmen find new sites, but Lee and Logue thought it wise to establish a Business Relocation Office, reputedly the first of its kind in the nation.[16] To run it the city hired on a part-time basis an experienced local realtor, Harry Sviridoff. He helped a number of firms to relocate and in various other ways represented the city to them.[17] Precise and reliable data on the fate of all the businessmen involved cannot be obtained,[18] but it appears that around 78 percent of them successfully relocated and the rest went out of business. Some of the latter were "mama and papa" businesses whose elderly proprietors took this opportunity to retire rather than face the rigors of building up a new clientele in a new location. It appears that a great many firms profited by their uprooting, which led them to take larger quarters and thus permitted substantial expansion.

[16] Several years later, it was still unusual for local public agencies to use realtors for relocation assistance. See William N. Kinnard, Jr. and Zenon S. Malinowski, *The Impact of Dislocation from Urban Renewal Areas on Small Business* (Storrs, Conn.: University of Connecticut School of Business Administration, 1960), p. 8.

[17] New Haven's business relocation activities were a good deal more extensive and helpful than those of other cities studied by Kinnard and Malinowski (*ibid.,* p. 41).

[18] Kinnard and Malinowski report similar difficulties (*ibid.,* pp. 20–21). The figure for relocation given in the text was supplied by Mayor Lee some years after the event.

Most of the best-established area merchants were in a shopping district along Congress Avenue. The largest of these was the M. H. Alderman Furniture Company. Logue concluded that Alderman would be a likely focal point of any organized opposition to the project. As a means of forestalling this possibility the city offered Alderman an opportunity to buy some project land and erect a sizable building to house not only his furniture business but a number of other tenants. The project boundaries were extended to provide a lot of about an acre, which Alderman bought for $83,900, considered a very good price for him. In addition to providing this opportunity, the Redevelopment Agency also left his old store standing a year after all adjoining buildings were torn down, which impeded surrounding demolition and new construction. As acquisition prices were manipulated to achieve the Agency's goals, it is likely that the price paid for Alderman's old store was a handsome one. The Agency insisted on approving the architectural plans for the new building, found the first submission unsatisfactory, and had the plans revised extensively by various city officials and members of Rotival's staff. The building cost $1,250,000 to construct. In addition to office and retail space and parking facilities, it included the radio and television studios of Station WNHC. Alderman eventually decided not to move his furniture business there, being satisfied with an interim location he had occupied after finally moving from his old store.

Parcel I, across the Connector from the WNHC building, had been scheduled for use by one of the displaced religious institutions in the project area. No firm plans materialized and the lot became available for other purposes. The City Plan Department recommended that it be limited to institutional uses because any commercial development there would be cut off from the CBD and thus likely to become a depressed local facility. Logue and Taylor disagreed, largely because of the "public relations implications": if displaced shopkeepers opened a commercial development there it would "be graphic evidence that we are interested in helping the small merchant and that the small man can benefit from redevelopment as well as the institution that can buy the big parcel." Using the land for commercial purposes meant that the project plan had to be amended, which required favorable action by the Redevelopment Agency and Board of Aldermen and, more important, by the URA, which took a long time to approve the change.

Meanwhile, the city had been working on a plan to form a group of displaced businessmen to develop this land, thus finding a use for Parcel I and a home for the businessmen, demonstrating how urban renewal could help the "small man," and incidentally helping exacerbate the divisions in the New Haven Republican party. The businessmen involved were largely minor retailers without experience in real estate development. Harry Sviridoff helped organize them into a syndicate, eventually called College Plaza, Inc., to buy Parcel I as the site of a commercial office building similar to the WNHC development. Sviridoff spent a good deal of time persuading, helping, and encouraging members of the syndicate.[19] Another person who played a major role in forming the syndicate, developing the property, and dealing with the city was George DiCenzo, Celentano's ally and former corporation counsel. I do not know if DiCenzo was hired by the merchants independently or suggested to them by the city, but he unquestionably worked amicably with redevelopment officials. He may also have been a means of influencing members of the syndicate. College Plaza bought two acres for about $140,000 and built on it a two-story building costing $750,000, with parking space for 150 cars. Here again city officials played an influential part in drawing up the plans. For example, they insisted on many more off-street parking spaces than the merchants were originally willing to provide.

The College Plaza and WNHC developments had two functions. They provided markets for unused land and they were a means of reducing opposition from displaced businessmen. City officials thought it much more important to avoid opposition than to get maximum prices for the project land. Moreover, the quick return of the land to the tax rolls was more important financially than the price received for the land: the federal government paid two-thirds of the subsidy, while the city kept all of the property tax revenues.

The city provided a third site for displaced businessmen on 21 acres of reclaimed swamp at the edge of town. This plot was owned by the Park Board but unused for any purpose except dumping. In hopes of developing the plot for a shopping center, the city had convinced the state legislature to authorize sale of surplus park land to private parties. When the original hopes fell through, the city decided to use this site for a business park, with priority to firms displaced by redevelopment. The CAC executive director, H. Gordon Sweet, was in immediate charge of this project and CAC members donated a great deal of technical assistance. After the soggy ground had been filled, lots were sold to former Oak Street concerns for the cost of site preparation. Within a short time there was more than a million dollars worth of construction on this formerly worthless land, and it was paying over $25,000 in property taxes as well as providing scores of jobs in the central city.

Town and Gown: Indirect Influence

The Oak Street plan envisioned four re-use developments: the two commercial buildings, which were of secondary importance; the telephone company building; and the apartment complex. Arrangements for all but the last of

---

[19] In addition to the Redevelopment Agency, other city agencies helped this project along. One member of the syndicate was given a tax abatement of several thousand dollars.

these were concluded rather easily, in good measure because the city offered desirable land at low prices. This formula could not be applied so easily to the apartment land, however, because of political considerations that complicated negotiations with Yale and contributed to another solution for the three blocks. This solution in turn led to numerous difficulties that plagued the project for years.

The project's feasibility was guaranteed by three events in 1954 and 1955: the state's agreement to build the Connector, the telephone company's decision to build in the project, and Yale's willingness to buy the remaining major parcel. The latter two decisions insured that the land would not lie idle after clearance and thus dispelled a principal source of reservations about the project.

Yale officials were concerned about the supply of accessible and attractive housing for junior faculty and felt that its relative scarcity hampered recruiting. Like almost any university, Yale also lacked adequate cheap housing for married students. These needs suggested to Lee and Logue that Yale would be the ideal customer for the redevelopment land on its doorstep. At the time there was scarcely any interest in New Haven affairs at Yale. While various officials were receptive to the idea of participating in the project, the governing body, the Corporation, was distinctly cool. After several exposures to the artful persuasions of the mayor, Logue, and Rotival, the Corporation warmed up to the goal, but remained dubious of its ability to finance an apartment development on the three blocks. Lee and Logue then brought Roger L. Stevens, a nationally prominent real estate operator, into the picture as a potential partner for Yale.

By mid-1955 the city had reached an agreement in principle with Yale and Stevens. Yale would buy all three blocks, put up a high-rise apartment house on one block, and lease the other two blocks to Stevens, who would construct similar buildings and "service" retail facilities for the project residents. Altogether there would be more than 700 apartments with 560 off-street parking spaces. Rents in the Yale building would be pegged low for students, faculty, and staff. Stevens' buildings would be commercial ventures. All property would be subject to municipal taxation.

The plans became clearer and changed somewhat in detail, but they were sufficiently far advanced to be described in several *Register* articles in July 1955. Although Yale and Stevens were not identified by name, it was easy for many knowledgeable residents to guess that the university was involved. A few weeks after the *Register* series the sale of the high schools to Yale was announced and became the main theme of the unsuccessful Republican mayoralty campaign that fall. Despite Lee's enormous majority, it was clear that his opponent's charges had aroused the resentment that a great many residents felt toward Yale. Public opinion polls years later revealed that the high school sale was Lee's most unpopular act. Doubtless the hostility would have been as great even if Yale had doubled its very generous price.

As the Yale-Stevens plans became known, rumors began to circulate that the understanding was collusion, another example of Yale exploiting the local people with the connivance of its former publicity director. Clearly, deals between the city and Yale were politically dangerous. This was reflected in the administration's negotiations with the university. A Yale official described the result of the mayor's fears:

> At one stage of the game...I was for pulling out of negotiations altogether because it was at that stage that the mayor and Ed Logue began writing into the contract more and more clauses defending...their reputations against Yale, as it were. Here they were in the paradoxical position of wanting Yale to come in as a bidder in order to make the whole Oak Street thing possible and in order to get all the credit from Yale in that respect and then at the same time wishing to disavow Yale and show the public that they were under no Yale influence and didn't even want to treat Yale the way they would an ordinary business venture.

As their dealings on the high schools revealed, Yale was a pushover for Lee, not his master. Yet the rumors flourished. Perhaps because they moved in a subculture where collusion was the order of the day, and had been raised on the belief that Yale represented Yankee disdain for immigrants, most New Haven politicians were convinced that the university was sure to get the land in an under-the-counter transaction. Probably the most primitive explanation for Lee's assumed complaisance was that he had been bribed, or simply cowed. A more sophisticated explanation was that the mayor had been seduced by hopes of receiving an honorary degree from his old employers (as he did in 1961). This attitude persisted despite the obvious fact that Yale's location and needs made it the "natural" buyer of the land.

Pressed by this irrational but dangerous public sentiment, Lee found his troubles multiplied as other possible developers took an interest in the three blocks. Perhaps inevitably, in some cases their contacts with the administration were heavily tinged with a variety of political pressure. One out-of-town group approached Lee through a prominent member of the New Haven Democratic organization who, when the mayor refused to give him a commitment, accused Lee of a pro-Yale bias. Another group made a somewhat similar suggestion, also accompanied by political threats. Not all potential buyers made such tough political appeals, but it was increasingly clear that the administration was in a serious dilemma. Regardless of the eventual buyer, Lee was faced with the problem of legitimizing the sale, protecting himself from the political backlash, and maintaining the integrity of his redevelopment program in the face of damaging rumors.

The best solution was an "objective" way to dispose of the land: an auction. The Redevelopment Agency secured the URA's permission to auction the land. Announcement of the auction had virtually no effect on the rumors of a deal with Yale; now the story was that the bidding would be rigged. Indeed, this seemed to be the point of the initial ground rules for the auction, which provided that after the high bid had been ascertained any other bidder could match this price, in which event the city could choose among them. One out-of-town group felt that this would let the city choose Yale no matter how the bidding came out and, it is likely, made use of its political connections to get the federal government to force the city to drop this provision. While some of the contenders evidently continued to believe that the city would contrive to give the sale to Yale, one group with a local political patron asked Lee to arrange a rigged "New York type" bid.

The auction was not held until May 1957. Providing adequate publicity and negotiating with bidders took some time, but the delay probably was due largely to the city's desire to get Stevens firmly committed on downtown redevelopment before the auction, so that if he and Yale lost, the consequences would be limited to the Oak Street Project. Some of the interested parties mentioned above dropped out and eventually there were four bidders sufficiently interested to put up the $50,000 deposit. To keep the maximum number of contestants interested, the city had managed to give each of the four bidders the impression that the proceedings were fixed so that they would win. The Yale-Stevens combine was particularly confident of the outcome.

One of the other bidders, S. Pierre Bonan, the president of a combine called University Towers,[20] had explained to the city that his firm lacked liquid assets and was interested in leasing rather than buying the land. It was agreed that University Towers could bid as if it intended to buy; if it won, the lease payments would be computed on the basis of its bid. The bidding began at the minimum of $700,000 and went up to $1,150,000, at which point Yale dropped out, leaving University Towers the winner. Yale and Stevens had agreed on an upper limit beforehand and had been unwilling to go far beyond it. They did not know that Bonan also had a limit almost identical to theirs and would have gone up just $10,000 more and then quit. Yale officials, feeling that they had been betrayed, were very bitter toward Lee and Logue. Later, they took the mellower view that perhaps it had been just as well, since town–gown relations would have been much worse if they had won, and the apartments were built anyway (but with higher rents).

The decisions that led to University Towers' control of the three blocks were a consequence of the endemic anti-Yale sentiment in New Haven. This episode was an example of what Dahl called "indirect influence": "elected leaders keep the real or imagined preferences of constituents constantly in mind in deciding what policies to adopt or reject."[21] It would also seem to be

---

[20] This firm is not one of the firms described earlier in my account of the political pressures invoked by potential developers.

[21] Robert A. Dahl, *Who Governs?* (New Haven, Conn.: Yale University Press, 1961), p. 164. In another context, Dahl described people opposed to the sale of the high schools as "politically unimportant" (p. 206). This judgment is correct in that their

a "nondecision," that is, a politician's avoidance of a particular course of action because of his anticipation of a hostile reaction to that action.[22] But the authors of the concept of "nondecisions" have explicitly stated that only anticipations of the reactions of small groups or individuals count as "nondecisions," for otherwise, "do we not necessarily prejudge that power in real-world situations will be widely dispersed?"[23] It is not necessary to make prejudgments about the distribution of political power to recognize that the administration's behavior in disposing of the land was powerfully affected by a desire to avoid appearing soft on Yale in the eyes of the electorate. This is a far more valid case of anticipated reactions than Lee's relations with the malleable CAC.

Yet it is one thing to recognize that this was "indirect influence" and another to know how to attribute political power on the basis of this episode. One great theoretical advantage to imagining that fear of the CAC constrained Lee is that the CAC can be construed as the embodiment of "the ruling class," a familiar term that is readily adapted to all kinds of formulations and assumptions. But how can one attribute power (as opposed to recognizing its exercise) when the electorate's "real or imagined preferences" constrain a politician? Thus the drawback of this mode of analysis is not that it requires a preconception, but that it presents insuperable problems of data interpretation.[24]

The Troubles of University Towers

On the day of the auction the possibility of leasing rather than buying the land was announced, but neither the city nor University Towers went out of its way to reveal their arrangement, and it did not come to public attention until nine months later.[25] When the disclosure was made it was greeted with a good deal of criticism. The lease agreement was not signed until March

---

opposition did not prevent the sale from being consummated, but it does not do justice to the lasting impact of their attitudes on Lee's future dealings with Yale.

[22] See Peter Bachrach and Morton S. Baratz, "The Two Faces of Power," *American Political Science Review* 56 (December 1962), 947–52.

[23] Peter Bachrach and Morton S. Baratz, "Decisions and Nondecisions: An Analytical Framework," *American Political Science Review* 57 (September 1963), 632–42. Both articles by Bachrach and Baratz appear in their *Power and Poverty* (New York: Oxford University Press, 1970).

[24] For further discussion see my "Nondecisions and the Study of Local Politics," *American Political Science Review* 65 (December 1971), 1063–80.

[25] The fact was mentioned in a short note on the auction in *Architectural Forum*, but evidently no one in New Haven except city officials noticed it.

1958, ten months after the auction. University Towers was to pay the city $69,000 annually for 50 years and also to make payments to it in lieu of taxes; that is, the city would not lose tax revenue on the land because it retained title to it. The lease payments would be more than adequate for the city to retire the loan it had obtained to finance the land purchase.

The principal source of capital for investment in such developments was institutions like insurance companies which required that the mortgages they bought be insured by the Federal Housing Administration. This raised a problem, for the FHA had valued the land at $700,000, the original re-use appraisal and the minimum asking price at the auction. More than four months went by while the city argued to the FHA that the $450,000 increase in the land price reflected rising property values resulting from the growing attractions of living in the new, redeveloped New Haven.

No sooner was this difference settled than another one arose: the FHA maintained that the market for high-priced apartments in New Haven had not been proven and that it would be prudent to test this market with one building rather than plunge ahead with all three. This decision was uncongenial to Lee, who for years had been talking about the fine new apartments which soon would replace the Oak Street slums and had, with the auction, announced speedy completion of the project's three apartment buildings. He tried very hard to change the FHA's position by invoking Senator Bush's intervention and bringing other pressure to bear, but he desisted when told that perseverance might result in a decision not to insure any buildings.

This struggle continued until a year had passed since the auction and several more months went by before the FHA actually granted the insurance. The Redevelopment Agency and Board of Aldermen then each held a public hearing on the lease agreement with University Towers, providing occasions for Republican opposition and hostile editorials in the *Register*.

Almost since the auction city officials had felt that University Towers was cutting corners and seeking every opportunity to save money and minimize risks. One example was the change in architects from a very well-regarded man to a firm which the city considered undistinguished. On hearing this news Logue summoned his staff as an audience and loosed a sustained and spectacular denunciation over the telephone to a University Towers officer, but the decision stood. After the FHA insurance was finally granted, another six months elapsed before construction began. The major cause of delay was a dispute over the size of the development's commercial facilities. Originally a few shops had been contemplated to serve the apartment dwellers. But as prospects of strong demand for the apartments faded, it appeared that this setback could be recouped by an ambitious expansion of the commercial side. University Towers submitted plans for a branch bank, numerous stores, offices, bowling alleys, a 200-seat restaurant, and a supermarket.

The last point became the focus of the struggle between city hall and Uni-

versity Towers. The city felt that a large store would create traffic and parking problems that would reduce the buildings' residential appeal. It insisted
that the size of the proposed commercial development be halved. This argument was settled by a compromise: the retail space would be reduced by half,
but some professional offices would be built. The first 250-unit apartment
building was finally begun early in 1959 and finished about a year later. A
second was started in June 1961, but by a new company. By the mid-1960s
the third apartment house and the ancillary commercial facilities were finally
finished.

The apartment development, which initially seemed rather untroublesome,
turned out to be the project's political Achilles heel. The belated revelation
of the lease and its possible disadvantages for the city, the delay of almost
two years before construction began, the enlarged commercial development,
and the disappointing demand for the apartments were detrimental both to
the project and to the administration. Disposing of the land by auction, while
apparently necessary for political reasons and perhaps also for the program's
viability, had unfortunate consequences for the project. In part these came
from the various troubles encountered by University Towers; they might not
have happened had Yale won the auction. Yet disposing of land to the
highest bidder has certain intrinsic implications. Any auction minimizes
design as a criterion of choice, because price is the only consideration.[26]
The apartments are architecturally undistinguished, although not as offensive
as the squat bulk of the nearby telephone company building, described by
the editor of *Architectural Forum* as "that great green hulk of a building
which looks like it was designed by the janitor."[27] The city did receive a
somewhat higher price for the land than it had expected, against which must
be put its loss in tax revenue due to the long delays.[28] These considerations

[26] To qualify for the auction, potential bidders had to submit preliminary plans
satisfying minimum design standards, but these were neither demanding nor binding.

[27] Quoted in the *New Haven Evening Register,* 19 February 1960, p. 1. This structure,
which cost about $12 million, was the largest office building in New Haven. It accom-
modated 2,500 employees, of whom about half were newcomers to the city.

Lee, Logue, and their subordinates cared about aesthetic matters, and at times
pressured developers into improvements. But they were primarily interested in action.
While they deplored the telephone company's building, I doubt that they tried to change
its design. As the very first building in a redevelopment project, it was important as a
sign of progress. In appearance as in the price of its site, the telephone company
building was a loss leader for the program. And of course, the company's support was
considered vital in the program's early days.

[28] As a general proposition, resale prices should not be the dominant consideration
in disposing of urban renewal land, because the principal returns will come from increased taxes and the presumably more socially desirable uses. Money made on land
sales may be lost many times over in lower property tax returns. Because of the federal
contribution, if higher project costs produce greater long-term local revenue, the result
is a federal subsidy of local government.

were a result of the same cause, widespread popular hostility to Yale and Lee's particular vulnerability to it. Thus the thousands of New Haven residents who thought that Lee had betrayed the public trust by selling the high schools to Yale had a durable influence on redevelopment progress.

The timetable of the Oak Street Project demonstrates the time required to complete a redevelopment project even in the hands of exceptionally able and determined men. The survey and planning grant was made early in 1952. Two years elapsed before Lee took office and a third before he began to pay much attention to the project. The URA approved the final project report in October 1955 and the loan and grant contract the following February. The city immediately began a second round of acquisition appraisals and by August was buying land. Demolition began in April 1957 and was substantially finished by the end of the year. Construction began on the telephone company building in the summer of 1957 and on the two commercial developments the following year. All of these and the College Street Extension were completed by the early fall of 1959, almost four years after the project was approved. The first apartment building was not ready for occupancy until the spring of 1960 and the entire development was still unfinished ten years after the award of the survey and planning grant.[29] The books were not finally closed on the project until 1971, with completion of a fourth luxury housing development, a 105-unit complex of apartments and townhouses. During the 1960s the plans for Oak Street were also amended to include major new buildings by Yale and the Connecticut Department of Mental Health, at a total cost of almost $9 million.

The slow pace might have caused serious political trouble for the administration, but by the time demolition was well under way on Oak Street, Lee had announced another project that dwarfed it—and almost every other redevelopment project in the country—in size, daring, and political peril. This was the Church Street Project, the keystone of New Haven's reconstruction and the subject of the next chapter.

---

[29] The project was achieving its purposes long before this. In June 1959 taxable property in the project area was assessed at more than $11 million; before clearance the entire area's assessment was only $3 million. By 1970 assessments in the area exceeded $20 million.

10 the Church Street Project

In the summer of 1957 Lee announced that the Redevelopment Agency would buy four blocks in the center of the downtown business district, demolish the buildings, and sell the cleared land to an out-of-town promoter who would build a number of lucrative commercial properties. In the months that followed, this drastic plan, apparently an act of political suicide,[1] was approved and a loan and grant contract was executed. Within two years the occupants of the area had moved out, many of them involuntarily, and the heart of the city's shopping district had become a stretch of vacant lots. Ten years later, after many ups and downs, the Church Street Project had given the city two new department stores, a hotel, an office building, a third high school, a mammoth parking garage, and various other facilities. By any standard of American local politics the project was a big achievement, and it is certainly the most important event in recent New Haven history. For my purposes the most important part of the story is the first part of the project, which ended with the demolition of much of New Haven's central business district. This chapter explains why and how this came about.

The Failure of Private Enterprise

The Church Street Project was an attempt to make downtown New Haven sufficiently attractive and accessible to compete on even terms with suburban shopping centers, and thereby maintain this essential part of the city's tax base. The CBD comprised less than 1 percent of the city's total land area and contributed more than a fifth of its taxes. But with the postwar suburban boom it attracted an increasingly smaller part of the retail market. Its share of all retail sales in the New Haven metropolitan area dropped from 28 percent in 1948 to 23 percent in 1954. In constant dollars, the CBD suffered a decrease in sales of almost 5 percent.[2] A 1956 survey of shoppers in the

[1] When Lee disclosed the plans for Church Street to a political associate, a successful businessman with a long record of governmental service, the response was, "What are you trying to do, lose the next election?"

[2] Source: U.S. Bureau of the Census, *U.S. Census of Business: 1954. Central Business District Statistics Bulletin CBD-25-New Haven, Conn.* (Washington, D.C.: 1956), pp. 12, 13. Unattributed data are from the New Haven Redevelopment Agency.

New Haven area, conducted by the Harris organization, revealed that 40 percent of the respondents visited the CBD less than they used to, while only 12 percent went there more frequently. In contrast, 56 percent shopped more often in the booming suburb of Hamden, and just 4 percent did so less often.

There were two principal reasons for the decline. Downtown New Haven had been laid out in the eighteenth and early nineteenth centuries. The enormous postwar increase in automobile traffic imposed a crushing burden on its narrow streets. It was an ordeal to drive through the area and difficult to find a parking space; 81 percent of the shoppers felt that downtown parking facilities were inadequate. The other problem was that New Haven was not well endowed with attractive stores. Dozens of low rent, low yield buildings occupied the choicest sites: "Bowery buildings in Tiffany locations." More than half the shops in the key blocks of the project area had been built before 1885. The city's only major department store, the Edward H. Malley Company, was widely considered unsatisfactory in merchandise, service, and appearance. It contrasted badly with G. Fox and Company, an aggressive Hartford store whose sales were four times larger and whose delivery trucks were often seen in New Haven suburbs. Fifty-one percent of the shopper respondents thought that New Haven needed a new department store.

New Haven's commercial position seemed on the point of eclipse. Early in the 1950s Sears Roebuck had abandoned its cramped old downtown store for a spacious location in Hamden—across the street from a brand new shopping center that did 33 million dollars worth of business in its first year of operation, mainly taken from New Haven stores. Plans were in the offing for a large shopping center next to an interchange of the new Connecticut Turnpike, a few miles outside New Haven. Downtown businessmen were doing little to improve their competitive position. From 1947 through 1956 there was only $720,300 worth of new construction in the entire Church Street Project area. Seventeen percent of the floorspace was vacant in the three project area blocks closest to the Green, the city's focal point.

In June 1953 came another ominous sign of the CBD's decline, when the Gamble-Desmond department store went out of business. This event turned out to be the origin of the Church Street Project, although some years passed before this relationship became apparent. Gamble-Desmond was a sizable but second-rank firm with a first-rate location on Chapel Street between Church and Temple Streets, facing the Green and straddling Gregson Alley, a narrow, two-block-long lane that ran south from the Green. Both the building and the lot were owned by the Trinity Church, a venerable Anglican institution with a thick portfolio of downtown real estate.

The next month the Harwell Corporation acquired the lease on the building and lot. This firm was a personal corporation owned by G. Harold Welch, the senior vice president of the New Haven Bank. Under the terms of the lease Welch assumed responsibility for property taxes, amounting to about $21,000 annually, as well as the $6,000 monthly rent. Welch demolished the old building, hoping to acquire adjoining property and develop most of the block, with the exception of the Malley Company, which occupied the western part of it. His hopes for a major project failed when he and the adjoining property owners were unable to agree on prices. The scope of his plans was reduced to the lot he controlled.

Any development of the Gamble-Desmond property, either by itself or as part of a larger effort, would be vastly facilitated if Gregson Alley, which bisected the site, were closed and merged with it. Soon after he acquired the lease Welch asked the city to close the alley. At first Lee was sympathetic, although Welch proposed that the city not only close part of the alley, but donate the land to him and then compensate the adjoining property owners, who, because they would lose this means of access to their back doors, were vehemently opposed to the closing. Lee's initial response was based on his realization that the Gamble-Desmond site offered a great opportunity to strengthen the city's fading commercial appeal. But Welch's plans shrank in grandeur as they become more concrete; the development he came to envisage for his property was very different from what he had first described to the mayor. Lee and Logue were disappointed, fearing that Welch's plan would accelerate the city's decline rather than arrest it. Welch had petitioned the Board of Aldermen to close Gregson Alley. Lee's eventual opposition precluded favorable aldermanic consideration and by the end of 1954 Welch withdrew his petition.

Welch already had invested a good deal of money in the lot, now just a hole in the ground. Having been frustrated twice, he was impatient to find a solution that would let him recoup his investment. He now proposed putting up low buildings on either side of the alley, backed by a garage. This idea was even more unsatisfactory to Lee and Logue. The narrowness of the surrounding streets was not the greatest of their reasons for opposing Welch's proposed garage, but they dwelt on this point in pressing him to defer immediate action. As inducements they could offer not only the possibility of a more lucrative solution for his lot, but also their power to make traffic regulations which would impair access to the garage.

The administration was coming to see the fate of downtown New Haven in the future of the Gamble-Desmond hole. The lot grew in importance as time passed; by providing a new commercial attraction for downtown New Haven, it could prevent the district's diffusion and stagnation. Lee and Logue became convinced that Welch did not have the resources to realize their conception of the property's importance. Assuring him that they would help find a solution to his problems, they asked that he wait a little longer while they looked for alternatives to his latest plan.

This search led the city to approach Roger L. Stevens, a well-known real estate broker and developer, backer of Broadway plays, and chairman of the Finance Committee of the Democratic National Committee in the 1952 presidential campaign.[3] Stevens had hired as a vice president of his development company James S. Lanigan, a former aide to W. Averell Harriman who had gone to Harvard with Ralph Taylor and had known Logue when the latter had worked for Bowles. At the beginning of 1955 Logue met with Lanigan and through him interested Stevens in examining the possibilities of commercial development in downtown New Haven. Stevens visited the city and talked with municipal officials and CAC members. He told Lee and Logue that it would not be worthwhile to think in terms of developing just the Gamble-Desmond lot, or even the entire block. A solution to the CBD's crisis would have to deal with all the factors contributing to the area's decline.

Stevens insisted on a large-scale development encompassing the three blocks from Chapel Street on the north to George Street on the south, bounded by Church Street on the east and Temple Street on the west (excluding Malley's). He would try to buy two blocks and build a department store, a hotel, and numerous shops. The city must build a large garage, preferably in the middle block, to provide parking facilities for thousands of cars. Considering the high cost of land, it would not be profitable for private enterprise to build this facility. As part of the plan Church Street would be widened and extended across the Connector to the railroad station. The administration's willingness to take these steps and its commitment to urban renewal were essential to Stevens's participation. Lee brought Freese, Hook, and several other CAC members into these conversations and gained their strong support. The First National Bank and Trust Company, in the process of considering a new building to replace its old one on Church Street, also participated in these talks, on Lee's initiative. The city brought the bank and Stevens together and used the Rotival organization to develop preliminary plans for coordinating their activities. Several months passed while studies were made and negotiations conducted before Stevens was satisfied that the CBD was potentially profitable ground for a major commercial venture and that there would be adequate local support.

By the spring of 1955 Welch had lost $200,000 on his investment and every month's delay cost him an additional $6,000. As he grew increasingly restive, Lee and Logue placated him by picturing his future profit from Stevens's success. Although the city could frustrate Welch's plans for a garage, it probably could not prevent his developing the lot for other possible

---

[3] An idea of Stevens's eminent position at the intersection of business, politics, and the arts may be gained from some of the public appointments he held in 1967: Chairman of the John F. Kennedy Center for the Performing Arts, Chairman of the National Endowment for the Arts, Director of the National Council on the Arts, Special Assistant to the President on the Arts.

uses that would impede any major project but make no substantial contribution to the health of the CBD. The alliances formed through the CAC helped keep Welch in line. At least one prominent CAC member told him that if he stopped cooperating with the city and went ahead with his own plans, he would find little sympathy in the business community. I think it likely that Welch was also restrained by a commitment to give him an interest in Stevens's development; in any event, Welch eventually did participate in the development of the project after clearance. After renewed complaints from Welch about his losses, the mayor asked Stevens to take an option on the Gamble-Desmond lease. On being reassured of the city's determination to proceed with its part in the proposed undertaking, Stevens agreed. In all, he carried the lease for almost two years and spent about $200,000 on it.

Stevens's efforts to do the project on his own by private purchase of the land began in the spring of 1955, with the assistance of the mayor and his redevelopment staff and big business allies. The latter had been drawn to support this enterprise by the familiar arguments about the importance of preserving the city's tax base. As usual, some of them were willing to lend their prestige, connections, and power to efforts in which Lee took the responsibility and initiative. By early 1956 Stevens had made virtually no progress. At that time he, Logue, and Lee had a series of fruitless conferences with representatives of property owners along Church Street. These negotiations collapsed because some asking prices for land were astronomical, in one case reportedly higher per square foot than Stevens had paid for the Empire State Building. Perhaps the highest prices were asked by the Bahr Corporation, composed of Robert and Herbert Savitt and their wives. It held a new building abutting on Gregson Alley which was occupied chiefly by the largest jewelry store in New Haven, owned by Robert Savitt. The Bahr Corporation also had quoted a high price to Welch when he attempted to assemble land and had been prominent in the opposition of adjacent property owners to the proposed closure of Gregson Alley.

Stevens began to realize that he would be unable to buy the land he wanted at satisfactory prices. In May 1956 he and the city abandoned their efforts to assemble land privately. This failure did not put an end to efforts to modernize downtown New Haven because Logue had, more than a year before, provided an ace in the hole, a redevelopment project to do what Stevens had been unable to accomplish by private means.

The South Central Project

It is necessary at this point to examine a parallel series of events. In 1955, a year before abandonment of the plan for private land purchase, there were two redevelopment areas with roughly equal priority for action after Oak

Street: Wooster Square and South Central. The South Central district, shaped like an inverted wedge, extended from the intersection of Church and George Streets south to the railroad station. As far back as 1910 there were plans to build a broad road through this district to provide an easy route from Yale and the CBD to the station. In the 1940s these proposals were expanded to include parking for downtown shoppers. The area was a maze of short, narrow streets, slums, and the wholesale produce market. The buildings housing the 51 produce merchants had been built for other purposes. They were badly dilapidated, infested with rats and vermin, and full of fire and sanitation hazards. From 1949 onward there were various proposals to demolish them. There were also proposals that a junior high school be built in the area southwest of the produce district for "the Hill," that part of the city lying south of the CBD along the west side of the harbor. This area became one of the nine sections designated as redevelopment areas by the City Plan Department and the Board of Aldermen in 1950. The focal points of the plans for the South Central district were the road to the railroad station, which would be an extension of Church Street, and clearance of the market area. Lack of financial resources kept these proposals in the stage of vague planning.

The South Central Project's northern boundary was George Street. No one had contemplated including the three commercial blocks from there to the Green, between Church and Temple Streets. These blocks, in the heart of the CBD, were not in any of the nine redevelopment areas. The Short Approach Plan had recommended public construction of access roads and parking facilities for the CBD, but saw commercial reconstruction as a job for private interests which could best occur east of Church Street. When the Rotival organization began preliminary planning on the South Central Project in the fall of 1954, attention was concentrated on the area south of George Street.[4]

In March of 1955, when the URA's favorable response to the Oak Street plans convinced Logue that the project was on its way, he "began to look around for another one." The problem of the Gamble-Desmond hole drew his attention to that area and Welch's impatience forced his hand. Early that summer, without telling anyone but the mayor, Logue amended the boundaries of the South Central survey and planning grant application to include all of the area being discussed with Stevens: the three blocks between George, Chapel, Temple, and Church Streets, excepting Malley's department

---

[4] This history of fruitless planning was often invoked to give the Church Street Project a heritage dating back to 1910, in an attempt to soften the impact of the city's drastic proposal to demolish so much of the CBD. In fact, however, this heritage was spurious, because these earlier plans had not included the crucial blocks closest to the Green. Here, as elsewhere, Lee tried to soften his role as the initiator of plans and share the nominal credit with others.

store at the corner of Chapel and Temple. Logue did not then expect that these blocks would stay in the project; they were included as a precaution against Stevens's possible failure, so they could be developed this way if necessary. It is likely that Lee and Logue soon told Stevens about this step, for it does not seem probable that Stevens would have committed himself to assuming the obligations of Welch's lease without a stronger reason than an unsupported hope of private purchase of the adjoining land. But otherwise the city seems to have kept quiet about the inclusion of these blocks in the South Central Project; Freese, for example, did not know about it until matters had progressed a good deal farther.

The survey and planning grant application for the enlarged South Central Project was submitted to the Redevelopment Agency in July 1955. Logue avoided possible concern about the scope of the proposal by minimizing the significance of the project area boundaries, that is, the inclusion of the area north of George Street. Stimulated by the administration's energy on the Oak Street Project, Agency members were enthusiastic about redevelopment and welcomed this evidence of further progress. The Board of Aldermen approved the application a few days later and then passed it again in September. (The double approval was necessary because federally-required procedures had not been followed the first time.) Not a word acknowledging this remarkable document was uttered by Democrats or Republicans, due partly to a fairly wholesale failure to read the application. Since 1950 there had been so many official announcements about imminent progress on clearing Oak Street that most people in New Haven undoubtedly were convinced that the project would never take place.[5] At this stage there were few tangible reasons for thinking that the Lee administration was any more in earnest about urban renewal than its predecessor had been. Little wonder, then, that a proposal to raze the central business district seemed to be the stuff of fantasy.

Lee and Logue could not expect that this air of unreality alone would continue to hide their plans for Church Street, so they took pains to conceal their intentions. The project was conceived and brought to fruition in secrecy, as were subsequent urban renewal projects, which were never disclosed until plans were completed and ready for formal ratification. Redevelopment offi-

---

[5] Refusal to believe that an urban renewal project will actually force one to move seems to be a fairly common phenomenon. For examples in other cities see Webb S. Fiser, "Urban Renewal in Syracuse," in *Cases in Local Politics*, ed. Richard T. Frost (Englewood Cliffs, N.J.: Prentice-Hall, Inc., 1961), p. 338; and Herbert J. Gans, *The Urban Villagers* (New York: The Free Press, 1962), Chap. 13.

Even after the New Haven administration had given ample proof of its determination, people in project areas often seemed unable to realize that plans would be carried out. In the summer of 1957 the Redevelopment Agency informed Church Street shopkeepers by letter that it would begin to acquire their places of business in a year. About eleven months later the merchants received notices that the city would take their property in a few weeks, and began to protest that they were being rushed out without warning.

cials compared their tactics to a submarine: they "came to the surface" only to secure formal approval of a major step, then "dived" until another milestone was reached. There was almost total secrecy on incomplete plans and incessant, imaginative publicity after disclosure. The public was never allowed to see what plans city hall was working on and never allowed to forget what it had completed.

A decade later the pressures for "community participation" would make these methods politically impossible. "Submarine" tactics did have merits, however, particularly when the mere fact of plans for possible renewal could be a major influence in business calculations. Because such plans inevitably would change a good deal before they were completed (consider the many amendments in the Oak Street and Church Street Projects), disclosing them would unsettle many more people than those who would actually be affected by the final plan. The New Haven method spared people alarm and uncertainty during the planning stages of a project:[6]

> It's doing a retailer no favor to tell him three years in advance of the possible acquisition of his property, if the federal government and all the local bodies happen to approve it and the money happens to be available and Eisenhower hasn't given up the ghost on urban renewal—to tell that poor guy that he's going to be out of business or that you're going to force him to move.... If we had two years of uncertainty during which the city was arguing whether the area north of George Street was or was not a blighted area, can you visualize the impact on the business community?

> People say in a democracy that you should not be secretive in any of your public acts, but, you know, when you are dealing with top-priced real estate... you have to realize that if you talk about wholesale relocation and demolition, then the people who just signed their leases would be filled with fear and frustrations, and it would upset them, and the people whose leases run out in six months will immediately scurry, even though the project is five years away; and you will cause property owners, who should fix up, to abandon all attempts to invest, even though their investments would be returned when the properties finally are purchased. So, all in all,... while we explore very carefully all the implications of every project,... we have to be very careful not to have any public discussion until we are absolutely satisfied that we are right....

Boston's West End Project illustrates the damaging effects of public announcements made far in advance of action. When the project was first announced in 1950, property owners were advised not to make further repairs. Eight years passed before the first land was taken, however, and in the

---

[6] These and other unattributed quotations are from interviews with major city officials.

interim little maintenance or repair was done and considerable deterioration resulted. Many buildings were vacated as businesses and residents moved out. Property owners could not be compensated for rents lost this way. The cost in anxiety and social disintegration was considerable, if incalculable. The long delay and the attendant confusion caused hostility toward the city and the project on the part of area residents and property owners.[7]

Neighborhood reaction is only part of the effect. Announcement of a project in its early planning stages immediately evokes public controversy, protests by the affected persons, and attacks by political opponents. If project plans are still fairly tentative, the criticisms generally are more destructive than constructive. In addition, it is difficult and time consuming to defend such uncertain intentions, and embarrassing if they are changed or delayed.[8] In short, secrecy saves time explaining and replying:

> I've seen enough of government... so that as far as I'm concerned, it's debate and discuss and everything else and nothing gets accomplished—that's the history of urban redevelopment in 99 per cent of the cities in America and they haven't got a goddamn thing to show for it.... You just read Mrs. Cook's campaign statements and she'll tell you what's wrong with it. She'll say it's dictatorial, it's irresponsible, but I say two years is a hell of a short time and if people don't like it, they can throw us out.[9]

[7] See Gans, *The Urban Villagers,* and also his "The Human Implications of Current Redevelopment and Relocation Planning," *Journal of the American Institute of Planners,* 25 (February 1959), 17, 21. The authors of an extensive study of business relocation across the country reported that both local redevelopment officials and businessmen considered the long time lag between announcement and actual acquisition the greatest problem in urban renewal. By reducing the lag, the New Haven secrecy policy ameliorated some of its effects. See William N. Kinnard, Jr., and Zenon S. Malinowski, *The Impact of Dislocation from Urban Renewal Areas on Small Business* (Storrs, Conn.: University of Connecticut School of Business Administration, 1960), p. 2.

[8] For example, the delays in federal approval of the Wooster Square Project caused by the city's attempt to include Sargent's and the changes in land disposition methods of the Oak Street apartment land occasioned partisan criticism. Such attacks would have been far more frequent if the Republicans had known about other delays and changes of plan.

[9] Another less prominent city official, explaining why few people were involved in planning the Church Street Project, said, "I have the greatest respect for the so-called grass-roots level thing which involves lots of people. It would be nice to give them a sense of participation. It would take a large staff to do that, because it's a rather large scale con game to give these people the illusion that they're really doing something when they aren't."

These "con games" do not necessarily require a large staff, however. While planning the Wooster Square Project the Redevelopment Agency operated a successful game with one skilled "community relations officer" who worked closely with the Wooster Square Neighborhood Committee, satisfying its members' desires for stop signs and the like, soothing their impatience at the slow pace of project planning, and concealing from them the true reasons for the delay. The high point of this committee's influence was reached when it vetoed a sidewalk café in the project.

These considerations applied with particular force to the Church Street Project, with its unprecedented solution to a delicate and important problem. It was feared that controversy would frighten away some of the businessmen whose assent or support was essential to the project's success. Yet in spite of the administration's best efforts, a diligent investigator—or even an attentive listener at aldermanic meetings—could have learned the boundaries of the South Central Project as stated in the survey and planning grant application.[10] In 1955 this document may have had an air of fantasy, but there was a quality of real, fiscal substance to the board's subsequent appropriation of funds for designing the Church Street Extension. Nonetheless, the aldermen who voted the money seemed unaware of the implications of their act. Thoroughgoing inspections of all the buildings in the project area, required for submission of the final project report, might have alerted businessmen to some sort of impending event, but almost every merchant in the area reported that he first learned of the project by reading the announcement in the newspapers.[11]

Eventually rumors about downtown redevelopment—some of them very accurate—did begin to circulate. Had the newspapers picked them up, the information might have led to troublesome and premature inquiries. But New Haven reporters, despite their employer's uncompromising hostility to Lee and all his works, rarely dug hard for a story that was not summed up in a press release. Some of the businessmen who knew about the city's plans through attempts to induce their participation and/or support were hostile to the project and could have revealed it to the press. But such opponents hoped to deal with the city or Stevens and were unwilling to prejudice their chances by making trouble.

The South Central survey and planning grant of $127,090 was approved by the URA in March 1956, while Stevens was still trying to assemble property on his own. When he gave up two months later, Logue suggested to the mayor that the city "go federal" on downtown modernization. Lee agreed and the two men convinced Stevens to stay with the project.

Late in the summer of 1956 Logue and Taylor met at Logue's house one night and decided on the outlines of how the cleared land would be used. Stevens would buy most of the four blocks north of the Connector and build a department store, the great magnet of any shopping center; a hotel, to attract conventions and supplement the city's meager resources in that line;

[10] That the boundaries remained secret is all the more remarkable because Francis Kelly, the intelligent and wary executive director of the Taxpayers Research Council, customarily attended meetings of the Board of Aldermen.

[11] This information is from a survey of several dozen merchants in the Church Street Project area conducted by Pamela Jewett for a master's thesis written for the School of City Planning of the University of North Carolina. I am indebted to Miss Jewett for other information about these businessmen.

office space; and a number of shops. The New Haven Parking Authority would build a 1,300-car garage along Temple Street with direct access to the Connector, and facilities for the same number of automobiles in the block south of the Connector. The Connector provided the high-speed access and far-flung highway connections necessary for competition with suburban centers served by the Connecticut Turnpike and other fast roads.

The extension of Church Street, crossing the Connector on a bridge paid for by the state highway department, would be built to the railroad station and eventually all the way to the Turnpike along the harbor. It would cut through the decrepit produce market area, which would be replaced by a new state-built facility next to the Turnpike. The tangle of slums and run-down business properties between George Street and the station would be cleared, replaced by a rational street pattern, 19-acre commercial park, and perhaps by apartment buildings. The Hill neighborhood would get its new junior high school and recreation center. A somewhat extraneous four-block strip of homes at the southwestern edge of the area was scheduled for rehabilitation. In all, the project area encompassed 96 acres. The city would ask for a federal loan of $25,921,662 and a grant of $13,287,842. The value of Stevens' development was estimated (perhaps loosely) at $34 million. The Parking Authority would spend over $5 million on the garage, which would eventually pay for itself.

The city expected to gain a number of financial advantages from the project. It was estimated that for the crucial four blocks the annual tax revenue would increase from $400,000 to $1,080,000. The area's inadequate sewer system would be replaced by new sewers worth $1.4 million for which the city would receive credit as a non-cash contribution toward its one-third share of the net project cost. The cost of the Church Street Extension, estimated at $280,000, would also be credited to the city. The site for the new junior high school would be acquired for $500,000; otherwise, this land would have cost about $1.9 million. The Parking Authority would buy sites from the Redevelopment Agency at a writedown. Without the subsidy offered by urban renewal, it might not have been able to operate its facilities at competitive prices.

The Housing Act of 1949 envisioned redevelopment as a means of replacing slums with decent housing and thus limited federal aid to project areas that were "predominantly residential in character" before or after clearance. This was generally taken to mean more than half residential use.[12] The Housing Act of 1954 relaxed this requirement in several respects, notably the "10 percent exception" which permitted 10 percent of appropriated funds to be used for projects that had only a "substantial number" of substandard dwellings. The four-block strip of homes constituting the rehabilitation section of the Church Street Project had the virtue of raising the residential charac-

---

12 Ashley A. Foard and Hilbert Hefferman, "Federal Urban Renewal Legislation," *Law and Contemporary Problems*, 25 (Autumn 1960), 662–65.

ter of the entire project area to a level sufficient to qualify for federal aid under the 10 percent exception provision.

While the area *as a whole* was technically eligible for federal aid, it was another matter whether the URA would approve a project that was so obviously directed at commercial rather than residential problems. The area from Chapel Street to the Connector was not blighted. That it was an unappealing and inefficient city center was not pertinent to the URA's regulations. Furthermore, the project would be very costly; at the time of its approval the Church Street capital grant was the second largest in the country for any project in the action stage. No other city had proposed a project which involved such a central area and the destruction of so many sound buildings. Hesitating to approve this daring scheme, the URA delayed action on the survey and planning grant for months. For more than a year city and federal officials battled over retaining the key commercial section, the blocks north of George Street.

Logue and Taylor devised a number of arguments to "prove" that the area was blighted and hence eligible for redevelopment: (1) An engineering study showed that more than half the buildings were substandard, that is, that they had three or more basic structural deficiencies. (2) The area was underdeveloped; only 33 percent of its total assessment was on improvements. (3) The street system was narrow and congested. The Oak Street Connector would make new demands on it and also offered traffic opportunities which the city should exploit. (4) The area south of George Street could not be developed as a new retail center without making the CBD too diffuse, ruining the northern blocks and destroying the Green as the center of the city. The first block south of Chapel Street was the most important one, because it was next to the Green, but it was also the least deficient block of all, even from a commercial point of view. It was argued that this block was necessary to make an "adequate unit of development," a concept, embodied in state law, that authorized the destruction of sound properties. These assorted technical arguments were powerfully supplemented by pressure from Senator Bush.

Still another problem plaguing the redevelopment staff was the financial plan. When it was worked out, it became apparent that the city's one-third share of the net project cost would be prohibitively high. L. Thomas Appleby, the Redevelopment Agency's assistant director, thought of claiming the Parking Authority's $5 million garage as a noncash contribution. The city asked for 100 percent credit for the garage, claiming that the entire cost should be counted as part of its share. This caused another major argument with the URA, with Bush again intervening on the city's side. The two parties arrived at a compromise figure of 60 percent, thus saving the city several million dollars in cash and removing the possibility that the city could not finance its share of the net project cost.

Despite the determination and technical ability of the redevelopment staff in solving these controversies with the URA, the project was jeopardized by the delays, for all this time Stevens was losing money. After the vain attempts to assemble the land privately, Logue had asked Stevens to retain his option on the Gamble-Desmond property while the city explored the possibilities of a federally-aided project. Members of Stevens's organization were dubious about the feasibility of this and urged him to cut his losses by limiting his investment or withdrawing. In the fall of 1956 Stevens and New Haven officials met in the New York office of Walter Fried, the regional administrator of the HHFA. Fried assured the restive Stevens that the project area was eligible for federal aid. In February Stevens sent the city a letter (drafted by Logue) stating what he proposed to do in the project.[13] In December 1956 the preliminary project report was approved by the URA.

Stevens's impatience with his unprofitable situation spurred city officials' efforts to complete the mountain of paper work involved in finishing the final project report. Through professional contacts with other redevelopment officials Taylor learned that the Housing and Home Finance Agency (the URA's parent agency) was conducting a study of redevelopment administrative procedures. He obtained a copy of the study group's recommendations for simplifying federal requirements and followed these proposals in preparing the final project report. Then, learning which study group recommendations would not be accepted, he modified the report accordingly. He managed to secure the URA's permission to submit the report, although the reforms had not yet been promulgated, and induced the URA to direct its New York branch office to accept the new-style report. This gamble cut months off the time which ordinarily would have been required to complete the final project report. In May 1957 the city finally learned that the report would be approved. Considerable effort was then expended in setting the stage for public announcement and local approval of the project.

Mobilizing Support

The danger and opportunity presented by the Gamble-Desmond lot had led to the city's concern with downtown development as a practical, immediate matter. Welch proved unable, either on his own or with the benevolent cooperation of the city, to make a significant contribution to arresting New

---

13 The city never made a serious attempt to interest other developers in the four blocks. Only a very few organizations could undertake a project of such magnitude. It would have been almost impossible to interest another developer if competitive bidding had been required, for a meaningful bid could be made only after a number of expensive preliminary studies of potential demand, architectural plans, and so on. As time went by Stevens's equity in the project increased and with it his interest in remaining. By the time the loan and grant contract was approved it was estimated that he had spent over $400,000 on the Gamble-Desmond lot and preliminary studies.

Haven's commercial decline. On the other hand, Lee was able to prevent him from actions which might have accelerated that trend. The city then brought Stevens into the picture. With the government's role expanded to that of a participating partner, Stevens, too, was unable to achieve a satisfactory solution, although he broadened the scope of the goal. The next attempt was an alternative chosen autonomously by Logue and prepared by the city with no participation by outside groups—the qualification of the project area for a federal survey and planning grant. The administrative requirements for federal approval of a redevelopment project were subsequently satisfied by the Redevelopment Agency staff, assisted by political intervention instigated by Lee. Perhaps the most difficult aspect of this project was not a successful negotiation of the URA's bureaucratic obstacle course, but local acceptance of the project's unprecedented and drastic provisions.

At the same time that the city and Stevens were devising the project, Lee and Logue were building political support for it in New Haven. Lee used his CAC allies to aid his negotiations during the planning stages of the project, as well as to build a coalition of interest groups to support the completed undertaking. Two types of interests were particularly relevant: intrinsic ones, affected directly and individually by the project; and a larger, more general public, the city's business community. The two most important intrinsic interests were New Haven's largest commercial bank and its only major department store. The bank became a powerful and active supporter of the project. The store's eventual opposition was ineffectual because of its isolation from the bulk of the business community.

The First National Bank (subsequently known as the First New Haven National Bank after its merger with the institution of which Welch was a vice president) owned and was the principal occupant of a large building in the Church Street Project area. As the bank's business increased, its officials grew more and more dissatisfied with their building and tried, unsuccessfully, to sell it. They also acquired adjacent land as a step toward construction of a new building or an annex to the old one. A redevelopment project could be an ideal way for the bank to get rid of its unwanted building at no cost, but it would be difficult to find a suitable new home without building it to order; unlike a small retail store, the bank could not quickly find new quarters if it were turned out of its old ones. The bank officers seemed to look favorably on Stevens's private development plans (which might have included the bank's property). What would they think of a federally-aided project?

Lee and Logue considered the bank's support for the Church Street Project invaluable and its opposition fatal, for the rest of the business community would not lightly oppose the area's greatest financial power and the project could not succeed without business backing. Assuring the bank that it would not be displaced without a place to go was a prerequisite to gaining its support. When Stevens's failure became apparent, Logue sought a meeting with the bank's officials and presented to them the best plan for private development that could be devised without the property owned by Savitt and the other merchants with whom Stevens had been unable to make a satisfactory deal. The bank's interest was to remain in the Church Street vicinity and hence in making the neighborhood as attractive as possible. It was also interested in minimizing its expansion costs.

On seeing Logue's presentation of the best plan attainable by private enterprise, and knowing that one alternative was a redevelopment project, one of the bank's officers urged Logue to "do it right." Logue replied that redeveloping the Church Street area would be an enormously daring and difficult job and that "the mayor can't walk down Church Street naked and alone, he needs help." The bank agreed to support the city in an attempt to secure approval of the Church Street Project. Its own specific participation would be to erect a new building in the project area. It wanted the site to be at Church and Chapel Streets, New Haven's prime commercial location, but the city wanted this corner location for a hotel and instead agreed to sell the bank a lot where the Gamble-Desmond store had been, and to delay taking the old bank building until the new one had been constructed. It would pay the bank $1,350,000 for its old building and lot and sell it the new lot for $500,000. (These prices were not settled at this time.) This was a good deal for the bank, saving it from taking a loss on its discarded quarters. In turn, the bank's active support of the project was very useful in winning over many influential local businessmen. The bank, while championing the project, hedged its bet on redevelopment by continuing to buy land on which it could build new facilities on its own, rather than depend on the city, Stevens, and the URA.

The bank's participation in the project was due to the accidents of its location and the age of its building. Its counterpart in New Haven commercial life, the Edward H. Malley Company, was also in a crucial location, occupying the northwestern corner of the project's northernmost block. Even more important, Malley's, as the city's only major department store, could hardly avoid being affected by such sweeping changes in the CBD's parking and retail facilities. It played a complicated role in the Church Street Project; first a reluctant maiden, it then opposed the project like a woman scorned.

A big department store casts a long shadow in a city's commercial life. It is the main event drawing people downtown. If the store does not attract a sizable and heterogeneous clientele, the whole commercial district suffers. Malley's did not have such drawing power.

If the Church Street Project were to be successful, it would have to meet this deficiency. The ideal solution would be for an outside, established firm to open a New Haven branch in Block D, just above the Oak Street Connector. The new store would be an adequate drawing card in itself and, hopefully, would stimulate Malley's to match its appeal. Stevens had interested the R. H. Macy Company in the project and was counting on its participation by the time the project was announced in June 1957. The prospect of competition from a new and glamorous store was scarcely appealing to the Malley management. The president, Richard Edwards, was strongly opposed to Macy's coming to New Haven, although he professed to believe that it would never happen.

Lee and Logue were concerned about the consequences if Edwards tried to mobilize all-out opposition to the project in the local mercantile community. They hoped to disarm him by offering to sell project land for a new Malley store. Edwards rejected this proposal and said that Malley's could participate in the project only if the city bought and demolished the old store. With the proceeds of this sale, he would be willing to build a new store in the project area. The city was afraid that the URA would not approve amending the project boundaries to include the existing Malley store, if only because it would cost almost $3 million to do so. It is also likely that city officials (and perhaps Stevens, too) thought that Macy's would be a better drawing card and so preferred that it operate the department store in Block D. They denied Edwards's request, using federal requirements as the excuse.

This left the project a considerable threat to Malley's, and Logue and Lee still did not want to arouse Edwards's active opposition. They made at least two concessions to him: they would not reveal the shopper survey's report of Malley's widespread unpopularity, and they agreed not to announce that the project would have a department store until Stevens actually had one signed up. Edwards felt it would harm Malley's reputation if the city announced that a new department store was coming, even if this promise subsequently fell through. Lee and the redevelopment officials often dealt with Edwards through their big business allies, particularly Rowe and O'Brion; they almost never saw Edwards without one or both of these men present. In written communications they took care to remind Edwards of the eminent businessmen on their side, a practice they followed in all their dealings with businessmen on the Church Street Project. After the city refused Edwards's request to be included in the project, the issue rested for the moment.

Lee developed concentric circles of business support. Rowe and O'Brion were his major day-to-day helpers; Rowe in particular used his institutional position in Lee's behalf. These men attended to specific problems, such as Malley's. Lee also needed more general support, which he built through the CAC. Several members of the CAC, because of their prominence or closeness to Lee, had known about the project before Stevens's failure. The mayor approached the problem of informing the CAC as a whole with his customary careful preparation. In the late summer of 1956 he drew the CAC's attention to the CBD's decline. One CAC response was the formation of a seven-man committee on downtown problems, appointed by the mayor. This group was informed of the city's plans. At each succeeding CAC meeting there was progressively more specific discussion of the CBD's needs and ways of meeting them. At the March 1957 meeting the results of the shopper survey were presented and the commission discussed "action" to solve the problems suggested therein. The next month Lee announced the complete Church Street plan, which had not yet received URA approval.

The Redevelopment Agency posed another type of problem for Lee. O'Brion had known about the plans for Church Street at least since the middle of 1956 and had participated in negotiations with various business interests. Other members of the Agency had played no active role in creating the plans for the project or building support for it. One of the nonvoting members was a Republican alderman, Louis Raggozino, who could be counted on to be hostile to the administration. This was important because the Agency had to approve the final project report before it was submitted to the URA, which would give Raggozino a chance to learn the project's scope. Around the end of 1956 Taylor and Logue told each of the voting members about the project, one at a time. Early in 1957 the plans were presented in great detail to all of the voting members, with Logue and Taylor taking pains to answer every question. At the same time the members were told that a formal vote would be required at the next regular meeting, in February, at which nonvoting members would be present. At this meeting Taylor proposed approval of the final project report and then, instead of giving each member a copy of the report, as was customary, he read excerpts aloud from the stencils. Taylor suggested that the proposed motion was only a formality. Reading quickly, he omitted figures that would have revealed the scope of the project. The Agency passed the motion unanimously. Raggozino was present but did not object, nor did he raise the alarm subsequently.

Step by step Lee and Logue enlisted the active support of those persons who were already involved with the project. In the beginning this involvement mainly reflected support of Lee's general program; such was the case with Freese, Rowe, and O'Brion. As time went on and other interests agreed to participate, they became motivated to help bring the project about. The bank, of course, became a powerful ally because the project would be beneficial to it.

As the time drew near when the URA would approve the final project report, the mayor grew increasingly concerned about the setting for public revelation. He wanted to tell various people about the project just before the public announcement, particularly the Chamber of Commerce (a few of its officials had worked on the plans) and the major property owners in the project area, yet premature disclosure of the city's plans would be a disaster. Inevitably people opposed to the project learned of it and threatened to reveal the secret. The *Register* intended to break the story early, but Lee rallied a group of officers and directors of the First National Bank for a meeting at which Jackson was induced to wait for the city's deadline. A prominent realtor hostile to the project threatened to express his opposition openly and was curtly told by Rowe, whose firm gave him a good deal of business, that Rowe supported the project. The business interests favoring the project were now so numerous and powerful that potential opponents kept the peace for the moment. The stage was set for the grand opening and Lee was determined that no one raise the curtain ahead of time.

The federal government formally approved the final project report on June 10, as the administration had anticipated. Recognizing that the project's debut on the public scene would have a great deal to do with its popularity, the administration prepared for this event with great care, imagination, and thoroughness. The secrecy that had characterized the planning of the project would heighten the dramatic impact of its disclosure; never again would so much public attention be given the project as at the time of its announcement and never again would attitudes toward it be more malleable. Lee planned to make the biggest possible splash with the disclosure and follow it with a sustained barrage of publicity, hoping to exploit the monopoly of attention he would enjoy before the project's potential opponents could manage coherent public statements, so that attitudes would be formed without competition from hostile publicity. The Republicans were likely to seize on any weakness in the project, for 1957 was an election year. Business interests adversely affected by the project were another expected source of attack. Preparation for the announcement and management of the hearings were the primary assignment of two city employees for several months prior to federal approval. The mechanics of the announcement also received the attention of many others, including several members of the publicity department of the Southern New England Telephone Company, whose services Rowe made available to the administration.

On June 7, five days before public disclosure, Lee and several aides gave the executive committee of the CAC a thorough briefing and discussed ways to organize widespread support for the project. On June 10 and 11 the major property owners in the project area were informed in the mayor's office. The press was briefed on the day before the public announcement, to give reporters time to digest and present the story fully. Elaborate press kits were prepared for the briefing, which was attended by representatives of all local media, New York and Connecticut papers, and the wire services.[14] Lee, Logue, Stevens, and O'Brion spoke and answered reporters' questions for more than two hours. The Board of Aldermen and city department heads were informed on the night of June 11.

[14] The project was generously covered in *Time,* which also published a photograph of Lee (24 July 1957, p. 24).

The project was formally disclosed at noon on June 12 at a Lawn Club luncheon attended by over 400 persons: CAC luminaries; important contributors and officers in the United Fund (Rowe had been its president); leaders in labor, social welfare, and ethnic groups; representatives of the Hill neighborhood (site of the proposed junior high school); officials of the state highway department, Senator Bush, and federal redevelopment figures, including G. Albert Cole, the Housing and Home Finance Administrator. Lee made the principal announcement and was given a standing ovation. Other speakers included Stevens and O'Brion, whose position as a bank president added authority to his discussion of the financial details.

At the Lawn Club and in the press releases major emphasis was given to the size of the undertaking, described as "an $85 million project," and to the new construction it would bring: an 18-story hotel-office building, a bank, "retail shopping structures," and a 1,600-car garage, among other new buildings. The amount of federal aid was featured, as was the city's comparatively small cash contribution and the fact that the project was to be completed without a tax increase and would eventually double or triple tax revenue from the area. There was no explicit explanation of the project's relationship to New Haven's commercial decline and little was said about the demolition of a major portion of the central business district. It was mentioned that the Redevelopment Agency hoped to acquire land by Labor Day, but the fact that hundreds of businesses would be uprooted was soft-pedaled. The entire project would be completed in three-and-a-half to five years.

The *Register* gave the project most of its front page under a banner headline and devoted more pages to the announcement details and half a dozen feature stories. In the lead editorial that day the paper's booster spirit (and perhaps Jackson's heavy downtown real estate holdings[15]) held a shaky ascendancy over its hostility to Lee and government spending: "The major virtues of the project are excitingly obvious." But it warned that the merchants in the area "deserve, and must have, every consideration of their own rights and needs," and took an option on future criticism: "The application of the program, of course, now presents the City with a challenge at least as great as that posed by the original planning."[16] Another noteworthy response was a full-page advertisement by Malley's congratulating Lee, Stevens, the redevelopment staff, and other participants, and pledging the department store's cooperation. The administration intended to secure complete local approval of the project in the shortest possible time; that afternoon the Redevelopment Agency set its public hearing for June 28.

A comprehensive campaign directed by the telephone company's publicity chief made use of television interviews, press releases on details, and other

---

15 The assessed value of John Day Jackson's property in the CBD, five parcels in five blocks, was $456,325.

16 *New Haven Evening Register,* 12 June 1957, p. 20.

material to keep the mass media supplied with a steady diet of information. Lee and his helpers set about winning the support and public endorsements of innumerable community groups. Leading figures in many of these groups had been contacted before the public announcement. Perhaps flattered by sharing the momentous secret and undistracted by any criticism of the project, they had agreed to secure their groups' endorsements. The extent of Lee's effort in this respect may be appreciated by reference to this partial list of the organizations whose leaders registered support for the project at the Redevelopment Agency's public hearing: New Haven Chamber of Commerce, New Haven Clearing House Association (composed of commercial banks), New Haven Real Estate Board, Connecticut Labor Council, New Haven Central Labor Council, New Haven Junior Chamber of Commerce, New Haven Council of Social Agencies, United Fund, New Haven Council of Parent Teacher Associations, League of Women Voters, New Haven Joint Council of Municipal Employees, New Haven Teachers League, New Haven Council of Churches, New Haven Area Tuberculosis and Health Association, and the Home Builders Association of New Haven County.

Again with the aid of the telephone company's publicity department, the city prepared a brochure on the Church Street Project and mailed more than 12,000 copies before the June 28 hearing. The Chamber of Commerce, Jewish Community Center (whose business manager was a member of the CAC executive committee), League of Women Voters, and Council of Social Agencies had all stuffed and addressed envelopes containing the brochure to their respective members. School teachers, political figures, city officials, Yale bigwigs, and all CAC members were also on the mailing list.

The Church Street Merchants

New Haven Republicans, searching for a candidate to run against Lee that fall, at first had little to say about the project; they waited until they could discern the course of events and opinions. One other group did not wait for the dust to settle—indeed, could not afford to. The merchants in the area north of the Oak Street Connector became the project's principal public opponents. Because they were the major interest *group* directly affected, their activities are worth describing in some detail. Their almost complete failure to impede the city's plans is interesting in view of the ability of similar groups to forestall redevelopment projects elsewhere.[17]

Several hundred businesses, almost all of them small, were located in the

17 *New England Business Review* (published by the Federal Reserve Bank of Boston), June 1959, p. 2. That May the voters of Winsted, Connecticut not only canceled a proposed renewal project but abolished the city's redevelopment agency as well. Opposition to the project was led by a group of merchants whom it would have displaced. See the *Hartford Courant,* 10 May 1957, p. 1.

project area north of the Connector.[18] Only 10 were branches of larger con-cerns and only 9 owned the premises they occupied. Among them were 103 first-floor firms, including 38 clothing stores; these are the focus of my atten-tion. Few of these shops had more than half a dozen employees. Most were family businesses run by young and middle-aged people,[19] almost all of whom were Jews. Customarily there was a good deal of visiting back and forth between stores during slack hours.

The merchants first learned about the project from the newspapers. Over-whelmed by the announcement, they were confused and completely unaware of how to deal with this terrifying prospect. The immediate reaction was a realization that they would have to move from their present locations, but more specific grievances and questions soon came to mind. Most of them had made considerable improvements to their stores, but in almost every case their leases contained "eminent domain clauses" releasing the tenant from any claim on the price paid the owner in the event the property was taken by the government. If the merchants moved elsewhere they would also lose much of the clientele they had slowly built up over the years. Would the government compensate them for either of these losses? When the new Stevens development was completed, would they be allowed to rent stores in it? If so, what would the rent be? And where would they go in the interim?

As the merchants pondered and discussed these questions, their shop-to-shop interaction increased. Singly and in groups they visited Lee and his redevelopment officials, who were sympathetic to their concern and unrespon-sive to their questions. Even more confused and unsure of what to do next, the merchants agreed eagerly with the suggestion of one of their number that they form an organization and hire a lawyer. They created the Central Civic Association and engaged the services of a prominent, experienced at-torney, Louis Feinmark. Feinmark was no more successful in extracting in-formation from the city than his clients had been and asked that approval of the project be delayed until his questions were satisfactorily answered.

The formation of the Central Civic Association was an event the city could not ignore, particularly because it was receiving excellent coverage in the *Register*. Lee responded with a series of releases about the "business relocation policy" for the project: although there was no federal or state obligation to help businessmen beyond giving each a relocation payment of up to $2,500 (later raised to $3,000), the city would bend every effort to ease their painful readjustment, as it had done with such great success in the

---

18 Most of these data on the Church Street merchants are from the Kinnard and Malinowski study, which was based in part on a sample of 43 of the firms north of the Connector. Other information is from the research by Pamela Jewett cited earlier.

19 Less than 5 percent of the businessmen in this area were over 60 (Kinnard and Malinowski, *The Impact of Dislocation on Small Businesses*, p. 30).

Oak Street Project. The Business Relocation Officer (the first in the country) stood ready to help merchants find new quarters. The city had been pledged the cooperation of the Chamber of Commerce and the Real Estate Board in finding suitable new stores for displaced merchants. (By so doing these two organizations made it clear that they supported the mayor and would not cooperate in any attempts to postpone or subvert the project.) Stevens had agreed to give the merchants priority in finding room in his new development and would give them a 10 percent reduction in rent. There would be no delay in approving the project, for the merchants' questions could not be answered until Stevens was sure that it was worthwhile to proceed with the drafting of detailed plans.

Some aspects of the situation were not publicized by the city. Unlike the Oak Street Project, there could be no permanent developments into which displaced merchants could move directly, because this would provide competition for the completed project. It was felt that many of the Church Street concerns were marginal enterprises that could not survive a move and the likelihood of higher rent, and that some of them were in businesses unsuited for a central downtown location. One of the causes of the CBD's uncompetitive position was the unappealing character of many of its stores; neither the city nor Stevens thought that the project would be a success if it merely offered the same old shops in new surroundings. In any event, it was not likely that many of the Church Street merchants could come back to the project area. Life insurance companies and other larger institutions that financed private developers like Stevens usually required that 65 to 70 percent of the floor area in the new development be leased to firms with credit ratings equivalent to a Dun and Bradstreet AAA classification. One of the prerequisites for an AAA rating was $1 million in net assets, a requirement that few Church Street merchants could meet.[20]

At its peak the Central Civic Association had perhaps 75 members, all small businessmen in the project area. Its members failed to enlist the support of other downtown businessmen. (Several substantial retail concerns in the CBD were opposed to the project, but expressed little sympathy for the Central Civic Association. Their opposition was not conducted in public.) They felt overwhelmed not only by the experts and data commanded by the Lee administration, but even more by the array of organizations endorsing the project. Feinmark's sarcastic comment at the second public hearing expressed this feeling:

As I listened at the public hearing before the Redevelopment Agency to the reports of every single city department, and the dire details of the calamitous condition of the center of the city of New Haven, and heard the impressive

[20] *Ibid.*, p. 63.

list of organizations and individuals who spoke in favor of this program, I suppose I should have been overawed at the idea that my voice would be the only one to have the temerity to even raise a question, or perhaps a series of questions, concerning this program.[21]

Largely isolated from other relevant groups, the merchants thought that "everything was rigged," the outcome already determined by widespread collusion that protected favored institutions like the bank. In this view the clinching piece of evidence was the exclusion of Malley's, which the merchants thought had been saved from demolition by favoritism. The department store's participation in the plot was proof that the Stevens development would not present it with any competition, that is, with a new department store. Confronted by this massive coalition, the merchants were painfully anxious to avoid the appearance of hostility to the project itself, as the following statement at the second hearing indicates:

First, let us emphasize that we are not opposed to progress for the city of New Haven; in fact, we are all for it. . . . But the fact that we happen to be in the direct path of this project poses some particular problems and raises many questions for us.

A good many merchants really believed that the project was in the best interests of New Haven. Furthermore, many of them were afraid to antagonize Lee too much, since they would have to deal with him. These reservations intensified their confusion about what tactics they should follow to protect their interests. Few of them were very sophisticated politically and for the most part they took no political action. Little thought was given to contributing money to the Republicans—most of the merchants were Democrats —or to collaborating with them in an organized attack on the administration.

The Public Hearings

Undeterred by the merchants' pleas, the administration proceeded to the first public hearing, held before the Redevelopment Agency just 16 days after the project was announced to the public. On the day of the hearing the *Register* said of their demands in an editorial: "If adjustment to their needs requires some change or compromise in the elaborate—but still theoretical—outlines that have been announced, such adjustment is both a moral obligation and a duty."[22]

The hearing was a carefully prepared production, designed to explain and

---

21 All quotations from these two hearings were taken from the official transcripts.
22 *New Haven Evening Register,* 28 June 1957, p. 18.

justify the project, make a strong legal case in the event of litigation, and demonstrate overwhelming public support. The audience was variously estimated at 400 to 600 persons. The hearing began with a statement by Lee outlining the need for the project and setting forth the city's position on the Church Street merchants: "We will do everything in our power to assist them and to minimize any hardships which this program may cause them." The mayor promised to make public a schedule of rents in the Stevens development by the end of the year. This promise had not been kept two years later, if only because the final blueprints for the development had not been finished.

The city's redevelopment and planning experts made a detailed and powerful case for the project. Representatives of 22 private organizations added their endorsements. In addition to the groups previously listed, the project was praised by several neighborhood organizations from the Hill. The testimony of other city officials, written for the most part in the redevelopment offices, followed a simple pattern: the Church Street area accounted for 20 percent of all arrests, 40 percent of all morals charges, and 14 percent of all fire damage; its housing had been adjudged substandard as long ago as 1944; and so on. The Director of Public Health, dwelling on the obsolete sewers and prevalence of venereal disease in the area, summed up his indictment in a memorable sentence:

> The single sewer system and the moral climate intertwined with the physical environment make the Church Street area definitely detrimental to the health, safety, morals and welfare of all the people in New Haven. Because of this, I endorse the redevelopment and renewal plans for the Church Street Project Area.

When Feinmark inquired how all these indices of blight were distributed between the sprawling decayed neighborhood south of George Street and the central shopping district to the north, Logue blandly replied:

> It is the position of the city in this project that the area as a whole qualifies for redevelopment under Chapter 55 of the General Statutes. The area as a whole. And we are not attempting to and did not attempt in any information here presented to break it down.

Feinmark made the only unfriendly statement, a request for more information and less haste. He also took pains to emphasize that the CCA was not opposed to the project, but only wanted a little more data. There were very few questions. It seemed that the project's possible opponents had not had time to gather their thoughts.

The Redevelopment Agency approved the plan a few days later, as expected. To make a good legal case that its findings had been reached after proper deliberation, it went through elaborate procedures before making this decision, and even made several minor changes in the plan. The candor of this behavior may be judged by noting that two of the Agency's five voting members had spoken in favor of the project at its public announcement.

The Central Civic Association's position hardened after the Redevelopment Agency approved the project. As the hearing before the Aldermanic Committee on Streets and Squares approached, association members circulated to their customers and other downtown shoppers a leaflet stating their position and asking readers to urge their aldermen to delay. Accordingly, the city expected a more determined opposition at the second hearing and prepared a more explicit defense of its position. Hours of testimony were planned, to overawe the opposition, court public opinion, and prepare for possible litigation. The drawn-out supporting testimony also had the effect of exhausting opponents' patience and stamina; the hearing ended after 1 A.M.

The hearing room again was crowded and included many hostile merchants. In his opening statement Taylor said that information about the size and type of stores Stevens would build and the rent he would ask for them would not be available until the developer conducted surveys and drew up detailed plans, and he would not go to this considerable expense until he was sure of getting the land, that is, until the plan was approved. The Redevelopment Agency would try to do the project in stages, but it had to begin demolishing buildings before new ones could be built and therefore could not say that retailers would be able to move directly from their old stores into new premises in the project. The tenant merchants had signed eminent domain clauses voluntarily, but the city would "do all we can" to ameliorate hardships resulting from such situations, although "to go beyond that statement at this time would be quite improper." As far as delaying the proceedings was concerned:

> It is our position that the delay sought by the merchants' association will not accomplish the purposes they intend, but will only succeed in holding up the entire project, including the work which will provide the answers to the questions they have asked us.

Finally, "we will discuss with them [the merchants] the provisions of the contract [with Stevens] which concern them, and will protect their interests in every way possible."

To this Feinmark rejoined that Stevens would hardly have committed himself to the ambitious undertaking described by the city without knowing "what stores he is going to construct, and what rentals he is going to get for them." The alternative, he said, was that Stevens was not really committed at all. In other words, the city's assurances were unsatisfactory:

I assure you, we have had plenty of sympathy. But every single time we have asked that sympathy be translated into dollars and cents, a sudden hush falls, and then we get no answers.

Feinmark asked that the project not be approved until his questions were answered:

> If it took all of these years of preparation and investigation, with ample financing and with all of the facilities of every single department at their disposal for this Agency to prepare its plan, are we asking too much when we say that six weeks is hardly ample time for the people of New Haven to digest this great proposal, for we people who are about to be especially hurt by it to try to find out what the facts are, in order to have proper consideration and discussion of those facts? And particularly so when the very Agency which has had all of this time and all of this ability to investigate and get the answers isn't itself able to give us the answers that we are asking for?

He concluded by invoking the doctrine of separation of powers, pleading with the aldermen:

> After all, you are the Board of Aldermen of the City of New Haven. You are co-partners and equal partners. You are not to be dictated to, nor have your authority imposed upon by any person or by any agency. You owe a duty to the citizens of the city of New Haven, and one of the duties that you owe is that you not act on a proposition having the magnitude of this kind unless the people who are proposing it to you are able to give you the facts about it.

Several Church Street merchants opposed the project, often very emotionally. They also participated in the question period, but were such inept debaters and advocates that they made virtually no impression and were easily rebuffed by the adroit Logue. A good deal of time was spent in pursuit of the erroneous point that favoritism for a big institution had resulted in "saving" Malley's.

The Republicans, despite the impending municipal election, had raised no objections at the first hearing. This time they contented themselves with two ineffectual appearances. Mrs. Edith Valet Cook, just nominated to oppose Lee that fall, made a brief statement: "What is the rush? Let's have a little more democracy in this town than we have had lately." A state assemblyman hoping to be his party's chief critic of Lee's redevelopment program fenced coyly with Logue and proved only that the Republicans were hopelessly outclassed.

And so the hearing ended. The chairman had announced that his committee would receive letters on the project and consider them in deliberating its report to the Board of Aldermen. Ten letters were received, nine endorsing the project and one opposed. In due course the committee submitted a favorable report, along with a minority report by its one Republican member opposing approval of the plan until Stevens was irrevocably committed to the undertaking and had answered the Central Civic Association's questions. To no one's surprise, the Board of Aldermen approved the project. As soon as the URA approved a loan and grant contract, the project would enter the execution phase.

The Project and the Campaign

The most important thing about the project's progression through the two hearings was not the resulting approval—for that was a foregone conclusion—but the favorable public reaction. The municipal election campaign that fall guaranteed that the Republicans would exploit any aspect of the project that offered a lucrative target. Lee wanted to avoid giving them such an opportunity and set about building a public image of the project which would make it impregnable to such an assault. Everyone expected he would win the election handily, but both his political interests and the welfare of the project required that it not become a liability which would cost him votes.

There was no slackening in the barrage of publicity about Church Street after the Board of Aldermen approved it. The project was still a good news topic and the mayor and his lieutenants were indefatigable in speaking about it before organizations of every description. When Lee resumed his question-and-answer television series that fall, there were several Church Street queries on every program.[23] The project was, of course, a prime theme in his campaign. The most spectacular device to publicize it was a large model of the Oak Street and Church Street areas showing how New Haven would look when these projects and the Connector were completed.[24] First displayed at a home show sponsored by the *Register,* the model, accompanied by a "New Look for New Haven" brochure, was a great success. From the home show

[23] While a few questions called in by viewers were answered on this program, most of the bona fide calls were boring and particularistic complaints about things like stopped-up drinking fountains or rutted streets. To make the program interesting and to use it for propaganda purposes, most of the questions that were answered were written in city hall. This practice led to the sort of minor problem that is commonplace in politics, for the names to which the planted questions were attributed could not be those of persons known to be part of the Democratic organization. Members of the mayor's staff thus had to nominate their unpolitical friends for this role. One such friend, now a distinguished political scientist, heard his name associated with: "Mayor Lee, I read in the *Reader's Digest* that...."

[24] This model, over 10 feet long, cost at least $5,000. Mrs. Cook bitterly protested the expenditure of public funds for partisan purposes.

it went to the Jewish Community Center, for Lee was concerned about a September Harris survey showing widespread Jewish sympathy for the Church Street merchants and a substantial decline in his popularity among Jews. Before election day the model appeared in other busy locations.

Lee's two campaign opponents did not discuss the project a great deal. Malkan, the "Independent Democratic" candidate who had attacked the big business composition of the CAC, also criticized the city's relationship with Stevens. But Malkan was not taken too seriously by the mass media and, lacking campaign funds, did not have an effective forum for his remarks about "secret deals." Oddly, Stevens's connection with the national Democratic party was not exploited by the Republicans, although this affiliation seemed to offer a tempting chance to accuse Lee of using the project for narrow partisan purposes. As the campaign wore on Mrs. Cook began to charge that Lee's conduct of redevelopment was characterized by secrecy, dictatorial methods, and unscrupulous propaganda, thus perverting a program "which was started by Republicans." But for the most part she was not specific about Church Street, although the project's history furnished illustrations of all these evils. Her major attempt to make political use of the project was promptly neutralized by the city's alertness and speed. This incident is an excellent example of the political skill with which the Lee administration conducted its redevelopment program.

In the late summer of 1957 the Connecticut General Assembly was to meet in a special session called in response to a serious drought. Mrs. Cook, a member of the lower house of the legislature, announced that she intended to place on the agenda of this session proposals to revise state law so as to: (1) guarantee that occupants of buildings in redevelopment areas be allowed to remain until demolition was about to occur; (2) keep property in project areas on the tax rolls as long as possible; and (3) compel public disclosure of the buyers of redevelopment land and the prices paid.

Lee learned about this from the *Register's* early edition (which he habitually read the instant it was available) and immediately had Taylor draft a letter to Mrs. Cook, for O'Brion's signature, saying that there was no need for such action by the legislature since the Redevelopment Agency's policy under existing law "accomplishes all of the objectives you seek." This reply was rushed to the radio and television stations in time for their 5 o'clock news broadcasts, along with a news release which noted that O'Brion was a Republican and a Celentano appointee. This fact was mentioned in the morning newspaper, which gave top billing to O'Brion's reply. That evening the story was relegated to the back pages of the *Register* and featured the refusal of Republican legislative leaders, who were no doubt wary of setting a precedent for the numerous municipal elections in Connecticut, to put Mrs. Cook's proposals on the agenda. Her subsequent attempts to draw a distinction between "mere policies" and enduring legislation were too fine for either the electorate or the newspapers' city editors. Such direct campaign participation by Lee's eminent Republican allies was rare, but the need was also infrequent.

The election results were a great personal victory for Lee, who received two-thirds of the total vote, despite losses as high as ten percentage points in some predominantly Jewish wards. Twelve percent of the Jewish respondents in our summer survey voted for Malkan (who was Jewish), but he won no more than 3 percent of any other ethnic group's vote. This election was the acid political test for the city's Church Street plans. Although the project would have been in trouble if a reading of the 1957 returns had indicated its unpopularity, in fact, elections scarcely ever provide politicians with "mandates" for specific policies. A Harris survey conducted in September 1957 provided more valid evidence of the project's popular appeal: 66 percent of the respondents approved of the project and 15 percent disapproved of it. (It was not as popular as the Oak Street Project, which was liked by 71 percent and opposed by only 6 percent.)

Business and Politics

Edwards, the president of Malley's, had had a rather obscure attitude toward the project since he and the city had rejected each other's offers in the spring of 1957. His firm's newspaper advertisement endorsing the project had been his only public statement. At the end of July Edwards complained to Lee about some aspects of the project. Shortly thereafter he arranged for several Church Street merchants to appear with him at a meeting of the board of directors of the Retail Division of the Chamber of Commerce. Lee learned of this and briefed some board members before the meeting. Forearmed, a majority of the directors, after an acrimonious session, rejected Edwards's motion to recommend that the city fully compensate displaced merchants for all losses caused by moving, including those resulting from disruption of business. A day or two later Edwards and the presidents of two other large downtown stores which may have feared increased competition from the project issued a public statement urging the city to "give more thought to the problems of the many merchants being dislocated."[25] Specifically, they asked for higher relocation payments than those financed by the federal government. At least one of these two other retailers had been associated with Edwards's attempt to attack the project through the Chamber of Commerce. Shortly after these episodes the city accused this man's store of serious smoke pollution violations and threatened legal action unless remedial action was taken. Failing to get help from the Chamber of Commerce,

[25] *New Haven Evening Register,* 30 August 1957, p. 1.

Edwards assured Lee of his support for the project and suggested that they discuss ways in which Malley's could participate in it. Lee then learned that Edwards was urging the federal government to reject the project. Nevertheless he dealt with Edwards carefully, for he did not want to stimulate further attacks on the project with an election pending.

Lee's desire to avoid provoking Edwards and the Church Street merchants was a factor in his decision not to announce Macy's participation in the project before the election, although the new department store was considered a key attraction and rumors of its involvement were already circulating.[26] After the election the city was anxious to pin Macy's down and planned to make the public announcement in January, despite a threat from Malley's to bring suit to enjoin further progress on the project if the announcement were made. Before the day arrived, the Macy management decided not to participate in the project. Revelation of the plan to have a new department store was postponed indefinitely while Stevens and the city began to search for a replacement.

In April 1958, the mayor announced further plans. Many occupants of the four blocks would have to move out by the end of January 1959, after the Christmas rush and the traditional January sales. A "Church Street Co-ordinating Committee" would be formed, chaired by Bell (the president of the power company) and with a majority of pro-Lee businessmen as members. Its task would be to study and make recommendations on problems that arose in the course of the project's execution. It was announced that there would be a major department store in the four blocks. The biggest news was the land disposition agreement with Stevens: he would pay $4.3 million for 230,000 square feet of cleared land which the city pledged to turn over to him by May 1, 1959.[27] When this agreement was signed Stevens

---

[26] Other considerations were the Central Civic Association's complaints and Stevens's feeling that announcing Macy's participation would weaken his bargaining position with the store. He was negotiating with other department store chains at the time, although Macy was clearly the prime candidate.

[27] It is difficult to assess this price. A prominent out-of-town expert appraised the land at $6 million, based on the income it was expected to produce. In 1957 Agency officials expected to get almost $5 million from Stevens. The Agency also imported a "disinterested" appraiser who reported that the land was worth $4 million, $300,000 less than Stevens's price. This was a useful bulwark for the city in the event of Republican charges that the price was too low. The URA had to approve all purchase and sale prices and was under some constraint because of scrutiny from the General Accounting Office. But because the national urban renewal program was still barely off the ground, the URA might have been reluctant to be too sticky about such matters for fear of adding more obstacles.

On the other hand, the price Stevens paid was many times higher than the cost of well-located suburban land served by utilities and with comparable parking and freeway access. The existence of such outlying centers as an alternative outlet for investment capital and retail firms and the scarcity of developers like Stevens all tended to depress

gave the city a check for $430,000. The first property acquisition also began in April.

In February Lee had announced his refusal to seek the Democratic nomination for senator, saying that he preferred to complete the program he had undertaken in New Haven. I do not know all the factors behind Lee's decision, but it is very likely that Stevens or a member of his organization intimated that he would withdraw immediately from the Church Street Project if Lee planned to leave town. Such an announcement would have made the project a fiasco and dealt Lee's political chances a grievous blow, while Lee's departure would have jeopardized the success of the project and thus endangered Stevens's investment.

The first demolition began in July 1958, clearing a section of secondary shops and "hot pillow" hotels below Church and George Streets to make way for the Church Street Extension. The Redevelopment Agency began buying property in the key four blocks about the same time. Clearance began along Church Street the following February and continued on schedule, with the exception of the building housing Savitt Jewelers.

The Determined Jeweler

Robert Savitt was the owner of one of Connecticut's leading jewelry stores and president of the Bahr Corporation, a family concern that owned the building housing his store. His building was located on the west side of Church Street and extended through the middle of the block to Gregson Alley, which was used for deliveries. Built in 1953, it also contained a cafeteria and office space. Ever since the old Gamble-Desmond store closed its doors, it seemed as if Savitt were playing the role of nemesis to downtown redevelopment. He was a leading opponent of Welch's attempts to close Gregson Alley and quoted both Welch and Stevens prices for his property which they considered astronomical.

Lee told Savitt about the URA's approval of the Church Street plan shortly before the public announcement and intimated that an understanding could be reached. Subsequently Savitt's lawyer suggested to the city that since the Bahr Corporation building was less than five years old, it should be preserved and incorporated in the project. Savitt persisted in this position

---

the Church Street price. For a discussion of these general topics see Raymond Vernon, "The Economics and Finances of the Large Metropolis," *Daedalus,* 90 (Winter 1961), 44–45. Vernon said that comparable suburban land "can usually be had for $15,000 or $25,000 an acre."

after being told that plans called for an 18-story hotel on the site,[28] that widening Church Street would cut 20 feet off the front of the building and development of the rest of the block would take 5 feet off the back, and that, in any event, the structure was not adequately fire-proofed.

Savitt announced his opposition to the city's plans to demolish his building, requested a delay in the proceedings, and threatened litigation. He also protested to the federal government, both directly and through Senator Purtell and Meade Alcorn, a Connecticut man who was chairman of the Republican National Committee, whose "interest" was felt by the URA. The city proposed a deal to Savitt: he would stop complaining to the federal government and attempting to stimulate political intervention and would drop any plans for litigation; in return the city would give him a chance to buy choice property in the project or lease a prime site from Stevens and would give him a good price for his building; $990,000 was suggested.

There were some indications in July that an understanding could be reached along these lines, but the deal fell through, for David Goldstein, Savitt's attorney, testified against the project at the aldermanic hearing:

> It would be a great waste of public funds to demolish this property for the substitution of another commercial building. . . . Insofar as the plan exempts Malley's and fails to exempt the Bahr Corporation, it is claimed that the plan is unreasonable, arbitrary, discriminatory and confiscatory. . . .

Negotiations were resumed. The city repeated its offer and again it was felt that Savitt would agree. But he continued to threaten legal action and to complain to federal authorities. In September the Bahr Corporation sued the city and the Redevelopment Agency. The suit asked the superior court to rule on two questions: the project's constitutional validity and the legality and propriety of the Agency's actions, which were alleged to be abuses of its power. These included improper procedures, gerrymandering the project area to qualify it as "substantially residential," the use of eminent domain for private profit, and giving improper notice of hearings.

It is likely that Savitt regarded the suit as a bargaining device to increase the price he could get from the city and perhaps enable him to relocate in the project or invest in it. Any such suit was disadvantageous to the city. As long as the project was hampered by litigation, the Agency could not obtain federal guarantees for borrowing money from private sources, and was forced to borrow money directly from the government at a higher interest rate. Moreover, the suit jeopardized the project by creating uncertainty about

---

[28] This proposal was later changed, as were most aspects of the re-use plan, in some cases more than once.

its viability and thus was likely to make it more difficult to attract investors and developers. Litigation encumbers affected property and prevents its transfer or use until the case is settled. A lawsuit can also be embarrassing, even when one is in the right, and the city's lawyers considered their case unassailable. Several of the principals in the suit did not want to take the stand and be exposed to cross-examination: Lee because he disliked uncontrolled exposure to opponents, and businessmen because they abhorred involvement in public controversy. Furthermore, the city was not anxious to reveal all the details of the project's origin and planning. Finally, litigation is expensive; it cost about $100,000 to fight the Savitt suit and others brought against the project. Redevelopment officials wanted to avoid giving the impression that they could be coerced by the threat of a lawsuit into giving a property owner a better price (as they could be); otherwise, they would be deluged with suits.

The Redevelopment Agency retained one of the city's two top-ranking law firms for all the Church Street litigation. A complex legal struggle ensued. The city moved successfully to change the proceedings from a jury trial to one conducted before a judge. Its "special defense" was then accepted by the judge. This included an account of all formal procedures followed in adopting the project and cited many legal precedents approving projects in which land acquired by eminent domain had been sold to private developers intending to make a profit. At the same time negotiations toward a settlement continued. After six months of maneuvering, the city, feeling that Savitt's lawyers were trying to enhance the pressure of litigation by delay, urged an immediate trial. Goldstein objected, but the judge agreed with the city and a trial date was set for early June.

On the appointed day the city's lawyers were confident of their case. Goldstein, apparently uncertain of the merits of Savitt's case, expressed a strong willingness to settle out of court and indicated that his major interest was the purchase price. City officials agreed to settle, but set certain other conditions for a deal, including the date when Savitt would vacate his building, a statement that he would issue admitting that his case was without legal validity, and an agreement on the procedure for determining the acquisition price which would have been advantageous to the city. Savitt and his attorneys were willing to consider these terms and the case was postponed until the afternoon. In a brief, abrasive hallway confrontation with Savitt, Lee threatened to launch a public attack on Savitt Jewelers as an enemy of progress in New Haven. After thinking about the city's offer, the Savitt forces realized that they could merely withdraw their suit without also restricting themselves by accepting the city's terms. They did so that afternoon.

The Redevelopment Agency resumed negotiations with Savitt, but was still unable to agree on a price and in the fall of 1958 condemned the Bahr Corporation property for $700,000. Shortly thereafter Savitt, having changed lawyers, again brought suit. This time Bahr argued that its case against the project could not be judged without considering the full background and therefore it needed to put a number of witnesses on the stand. The judge ruled that he would not consider evidence other than the record of the two hearings preceding local approval of the project. He found for the defendants and issued an order putting the Redevelopment Agency in possession of Savitt's property. The Bahr Corporation appealed both of these decisions to the state supreme court, which ordered that Bahr remain in possession of its property pending the outcome of the suit. This ruling prevented the city from transferring its new building site to the bank by the agreed deadline. In March 1959 the high court ruled that the lower court had been in error in refusing to accept new evidence and returned the case for further proceedings.[29] This was a considerable blow to the city, which was pledged to turn over the cleared block to Stevens by May 1.

Lee faced another election in the fall and was worried about the political danger of delayed reconstruction of the barren downtown blocks. He decided that the time had come for serious negotiation. Savitt offered to withdraw his suit for a total settlement of $1.3 million. Lee appeared to agree, but pointed out that the Redevelopment Agency had to approve the figure and suggested that he and Savitt appear before the Agency, where he would urge it to approve the price. Logue and Taylor were informed of this arrangement. Opposed to the price, they briefed O'Brion accordingly. Lee argued for his deal with the Bahr Corporation without giving the impression of boundless enthusiasm for it. The Bahr representatives left the room and Logue and Taylor then disputed Lee's case, finally "convincing" him of his error. The Agency voted to reject the $1.3 million figure and approved a counterproposal which did not mention price but offered Savitt several opportunities to participate in the project. Savitt replied with an offer of $1.1 million. The Agency accepted but the URA refused, citing a regulation which prohibited acquisition prices more than 10 percent higher than the highest appraisal. Savitt refused the city's offer of this maximum. The Agency then sought a new appraisal and gave the appraiser instructions which amounted to a strong hint that he increase his estimate. But he could only make a minor increase which raised the city's offer to $1,056,000, whereupon federal officials convinced Savitt's attorneys that a higher figure would never be approved. Savitt finally consented and on April 20, more than a month after the supreme court's decision, the agreement was announced. Although the city had agreed to turn over that block to Stevens by May 1, Savitt was given until June to vacate the premises. The city thus had to default, although Stevens did not take advantage of the failing. The lagging pace of construction in the project subsequently was blamed on the Savitt suit. It is conceivable that city officials

---

[29] *Bahr Corporation* v. *O'Brion;* 146 Conn. 237, 149 A. 2d 691 (1959).

did not press Savitt to move out by May 1 because they were pleased to have the excuse.

The Merchants Again

The Central Civic Association had failed to prevent speedy local approval of the project. Subsequently its goal changed from delay to winning concessions from the administration, first by attempting to rally public sympathy for its members' position, then by a lawsuit. Throughout the summer and fall of 1957 its attorney and officers issued statements that grew more critical of the project and hostile to the administration. Their statements usually were conspicuously placed in the *Register,* which expressed mild sympathy in its editorials. By November the Association was saying that the Redevelopment Agency was in a "state of complete confusion" and that the project should never have been "jammed through" until answers to its questions had been found. Somewhat contradictorily, the Association also said that the land should not be sold until it had been cleared—and then only by sealed bid. In mid-November the Association formally departed from its public position of approval of the project and announced its emphatic opposition not only to the city's plans, but to any other attempts at downtown redevelopment.

The city's response was a heavy barrage of publicity on the wonders of the new New Haven and a reiteration of its position on the merchants' demands: answers were unavailable and the city's good faith was evidenced by its unprecedented business relocation program. Harry Sviridoff, the genial business relocation officer, surveyed the merchants to learn their needs in new stores. In October Stevens opened a branch office in New Haven, an event which had been heralded for months. His local representative had little new information to disclose and spent a good deal of time hymning the advantages of the project to the Church Street merchants and urging them to drop their opposition to it. In private, Lee and Logue told Feinmark that the city had no legal obligation to help his clients. Any help they gave would be voluntary, they told him, which suggested that his clients would be more likely to profit from the city's indulgence if they behaved properly and stopped attacking the administration's motives and making the project a campaign issue.

Undoubtedly Feinmark realized that it was precisely his ability to embarrass Lee in this most vulnerable season that gave the Central Civic Association its best chance of success. Its complaints were influential in the decision to delay announcing Macy's participation in the project. They also stimulated a thorough study by the Redevelopment Agency of the possibility of doing the project in stages so as to minimize dislocation. (The conclusion of this study was that staging would be impractical and would not materially improve the merchants' lot.)[30] Under existing conditions, however, the little shopkeepers could not win a public debate with city hall. They could not even attract support from their fellow businessmen on the other side of Church Street, nor form a united front with Savitt or Malley's. They lacked the resources to match the administration's technical knowledge and public relations skills. Even with unlimited resources they could not have matched the city officials' single-minded determination. They were victims of the city's propaganda; most of them believed that the project would be good for New Haven and thus many of them were not as resolute as they might have been.

Failing to make a significant impact on public opinion, the CCA turned to litigation. In October, several weeks after the Bahr Corporation, six CCA members brought suit on behalf of themselves and their fellow merchants against the city and the Redevelopment Agency. They charged that members of the Redevelopment Agency had made up their minds about the project before its public hearing, which had been held in an unreasonably short time after the public announcement and without providing the affected merchants with adequate information; and that Blocks A, B, and C were unrelated to the rest of the project area, not substandard, and included for Stevens's profit. These paragraphs from the complaint summed up widespread criticisms of the project:

41. This Federal Act was not intended to permit the use of federal funds by local agencies to enable them to acquire wholly commercial areas for resale to private real estate operators for redevelopment as a commercial area.

42. Fully realizing that Federal funds are not intended for commercial developments, the Redevelopment Agency, seeking to technically qualify for the use of Federal funds, has artificially, improperly and illegally linked together two sections of separate character in the attempt, under the guise of redeveloping or renewing a residential portion of the city of New Haven, to meet the literal conditions as set out in the Federal Act.

43. The Edward Malley Company department store, in the perimeter of the area, just outside Block A, has been omitted from the Plan. This exception stands as an obvious and improper discrimination because the said store differs from the property leased by the plaintiffs in only one significant respect: it was not desired by Roger Stevens.

The suit requested the court to judge the project's legal and constitutional validity in view of these charges; in particular, to decide if the city and

---

30 One exception was the First New Haven National Bank, which was to be allowed to remain in its old quarters until its new building was completed. This can be regarded either as favoritism to the city's largest bank or recognition that there was no temporary relocation site for the bank.

Redevelopment Agency had not violated due process and taken private property without just compensation and for other than public uses. City officials assumed that this suit, like Savitt's, was intended primarily as a bargaining device.

The suit was the Central Civic Association's high-water mark. As the city began to negotiate to acquire property in early 1958, it soon was able to exploit conflicts between the individual merchant's immediate self-interest and his devotion to the cause of the Association. This conflict had been evident since the group's formation, for some of its leaders had been approaching the city seeking to make private arrangements. Some of the administration's most vehement critics played this double game, leading redevelopment officials to suspect that the CCA was being used as a means of attacking the city in the name of all affected merchants for the benefit of a few.

The city's best resource in dealing with individual CCA members was its ability to time condemnation. As almost all the merchants rented their business premises, they often could not move even when they found new quarters, for they were still bound by the leases on their old stores. This situation also prevented them from relocating before downtown rents went up, as they were doing under the influence of the project announcement. But their leases would be terminated when the city acquired the property, either by condemnation or negotiation. There was considerable flexibility as to when the city could acquire a parcel of land. It could manipulate appraisals to ensure condemnation and could time the proceedings to suit a tenant's convenience if he had a new location to which he wanted to move. The ability to time acquisition was a powerful weapon over the CCA, whose members' haste to move into new stores became a divisive force stronger than the Association's common interest—especially since the city showed no signs of meeting its demands. In effect this was a policy of favoring the tenant over the landlord, who might lose several months' rent through such early acquisition. The CCA suit doubtless had something to do with the city's adoption of this policy.

The first break in the CCA's ranks came early in 1958 when a merchant who had been a hostile witness at the aldermanic hearing asked the Redevelopment Agency to condemn his landlord's property at an appropriate time to permit him to move into a new location. Overriding the objections of some of his lieutenants, who wanted to treat a conspicuous enemy harshly, Logue made him an attractive offer, knowing it would induce other Association members to make similar approaches to the city. The Agency announced that it would give special help to those merchants who wanted to leave before the city's deadline, that it would break their leases by early condemnation. This policy was also followed to help shopkeepers whose business was disrupted by adjacent demolition and construction. As they, too, were constrained by leases, this was "the only way to free some of the merchants of their long-term leases and clear the way for them to relocate according to their wishes."[31]

One of the Association's original concerns had been what would happen between demolition of the old buildings and construction of the Stevens development where many of its members hoped to be accepted. About half the merchants in the area wanted to be included in the project. In April the city announced its decision against staging demolition and pointed out that dozens of empty ground floor retail locations in the CBD were available to displaced merchants. In addition, redevelopment officials had worked out a scheme for temporarily housing shopkeepers who would eventually move into the Stevens development. Under this plan, the shopkeepers would form a corporation to build and operate a prefabricated building to house their shops. The city would lease them the building site and a parking lot for a dollar a year, would agree to buy the building when the merchants moved from it to the Stevens development, and would pay this purchase price before the building was constructed, thus financing the construction.

Lee hoped to announce the CCA's consent to this plan in April, when he would also announce the signing of the land disposition agreement with Stevens and reveal that the project would contain a department store. The mayor thought that the first item would sweeten the merchants' reactions to the information about the department store. While reporters were gathering for the press conference on the land disposition, Logue was hurriedly conferring with Feinmark, trying to persuade him to withdraw the suit and offering to present the plans for temporary relocation as a joint creation of the Redevelopment Agency and the Central Civic Association (another example of Lee's tactic of trying to share credit—and responsibility—for his policies with groups that would be affected by them). Logue was unable to reach complete agreement with Feinmark in time for the press conference.

As many of the merchants began to find satisfactory new locations, their enthusiasm for the CCA flagged. The primary focus of the organization became temporary relocation. This was both the limit of the city's willingness to help and the topic of greatest interest to the Association's diminishing membership. They were becoming less vociferous, for they were reluctant to rock the boat as agreement with the city became more likely. When the hearing on the land disposition agreement with Stevens was held, no Association members spoke, although the subject was a central point of their lawsuit.

The suit was scheduled for trial at the same time as Savitt's. While the city and Bahr forces conferred outside the courtroom, Feinmark wandered up and down the hall alone. That afternoon his suit was continued for a week, a move to give more time for bargaining. Once again, although the

---

[31] This explanation by Taylor was quoted in the *New Haven Evening Register*, 18 May 1959, p. 7.

city's lawyers were supremely confident that they would win, they sought a settlement to prevent unnecessary disclosures and avoid controversy. Moreover, Lee and Logue wanted the goodwill of the merchants. They reached agreement with Feinmark and his clients on the plan which had been prepared for the Stevens announcement and proceeded to negotiate about the amount the city would pay for the building, that is, to what extent it would subsidize the construction of the temporary quarters. Agreement was reached before the case was due to come to trial again. The city also wanted a statement from Feinmark to the effect that his case was without legal foundation and that all aspects of the Church Street Project were entirely valid and lawful, because it wanted to avoid giving the impression that the suit had forced it to make the other arrangements. The city's anxiety to avoid litigation was an indication, of course, that legal action was an excellent way for an interested party to improve its bargaining position. Feinmark's willingness to recant did not extend far enough to satisfy Lee and Logue's desires for his self-flagellation (after all, Feinmark had his professional reputation to worry about) and, after some confusion, no statement was issued.

As it turned out, only nine merchants were interested in temporary relocation. They formed a corporation, with Feinmark as their attorney, to erect a $50,000 prefabricated building. The city's advance payment for the building was $25,000. The nine prospective tenants paid three months' rent in advance, another $9,000. The corporation borrowed the remaining money from a local bank and quickly put up its building. A 150-car parking lot was prepared next to the new stores, which opened for business in March 1959. A year later the bank loan had been retired with the proceeds from rents, which were then reduced to cover operating costs. From all appearances the venture was a success.

By the spring of 1960 the project had dislocated several hundred business concerns. Sixty percent of the firms which had been located north of the Connector had moved to other locations in New Haven, 7 percent moved out of town, and the rest went out of business. About half these discontinued concerns disappeared, but some information is available from the others. They were usually the smallest businesses, those least able to afford higher rents, the loss of customers, and the costs and strains of moving.[32] Forty-three of the relocated businessmen were interviewed. Most reported that both their rents and volume of business had increased in their new locations. About a third of the firms which were paid for the costs of moving received the maximum payment; many losses, for example, of improvements, were not com-

[32] Kinnard and Malinowski, *The Impact of Dislocation on Small Businesses,* pp. 50–51, 83–84. As few proprietors were elderly, at least in the firms north of the Connector, these figures do not reflect old folks retiring rather than moving.

pensable.[33] Most of the interviewed businessmen thought that the Church Street Project would improve downtown retail trade.

The Central Civic Association had some measure of success in pressing the city to take into account the individual interests of many of its members, by timing property acquisition and subsidizing the temporary building. This may have been its founders' principal motivation, but neither Miss Jewett's study nor other observers' impressions of the merchants suggest that many of them were thinking this cooly in the summer of 1957 when the stunning news of the project first reached them. At that time they were opposed to what the city planned and, when they had plucked up their courage enough to say so, they made no bones about announcing their dislike of any form of downtown redevelopment.

In other cities similar groups had succeeded in balking far more modest proposals for downtown renewal. Why not in New Haven? One reason, which hardly bears repeating, was the overwhelming political skill of the Lee administration, which left the CCA without significant allies in an opinion market already saturated with pro-renewal propaganda. Another is that the merchants thought that the project would be good for New Haven, which put them in the difficult position of opposing for selfish reasons something they considered in the public interest. Finally, they were weakened by their stake in the controversy: their tangible, personal, direct economic interests. It may seem paradoxical that a group with economic (as opposed, for example, to "ideological") interests of this kind would be handicapped by them, but the fact that their interests were so direct *and divisible* meant that they were vulnerable to being bought off and divided, which is just what the city did to them.

The third and least troublesome suit, in that it had no discernible effect on project execution, was brought by the Taft Hotel. The Taft was the city's only first-class hotel, although many people thought that it won this classification by default; 60 percent of the respondents in the shopper survey said that New Haven needed a new hotel. Stevens's intention to include a hotel in his development was generally considered the answer to a deficiency that kept New Haven from attracting conventions.

The owner of the Taft felt that what was good for New Haven might not be good for him. After the project was revealed his attorney contacted the New York office of the URA to present his client's feelings about the proposed new hotel. That fall he sent a letter to G. Albert Cole, Housing and Home Finance Administrator, formally protesting the plans for a hotel. These objections were rebuffed. In February the Taft filed suit against Cole and the city in federal court, asking an injunction to prevent release of loan and grant funds, claiming that the law prohibited the use of Federal Housing Adminis-

[33] *Ibid.,* pp. 36–37, 42, 56.

tration funds for hotel construction, and stating that there was not enough business for one hotel and that the project therefore constituted "commercial cannibalism." In effect, the Taft claimed that redevelopment was illegal if it hurt an established business. In May the suit was dismissed: the Taft's possible loss was not valid ground for a suit; the FHA was not involved in the project; federal funds were not to be used for building a hotel. Furthermore, in serving papers on Cole in Washington rather than Connecticut, the plaintiff had acted in the wrong jurisdiction. The Taft appealed, but this decision was upheld by the circuit court in January 1959 and by the United States Supreme Court later that year.[34] This ruling disposed of the last legal action against the project and so lifted the prohibition on borrowing from private sources.

Later Developments

After the Macy Company withdrew in January 1958, Stevens began looking for a department store. By the end of the year he had approached almost every large department store organization in the East, and found none willing to participate in the project. Having failed to attract an out-of-town firm, Stevens turned to Malley's as a possible tenant for the store he planned to build. His first thought was to include the old Malley store in the project, but Lee and Logue refused and told Stevens that any arrangements he made with Malley's would have to be private. Edwards's death in 1958 made dealings somewhat easier than they might otherwise have been. It was agreed that Malley's would lease the new store that Stevens would build, on land that the Malley Estate would buy and lease to him. Stevens would acquire the old Malley building, take a 99-year lease on the site from the Malley Estate, demolish the old building, and use the site and some adjacent land, which had been destined for the bank, as the location for the new hotel.

This change of plan would permit widening Temple Street and give the hotel a more desirable location, with a setback on Chapel Street to avoid traffic congestion. On the other hand, many people considered Malley's a rather lackluster substitute for a glamorous, big-city department store. There would also be a considerable delay in project completion, for construction of the hotel could not begin until Malley's moved into its new home, which would take several years to build.[35] As soon as this agreement was reached it

34 *Taft Hotel Co.* v. *HHFA*, 262 F 2d 307 (2d Cir. 1958), cert. denied, 359 US 967 (1959).

35 It took a year from September 1959 to get all 33 of the Malley heirs to sign the agreement. See Allan R. Talbot, *The Mayor's Game* (New York: Harper and Row, Publishers, 1967), pp. 123–24. Much of my information on developments in the Church Street Project since 1960 is from this source.

was immediately announced by the mayor, deep in his biennial reelection campaign and smarting from unaccustomed criticism from the business community for his handling of Church Street, including a strong critical statement from the president of the Chamber of Commerce.

The First New Haven National Bank's involvement in the project was powerfully affected by these events, which helped nudge it out of the project area altogether. The bank had never put all its eggs in one basket in looking for a new home; from the beginning there had been an element of reserve in its commitment to build in the area. Since the project's public debut in 1957 numerous problems had dampened the bank officers' enthusiasm. Some of them wanted more access room for drive-in tellers than Stevens was willing to grant. The bank's building site on Chapel Street included a slice off the back of Savitt's store, and his suit made the city miss its deadline for turning the complete site over to the bank. The west side of the bank's proposed new site abutted the Malley store and this posed certain technical problems for construction of the new bank building, including expenditure of over $100,000 to shore up Malley's foundation. The bank once again was up in the air while waiting for Stevens and Malley's to negotiate. When this deal began to take shape, a search began for another site for the bank elsewhere in the project, but no alternative really seemed to fit in with Stevens's plans. The bank's officials were becoming increasingly nervous and disenchanted with the prospect of tying their needs for a new building to the infinitely complicated and changing plans of the Church Street Project. By the time Stevens offered them an alternate site and compensation for their expenses if they would give up the Chapel Street location for the hotel, they accepted his offer but were undecided whether to remain in the project at all.

The situation remained cloudy for most of the summer. The bank, having been bounced from pillar to post by the city, Savitt, and Stevens, now had a surprise of its own. With no advance warning it disclosed that it would merge with another bank which owned a large office building with spacious ground-floor banking facilities. The First New Haven would have no need for a new building of its own and would withdraw from the Church Street Project, except perhaps for a small branch. Lee, taken completely by surprise, felt betrayed. A few weeks later the Antitrust Division of the Department of Justice warned the two banks that it would take action if the merger were consummated. Merger plans were cancelled, but the First New Haven stayed out of the project anyway.

Shortly thereafter Lee heard that the bank was planning its new building farther out Church Street, at the northern fringe of the central business district. Fearing for the effect on the CBD, for this was just the sort of diffusion that the project was designed in part to counter, Lee told the bank's officers that this location would put them "out of the mainstream of urban life." He showed them a rundown building for sale almost across Church Street from their old home and suggested that they buy it and build there. This was done and the new building soon rose opposite the still vacant project area. This solution was much easier for the bank than construction of a similar building in the project, subject to constraints from the city, negotiations with Stevens, coordination with his intricate schedule, and assorted other complications attendant on participation in an urban renewal project. Ultimately the bank profited from the project, for it disposed of its unwanted old building for $1.3 million. At the same time, it avoided the problems of construction in a redevelopment area, thus having the best of both solutions. For its part, the city benefited enormously from the bank's support in 1956 and 1957, when its help was invoked on several occasions to impress potential opponents of the project.

In 1957, when the Church Street Project was announced, Lee said that the four-block section would be completed in three-and-a-half to five years. This was based on the "hope" that the Redevelopment Agency could start acquiring land by Labor Day 1957 and an estimate that construction would begin in the fall of 1958. Two years later most of the four blocks had been cleared and turned into temporary parking lots but no building had begun. While Stevens sought a tenant for the projected department store the plans for the entire project were up in the air. In October 1959 the decision to invite Malley's to join the project and the subsequent withdrawal of the bank led to a wholesale public revision of the schedule: parts of the project would be finished by 1961 and all of it by 1963.

This was a bad month for the project and a bad month for the mayor. Another election was on. The Republicans dwelt on the absence of any construction, assailed Lee for "replacing thriving businesses with parking lots," and asked how long the business district would resemble a bombed-out city. Five weeks before election day the *Register* devoted a substantial part of its front page to a feature entitled "The Real Story of Church Street Redevelopment."[36] The main article recounted the changes and delays since the original announcement. An accompanying editorial strongly criticized the administration for extravagant claims, delays, mismanagement, and secrecy about the current situation. This was aid and comfort to Republican campaigners who were taking the same line. The newspaper mentioned and the Republicans deplored at length that "there is at present no iron-clad agreement in existence between Stevens and the City."[37] It was suggested that Stevens might be victimizing the city and could even walk out of the project. Lee felt that the lack of progress on Church Street hurt him in the 1959 election, in which his share of the total vote dropped from 65 to 62 percent.

These delays were also hard on Stevens, who had an increasing amount

36 *New Haven Evening Register,* 2 October 1959, pp. 1, 8.
37 *Ibid.,* p. 1.

of money tied up in New Haven. He had given the city a check for $430,000 when the first land disposition agreement was signed and had probably spent almost that much more on the Gamble-Desmond hole (before the city acquired it) and on preliminary studies, administrative activities, and architectural plans. (By the end of 1959 more than two dozen architectural schemes had been produced by John Graham, a noted architect.) The changes in plan and the city's default on the initial land disposition agreement in May 1959 led to a renegotiation of the agreement in the early fall. This was not expressed in a formal legal document, but in a "memorandum of understanding" initialed by both parties. Evidently this form was used because, while conditions were still too unsettled for a conclusive document, the political situation required some sort of authoritative public statement of the city's relationship with Stevens. The price per square foot remained the same, but because of street widenings made possible by Malley's participation, the total acreage was reduced somewhat. This agreement also let Stevens buy the land in pieces, instead of all at once. The agreement was announced to the public in October and obediently approved by the Board of Aldermen the same month.

In view of his investment in the project, it is hardly surprising that Stevens did not withdraw when the city defaulted on its original agreement to deliver his land in time. Shortly after the second agreement was announced, Stevens said he felt that "the City owes an adjustment of some kind for the hundreds of thousands of extra interest cost caused by the court action."[38] This resulted from a rise in interest rates while the Savitt case was before the Connecticut Supreme Court.[39] In an accompanying interview Logue replied that the new "memorandum of understanding" made no such provision.

Actually the "Stevens development" was to be built by a firm of which Stevens was half owner and president, the Stevens–New Haven Development Company, Inc. His partners were Graham, the architect; the Gilbane Construction Company, a Providence firm which would be the building contractor; and G. Harold Welch. In 1959 Stevens said that most of the company's initial capitalization of $1 million had been spent already.[40] This may have included Welch's early expenditure on the Gamble-Desmond hole, which may comprise some or all of his equity in the development company.

Welch's partnership in the development company at least opened the way to a return after his many lean years since taking over the Gamble-Desmond lease. At one point he suggested using the hole as a temporary parking lot until the time for construction arrived. The redevelopment staff concluded

[38] *Ibid.,* p. 8.

[39] Interest rates went from 4 percent in 1957 to 6 percent by the time construction began (Talbot, *The Mayor's Game,* p. 124).

[40] *New Haven Evening Register,* 2 October 1959, p. 8.

that the cost of preparing the lot would be far in excess of the expected return and Logue dissuaded Welch. Possibly the settlement with Trinity Church at the time the Redevelopment Agency finally bought the hole included some consideration by the church for Welch. His lease gave him no protection from being cut off by the church without a cent when the city acquired the land, despite his unremunerated expenditures. But the city intended to refuse coming to terms with Trinity Church on a purchase price unless the church gave Welch a share of its proceeds from the sale of the land. They did agree on a negotiated price, however, and the likelihood is that the church agreed to share with Welch.

By the summer of 1960 all land in the project area north of the Connector had been cleared, with the exception of the bank. The Church Street Extension bridge over the Connector was finished. That fall work began on the department store and Parking Authority garage, and progressed at a very slow pace. Across Church Street from the project area the framework of the new bank building was up. Until its completion the old building would impede construction. This was, however, only a problem for the future, for there were no immediate prospects for construction there.

Thus the only building was at the south end of the area, farthest away from the center of town. The section next to the Green was still bare of new structures and hence continued to be a political liability. In his embarrassment Lee produced a diversion that was almost a parody of his political style: the "New Haven Progress Pavilion." This cinder block building at the corner of Church and Chapel Streets "was built through voluntary contributions of labor and material by public and private groups in the City. It contains photographs, models and maps that explain how New Haven is building toward its future." It was staffed by municipal employees who dispensed promotional literature and optimism. Republican attacks on the administration intensified.

The project was delayed because Stevens was having great difficulty finding either tenants for his development's proposed retail facilities or the approximately $5 million he needed to finance construction. These troubles were due in part to the vast difference between the cost of the land he had bought and comparable sites in the suburbs. This handicap undoubtedly heightened potential investors' doubts about the success of the project, particularly in the face of increased competition from new suburban shopping centers. In September 1960 a 90-store center opened a few miles west of New Haven, adjacent both to the Merritt Parkway and to the new Connecticut Turnpike. A smaller development was opening a few miles east of town. To the north, Hamden Plaza, which drained a good deal of business from the CBD when it opened four years earlier, was being doubled in size. Stevens's money troubles were reflected even in the pace of what little construction there was. As its expenditures mounted far beyond payment, Stevens's partner, the Gilbane Construction Company, virtually stopped work on the new department store early in 1961.

It appears that there was considerable friction between Stevens and the city administration in this season of discontent. Promising that "I'll never go into another one of these things," Stevens complained to a reporter about city hall: "Some decisions about the Church Street project didn't make economic sense from the beginning, but they were politically necessary. Nobody has thought about the good of New Haven; they've all been thinking about their own political welfare. And I've been caught in the cross-fire."[41]

These were hard years at city hall. The project was almost completely halted, its principal achievement a $6 million garage that might not be needed because cars could park on what had been the city's prime commercial blocks. Many of the remaining merchants in downtown New Haven reported a disastrous decline in business. From 1957 to 1961 the dollar volume of taxable sales in the entire city had fallen 20 percent.[42] Lee's political career seemed to be plunging into disaster along with the project. In late 1960 he had to announce an increase in the tax rate of more than 10 percent, the first in his administration. That year he learned that he would lose Logue to Boston in 1961. In 1961 Lee reaped the electoral harvest of the project's stagnation; he squeaked through with 4,000 votes to spare, by far his smallest margin since taking office eight years earlier.

Public complaints and recriminations continued. The fifth anniversary of the project's announcement was marked by a bitter monument, a withering series of front-page articles in the *Register* entitled "Redevelopment: On Its Back or On Its Way?"[43] The series noted that when the project was announced Lee said it would be completed within five years, yet five years had passed and only Malley's new store and the garage were near completion. There was not even a beginning on the hotel, high school, shopping facilities, and other promised features. The project had been marred throughout by extravagant claims, changes of plan, and confusion. The only evident result to date was a ruinous slump in downtown trade.

On the public record this must have been the nadir of the project's fortunes, but in fact the tide had turned some time earlier. Stevens's money shortage had finally been solved by Yale's willingness to loan him $4.5 million, an arrangement which took almost 15 months to negotiate and was finally announced in March 1962. In the course of negotiating the loan, Lee had met a member of the Yale Corporation who was also a director of R. H.

41 *Wall Street Journal,* 17 January 1962, p. 12. This article also said that Lee was not planning to run for mayor again.

42 Source: data from the Connecticut Tax Department reported in the *New Haven Register,* 24 June 1962, p. 1. The comparable decline in Hartford and Bridgeport was only 5 percent.

43 *New Haven Register,* 22–26 June 1962.

Macy and Company. Through him the mayor renewed relations with the Macy management that spring and by the end of the summer Lee had negotiated an agreement for Macy's to build a $5 million department store in the project area. Stevens did not participate in these discussions, although he owned the building site in question.[44] These two events started the project on its way at last. Lee's electoral fortunes recovered also. He carried every ward in 1963 and maintained almost a two to one ratio over various opponents in his remaining elections.

By 1967 the key four blocks north of the Connector were rebuilt. In addition to the garage and two major department stores, this area included a covered 2-story shopping mall, a 19-floor hotel, and a 14-floor office building. Retail sales in the city increased 41 percent from 1963 to 1967. By the time Lee left office a variety of buildings were finished or under construction elsewhere in the project area. These included a $20 million municipal coliseum and convention center topped by a 2,400-car garage, an office tower to house the international headquarters of the Knights of Columbus, the Richard C. Lee High School,[45] a major medical office building, and 518 units of low-cost housing.

In 1964 Stevens withdrew as director of the four-block commercial development, although he retained a financial interest in the project. The Gilbane Company built the hotel and a local construction firm put up the office tower and the shopping mall. Stevens could scarcely have been sorry to reduce his ties to New Haven. He reportedly lost money on the project,[46] and he must have invested a disproportionate amount of time in it.

Conclusions

How can this long and complicated narrative enhance our understanding of local politics? A summary of the high points is one way to begin. The project's origins were as haphazard and dogged by false starts as its later stages. Although the city's fading commercial appeal was reflected in dwindling cash register receipts, local businessmen had not exerted themselves in behalf of either private or public solutions to the problem, with the exception of the stillborn Parking Authority. The closing of the Gamble-Desmond store drew Lee's attention to the CBD's plight and led to his attempts to be a broker between Stevens and local interests. Although these efforts failed, Stevens's involvement had brought about a second fortuitous development: at his

[44] Talbot, *The Mayor's Game*, p. 130.

[45] At some time along the way this had been changed from a junior to a senior high school.

[46] Talbot, *The Mayor's Game*, p. 134.

insistence, the scope of contemplated action was vastly expanded. Stevens's most important impact on the project came during its conception, for he rather than city officials first thought that the project had to be so sweeping.

Even before the failure of Stevens's attempt at private development, Logue had included the crucial blocks in an urban renewal project application, which became the vehicle for modernizing the CBD. Using the urban renewal process for commercial redevelopment of this magnitude required a certain amount of innovation by the Urban Renewal Administration, which was facilitated both by the technical expertise and aggressiveness of New Haven's officials and by the useful alliance with Senator Bush. Local support for the project was slowly built in the business community, layer by layer. As the administration's plans ripened new participants—and therefore allies—were acquired. Together with Lee's all-purpose supporters on the CAC, these businessmen converted or stifled potential opponents. The other specific local obstacle was public opinion. The painstaking preparation for announcing the project and defending it at its public hearings inundated local residents with favorable publicity and, for a time, overawed the project's "natural" opponents, the Church Street merchants. The same combination of technical skill, effective publicity, and interest group alliances, together with Lee's political power, maintained the project's momentum through demolition of the key blocks and the long years of stagnation. The deadlock about financing the project was broken by yet another fortuitous event: Yale's willingness to underwrite Stevens. The connection with the university then provided a bonus in the opportunity for Macy's reentry into the project.[47]

The project's history reveals that the business community, often viewed as monolithic, was in fact divided in a number of respects. From the closing of Gamble-Desmond to clearing the CBD, a variety of business interests were in conflict with each other or with city hall. Welch, who started it all, quickly found his plans balked by Savitt and other adjoining businessmen and, eventually, by the city. Stevens and the local businessmen whose endorsement Lee provided were frustrated again by Savitt and his neighbors. When the enterprise became an urban renewal project, it accumulated various enemies even before it was disclosed: the millionaire owner of the newspapers, the city's only major department store, its biggest realtor, and various other downtown businesses. When the project was disclosed it soon had new opponents, including almost 100 more downtown merchants and the Taft Hotel. With the exception of the press publicity given to their cases, there seems to have been virtually no coordination of tactics by these various groups. The most important reason for this was their diversity of interests; perhaps because most of them despaired of stopping the project, their behavior was

---

[47] The Church Street Project illustrates Yale's most important contribution to New Haven politics: it is a focal point for fortuitous events.

calculated instead to shape the city's execution of the project so as to benefit from it. Thus their opposition to the project was not a sufficient basis for an alliance. Moreover, some of these actors, notably the merchants in the Central Civic Association, seem not to have considered acting in concert with their most obvious potential ally, the Republican party. Initially, when the project was all bright plans, the Republicans hesitated to attack it. When the lack of progress after demolition became obvious, the Republicans leaped to the attack, but by then most of the project's other opponents had come to terms with it.

The administration used a variety of techniques to deal with its actual or potential opponents. Hostile businessmen were isolated by ostentatiously mobilizing friendly ones, either specific allies like the bank or general ones like the telephone and power companies. A combination of these tactics plus selective concessions was used on members of the Central Civic Association and on Savitt. The most important and basic defenses were the project's wide popularity, a result of the administration's political skill, and Lee's popularity and political strength. These advantages closed off every point of attack. The various municipal agencies that might have offered a foothold for criticism were tightly controlled by the mayor and his allies. As long as he and the project retained popularity, neither dissident Democrats nor Republicans could see much political reward in criticizing the project. Once matters had progressed to the point of wholesale clearance, the project's political vulnerability diminished. As the years went by without satisfactory reconstruction, the project suffered a drop in public esteem, but by then it was too late. The Republicans saw a promising issue and denounced the project vehemently, but once the area had been cleared, the project was irrevocable. The Republicans' real target was Lee, of course, and he was a good deal more vulnerable. He faced political disaster if he failed to put the Church Street area back together again, and could only press forward with the project.

The project's inception, development, and survival depended on four important advantages possessed by the Lee administration: technical skill, public relations talent, Lee's control of his government and party, and his alliance with businessmen and Yale. The great competence of New Haven's redevelopment officials not only gave them the benefit of the doubt with the federal government but enabled them to manipulate federal requirements. This same ability was an important consideration in attracting Stevens to New Haven and maintaining his participation. By the same token, it impressed the businessmen on whom Lee relied for endorsement and cooperation. Finally, of course, Lee's extraordinary ability contributed to the eventual success of what was, in comparison to other projects, a daring and fundamental effort to deal with municipal problems. Lee's talent for publicity had a good deal to do with the initial public acclaim that greeted the project's announcement and persisted at least until demolition was well under way. More basically, Lee's popularity helped maintain his position in his party and thus secured the project's political base. The combination of these two factors was responsible for immobilizing not only intrinsic opponents of the project but Republican politicians, who hesitated to attack it in its early years. Lee's success with public opinion in turn contributed mightily to his grip on the various organs of municipal government and hence made sure of coordinated public action on the project. The part played by his business allies is clear from the preceding narrative. And Yale, which had good reason to be wary of its involvements in New Haven politics, nevertheless was available to bail out the city and Stevens when no other source of financial support could be found. As before, the university was the most undemanding of allies.

The eventual success or failure of the project's assorted opponents varied as much as their interests. Some of them got very little of what they wanted: the newspapers,[48] the realtor, other downtown businessmen worried about competition from the project, and the Taft Hotel. This is not to say, however, that their opposition had no effect on the city, which at least had to take into account such considerations as press hostility. Savitt and many of the merchants represented by the Central Civic Association got part of what they wanted from city hall. After turning down various concessions and investment opportunities offered in hopes that he would not sue, Savitt did take the city to court and had enough success to raise the price for his building. His profit from this transaction was reduced by his considerable legal fees and the interest foregone by having to wait for his purchase price. I have no way of knowing how much money he netted by his dogged opposition, but it could not have been very much. His suit cost the city a good sum for legal expenses, as well as time, which, in the circumstances, was far more precious. It would seem that the damage Savitt inflicted on the city far exceeded his gains.

Many individual members of the Central Civic Association did very well out of their organization's activities. The threat the CCA posed induced the administration to time condemnation proceedings and in other ways look after the interests of particular shopkeepers. The CCA also pressed the city to subsidize the temporary building occupied by nine of its members. Some merchants displaced by the project went out of business and some became more prosperous. The CCA's activities cost the city money for legal fees and the temporary building, but do not seem to have affected the project as much as Savitt did. Savitt and the little merchants were the only local interests who were able to gain concessions from the city through their opposition;

[48] It did not appear that the elder Jackson's downtown real estate holdings had any restraining effect on his opposition to the project.

in both cases litigation was their principal tactic. Directly and immediately affected by the project, they had legal claims based on its impact. And they were the least prominent of the various business interests opposed to it.

Malley's had a somewhat different relationship to the project. Failing to get what he wanted from the city, Edwards was able to win a couple of minor concessions, such as keeping the shopper survey confidential, but he was totally unsuccessful in his efforts to defeat the project. Malley's opposition to the project subsided and, with Stevens's failure to woo an out-of-town department store, Malley's became a part of the project on very favorable terms. This lucrative arrangement was not, however, a product of Malley's earlier opposition; in no sense had it forced concessions from Stevens and the city, who were overjoyed at its participation. The favorable deal with Malley's, then, was not part of a zero-sum game reflecting a commensurate loss for the city (although it cost Stevens money), nor did it reflect the department store's political power.

These outcomes nicely illustrate the deficiencies of treating the question "who benefits?" as synonymous to "who governs?" Those who profit from governmental decisions often do not do so by virtue of their political activity or reputed political power.[49] Malley's did very nicely out of the Church Street Project—some years after the total failure of its efforts to kill the project. Stevens, whose ideas about how to redevelop downtown New Haven were responsible for the project in the first place, ended up losing money, despite the influential role he had played. The Jackson newspapers, which had harassed the project almost from its announcement (after being narrowly dissuaded from prematurely disclosing the secret), now receive an estimated half million dollars annually in Macy advertising. Yet at the height of Lee's negotiations with Macy's they carried a long and relentlessly hostile series of articles suggesting that the project was a disaster. In short, there were major discrepancies between the degree of control over project decisions exerted by private interests and the benefits that these interests eventually derived from the project.

While identifying the beneficiaries of a public policy can be helpful in understanding how that policy came about, limiting such a list to private interests would be a serious mistake. Insofar as understanding the origins of the Church Street Project is concerned, the principal beneficiaries of the project were public rather than private figures; their rewards were prestige, fame, and career advancement. The most important of these beneficiaries were, of course, Lee and his lieutenants in the city's urban renewal officialdom. The announcement of the project marked Lee's entry on the

---

[49] It might be noted that although the Church Street Project was designed to keep business away from suburban shopping centers, suburban interests apparently did not attempt to influence any decisions connected with the project.

national political scene. It also was the biggest factor in establishing the reputations of Logue, Taylor, Appleby, and their assistants.

Another noteworthy aspect of the project's history is the apathy of most businessmen to the public remedies, ranging from the Parking Authority to urban renewal, that could be devised to deal with the CBD's decay. With some ineffectual exceptions, these men did not seek public solutions to the trends that were eroding their livelihoods. More generally, it appears that many individuals and groups whose interests can be significantly affected by governmental policies are ignorant of those policies that can or do affect them. This ignorance and indifference are not limited to the poor, but extend fairly generally, if not equally, across the social and economic spectrum of American life.

A politician can use this situation to enhance his own position; to win votes, fame, campaign contributions, and help with his substantive programs. He can do this not only by satisfying the explicit demands of the electorate, but by stimulating demands which he then satisfies. The process of satisfaction may begin even before the corresponding demands are elicited. In other words, a politician can not only choose certain alternatives on the "agenda" of public issues, but can also put alternatives on the agenda.[50]

In generating demands and devising policies to gratify them, the politician has some scope for action that does not infringe on politically dangerous opposed interests. (This is not to say that even unopposed progress is easy, but only that Newton's second law is not always valid in politics.) This proposition runs counter to the view that all relevant actors already have an opinion on every issue, or, as David Riesman puts it, "so intractable is the political world of the veto groups that opinion as such is felt to be almost irrelevant."[51] On many issues in New Haven, including almost everything

---

50 By "agenda" I mean that set of possible courses of action under consideration by members of the polity. There is a difference, difficult to define but nonetheless crucial, between statements of ideal goals and proposals that can reasonably be expected to occur. Clearing the Oak Street slums was first suggested in the Gilbert-Olmstead plan of 1910, but at that time it was just a good idea, a specific variant of the pious wish that the city's slums would disappear.

The community agenda of issues is an important subject in discussions of political power and "nondecisions." See, for example, *Who Governs?*, pp. 92–94, 126–28; Dahl, "A Critique of the Ruling Elite Model," *American Political Science Review*, 52 (June 1958), 469; Jan G. Deutsch, "Neutrality, Legitimacy, and the Supreme Court: Some Intersections Between Law and Political Science," *Stanford Law Review*, 20 (January 1968), 254–57; Peter Bachrach and Morton S. Baratz, "Two Faces of Power," *American Political Science Review*, 56 (December 1962), 948–49; and Nelson W. Polsby, *Community Power and Political Theory* (New Haven, Conn.: Yale University Press, 1963), pp. 133–35.

51 David Riesman, Nathan Glazer, and Reuel Denney, *The Lonely Crowd*, Anchor ed. (New York: Doubleday & Company, Inc., 1953), p. 259. This notion that American

connected with urban renewal, this clearly was not true. Indeed, most of these concerns had barely entered the consciousness of most local political actors. Thus the tolerances of opposing interest groups did not confine Lee on dead center.[52] The ratio between the distance a politician can actually move and the effective opposition his policies arouse is partly a function of his ability to formulate policies so as to minimize their apparent cost to specific groups. In good measure this is a matter of the politician's skill at exploiting the "dazzling opportunity" of what Dahl calls "slack in the system": "most citizens use their resources for purposes other than gaining influence over government decisions."[53] Lee also exploited the relative novelty of urban renewal, which was so new an issue that habits and coalitions about it had not yet formed.

Effective support and antagonism for a policy are by no means a function only of its inherent properties. Some actors supporting the Church Street Project (or any other public policy, for that matter) might be called *intrinsic* elements of the coalition: their support was motivated by their attitude toward the project itself, and their participation was explicitly directed toward forwarding the project. The Chamber of Commerce is an example of this aspect of the project coalition. The motivations of the telephone and power companies, while not limited to this one project, were largely intrinsic.

The motivations of other elements of the coalition were *extrinsic*. Their support was fully as essential as that of the Chamber of Commerce, for example, but it was not given because of attitudes toward, or benefits from, the project. Perhaps the most important extrinsic part of the project coalition was the Democratic organization. While the machine's support produced the aldermanic majorities that were essential to the project, this support was not induced by favorable attitudes toward Church Street redevelopment. Within very broad limits (discussed in Chapters 7 and 11), the organization supported Lee's policies almost irrespective of their substantive content. Many party figures were indifferent to the mayor's policies and at least a few were opposed to the scope of his urban renewal program. But policy was far less important to them than patronage. They supported Lee because his candidacy guaranteed them access to the spoils at city hall. Thus the Democratic organization could agree on its mayoral candidate but not on his policy choices. By endorsing the candidate, they contributed to the success of his program, as well as to their own share of the patronage.

---

politics is dominated by "veto groups" is, of course, derived from the recurring discussions of "concurrent majorities" associated with the thought of John C. Calhoun.

[52] This conclusion is often implied in Arthur F. Bentley, *The Process of Government* (Cambridge, Mass.: Harvard University Press, 1967), pp. 436ff. See also Philip Monypenny, "Political Science and the Study of Groups: Notes to Guide a Research Project," *Western Political Quarterly,* 7 (June 1954), 188–89.

[53] *Who Governs?,* pp. 309, 305.

To a significant but indeterminate degree, people who voted for Lee also were part of the project coalition, because his electoral majorities were an important factor in his ability to win acquiescence for his policies.

The motivations of intrinsic supporters were specific to the project, but the consequences of their support were more extensive. The political fortunes of the mayor and other local Democratic candidates reflected the project's popularity; thus whatever helped the project also helped the Democratic ticket. The converse of this proposition was also true, however. The continuation of Lee's big electoral majorities was good for the project, and some people with an interest in downtown renewal therefore contributed to his campaigns to help protect their investment.

All these observations were true in reverse for the project's foes. Some, such as Malley's, opposed it because of its intrinsic features. Others, like the Republican politicians, criticized the project because it was the handiwork of a Democratic administration.

Policy coalitions may be classified according to the respective importance of their intrinsic and extrinsic elements. One might hypothesize that innovation is easier when the extrinsic elements of a coalition predominate, that is, when the innovators do not have to build a new coalition from scratch for each program, but can rely more heavily on their "built-in" support. Extrinsic coalition elements tend to be relatively durable. In New Haven the Democratic organization and voters attracted by Lee's personal qualities and achievements were a staple item of the coalitions supporting his various programs.

Extrinsic elements are political resources that can be cumulated and transferred. Gathered in one arena for one reason, they may be exploited elsewhere for entirely different purposes. The commonest devices for cumulating and transferring power are the political party and the popularity of elected officials. From the standpoint of an innovative politician, the most useful political support is that which can be most easily converted from one arena to another and is freest of encumbrances in the form of reciprocal obligations. Any elected official receives some convertible support without having to "pay" a commensurate amount in return, because of his party affiliation and his personal popularity. Other support requires some sort of "payment" in exchange, but still does not foreclose policy options; patronage is an important example. Even most groups with substantive policy goals are interested only in a fraction of the total spectrum of current political issues, yet if these limited considerations lead them to help a candidate, their support is given to the whole man, not just to that slice of him that carries out the policy important to them. Their support may be given in anticipation of satisfactory performance in a single policy area, but it is just as good as if it were bestowed after approval of the candidate's entire program. In short, the transaction between politician and supporter is seldom an exchange by which the politician commits himself to as great an extent as the supporter. The motivations of supporters are usually far more limited than the consequences for the politician.

The more a leader can rely on supporters who do not expect commensurate policy commitments, the greater his freedom of maneuver. This convertible feature of political resources lets elected officials do many things that are intrinsically unpopular. Examples of unpopular discrete acts in New Haven include the interagency coordination under Logue's direction, relocating displaced blacks into white neighborhoods, and keeping G. Harold Welch from developing the Gamble-Desmond site. Judged independently, these and other acts would not have received much popular affirmation. But Lee was not hurt by these actions because of his personal popularity and the network of alliances he had built. Lee's strategy of buying time for grand achievements with cheap and easy projects like playgrounds further illustrates the convertibility of power resources. The more fields of action in which a politician operates, the more opportunities he has for accumulating power resources through discrete commitments that can then be mobilized to further policies that could never be sustained by their own intrinsic support.

These categories and propositions are reminiscent of supposed similarities between money and political power, a theme that has received the attention of some of the more prolific taxonomists in the social sciences.[54] The analogy has some major limitations that are neither acknowledged nor adequately faced by its champions.[55] Money is a possession, while power seems more usefully conceptualized as a relationship than as an object. If one prefers the power-as-relationship definition, one can surmount this objection by comparing money not to power but to power resources. Other major dissimilarities between money and power resources remain, however. There is no common medium of exchange in power relationships of the sort that money provides. If only for this reason, there can be no standardized unit of measure for power and thus no way of comparing the "value" of exchanges in power transactions.[56]

While the analogy is thus imperfect, there are important areas of similarity. Like money, power resources can be accrued, retained, and transferred;

[54] For example, see Karl W. Deutsch, *The Nerves of Government* (New York: The Free Press, 1963), pp. 116–27; and Talcott Parsons, "The Political Aspect of Social Structure and Process," in *Varieties of Political Theory,* ed. David Easton (Englewood Cliffs, N.J.: Prentice-Hall, Inc., 1966), pp. 71–112.

[55] For a detailed and cogent critique of the money-as-power school, see David A. Baldwin, "Money and Power," *Journal of Politics,* 33 (August 1971), 578–614. A recent article by James S. Coleman also rejects the analogy, but is concerned only with formal power and explicitly excludes informal power from consideration. See Coleman, "Political Money," *American Political Science Review,* 64 (December 1970), 1074–87.

[56] For a discussion of other problems in comparing different aspects of power, see my "Nondecisions and the Study of Local Politics," *American Political Science Review,* 65 (December 1971), 1063–80; and my "Rejoinder," *ibid.,* 1102–4.

gained for one purpose, they can be used for other purposes. This point might seem so transparent as to be unnecessary, were it not for various contradictory notions abroad in the literature. Consider, for example, the proposition that government agencies can rely only on their own clienteles to support their policies and cannot expect political backing from their chief executive. This view of the political autonomy of discrete programs is well stated by Norton Long:

> Power is not concentrated by the structure of government or politics into the hands of a leadership with a capacity to budget it among a diverse set of administrative activities. A picture of the Presidency as a reservoir of authority from which the lower echelons of administration draw life and vigor is an idealized distortion of reality.[57]

Long's assertion does recognize that mayors, governors, and presidents do not have such a large "reservoir of power" that they invariably can lend some to needy subordinates. Programs to which the chief executive assigns a low priority may sink or swim without his intervention. However, the need for individual agencies to rely on their own clienteles for political support does not mean that the chief executive necessarily cannot help them out, but only that he may think that he has better uses for his limited resources. Thus Lee did not (during the period of our study) concern himself much with the affairs and controversies of the New Haven Housing Authority, but he did dip into his reservoir of power to help the Redevelopment Agency through a number of unpopular steps.

The money–power analogy suggests that it is useful to win elections by big margins. Popularity, as demonstrated by a landslide and (usually) manifested in sizable legislative majorities, is a useful resource in dealing with other leaders in one's party, with the opposition party, and with interest groups. Here again, the obverse of this apparently self-evident proposition is a persistent theme in American political science. E. E. Schattschneider, for example, wrote that "the perfect party victory is to be won by accumulating a relatively narrow majority, the mark of the skillful conduct of politics,"[58] because more votes can be won only by more commitments:

> Fifty-one per cent of the vote will give any party all there is of the power to govern. A larger number of votes will add nothing to the victory.... As purchasers of political support the parties are bound to feel that *a landslide is simply political extravagance.* From the point of view of the interests participat-

[57] Norton Long, "Power and Administration," *Public Administration Review,* 9 (October 1949), 258.

[58] E. E. Schattschneider, *Party Government* (New York: Holt, Rinehart and Winston, Inc., 1942), p. 96.

ing in the political venture, it is more profitable to share a victory with a narrow majority than it is to partake of the spoils of victory with a larger number, for the smaller the number of participants the greater will be the share of each.[59]

Similar statements about the virtues of "minimum winning coalitions" appear in the writings of more contemporary political scientists.[60] While these arguments are often carefully qualified, they are sometimes interpreted into much the same sort of statement as Schattschneider's: because party coalitions are cohesive and votes for a candidate are in direct proportion to his "commitments" to voters, large majorities for a party ticket are undesirable in that they reduce the regime's subsequent freedom of action and do not confer any compensating advantages.

In the passage quoted above and elsewhere in his discussion of this subject, Schattschneider stated or implied a number of propositions about the behavior of voters and candidates that also seem implicit in the arguments of the coalition theorists:

1. Skilled political leaders do not try to maximize their share of the vote when they are assured of electoral victory.
2. Winning by a big majority does not improve the victor's chances of accomplishing his policies.
3. The vote for a candidate is in direct proportion to the commitments he has made to interest groups.
4. Such commitments all concern substantive policy.

None of these propositions appears to be true. Contrary to the first one, Lee did try to maximize his majority in each of his campaigns, where his goal was to roll up huge pluralities to strengthen his intraparty position, testify to the appeal of his policies, sweep as many legislative candidates as possible into office with him, and enhance his chances for higher office. Except for the last reason, similar considerations have motivated presidential candidates assured of victory, such as Lyndon B. Johnson in 1964.[61]

---

[59] *Ibid.*, pp. 95–96 (emphasis in the original).

[60] Perhaps the best-known of these statements—and also one of the most carefully limited—is William H. Riker, *A Theory of Political Coalitions* (New Haven, Conn.: Yale University Press, 1962).

[61] Franklin D. Roosevelt explained his 1932 campaign goals in much the same terms. See Rexford G. Tugwell, *The Brains Trust,* Compass ed. (New York: The Viking Press, Inc., 1968), pp. 444–46.

Even if the postelection virtues of the "minimum winning coalition" were as great as has been claimed, the idea has limited practical relevance to electoral politics, for it assumes a high degree of predictability of the gain in votes that will result from each discrete campaign appeal. The multiplicity of such appeals, the imperfection of voters'

The second proposition assumes complete party loyalty by legislators and other officials, a condition that is not attained even in England, much less in this country. Thus a larger legislative margin gives the majority party a cushion against potential defectors.

The last two propositions contradict a variety of well-established findings from voting behavior research, which show that votes for a candidate are powerfully motivated by party identification, his perceived personal qualities, and the image of the other party and its candidate. Partisan loyalties and candidate popularity are political resources that can be used in behalf of the winning candidate's programs and do not rigidly constrain his policy choices. The same is true of support that comes as a result of explicit commitments made by the candidate to interest groups, outside the area of each group's concern. In short, it appears that politics is not an appropriate context for Mies van der Rohe's famous architectural slogan, "less is more."

Thinking of power resources as money is also helpful in considering another topic: do policy achievements, by arousing resentment and using up resources, impose a built-in limit on what a mayor, governor, or president can accomplish? There is an impression among many political scientists that as more and more measures are enacted by a regime there will be a progressive alienation of more and more groups and individuals. Thus the politician gets things done by spending his resources, and when they are depleted, his innovative days are over. Yet one can argue that the politician can invest his resources as well as spending them and that a wise investment policy brings political returns that replenish his stock of resources. Some policies produce a net gain in power because they bring in more support from people who enjoy the benefits than opposition from people who consider themselves disadvantaged. (Financial aid from outside the local decision-making arena will often produce net gain for obvious reasons.) Moreover, some voters who pay no attention to struggles over the adoption of a policy will be favorably impressed by its successful realization. In New Haven this seems to have been particularly true of the Oak Street Project.

As I have argued in these last pages, the ability to accrue and convert power resources is a crucial aspect of policy innovation. There are, however, institutional and procedural limits to the convertibility of resources to achieve enactment of unpopular measures. The most obvious of these is the referendum. As we shall see in the next chapter, Lee's highly unpopular attempt to

---

perceptions, the strength of traditional partisan alignments, and the limited number of voter responses (yes, no, abstain) all infuse campaign calculations with a very high level of uncertainty. Since candidates can have only the vaguest notions of the consequences of particular appeals, no candidate could devise his campaign to garner only the minimum number of votes necessary to win and no more. Faced with so much uncertainty about the effects of what he says, the candidate must appeal to more than a bare majority of the electorate.

revise the city charter was successful as long as the issue was a matter of decisions made inside city hall by reluctant but coercible politicians. But when the proposed revision was submitted to the city's voters, it was soundly defeated.

11 the charter revision campaign

Lee won 65 percent of the total vote in the 1957 election against two opponents and in the following months went from triumph to triumph. He was the subject of flattering articles in two national magazines and the Israeli government invited him on a red-carpet tour.[1] Before leaving New Haven he announced the 235-acre, $37,000,000 Wooster Square Project to an enthusiastic crowd. On his return later in the summer he dedicated the city's two new high schools. Substantial and tangible progress was made on Oak Street and Church Street. But in the fall of 1958 the voters overwhelmingly rejected a proposed revision of the city charter that Lee initiated, supported, and identified with his many achievements.

Just as the Church Street Project demonstrates the opportunities for mayoral leadership, Lee's failure at charter revision suggests some of the limitations. The attempt to change the charter had two distinct phases; the contrast between them is also suggestive. In the first phase Lee's efforts were exerted in the "inside" world of politicians and he was able to get his way despite strenuous opposition. His tactics, appeals, and resources resembled those that had been so successful in urban renewal. But in the second phase, when the struggle moved to the electoral arena, the mayor failed dismally, to the surprise of almost all observers. The reasons for his defeat help to illuminate the sources of his success in other issue areas. Because of the heuristic value of the contrast between the two phases of the charter revision campaign, I have divided the narrative into two parts, one dealing with the internal struggle, the other with the election.

Success: Inside Politics

Charter revision had been a hardy perennial in New Haven politics for a dozen years. Between 1947 and 1952 there were six unsuccessful attempts

1 The Israelis invited Lee to their country to "discuss development." They were probably motivated by the hope that he would be a source of favorable propaganda on his return to the United States. Lee spent ten days in Israel and took advantage of the trip for lengthy stopovers in Ireland and Italy, the ancestral homes of the city's two other most numerous ethnic groups. Perhaps as a sop to the outnumbered Yankees, the mayor stayed a day or two in England also. The trip was a source of identification

by charter commissions, aldermanic committees, and citizen groups to institute council-manager or "strong-mayor" plans. These efforts generally were opposed by organization politicians of both parties and were rejected by the Board of Aldermen, the state legislature, or the electorate. In 1951 a committee of 23 aldermen codified the existing charter and a number of modifying state legislative acts and city ordinances into a document which became, in 1952, the Charter of the City of New Haven. It continued the city's "weak-mayor" form of government.

Early in 1954 Lee fulfilled a campaign promise by appointing a commission of 15 prominent citizens to draft a revised charter. Often meeting twice a week, this group deliberated for 18 months, hearing the testimony of several experienced consultants. The resulting draft, a thoroughgoing revision of the 1952 charter, prescribed a "strong-mayor" government. It was passed with some amendments by a reluctant Board of Aldermen and was submitted to the voters in the 1955 municipal election. Lee underwent two major operations that year and spent most of the fall in the hospital. Preoccupied by his health and his own reelection, he had no time for the charter, which he mildly favored. The campaign for approval of the charter suffered from the covert opposition of the Democratic and Republican organizations. Although the draft received 9,415 favorable votes to 6,523 negative ones, it failed of adoption because existing state law required affirmative ballots from 26 percent of all those voting in the election. Against this background of recurrent failure the next attempt at charter revision was made.[2]

It originated in the late summer of 1957, when Lee's second reelection campaign was beginning. The initial impetus for the new attempt was Logue's fear that Lee, the most formidable candidate for the Democratic nomination for United States senator in 1958, might leave New Haven. Logue's crucial role—directing the activities of a number of boards and departments—was based not on ordinances or the charter, but on Lee's delegation of extraordinary powers. Logue worried that Lee's successor would lack his skills, ambition, and strength and would adopt the machine politician's approach to urban renewal, treating it primarily as a source of jobs, contracts, and favors. Logue was unlikely to remain in New Haven long after Lee departed. In any event, his office doubtless would be abolished or severely circumscribed unless it could be based on more durable authority than a mayoral executive order. Logue was under no illusions about the importance to redevelopment of

---

and appeal to innumerable audiences: Lee had an audience with Pope Pius and hence could not be denied a front-page story when the Pontiff died; on Memorial and Veterans Days he reminisced about his visit to the American Cemetery at Anzio; and so on.

2 I am grateful to William Flanigan, William Foltz, Morton Halperin, Sarah McCally, Richard Merritt, Leroy Rieselbach, Bruce Russett, Peter Savage, and Allen Shick for information from their seminar papers on aspects of the charter revision campaign. Charles Blitzer gave me useful information about the Board of Aldermen's role.

Lee's popular leadership, public relations abilities, and influence with the Democratic organization. These were essential to the adoption of new projects. But he felt that in Lee's absence it might be possible to protect the existing urban renewal program from machine influence and so permit the completion of the ambitious agenda to which the city would be committed by mid-1958. In the winter of 1957–58 Logue and his staff began to discuss a revision of the charter to accomplish this objective.

Their idea was to institutionalize the existing ad hoc system of administrative relationships and make the entire urban renewal operation as autonomous as possible. The eventual solution embodied in the draft charter was to include all aspects of urban renewal in a single Development Department, directed by a development administrator under the aegis of a Development Board. The administrator, the key man, would be appointed by the mayor and removed by him, but otherwise would have considerable powers, which would be stated in the charter, not based on the mayor's fiat. The board would replace four semiautonomous bodies: the City Plan Commission, the Redevelopment Agency, the Parking Authority, and the Capital Projects Committee. The new department would perform the functions of these old agencies as well as those of the Department of Traffic and Parking, the Building Department, and the Bureau of Environmental Sanitation. The new urban renewal establishment would also include a Zoning Board of Appeals, two of whose voting members would be officials of the Development Department.

The proposed department would encompass a wide range of governmental functions. Staffed by able officials, headed by a man of ability and determination, and, doubtless, allied with a Citizens Action Commission representing interests with material or prestige stakes in the city's redevelopment program, this new agency would be a formidable adversary for the machine politicians who would succeed Lee. To be sure, a determined mayor could in these circumstances still exert considerable influence on the course of redevelopment. In alliance with the Board of Aldermen, he could prevent the initiation of new projects and affect major steps in existing projects, such as land disposition agreements. But it would be much more difficult for a mayor to interfere with the administration of ongoing projects, short of removing the development administrator and appointing someone more to his liking. This would involve some risks in view of the program's popularity. Hopefully the new superdepartment would have the same degree of independence that various agencies had enjoyed during the Celentano administration.

Although Lee removed himself from the Senate race in February 1958, Logue did not forget about charter revision. Suggesting it to Lee early that year, he sweetened the proposal by adding that this would be an ideal opportunity to seek four-year terms for the mayor and other elected officials. Considering the strain of electioneering, any official would welcome halving the number of these ordeals. This was especially appealing to Lee, who planned to run for governor in 1962 when, it was generally assumed, Governor Ribicoff would try for the Senate seat held by Prescott Bush. Lee's chances for the Democratic gubernatorial nomination were likely to reflect the size of his electoral majorities in New Haven, these being taken as an index of his vote-getting abilities. Lee believed that he would reach a point of diminishing returns in local popularity when the votes his policies won were outweighed by the defection of voters injured by those policies or disenchanted by delays in urban renewal.[3] There was also the possibility that members of his administration would be involved in a damaging scandal. Lee's feeling that he could not afford a reduced majority imposed an additional strain during campaigns. He feared that Celentano could not continue his waiting game indefinitely and would be forced to choose between running against Lee in 1961 or seeing his name fade from public consciousness. Lee was confident that he would defeat his predecessor, but anticipated that he would do so by a diminished majority.[4] All these considerations, added to Lee's passion for orderly arrangements, and in the absence of any evident disadvantages, led the mayor to be receptive to Logue's proposal of another attempt at charter revision.

Success was taken for granted, particularly since the 1957 passage of a Connecticut Home Rule Act established somewhat easier procedures for charter revision, including a provision that a draft charter needed only the approval of a majority of the electors voting *on it* in a general election. Lee controlled the Board of Aldermen, which had 32 Democrats and a lone Republican. His enormous election majorities and the widespread appeal of his policies convinced him that his endorsement would sway most of the electorate. Furthermore, there was always the Democratic machine, now much more responsive to his influence than in 1955, to do precinct work.

In late winter Lee and Logue put the question of charter revision to Barbieri, outlining the four-year term, the Development Department, and the other principal innovation, a Department of Administration to coordinate various fiscal agencies. Logue was the main advocate, arguing that the new charter would make it easier to do a good job of redevelopment and gain the resulting popular acclaim, and that a four-year term would reduce the strain of elections on the organization and have the particular advantage of exposing Lee to the voters only once more before he ran for governor in 1962. It was very much in the New Haven organization's interest to have Lee elected

---

3 For example, a decline in the Jewish vote for Lee of 11 percentage points from 1955 to 1957, attributed to resentment at the displacement of the Church Street merchants.

4 Although Celentano did not run again, Lee still had his closest call in 1961, winning by only 4,000 votes.

governor. This would both get him out of town and give the organization a privileged position in the disposal of state patronage. Barbieri appeared dubious, predicted considerable opposition from the organization, and reminded Lee of the 1955 failure. The mayor replied jocularly that the defeat had resulted from Barbieri's efforts and expressed the hope that his support would guarantee success in 1958.

The Democratic machine's position was crucial in 1958; its reasons for resisting charter revision virtually sum up the motivations of the interest groups that opposed the charter. Lee's effective power came in part directly from his position as mayor and in part from his influence in the Democratic organization; the latter was a result of his shrewd use of the resources available to him in his former role. Under the proposed charter the official, mayoral role would have been vastly strengthened by additions of formal authority. The existing de facto governmental centralization which Lee had achieved informally through patronage and popularity would become the formal prerogative of the mayoralty.[5] The resources required to exert centralized governmental control would be reduced considerably. The party organization would become less necessary to both weak and strong mayors. Declining in importance relative to elected officials, it would therefore have a weaker claim on the spoils of office. The four-year term would halve not only the mayor's need for the organization's campaign support, but also its leaders' opportunities to collect contributions.

These considerations were most pertinent to the proposed Development Department, whose head would be more independent of the party, particularly if he developed a strong relationship with the business community, and more resistant to the organization's claims for patronage and favoritism.[6] The Board of Zoning Appeals, the Building Department, and the Bureau of Environmental Sanitation (charged with housing code inspections) would be lost as sources of privilege directly responsive to the organization. Lee had "kept [machine] politics out of redevelopment" because the program's image

---

[5] Edward C. Banfield has drawn a similar distinction. In his terms the proposed charter would increase the mayor's "costless formal authority." See Banfield, *Political Influence* (New York: The Free Press, 1961), pp. 240–41, 344. Banfield emphasized the costs to a chief executive of exercising central control through informal means. Lee's expanded and strengthened grip at city hall did not extract a cost by limiting his range of alternatives in those areas in which he had chosen to make his mark. This was partly because of the lack of interest in substantive policy of the machine politicians through whom he achieved coordination, and partly because of his ability to recoup, limit, or compensate his "costs" because his electoral majorities gave him a strong bargaining hand. But because exerting this control took time and resources, Lee was to some extent forced to restrict the fields in which he brought about major innovations.

[6] Or, to anticipate the future more realistically, the development administrator would be in a stronger bargaining position to win concessions from the organization in return for favors given to it.

was his ticket to political success in New Haven and the fame he hoped would lead him to higher office. The urban renewal program was offensive to organization Democrats, and the proposed charter would maintain its distasteful features indefinitely by keeping the program's spoils away from them.

The Redevelopment Agency bore the main operational burden of the program on which Lee built and staked his political career. Its key officials were well-educated professional men, most of them career administrators. None was from New Haven and, while they were alert to the political aspects and prerequisites of their duties, they owed nothing to the local party organization and were loyal to Lee and to their sense of professional ethics. Few of them expected to spend their careers in New Haven (and not one remained there). The same was true of several other officials brought in by the mayor. Their goals, identifications, and personal styles all grated on the local politicians with whom they dealt. To the politicians, the new charter symbolized the distasteful governmental approach of men like Logue and Heman B. Averill, the city's director of administration and the likely first head of the Department of Administration, whom Golden had scornfully called "boy scouts."

In the course of extending his influence to its bureaucratic limits, substituting the exigencies of his program for patronage and favoritism, explaining and defending his complicated plans, and serving as the mayor's hatchet man, Logue had come into repeated, abrasive contact with many organization figures. As the agent of a massive expansion of executive influence which greatly restricted their bargaining power and participation, he was bound to have enemies. This "natural" hostility was exacerbated by Logue's personality and interpersonal tactics. His strategem of feigning rage when confronted with opposition, for example, did not endear him to local politicians. Logue did not suffer fools or opponents gladly, and thought he saw both in the Democratic organization, where he was considered arrogant and arbitrary.

Many of these observations also applied to Averill's relations with the organization, but with much less force: he had been in New Haven for a shorter time, had a less abrasive style, and was concerned with facilitating routine decisions consequent to settled policies rather than creating vast innovative projects that disrupted previous political arrangements. Doubtless both men were lightning rods to divert resentment away from the mayor; some of their unpopularity could be attributed to Lee's practice of Machiavelli's maxim that "princes should let the carrying out of unpopular duties devolve on others, and bestow favors themselves."

Despite Barbieri's reluctance, Lee decided to try to revise the charter. His principal goals were the redevelopment reorganization and four-year terms for all elected officials. Consolidation of various fiscal agencies under a single head was less important, but still to be sought. Only the four-year term was really in Lee's political interests. The other goals were already features of his administration. What would happen in these respects after he left office was scarcely of prime concern to Lee. Personally, he would also have preferred more thoroughgoing reform to reduce the size of the Board of Aldermen and make the wards more uniform in size, abolish the Board of Finance, shorten the ballot (each voter voted for 15 city officials), reorganize the Board of Assessors, and make various other drastic changes of conditions that had agitated good-government reformers for decades. But he felt that such proposals would turn his party against him. Consequently he settled for the greatest changes that he thought he could achieve.

He sent to the Board of Aldermen, for consideration at its April meeting, a letter calling the 1952 charter "obsolete" and urging the establishment of a commission to draw up a new charter. His letter contained this passage:

I would recommend no change in the following:
a. The powers, duties, and numbers of the Board of Aldermen.
b. The number of elected officials.
c. The powers and duties of the Board of Finance.

Attached to the letter was a draft resolution for the aldermen, authorizing the mayor to appoint a charter revision commission that would include the president of the Board of Aldermen and the "minority leader," the only Republican member, and directing the commission to report its proposed draft charter to the aldermen no later than July 7. The Board referred the letter and draft resolution to the appropriate committee, which was expected to report it at the board's meeting the following month. At its May meeting the aldermen reluctantly passed the draft resolution and the charter commission quickly began work.

By the time the mayor had written to the aldermen in April, he and Logue had a fairly clear idea of what they wanted and thought they could get in a new charter. While waiting for the aldermen to authorize the commission, Logue thought about people to appoint to it. The commission's membership is of some interest, for this body, along with the aldermen and the electorate, constituted the obstacles that the draft charter had to pass to be enacted. The motivations of the commission's members demonstrate some of the political resources available in a city like New Haven.

The charter commission

The problem in selecting commissioners was to appoint people of stature who would go along with the administration and forestall expected opposition, particularly from the Democratic organization. By law no more than a third of the commission could be public officeholders and only a simple majority could belong to one political party. Logue or another official sounded out each prospective commissioner before issuing a formal invitation, to ascertain not only willingness to serve, but agreement, or willingness to agree, with Lee's ideas on charter revision. In some cases potential commissioners had open minds about the merits of the issue and were expected to base their support on their calculation of future advantage that might be gained from their participation on the commission.

Two members were included by the mayor's draft resolution. William O'Connell, president of the Board of Aldermen, was well known to Democratic party workers. His participation was intended to commit him to the commission's work, satisfy the aldermen, and reassure the fearful party regulars. He was not enthusiastic about the proposed changes but agreed to go along with Lee. Michael DePalma, the lone Republican alderman, had often cooperated with the administration and seldom made effective attempts to embarrass it from his aldermanic rostrum. The Wooster Square Project encompassed virtually all of DePalma's tenth ward. Barbieri was included on the commission for much the same reasons as O'Connell. His membership was considered important as a sign that party workers would not oppose the charter as they had in 1955. It would also let him participate in drawing up the document which he was to support and would let him protect his immediate interest in the Public Works Department.

George DiCenzo, who had served on previous charter commissions, was appointed to the new commission and became its chairman. His appointment was expected to exacerbate the Republican schism and weaken his effectiveness as a partisan Republican by further associating him with the Lee administration. As one city official described the relationship:

> The chairman was appointed after an agreement as to the goals and aims of the charter commission and with full recognition by the mayor and everyone else that George would carry through on it. He was actually in agreement with it all before it started.

The New Haven League of Women Voters' long interest in charter reform and its high prestige made Lee and Logue want to involve it in the commission's work. The League leadership was disappointed by the restrictions placed on the 1958 commission, but approved Lee's charter suggestions and had often given him favored treatment in the past. Logue asked the League to nominate two of its members to serve on the commission. The first suggestions were not acceptable to the administration and the League then submitted a list of names from which Logue chose Mrs. Robert E. Lane and Mrs. Bernard R. Swan. Mrs. Swan was chairman of the Local Affairs Committee of the League. Mrs. Lane had been prominent in League affairs and she and her husband, a Yale political scientist, had been active in Lee's early campaigns. Both women approved of Lee's policies and relied heavily on his and Logue's ability and integrity. Named to the commission as representatives of the League rather than as individuals, their presence was expected to bring League endorsement of the commission's product.[7]

The other six commissioners are best discussed jointly. Russell Atwater, a former Republican alderman and a prominent attorney, had been chairman of the 1955 commission. Maurice Bailey, a nonpartisan Republican, was a member of the Board of Finance; his extraordinary doggedness had helped make him the most influential member of that body. William C. Lynch, a young attorney, was treasurer of the 1957 Citizens for Lee. Eugene V. Rostow was dean of the Yale Law School, a prominent "citizen" supporter of Lee, and had been vice chairman of the 1955 commission. Joseph Rourke, another Lee backer, was secretary of the Connecticut Labor Council and former president of the state AFL. Orville Sweeting, a chemist at the Winchester plant, was chairman of the Citizens Advisory Committee on Education. Rourke and Rostow were members of the board of directors of the CAC. Some of these men were closely identified with past attempts at charter revision, favored the mayor's proposed changes, and were interested in seeing their past labors bring fruit. (It was clear that the 1958 charter would bear a strong resemblance to the 1955 draft.) The commissioners tended to be Lee supporters who approved the mayor's achievements and wanted to give him a hand, even though they may have realized that the commission would be little more than a rubber stamp. Lee's control of such municipal powers as zoning, his influence in the court system and on political nominations and appointments at several levels of government, and his influence with numerous concerns doing business with the city all could be turned to the advantage or disadvantage of several commissioners.

The commissioners were chosen in part to lend prestige of a nonpartisan sort to the commission. The most prestigious members tended to be least in evidence; it is likely that one such commissioner attended no working meetings. Some commissioners were little more than fillers (one unguarded synonym was "patsy"). One or two were picked to be effective advocates and one was thought of as a chairman who would hurry matters along. Six of the commissioners were Democrats, four were Republicans, and two were independents.

The mayor announced the names of the commissioners on May 23 and scheduled the first meeting of the commission for May 28. Because the resolution set a deadline of July 7 for the commission to complete its work and report to the aldermen, it was not difficult to see that there would be little time for deliberation. This point was exploited by Republican spokesmen who charged that the charter must already be written and needed only the commission's stamp of approval.

Such critics were right. Lee and Logue had decided to use the 1955 charter

---

[7] As it turned out, the League voted that fall not to support the draft charter. It is doubtful that this had any significant influence on the outcome of the referendum.

as a base, making what modifications they considered necessary. They also decided that the commission need not consult a variety of experts nor hear the views of numerous department heads, steps that would impede the job of ratifying the administration's desires. This excluded, among others, Francis Kelly, executive director of the Taxpayers Research Council. Kelly probably felt slighted by this move and his hurt feelings may have strengthened his subsequent vigorous hostility to the 1958 proposal.

The first commission meeting was held May 28 in the mayor's office. Lee, presiding, went over the areas of proposed major change. He suggested using the 1955 charter as a base for consideration and "made available" Logue, Averill, and their assistants as a staff to present drafts for the commission's approval. Several commissioners expressed concern about the Democratic organization's attitude, citing as evidence Barbieri's absence from the meeting. O'Connell's remarks about the party's likely reluctance evoked gloom. Lee responded with a strong rallying statement about the desirability of the contemplated changes and his and Barbieri's ability to sell these measures to the party. The meeting broke up shortly, with one commissioner remarking to Logue, "You just keep putting the stuff out and giving it to us, Ed, and we'll approve it."

During the meeting the man whom Lee and Logue had tabbed as chairman objected to several of Lee's proposals. For a long time after the meeting he continued his debate with Logue and Averill. This jarring note caused a change in plans, and DiCenzo became chairman.

The 1958 charter commission met 12 times in the five weeks from May 28 to June 30. Seven to nine commissioners usually attended. The staff presented draft sections, pointing out the differences from the existing charter and the occasional divergences from the 1955 proposal. The commission debated, modified, and accepted the drafts. It made no important substantive changes, with one exception to be discussed shortly. Usually issues were decided by a "sense of the meeting" and formal votes were rare.

The major provisions were (1) creation of the urban renewal establishment described above; (2) creation of a Department of Administration including fiscal, purchasing, and personnel functions, whose director would also supervise all other city departments except those in the Development Department, and would, in the mayor's absence, cast his vote on a number of semiautonomous boards; (3) four-year terms for elected officials; and (4) reduction in the powers of most boards to make them largely advisory, while their membership would be increased. These changes had the double advantage of concentrating executive power and providing more positions to reward the politically deserving without giving away any freedom of decision.

The first business meetings of the commission were marked by very little progress, largely because one commissioner argued over many minor points, questioned most staff recommendations, and made numerous unacceptable suggestions of his own. This haggling, expressed with great force and stubbornness, became so serious an obstruction that two commissioners considered resigning, an action which also was often threatened by the obstructionist, who gave the impression that he intended to sabotage the commission. The mayor suspected that Barbieri and Golden had inspired these tactics. Lee asked Barbieri to advise the obstructionist to calm down. His warning, which served to remind both men of their obligations to the administration, eventually took effect.

The administration failed to get its way only on the issue of a four-year term for aldermen. One commissioner insisted that the aldermanic term should remain at two years to provide for "separation of powers" and afford an opportunity for public assessment of the administration's performance. He pressed his point by threatening to submit a minority report. DiCenzo supported him, presumably to avoid looking like a rubber stamp. Realizing that the Board of Aldermen could always change the draft charter to provide for a four-year term, and wanting at all costs to avoid the precedent of a minority report, Barbieri cast the deciding vote in favor of the shorter term. He later had assurances that if the aldermen lengthened their term the charter commission would accept this change; the earlier vote would have served its ceremonial purpose and demonstrated DiCenzo's "independence."

A two-year term for aldermen would present numerous problems for New Haven politicians. Campaign organization and fund raising were centered on the race for mayor and the aldermanic vote in each ward reflected this key contest. Without the popularity and campaign support that the mayoralty candidate gave to his aldermanic ticket, the aldermen might become more autonomous as a result of their need to make an appeal independent of the mayor's record in the midterm election. But without the salient mayoralty campaign to stimulate workers and contributors, it would be difficult to mobilize centralized campaign support. This would greatly benefit the party which did not control city hall, as its aldermanic candidates in midterm elections would not have to compete with a popular opponent at the head of the ticket. Thus the mayor would face the possibility of losing control of his legislature in the midterm election. To counter this danger he would have to campaign energetically for his party's ticket. This would vitiate the four-year term for citywide officials, because the mayor might find himself working as hard for his legislative ticket as for his own election, at the same time realizing that he could not bestow all his popularity on it. In Lee's case the likely loss of some seats in the midterm aldermanic election of 1961 might be taken as evidence of his declining popularity—the very event that the four-year term was planned to avoid. Lee and Barbieri did not like the two-year aldermanic term at all, but they were sure that this provision would not survive the attention of aldermen, who would be more concerned with tenure than possible increments of autonomy.

With the exceptions described above, the deliberations of the Charter Revision Commission proceeded without major controversy. O'Connell and DePalma limited their contributions in commission meetings to a jealous but not entirely successful guarding of aldermanic jurisdictions. Similarly, Barbieri was interested in protecting his Department of Public Works from possible encroachment.[8]

The commission completed its work at the end of June and submitted a draft revised charter to the Board of Aldermen. At the same time the commission's recommendations were made public.

The charter in public

From the first public step toward charter revision (the mayor's letter to the Board of Aldermen) vociferous opposition had been expressed by the *New Haven Register* and the Republican "Watchdog Committee," a group established after the debacle of the 1957 elections to comment on Lee's stewardship. For lack of any other target, early criticism was directed at the limitations suggested by Lee's letter, which were taken as evidence that he was motivated by "political considerations" rather than a desire for "real reform." Nine editorials questioning Lee's motives and the need for charter reform appeared in the *Register* from April to the approval of the draft charter by the aldermen in early September. As the terms of the proposed charter became known during the summer, the Republicans charged that they were intended to establish dictatorial government and perpetuate Democratic control of city hall. The *Register* carried several articles describing defects in the draft discerned by various observers.

The state Home Rule Act required the charter commission to hold at least one public hearing in the course of its work. The purpose of a hearing can be either to gather information or to present a proposed policy for comment by the public. Since Lee and Logue wanted to avoid controversy and deny their opponents opportunities for publicity, they decided to schedule the hearing in early June and characterize it as an attempt by the commission to solicit suggestions. This would prevent use of the hearing as a rostrum for criticism and protect the commission from possible charges that it had not made an earnest attempt to collect opinions from the public.

This strategy worked perfectly. The hearing, held on June 11, was attended by 35 persons, most of them administration insiders. DiCenzo announced that the commission would "make no expression tonight. We are here for the

---

[8] A major source of patronage, the Public Works Department usually was headed by the ruling party's political manager. This was distasteful to good-government forces, which advocated a statutory requirement that the director of public works be a licensed engineer.

purpose of receiving suggestions." The president of the League of Women Voters read a short statement containing several recommendations similar to major points in the draft charter and gently expressing her regret at the limitations placed on the commission. A Republican spokesman observed that the scanty attendance indicated no great public desire for charter revision, opposed a four-year term, endorsed several suggestions made by the preceding speaker, and urged more sweeping changes on the commission.

The head of a group composed of the police, fire, and school unions expressed his frustration at the shadowy substance of the hearing:

> You could help us, if the committee is in any position to, if you do have any ideas, if there is any substance to those rumors, by telling us just a little bit about a few questions that we have. . . . I thought that you might be able to give us something to sit down and consider.

DiCenzo replied that rumors were unreliable and that the commission was there to hear suggested changes. The two men engaged in a lengthy colloquy, each asking for the other's thoughts. After two indignant but trifling protests, the meeting adjourned. The administration had avoided giving its enemies an opportunity to make a public case.

The aldermen and the charter

Most members of the Board of Aldermen had viewed the mayor's letter with suspicion. They quickly learned that Logue was playing a prominent part in the affair and what kind of revised charter he and the mayor had in mind. Neither of these discoveries pleased them, but they complied with Lee's wishes in passing the draft resolution. They were less complaisant when they received the commission's report in July, for reasons that must be explained at some length. For one thing, the aldermen were mostly part of the Democratic organization and thus took its view of the proposed charter. Moreover, the redevelopment program represented the peak of aldermanic impotence in the Lee administration. The board's only role was to approve the plans and agreements presented to it by the administration. The aldermen saw the 1958 charter as an attempt to formalize and perpetuate impersonal, bureaucratic procedures and powers in a monolithic executive that would further erode their power and prestige.

This impression was given force by, and was often expressed as, their antipathy to Logue and Averill, whom they saw as the instigators and authors of the new charter. In large measure the objections the aldermen raised to specific provisions were expressions of their general resentment; naturally the points they singled out for criticism were those that embodied this strengthening of the executive. Some of their indignation may have been in compensation for their feelings of impotence. After these grievous potential injuries they felt insulted that they had not even been given a four-year term, but were forced to ask for it themselves. All the aldermen resented this enforced supplication; some suspected that the administration had deliberately omitted the provision in order to use it as a bargaining point.

The aldermen were deeply disturbed that two elected officials—the tax collector and treasurer—would be subordinate to an appointed official as division heads in the Department of Administration. The subversion of the elective process which these provisions seemed to represent was enhanced by the fact that the two elected officials doubtless would be loyal organization regulars, while their boss, a bureaucrat, was not even required to be a resident of New Haven.

It should not be thought that all aldermen were deeply committed to these opinions, nor that the indignation of many of them could not be assuaged by contemplation of the rewards that they hoped to gain from acceding to the mayor's pressure. Certainly their political futures were more salient than the proposed charter to at least the "leaders" on the board. Most aldermen, however, were sufficiently stubborn to require considerable persuasion.

A few days before the board's July meeting Lee called half a dozen aldermen to his office. Calling them the "key members" of the board, he said that he wanted to be sure of their support and proceeded to outline the major provisions of the draft and its political advantages. The latter centered on Lee's fear that his electoral majorities would dwindle and his suggestion that the fortunes of his audience were bound up with his own. Barbieri admitted his hostility to the 1955 charter proposal and added that he had participated in the 1958 commission's deliberations and heartily endorsed its recommendations, which he felt would be beneficial to the party. He also explained his strategy on the issue of two-year terms for aldermen. O'Connell added a few lukewarm sentences. It was clear that the aldermen were dubious, as well as ignorant of the legal procedures for charter revision.

The Board of Aldermen referred the commission's report to its Committee on Legislation, which scheduled a hearing on July 23. This lively event was attended by about 125 people. The mayor and a parade of interest group representatives endorsed the draft charter, although many speakers appended reservations about specific provisions. A number of Republicans attacked the draft vigorously, concentrating on the two big departments, the four-year term, the lack of more thoroughgoing reforms, and the absence of a provision prohibiting aldermen from holding city jobs. The gist of their remarks was that the last two points revealed the mayor's scheme to use the two departments and the four-year term to entrench himself and his cronies in office. The final speaker charged that Lee had disguised his real motives with a phony bipartisanship by appointing to the commission only members of a "minority faction" of the Republican party.

Subsequently the draft charter was considered by the board meeting as a committee of the whole, which permitted the board to split up the sections of the charter for study by groups of members in the same room. The aldermen were vigilant for errors, which were common in the hastily-drawn document. The tone of the proceedings is indicated by their habit of referring to the constitutional positions of development administrator and director of administration as "Logue" and "Averill" respectively, and the glad cries of "look at this boner!" when minor mistakes were found. One incident from these deliberations may illustrate the spirit of the board's objections to the charter. An alderman with a small business noticed a provision requiring that all city purchasing be done through the purchasing officer, who presumably would see that orderly procedures were followed. He explained to his colleagues that this would impose a considerable hardship on him. He did considerable business with local government agencies whose bookkeeping methods were sufficiently casual so that he often was paid before delivery. He had come to count on this and used the money to buy the supplies necessary to fill the order for which he had been paid. The other aldermen agreed that his grievance was just and struck out the offending provision.

In early August the aldermen returned the draft charter and their proposed revisions to the charter commission. This body was to consider the aldermanic proposals and refer a final draft charter back to the board, which could only accept or reject the document as a whole. The major aldermanic changes were the following: (1) a four-year term for the Board of Aldermen; (2) authorization of salaries for aldermen, with the amount unspecified; (3) the two aldermanic members of the Development Board were given voting powers; (4) the development administrator was deprived of his vote on this board; (5) the directors of the Divisions of Planning and Zoning of the Department of Development lost their votes on the Board of Zoning Appeals; (6) the director of administration was deprived of his power to cast the mayor's vote on various boards in the latter's absence; (7) the right of the Board of Aldermen to approve redevelopment plans was expressly stated. The first two of these changes represented the desire of the aldermen to "get something" from charter revision equal to the benefits conferred on other officials. The other provisions were attempts to restrict the power of Logue and Averill, limit the hierarchical organization of the city government, and give the Board of Aldermen a place in policy making. Points four and six also expressed a belief that appointed officials should not vote on the boards to which they were constitutionally answerable. The rationale for point five was the unfairness of letting officials help decide appeals of their own decisions and recommendations. Six aldermen appended a minority report calling for a prohibition of dual job-holding, that is, situations where an alderman worked for the city. For obvious reasons this proposal did not attract more support.

As the *New Haven Register* pointed out in an afterthought[9] to its original praise of the aldermen's "independence," these changes did not really make much difference in the draft charter, whose centralizing, hierarchical provisions were largely unmodified. No changes the aldermen could have made, short of a complete and drastic alteration, would have met their objections to the document produced by the commission. Their amendments were like so many other decisions connected with this issue, including Lee's original goal of limited reform—half-measures that aroused opponents and yet did not go far enough to satisfy advocates of real reform. Few aldermen would have become enthusiastic about the revised charter if all their suggestions had been accepted by the administration. Consequently the rejection of some of their proposals only made them a little more sullen.

Proceeding according to plan, the commission accepted the four-year term for aldermen. It also accepted the principle of another aldermanic change by authorizing annual $500 salaries for aldermen, but stipulated that no alderman could draw this pay if he held a city job. The aldermanic members of the Development Board were given the right to vote and the powers of the Board of Aldermen to approve redevelopment projects were explicitly stated. The other amendments were rejected.

It was now up to the Board of Aldermen to approve or reject the draft charter as a whole; no revisions were possible. The mayor called a special meeting of the board for a date six days after the commission's final report. During the summer Barbieri had been urging the aldermen to pass the charter. As their changes indicate, he had not been completely successful, but the only critical decision was now at hand. Barbieri intensified his pressures, although their effect was vitiated by the feeling of many aldermen that his heart was not with the new charter. There was no question about Lee's dedication, however, and the day after his return from Israel he presided over a seven-hour caucus. On this occasion he expressed himself forcefully, emphasizing his dedication to charter revision and the political benefits that it would bring to the party. Lee also had private talks with most aldermen during which he made more specific threats and promises. Under the stimulus of Lee's presence Barbieri grew more active, contacting people to whom individual aldermen were obligated and organizing pressure in particular cases. Lee felt that to demonstrate his determination to the party, he could not allow doubters to abstain: they must show up and vote.

The results demonstrated Lee's success. Although scarcely any aldermen had favored the charter, the vote to approve it was 29 to 4. Of the four dissenters, one did not run for renomination in 1959. Another, Salvatore Ferraiuolo, represented B. Fred Damiani's twelfth ward and had consistently

9 *New Haven Evening Register,* 6 August 1958, p. 1.

opposed Lee. A third dissenter was one of the very few aldermen who did not receive monetary compensation in any form from the city; subsequently he became an employee of the Redevelopment Agency. The fourth, Bartholomew Guida, had long been a maverick.[10] The final aldermanic decision was made before an audience of five persons.

With its passage by the Board of Aldermen the draft charter moved into another arena, one where new bases of power were required. Up to this point Lee had gotten what he wanted in the face of determined opposition by making skilled use of a number of resources: patronage and contracts, police and regulatory powers, the dedication and technical ability of his staff, his popularity, and his ability to identify his goals with those of others. The relevance of these elements to the demands of the situation that the charter now entered will be discussed in the second part of this chapter.

Failure: The Election

Lee planned to sell the charter to the voters on the strength of his endorsement, using Democratic precinct workers as door-to-door salesmen. While the document was being drafted its backers assumed that Lee's two-to-one victory in 1957 assured its automatic success if only the fact of his support could be widely communicated. But as presidential experiences with congressional elections demonstrate, there are limits to a leader's ability to make his popularity effective in an election in which he is not a candidate. It seems likely that this power is greatest in changing situations where familiar criteria and points of reference are absent or irrelevant. Thus Charles DeGaulle's endorsement secured an overwhelming popular majority for the Constitution of the Fifth Republic; but a decade later, in rather settled conditions, the French electorate found his support irrelevant in another (rather trivial) referendum. In 1959 Fidel Castro doubtless could have obtained almost any conceivable election result by announcing his preference to Cuban voters. But New Haven in 1958 was not in a state of flux; there were criteria relevant to the proposed charter and autonomous groups that could judge their own interests in relation to it. Many voters who supported Lee as a mayoral candidate had not abandoned all standards of judgment in favor of unreserved support for anything he proposed. Thus his endorsement was not sufficient to overcome either the hostility of groups that considered the new charter a threat to their interests or a more general and widespread public opinion that the charter was a partisan attempt to give the mayor too much power.

---

10 Guida, perhaps the most independent alderman during the period of our study, was often at odds with Lee and the party organization.

The Campaign for the Charter

On September 24 the Charter Revision Commission marked the successful completion of its work at a lunch arranged and attended by the mayor and those city officials who had served as the commission's staff. During the meal DiCenzo suggested that the commissioners continue the fight for charter reform by reconstituting themselves as a committee to work in the impending electoral campaign. It is a safe assumption that this idea originated in city hall. The assembled commissioners agreed with their chairman and the Citizens Charter Committee came into being. Except for DiCenzo, the commissioners contributed little to this committee but their names. The "committee staff"—Logue, Averill, and their assistants—played a very active role. DiCenzo signed almost one hundred fifty letters to citizens asking for their endorsement of the charter and contributions to help publicize it. Forty-nine recipients responded favorably. Four to five hundred shorter notes were mailed out asking for money and conversational support of the charter. These efforts yielded the committee a few hundred dollars, a small proportion of a total budget in the vicinity of $20,000. The rest of the money came from Lee, who raised it mainly from CAC members and other businessmen. His increased involvement with Jewish civic causes—a result of his trip to Israel—seems to have been helpful in this respect.

A number of news releases were written in the name of the committee. The *Register* carried parts of five of these in its back pages and the *Journal-Courier* printed three, similarly buried. Almost 40,000 brochures were mailed out or given to the Democratic organization for door-to-door distribution. Seven five- or six-column advertisements were taken in the *Register* and one in the *Sunday Herald* during the week before the election. DiCenzo and Mrs. Swan each appeared in one *Register* ad. The message in each ad was a general assertion of the desirability of the three main points of the new charter: the four-year term and the two super-departments. The other ads contained Lee's picture; in three of them the theme was the old charter's "indifference" to slums, in the others it was the dozens of "improvements" embodied in the new charter. On one local radio station 20-second spot advertisements carried the committee's message every hour from noon of the preceding Saturday to noon on election day. These were mainly short talks by Lee linking the new charter with his efforts to build a new New Haven. There were a dozen similar ads on a second station. The one local television channel had twelve 60-second spots, mainly a brief talk by the mayor and a demonstration of the mechanics of voting for the charter on a voting machine.[11] The committee established a speakers bureau and arranged for a number of speeches, chiefly by Lee and

[11] Mechanical problems of one sort or another were too much for some voters. The lever for the charter question was in a normally unused space on the voting machine. This obscure location and the necessity of pulling the various levers in proper sequence frustrated, among others, several members of the Yale political science faculty. Evidently

DiCenzo. The mayor devoted most of his campaigning efforts in 1958 to the charter. He spoke for it dozens of times, concentrating much of his attention on party workers in the wards, attempting to rouse them to support it actively. In addition, Democratic headquarters sent men to distribute bundles of literature and on election day assigned people to urge affirmative votes on citizens approaching the polls.

In all these presentations the major effort was to communicate Lee's endorsement of the charter. It was thought that this was the best easily-dramatized selling point—and perhaps the only one. Lee seldom bothered to explain the measure that he praised so heartily. The charter could be sold on its merits only by complicated arguments that few voters would listen to or understand. The four-year term was difficult to present in a favorable light. Asking for "enough time to do a good job" was not very vivid compared to the opposing argument that the longer term was a grab for power. The administrative reorganization in the new charter was equally devoid of mass appeal. Lee might have dramatized the existing bureaucratic tangle by pointing to the opportunities this opened for patronage and favoritism, but an attack on machine politics was clearly out of the question, particularly because the Democratic machine's support was crucial. He might have tied redevelopment to the new charter, but both his claims and his achievements precluded assertions that the old charter was holding up urban renewal. Lee's main substantive theme was an attempt to squeeze by on this issue: the present charter "did not care" about slums because it did not clearly give responsibility for dealing with them to one department; the city's present great progress was due to an "emergency program," but for real long-range success thorough reorganization was needed. This argument doubtless was neither comprehensible nor convincing. As the *Register* frequently pointed out, the old charter had been good enough for enormous renewal projects. The popular response probably was similar. Furthermore, if Lee could commit the city to so much with the existing charter, a document with fewer checks and balances might give too much scope to executive leadership.

Virtually all impetus for procharter campaigning came from Lee and Logue. On Lee's request the CAC executive committee voted unanimously to endorse the proposed charter at its October meeting. (Golden was not present.) The motion of endorsement and a covering statement were sent to all CAC members and to the newspapers. The *Register* printed the news in a three-inch story on page 5.[12] While the paper always seemed to feature anticharter news in biased articles on page 1 and to bury material from procharter

---

voters often fail to notice when a referendum item appears on the face of the voting machine. See Jack L. Walker, "Ballot Forms and Voter Fatigue: An Analysis of the Office Block and Party Column Ballots," *Midwest Journal of Political Science,* 10 (November 1966), 451.

[12] *New Haven Evening Register,* 30 October 1958.

forces, its policy is only a partial explanation of its treatment of this item. The CAC's public image was not so relevant to the charter. The businessmen who predominated on the CAC did not care very much about charter revision, nor did they want to become involved in a partisan controversy, nor was their endorsement relevant here, as it was in the "businesslike" field of redevelopment. Other than their campaign contributions, they had no vote-getting resources which the mayor did not already possess.

Opposition to the Charter

The Democratic organization was easily the most important interest group involved in the charter controversy. Its enthusiastic, unified support might have put the new charter across; the defection of most of its members insured Lee's defeat. At the beginning of the campaign Lee and Barbieri called a meeting of the Democratic Town Committee to secure official party approval of the new charter, enthuse the ward workers, and inaugurate the campaign. The committee dutifully but reluctantly gave the mayor its formal endorsement, but it was clear that the party workers were not likely to cooperate with his plans for an energetic neighborhood campaign for the charter. One ominous sign was Golden's conspicuous absence from the Town Committee meeting. Perhaps because he wanted to minimize chances of a protracted party split, Golden chose this method of indicating his opposition to the charter. Subsequently he passed the word that he was against the charter but would not think ill of anyone who supported it. Undoubtedly his great prestige and popularity in the organization, as well as his statewide connections and vast store of credits for past favors, encouraged many party regulars to vent their dislike of the charter.

The mayor spent a good deal of time trying to sell the charter to the organization, both directly and through Barbieri. Barbieri's vociferous, well-publicized support of the charter may have helped spread the impression that the Democratic party was in favor of it and hence may have won some votes from people whose main point of reference was their party identification. (But even here many insiders had the impression—perhaps fostered by Barbieri himself—that his heart was not really in his work and therefore he would not be vengeful to those who opposed the charter.) He and the mayor addressed the Democratic Town Committee on the benefits the new charter would bring the party and urged hard work to put it across. Lee spoke to almost every ward committee in behalf of his proposal and also pressured most ward chairmen individually. Despite all these efforts the ward leaders were not sold. Lee had some success with leaders who were closely associated with him or owed their positions in the party to his personal beneficence. Some of these men supported the charter, although few of them had a clear idea of its provisions or could find any advantages in it except Lee's endorsement.

Since so many party workers had economic relationships with the city government, fear of the mayor's retribution kept many of them from working openly against him, but they were able to avoid doing anything very positive either, and they talked against the charter to their families and friends. Few ward organizations distributed the procharter literature sent to them from headquarters. In some cases the ward leaders hired people to pass out the charter committee's brochures and then urged their constituents to vote against it. On election day many party workers driving voters to the polls advised their passengers to vote against the charter and there was a certain amount of anticharter effect in the "help" that poll watchers often gave to people unfamiliar with the voting machines.

Other than noting that the 33 Democratic ward organizations varied from vigorous support of the charter through sullen passivity to outright opposition, it is difficult to determine with any precision the extent of each of these attitudes.[13] The best index of the direction of precinct work is the absentee ballots turned in to the registrar of voters by each party organization in each ward. Connecticut laws permitted the blank ballots to be taken to voters by party workers. After the ballots were filled out they could be taken from the voter to the registrar of voters by the same intermediaries. Most ballots were not from soldiers and traveling salesmen, but from the sick, aged, and incompetent. Given the number of precinct workers in New Haven, it is not surprising that the absentee ballots represented for each party a pool of sure votes, subject, as politicians freely conceded, to the preferences of the party worker who collected them.

In the 1958 election 2,576 absentee ballots were cast in New Haven. In 18 of the 33 wards these ballots can be classified according to which party turned them in. The votes on these ballots concerning the charter reveal the extent of the Democratic ward organizations' revolt. Only 65 percent of the Democratic absentee ballots had votes on the charter issue, compared to 83 percent of the ballots turned in by Republican workers. This silent treatment of the charter by the Democratic workers doubtless extended to other forms of precinct work. As one Democratic ward chairman remarked, "When a thing is so confusing that you can't even understand what it means, you aren't going to work too hard for it."

Many Democratic precinct workers did more than ignore the charter; they actively opposed it. Of the charter votes on the Democratic absentee ballots, 30 percent were cast against the party's official position, compared with less

---

[13] Thirteen of the thirty-three Democratic ward chairmen were interviewed early in 1959. Each was asked his position on the charter and what he did on this issue during the campaign. On the basis of these interviews five chairmen can be classified as active supporters of the charter, six were passive, and two were active opponents.

than 8 percent antiparty votes on the Republican ballots. When votes are computed on a base of all absentee ballots, less than half the Democratic absentee ballots were cast for the charter, while more than 75 percent of the Republican ballots carried opposed votes. As might be expected from the diversity of positions taken on the charter by different Democratic organizations, the vote in favor of the charter on the Democratic absentee ballots varied from 5 percent in one ward to 79 percent in another.

The Republican party was virtually unified in opposition, as the figures cited above indicate. Its politicians had the same motivations as their Democratic opposite numbers for resisting the charter. They also feared—probably correctly—that the new charter would put them at a further disadvantage to the Democrats. The longer term of office would be useful for Lee, while the administrative reorganization would make it easier to carry out vote-getting programs and also would remove a source of possible embarrassment: city officials' quarrels over jurisdictional matters.[14] Furthermore, the whole affair was a fine opportunity to embarrass Lee, for the charter's origins provided ample material for charges of dictatorial conduct. The presence of four Republicans on the charter commission did not inhibit Republican criticism of the charter nor induce major elements of the party to support it. Atwater had virtually retired from active party participation. Bailey was not active in the Republican party; he was a member of Lee's Board of Finance and a known political ally of the mayor. De Palma was not in the inner circle of Republican leadership and also had cooperated with Lee on many past occasions. DiCenzo was not close to the "regular" Republicans and his friendly relations with the administration further weakened his standing with his party. Both the Republican Town Committee and the "Watchdog Committee" voted unanimously to condemn the charter. Republican spokesmen made vigorous attacks on it in speeches and public statements. They printed some brochures for distribution in the wards and bought three 15-minute television programs to express their position. Aside from these efforts the Republicans did not conduct an elaborate campaign against the charter. The party was impoverished and disorganized by its factional division and repeated electoral catastrophes. Many ward leaders were completely inactive and did little but express their opinion to those voters who requested it.

The *Register's* opposition to the charter was manifested early and often. In the eight days before the election it reached its peak with seven editorials, of which the pièce de résistance was a five-part series titled "Politics without Reform." (During this week the Citizens Charter Committee had an adver-

---

[14] That year, for instance, there were several squabbles involving the Building Department's willingness to issue building permits for construction which the City Plan Department disapproved.

tisement for every editorial. Perhaps this timing was coincidental; perhaps it was due to Lee's excellent intelligence system at the *Register*.) The *Register's* news stories regularly implemented its editorial policy. The procharter forces had difficulty getting their statements in print, even in the back pages, while their opponents regularly made the front page.

An important source for the *Register's* stories and editorials was a series of bulletins issued by the Taxpayers Research Council, an organization financed by almost 500 businessmen members, with an annual budget of about $21,000. The TRC's professed purpose was to minimize government expenditures by recommending efficient procedures to public officials and reinforcing these suggestions with material distributed to members, political figures, and the press. Formally TRC policy was set by a ten-man executive committee and carried out by its executive director, Francis J. Kelly. As often happens when citizens give a small proportion of their time to sitting on a committee, the executive director ran the show. An intelligent, self-educated man, Kelly had a good command of orthodox municipal administration doctrine. He combined an inside-dopester air with a belief that the main problem in government was value-free efficiency, a goal perpetually threatened by politicians' machinations. Numerous subordinate and out-of-power political figures brought him information and asked him for advice.

Kelly had long taken an interest in charter revision. He spent a great deal of time as a consultant to the 1955 commission and evidently was influential in writing the draft charter. Knowing what they wanted and not having much time to get it, Lee and Logue decided not to include Kelly in 1958, a decision that Lee later considered unwise. There is no doubt that this exclusion hurt Kelly deeply and was an important cause of his bitter opposition to the charter. Some observers thought that he was also motivated by jealousy and dislike of the mayor.

In the middle of June Kelly wrote to DiCenzo offering his help in drafting the charter and presenting an "outline of fundamentals" to guide any charter revision attempt. These principles included the three points which the commission avoided, several important changes that it did make, and the appointment of an official who would be in effect a city manager, with power to hire and fire important supervisory personnel and the members of all boards and commissions. A month later, after the commission's report to the Board of Aldermen, the snubbed Kelly circulated a list of 156 "deficiencies, inconsistencies and omissions" in the draft. Both of these releases were front-page news in the *Register*.[15] During the summer Kelly conferred with many aldermen and the heads of the fire, police, and city employees' unions, offering them advice in their campaign against the charter. On October 23 he circu-

[15] *New Haven Evening Register*, 24 June and 25 July 1958.

lated the first of a series of mimeographed "Charter Bulletins," criticizing various aspects of the charter. These were mailed to almost 700 persons and were prominently reported by the *Register*. It is difficult to avoid the impression that these efforts were intended to hit the charter as hard as possible rather than to express a consistent point of view. Among other criticisms Kelly said that the proposed director of administration was put in charge of more agencies than he could handle; this did not fit well with his summer proposal that *all* departments should be subordinated to a single chief administrative officer. Later bulletins charged that the important positions in the two proposed super-departments would be "patronage jobs," because they would not be subject to civil service provisions. Lee then wrote a blistering letter to the TRC Executive Committee, claiming that the bulletins did not represent the attitudes of the TRC membership, which was "allowing a paid staff director to use the good name of this distinguished group as a cover for this political performance."

A committee meeting coincided with Lee's letter. The committee members representing the United Illuminating Company and the Southern New England Telephone Company urged in very strong terms that the TRC abandon its anticharter campaign; in particular, that it not issue its sixth and last Charter Bulletin. It would not be unreasonable to conclude that the mayor had inspired this action. Not wanting any dissension in the TRC, particularly from two such powerful members, the committee decided to withhold the last bulletin. This decision was also influenced by the realization that the election was only a weekend away and that the committee's answer to Lee would doubtless receive good coverage in the *Register*. Their reply said that the TRC supported Kelly and agreed with him completely; it rebuked Lee for trying to divide the TRC and its executive director.

A number of important city officials opposed the charter because they feared that subordination to the development administrator or director of administration would reduce their independence and prestige. One of these executives, who did not get along with Averill, lobbied against inclusion of his department under Averill's jurisdiction until Lee peremptorily ordered him to stop. Another official spoke against the charter to his citizen commission and virtually had them resolve to oppose it.

With few exceptions city employees of all ranks thought that the charter was prejudicial to their interests and were opposed to it. The policemen and firemen's unions, which cooperated closely with each other, were hostile to the charter for several important reasons, primarily because of their dislike of the four-year term. These unions made their demands for salary increases during the summer and fall when the budget was prepared and approved. Every other year this procedure coincided with the municipal elections, a combination that gave the two groups, with more than 800 highly-politicized members, a potent negotiating weapon. If elections were only half as frequent, their opportunities for bargaining would be cut in half.[16]

Most policemen and firemen had "sponsors" in the party organization. Appointments, promotions, and transfers, made by the politically-appointed Fire and Police Commissions, were based in large measure on these connections. Both policemen and firemen are on duty all over the city, come to know their neighborhoods well, and have numerous opportunities to express their political beliefs in the course of their duties. These local orientations and the "sponsor" system result in extensive contacts between the two groups and the Board of Aldermen. When the government and the party organizations are less hierarchically structured than under Lee the support of the policemen and firemen could be very important for many aldermen. For these reasons, and because the mayor and the police and fire chiefs are always "management," against whom the aldermen and party organization are often a useful and willing balance, the interests of the firemen were threatened by weakening the latter groups. The new charter's provisions giving the chiefs the powers of appointment and promotion, then largely exercised by the commissioners, were very unwelcome. The firemen also resented the provision placing fire inspection under the control of the development administrator, and both services disliked the power the director of administration would have on the Civil Service Board. In short, these groups were opposed to proposals to centralize the government and thus reduce their bargaining power.

The two unions, acting through their joint council, presented the Charter Revision Commission with a list of fifteen suggested provisions. All but one of these were rejected. Some of these proposals involved bitter personal situations that intensified the hostility of the unions. The most important of the proposals pertained to a provision under which the mayor had blocked the promotion of Sergeant Everett Shaw, the head of the police union. Even with this personal motivation aside, the members of both unions were well aware of the import of the four-year term and were determined not to support it.

Shaw and his fireman colleague, Henry Longyear, offered to urge their allies on the Board of Aldermen to support the mayor's proposed 1959 budget in return for two more paid holidays a year. Lee said he would give them the holidays if they would support the charter as well. The leaders replied that

---

16 The bargaining power of city employees diminished as more and more of them moved to the suburbs. Since the firemen and policemen were the most politicized, their ability to press their labor demands on the administration was most affected by the suburban exodus. As this suggests, residence requirements for policemen specifically and municipal employees generally are an issue that cuts both ways ideologically. If most policemen live outside the city in which they work, they may therefore be less "involved in the community" they police, but they also are less able to participate in the city's electoral processes.

they would support it only if they were given Blue Cross and Connecticut Medical Service coverage. The mayor declined, pointing out that this would require giving similar coverage to all city employees, which would be prohibitively expensive. A few days later Lee offered the two holidays in return for support of the budget and an agreement not to oppose the charter. Shaw and Longyear asked if Lee wanted to raise the ante and win their active support. He answered that he did not need it and would be content if they would not campaign against him. The firemen and policemen agreed with his prediction and were content with their bargain.

The other city employees, enrolled in several locals that constituted the New Haven Municipal Employees Association, were much less politically conscious *in their roles as employees;* their political demands, if any, were based on identifications as *party* workers. Attempts to make a political instrument of the Employees Association failed, in large measure because its members were drawn from a wide range of jobs and had no common bonds comparable to those of the policemen and firemen. Hence the association leaders did not see the charter campaign as an opportunity for bargaining with the city and did not become involved. Most employees, with the possible exception of the school teachers (although politics was a consideration in appointments, assignments, and promotions in the school system), were hostile to the charter. Lee was a much tougher boss than Celentano. While his personnel *policies* were more liberal and resulted in considerably increased salaries and other benefits, he kept tighter control over his administration and allowed less scope for factional maneuvering. Moreover, his fussy intervention in innumerable minor details must have earned him many enemies. The employees were somewhat fearful and resentful both of the mayor and of his plans to put many of them under Averill's or Logue's direction. Workers in the older agencies were often jealous of the departments involved in redevelopment and resented what they considered the favoritism shown even the stenographic help there. Thus, while the Employees Association did not participate in the campaign, most of its members and their immediate families undoubtedly voted against the charter.

The Outcome and Possible Causes

On November 4, 1958, 62,386 residents of New Haven voted for candidates for state office, the United States Senate, and local and at-large congressional seats. Led by the popular incumbent Governor Ribicoff, Democratic candidates carried the city by two-to-one majorities. Forty-five percent of the total voting population also voted on the charter, which was defeated by 9,915 votes to 18,411.

Unfortunately, information adequate for a conclusive explanation of this outcome is not available. The only survey data come from a study of 192

New Haven residents who voted in the 1958 election, conducted three months after the election. The sample size, the time lag, and various other aspects of this survey make it useful only in a few instances where the differences are very large.[17]

Voting decisions on the charter question cannot be explained at all by demographic variables—income, occupation, education, ethnicity, and age— either in the survey data or in ward-by-ward correlations.[18] Party identification is a more useful variable, but only for one party. There was a strong relationship between Republican allegiance and a negative vote. Only three Republican survey respondents voted for the charter, while Democrats and independents were more evenly divided pro and con. For 32 wards[19] the correlation coefficient (Pearson's r) between the Democratic vote[20] and votes for the charter was .72. City employees are another group of some size who probably voted almost unanimously "no." Most of the 3,000 municipal employees lived in New Haven and were married. Because they had the voting habit and were highly conscious of the political framework in which they worked, they and their families must have taken pains to express their feelings on the proposed charter. One can guess with confidence that they made up a sizable anticharter bloc in addition to the solid Republican vote.

These two groups aside, the task of explaining the charter's resounding rejection remains.[21] The best clue is the manner of its conception. In no sense a response to public demands, it was initiated and put on the ballot by the mayor and a few of his lieutenants. Lee did not seriously attempt to identify the charter with the interests of specific groups, with the exception of the Democratic organization; nor did he seek group support by bargaining. On the other hand, the charter was viewed with alarm and distaste by important

---

[17] This survey was directed by William Flanigan, to whom I am grateful for help in analyzing the data. The study is Survey No. 1 in the Yale Political Science Research Library.

[18] Ethnicity was a variable only with respect to Negroes, who were concentrated in the three wards where the charter fared best. These wards were in Lee's home neighborhood, where he had friendly relations with local leaders. The aldermanic majority leader, John Reynolds, campaigned energetically for the charter in this section. In 1959 he was appointed to one of the new state circuit court judgeships.

[19] Official voting returns for one ward were erroneous.

[20] The "Democratic vote" is an average of the votes for the Democratic candidates for lieutenant governor and secretary of state.

[21] In addition to Republicans, other groups of survey respondents who were almost unanimously against the charter were those who voted against Lee in 1957, did not say that redevelopment was good for New Haven, or thought Lee had done a fair or poor job as mayor. The hostility to the charter of anti-Lee respondents suggests that the mayor's strategy of putting it across by his personal endorsement worked only in reverse; his opponents were far more likely to be impressed by this argument than his supporters.

elements in the city: the Democratic and Republican machines, hard-core Republican voters, city employees, and the newspapers. These groups together were less than a majority of the electorate (although they may have constituted a larger proportion of those who voted on the issue), but they commanded important vote-getting resources.

Except for the municipal employees, economic groups do not seem to have had much influence on the outcome. Indeed, positions on the issue were not related to social class differences, as both our survey data and ward-by-ward correlations show.[22] One manifestation of big business, the CAC, came out in favor of the new charter. This endorsement went almost unnoticed and had no discernible effect on the vote, although its later repercussions on the CAC itself were considerable (see Chapter 8). The Taxpayers Research Council's well-publicized stand against the new charter seems to have reflected more Kelly's predilections than the economic interests of its business members, some of whom eventually restrained Kelly. In any event the TRC, for all its activity, does not appear to have made much difference, as even Kelly agreed. Less than half its membership lived in New Haven and for this reason, as well as their rather limited numbers, they were an inconsequential voting bloc. There is no evidence that they themselves worked against the charter, and they certainly did not go so far as to put pressure on their employees— which cannot be said of the City of New Haven. Lee spent much more money promoting the charter than his enemies used against it. If the TRC was influential, then, it was because it acted as a center of information and propaganda, through Kelly's letters and bulletins. Its publicity activities had no direct impact on the electorate; only 2 of the 192 survey respondents were aware of its position. It is unlikely that Kelly's output added much to the effect of the *Register's* attacks. These began long before the TRC openly opposed the charter and did not gain much in information for all of Kelly's facts and figures.

It is generally supposed that newspapers play a larger part in referenda than in candidate elections because of the absence of personality factors and the orienting influence of the party label.[23] The *Register's* influence is difficult to measure. Nine out of ten respondents in our summer survey read the *Register* and 38 percent said that newspapers were their primary source of information about charter revision. Undoubtedly the *Register's* publicity for the Republican position let that party's voters know what the line was.

---

[22] Because voting was not differentiated along class lines, the New Haven data contradict Robert H. Salisbury's proposition that attitudes toward municipal structural change reflect social class divisions. See Salisbury, "The Dynamics of Reform: Charter Politics in St. Louis," *Midwest Journal of Political Science*, 5 (August 1961), 274.

[23] For interesting but inconclusive contrary evidence see John E. Mueller, "Voting on the Propositions: Ballot Patterns and Historical Trends in California," *American Political Science Review*, 63 (December 1969), 1204–6.

Probably it helped disseminate the simple and convincing arguments against the charter. One can only guess what might have happened if the *Register* had been neutral or had supported the charter. Generally in that era the Jackson papers were conspicuously unsuccessful in convincing politicians or voters to follow their advice.

How important was the defection of most of the Democratic organization? The effect of its position could be any combination of these: failure to persuade Democrats to vote on the charter question, failure to argue for the charter, and, most extreme, electioneering against the charter. While I cannot tell whether the machine could have put the charter across had it been solidly behind it, the available data do suggest that the organization's precinct work had an important influence on many citizens' votes on the measure. For example, in those wards where the Democratic chairmen reported that they worked hard for the charter (see note 13), the proportion of "yes" votes was more than twice as large as in those wards where the Democratic chairmen actively opposed the charter. Where little or no electioneering on this issue was reported by the chairmen, the percentage of affirmative votes fell between these two poles. These data are presented in Table 11-1. To control

TABLE 11-1.   Charter voting and avowed campaign activity of Democratic ward chairmen

| | Chairman's Activity on Charter | | |
	Active Support (N = 5)	No Action (N = 6)	Active Opposition (N = 2)
	%	%	%
Vote in favor of charter	47	37	22
Democratic vote	71	69	58
Vote for charter as percentage of Democratic vote	66	53	38

for the effect of Democratic sentiment on these differences, the procharter vote in each group of wards is also presented as a percentage of the Democratic vote. The Democratic vote was virtually identical in the "active support" and "passive" wards, but the procharter vote was 10 percent higher in the former group. Where Democratic ward chairmen campaigned against the charter, the Democratic vote–charter vote ratio was 38; where they worked for it, it was 66.

For five of the wards both interviews with Democratic ward chairmen and Democratic absentee ballot returns are available. A comparison of these two types of data provides further evidence for the proposition that absentee ballots are a valid index of local party activity. In one ward where the chairman reported his active opposition to the charter, only 26 percent of the absentee ballots favored it; in two wards where the chairmen said they actively supported the charter, 62 percent of the absentee ballots were cast for the charter. In the two wards where the chairmen reported little or no action, 36 percent of the absentee ballots were in favor.

I will use the charter vote on the Democratic absentee ballots from all seventeen wards as an index of precinct work by the party organizations in those wards. A ward organization that turned in a 79 percent "yes" vote on its absentee ballots will be assumed to have worked for the charter in all its electioneering, while the organization that produced "yes" votes on only 5 percent of its absentee ballots will be taken as hostile to the charter in other activities as well. By correlating the votes for the charter on these seventeen wards' absentee ballots with the procharter vote cast on the wards' voting machines on election day, the degree of association between precinct work and charter voting can be determined.

For the 17 wards the correlation coefficient (Pearsons's r) between the vote in favor of the charter on the ward's voting machines and procharter votes on the Democratic absentee ballots is .73. The relationship between these two values can be isolated by a partial correlation that holds constant the only other discernible independent variable, the level of Democratic sentiment. The partial correlation coefficient of the absentee ballots with the procharter vote on the voting machines is .58; this explains about 34 percent of the variance. Precinct work by the Democratic ward organizations was strongly associated with voting behavior and may be assumed to have had an important influence on the outcome of the charter election. Because less than half the voters in the 1958 election pulled either voting machine lever on the charter issue, we might also conclude that the Democratic electioneering affected voting intentions and did not consist merely of bringing favorably inclined voters to the polls.

This effect on the charter outcome is markedly greater than any results reported in other studies of the consequences of precinct work.[24] Research on this topic, however, has been concerned mostly with partisan elections.

---

[24] Representative studies include William J. Crotty, "Party Effort and Its Impact on the Vote," *American Political Science Review*, 65 (June 1971), 439–50; Daniel Katz and Samuel J. Eldersveld, "The Impact of Local Party Activity upon the Electorate," *Public Opinion Quarterly*, 25 (Spring 1961), 1–25; and Peter H. Rossi and Phillips Cutright, "The Impact of Party Organization in an Industrial Setting," in *Community Political Systems*, ed. Morris Janowitz (New York: The Free Press, 1961), pp. 81–116. This problem is the topic of my "The Influence of Precinct Work on Voting Behavior," *Public Opinion Quarterly*, 27 (Fall 1963), 387–98.

These contests are far more conspicuous than the charter issue, and the party label provides a cue to voting decisions that is of overriding importance to most of the electorate. This suggests that precinct work is likely to be most effective when information, attention, and partisan cues are minimal. Aside from referenda, which seldom elicit much activity from regular party organizations, the most common example of such elections is, of course, primaries. These findings thus reinforce the conventional wisdom that political machines find it easier to influence the outcome of low-turnout elections.

After his defeat Lee remarked that some people would always be against reform and so it was wise for the reformer to give the rest of the electorate something to be for. This assessment seems cogent, if belated. Lee's original decision to limit revision and his subsequent tactics tainted the whole enterprise, and more drastic changes probably would not have increased the effective hostility of the opponents of any revision.

In the context of the 1958 election the opponents had much the better case for mass appeal. It was difficult to make a simple, compelling argument for the proposed new charter. Its advocates made no serious attempt to give uncommitted voters any reasoned explanation for the proposal. They limited themselves to unconvincing generalities and Lee's featured message: "I'm for it." The simple, compelling themes were against him: a grab for power, dictatorial bureaucrats, patronage, dual job-holding, and so on. Few survey respondents who favored the charter could give any but the vaguest explanation for their votes, while numerous people on the other side readily produced a simple and accurate rationale: the proposed charter would markedly increase the power of the mayor and of "bureaucrats." It appears that most of the people who understood the charter were against it. This reflects not only the rhetorical advantage held by the opponents but also the fact that all the affected and mobilized interest groups were opposed. In short, the proposal suffered from a double handicap: few natural allies and a weaker appeal to "disinterested" public opinion.

These problems might have been less crucial had Lee involved more of the community in the charter revision process to neutralize the opposition from the party organizations. Instead, he relied on two factors whose potency he badly overestimated: his personal endorsement and his control of the Democratic machine. Perhaps he should have begun the revision process a year earlier and attempted more thoroughgoing changes. But as it was, the absence of any direct attack on machine politics in the new document, coupled with Lee's tactics in bringing the proposal to the referendum stage, gave it the worst of both worlds: the opposition of the party organizations *and* an image of "bossism." As Lee had hoped to placate the Democratic organization and had thought that he would win the referendum, he was in no position to rally an emotional reform vote to put the charter across.

Some Lessons from the Charter Episode

More general explanations for the contrast between the fiasco of Lee's defeat on the charter and his striking successes in urban renewal may be found by examining two factors: the issue and the arena.

The issue was not a substantive policy but a structural change. The outcome supports the generalization that substantive policies are easier to achieve than structural or procedural reforms that are intended to gain those policies.[25] One of the most striking examples of this phenomenon in national politics is the contrast between the remarkable success of congressional liberals in passing meaningful civil rights legislation in the 1960s and the total frustration of their attempts to weaken the senatorial filibuster, a device known primarily as a weapon against civil rights bills.[26]

There are several possible explanations of this higher threshold for structural change. Such revisions are almost invariably harder to dramatize than are substantive policy proposals (with the exception of reforms explicitly aimed at blatant corruption) and thus are not so likely to be the object of widespread public attention. That structural change often has policy significance should not lead one to overlook its nonpolicy implications. Indeed, it may well be that the clients of government can more easily adapt to different forms and procedures than can politicians themselves, and thus organized interest groups will be likely to save their political resources for attempts to shape those substantive policies of immediate concern to them. The principal vested interests with respect to governmental structures and processes are usually not private groups, but politicians. Forms and procedures are the context, constraints, and opportunities of politicians' ambitions, and therefore are of constant and direct importance to them. Having based their career calculations on the existing ways of doing business, politicians generally can be moved to changes in the status quo only by pressures both less likely and more compelling than those that animate them on substantive issues. Thus the alignments in the New Haven charter fight reflected not social or economic divisions, but political ones.

Despite these handicaps, however, Lee's charter revision efforts were successful as long as the fight was waged within the government, with decisions made by politicians. In this respect the charter resembled some intrinsically unpopular aspects of the urban renewal program that were achieved through the conversion and deployment of political resources to overcome specific opposition. The crucial difference on the charter was the arena in which the

---

[25] This proposition is stated by Salisbury, "The Dynamics of Reform," p. 275.

[26] See Raymond E. Wolfinger, "Filibusters: Majority Rule, Presidential Leadership and Senate Norms," in *Readings on Congress,* ed. Wolfinger (Englewood Cliffs, N.J.: Prentice-Hall, Inc., 1971), pp. 286–305.

final decision was made. Lee was defeated when the arena shifted from "inside" politics to the referendum, a decision-making mode in which convertible resources often cannot be effectively exploited. When a single issue is decided by the electorate, that issue stands alone. Group alliances, special appeals to voting blocs, and even publicity are often less effective than in candidate elections. The proponent is selling a single item. Personal popularity, multiple-issue coalitions, and party loyalty are far less relevant to the voter's decision. By virtue of its subject matter, the proposed charter had scant intrinsic voter appeal. It was the wrong issue in the wrong arena.

In the prereferendum phase, as in most other issue areas, the Democratic party organization had been a primary means for Lee to accrue, convert, and deploy his political resources. Why was he unable to control the organization in the charter election? One explanation reminds us of the reasons for the Board of Zoning Appeals' stubbornness: Lee asked the organization to do something that seemed self-destructive. Unlike urban renewal, to which party workers were largely indifferent, charter revision elicited deep hostility because it would hurt their interests. To be sure, the centralization prescribed by the new charter already existed in practice, but this condition reflected Lee's unprecedented use of various informal powers and was likely to pass from the scene when he did. The new charter would change a temporary irritant to a permanent injury.

Nevertheless, the mayor did succeed in forcing the Board of Aldermen to accept the charter. But most aldermen were passive during the ensuing referendum campaign, or actively opposed the charter. Of ten aldermen interviewed after the election, only one reported working hard for the charter in his ward, one of two which returned a majority for the charter. The form of opposition to the charter was vastly different in the campaign than when the aldermen were considering it. Opposing the administration in the latter situation involved a conspicuous, categorical, and revocable act: voting no. This was not the case in electioneering, where a great deal of opposition could be expressed clandestinely, where the actors to be controlled were not a handful of aldermen but hundreds of precinct workers, and where the fixed date of the election gave the rebels an advantage: there was only one election and no possibility for reconsideration. Many defectors were cautious and inaction probably was more common than outright opposition. Dissidence on the charter was easier because defeating the mayor on this issue would not turn the party out of city hall. In a candidate election, on the other hand, Lee and the organization had a complete community of interest: office for him and spoils for it.

Lee could not discipline the defectors, for they were too numerous and his position's unpopularity had been revealed by the outcome of the election. (Before the election, most politicians thought that the charter would pass.) In the aftermath his aim was to heal any wounds in the party and avoid possible further consequences of his defeat. Golden had encouraged organization dissenters but also had been careful to prevent lasting divisions over the issue. The same was true of Barbieri, who seemed relieved that a party split had been avoided. This probably had been one of his principal concerns from the outset; he certainly had not been an enthusiast for charter revision. Thus once the campaign ended it was in everyone's interest to forget about it. Lee, Golden, and Barbieri resumed their previous wary alliance: each contributing to the fortunes of the Democratic party according to his abilities, and benefiting according to his needs. As each man had different needs and abilities, all three managed to get along as before.

IV beyond
New Haven

12 *conclusions and alternatives*

New Haven's political and social context is fairly typical of other northeastern cities of comparable size. The atypical policy achievements in New Haven during the Lee administration can be accounted for largely by the unusual quality and tenure of Lee's leadership. The implications of this with respect to expectations of broad-scale change in other American cities are profoundly discouraging. In this chapter I will discuss some aspects of the career patterns of mayors which help to explain why Lee was so unusual. I will then examine an alternative to mayoral leadership.

The Prospects for Mayoral Leadership

Lee can be compared to other mayors on three dimensions: his skills, incentives, and opportunities. "Opportunity" is used here simply to mean time in office. Lee was mayor for 16 years, which gave him a chance to accomplish things. For example, federal approval of the Church Street Project application was announced in his fourth year in office. If Lee had left city hall at the end of that term, he would have served as long as most mayors, yet it is hard to believe that the Church Street Project would have survived his departure. Longevity in office is important for several reasons. It takes time for a mayor to learn his job, to locate and learn how to use his power resources. It also takes time for officials and private citizens to develop enough confidence in him to entrust major enterprises to his direction, as Chapter 8 illustrated. Unless a mayor has a reasonable expectation of being in office for an extended period, he is not as likely to undertake long-range projects, because he will not benefit politically from their realization. This proposition is important enough to bear repeating: Lee could achieve so much because he had opportunity: time in office and the experience it provided.

What is the likelihood of finding in other cities mayors with Lee's skill and ambitions and sufficient time in office to produce—or even launch—major achievements? Although (in company with other observers) I think that Lee was an extraordinarily accomplished politician compared to most mayors, there is no way to prove this belief with any degree of rigor. It is, however, possible to be much more systematic on the question of opportunity. While only this one point of comparison can be pursued conclusively, doing so

393

provides a useful basis for speculation about the dimensions of skill and incentive.

Mayors of most American cities are lucky to be in office for as long as four years and thus seldom have the opportunity to plan and carry out ambitious projects of any sort. Moreover, mayors rarely go on to more important public posts. The short and uncertain tenure of American mayors, together with the obscurity of their subsequent careers, suggests that the job seldom attracts the ablest politicians or provides them with opportunities to make ambitious strategies realistic. In these circumstances, most mayors do not run the risks of starting comprehensive innovation, for their interests are not likely to be served by doing so.

The most extensive study of turnover in city hall is by Eugene C. Lee, who sent questionnaires on municipal election results to all 729 cities with 1960 populations over 25,000.[1] One-third of the mayors of these cities did not run for reelection in the campaign before December 1962. A third of the mayors who did seek another term were defeated. Thus 56 percent of these cities had newcomers in the mayor's office. If communities with city managers are excluded the result is the same. Only 49 percent of those cities using the mayor-council form of government (where the mayor is really the chief executive rather than a ceremonial figure) had an incumbent in office after their most recent election. The mortality rate in the larger cities was even higher. In the 25 reporting cities with populations of more than 250,000, 32 percent of the mayors did not run for another term and 28 percent more were defeated for reelection. In other words, three-fifths of the mayors elected in these cities were nonincumbents.[2]

More recent research reveals the same high turnover rate. The *Municipal Year Book* annually lists the names of all mayors as of the first of the year, and one can compare these lists for various time periods and types of cities.[3] In 1965, 61 cities of more than 100,000 population used the mayor-council form of government. Thirty-four (56 percent) of the mayors of these cities in 1965 were still in office on the first day of 1969. During 1969 thirteen of the thirty-four were defeated or decided not to run for reelection, including such well-known politicians as Lee, Jerome Cavanagh of Detroit, Arthur Naftalin of Minneapolis, and Ivan Allen of Atlanta. Thus only 34 percent

---

[1] Eugene C. Lee, "City Elections: A Statistical Profile," *1963 Municipal Year Book* (Chicago: International City Managers' Association, 1963), pp. 74–84. Lee's findings are based on a 79 percent response rate.

[2] Lee's data strongly contradict Robert H. Salisbury's well-known article on trends in city politics, which dwells at length on the ease of mayoral survival: "It is difficult for others to challenge successfully the incumbent mayor for re-election...the mayor, once elected, may serve a good many terms." See "Urban Politics: The New Convergence of Power," *Journal of Politics,* 26 (November 1964), 789–90, and 793–95.

[3] Sally Ferejohn did the tabulations reported here on mayoral turnover and the research reported later on ex-mayors' subsequent careers.

of these cities entered the 1970s with the same mayor they had had in 1965.

The retirements of Lee, Cavanagh, Naftalin, and Allen, announced in the summer of 1969, led to a spate of articles on the presumed increase in the number and intensity of problems confronting local governments.[4] It seems reasonable that all the problems associated with the political trends of the late 1960s—notably growing black populations and black militancy—might make local government a less attractive career than before, and thus that these data on mayoral turnover may reflect contemporary developments. This proposition can be tested by duplicating the 1965–69 comparison for 1961–65. This tabulation shows, however, a much *higher* rate of turnover in the earlier period: only 18 of 59 cities (31 percent) had the same mayor in 1965 as in 1961. (There were 59 cities in the earlier period because two cities adopted the mayor-council form between 1961 and 1965.) This finding suggests that, whatever additional discouragements may have developed in the late 1960s, the job of mayor of an American city was already short and/ or unattractive in comparison with other outlets for political ambitions.

The brief duration of individual mayoralties is a consequence of both electoral defeat and voluntary retirement. Such retirements may occur in anticipation of impending defeat, as in the case of Robert Wagner of New York in 1965, or because the job itself is unrewarding. (A third possibility is that mayoral careers are brief because the incumbents go on to higher office. As I will show, this is not the case.) Retirement in both situations stems primarily from the gap between voters' expectations and governmental performance. This gap is wider and more salient in cities than at any other level of politics. The result is that the mayor's official life is more unpleasant and uncertain than that of other public officials, particularly those in legislative positions. These less attractive aspects of mayoral careers are a consequence of three inherent characteristics of American municipal government.

1. Municipal government has a particularly direct, immediate, and observable impact on everyday life. Garbage collection, snow removal, traffic control, playgrounds, schools, parks, police, libraries, and streets are seen and experienced by most voters, who can easily assess governmental performance in at least some aspects of these functions. Many people daunted by the distant and abstract quality of national political issues have no trouble understanding and judging city hall's performance on keeping the streets clear of snow, for example. The point of impact is direct and the line of responsibility clear—or apparently so. Thus, while only 7 percent of a sample of American adults reported that they understood national issues "very well," fully three times as many made this claim about local issues.[5]

---

4 For example, see Fred Powledge, "The Flight From City Hall," *Harper's Magazine* (November 1969).

5 Robert A. Dahl, *Modern Political Analysis,* 2nd ed. (Englewood Cliffs, N.J.: Prentice-Hall, Inc., 1970), p. 84.

2. The mayor is held accountable for the performance of municipal government, although he may lack both formal and effective control over much of what it does. Responsibility without commensurate power is a familiar theme in American politics; it reaches its peak in local government. American cities vary considerably in the formal powers wielded by their mayors. At one pole are communities like Minneapolis, which have elected mayors but grant them virtually no administrative authority or other power beyond what can be extracted from being the city's most conspicuous official. Yet despite his paucity of resources, the mayor of Minneapolis finds that all the city's problems tend to become campaign issues when he is running for reelection. He is associated with these problems in the public mind because he is the most visible embodiment of city hall.[6] Wallace Sayre and Herbert Kaufman observe that in New York mayors are "the central focus of responsibility and accountability for all that occurs in the city" and "the visible and vulnerable targets of blame for failures."[7]

3. The mayor is readily accessible to his constituents. He is there in the same city with them, walking the same streets and going to the same meetings, and the issues are less remote and forbidding than state or national issues. The result is that many people who would not venture into the deeper and muddier waters of national politics attempt to influence the outcome of local decisions: 28 percent say that they have tried to influence their local government, while only 16 percent report this about national government.[8] Similarly, 28 percent report that an attempt on their part to change a proposed local measure would be "very likely" or "moderately likely" to succeed, compared to 11 percent with such feelings of efficacy about a proposal at the federal level.[9]

In addition to exposing him to a more volatile and self-confident electorate, the mayor's accessibility introduces into his life an element that is muted in the experience of state and federal officials: he is vulnerable to complaints and abuse from citizens outraged by real or imagined lapses in municipal performance who turn to a handy and plausible scapegoat. For example, sluggish snow removal following a blizzard in the winter of 1968–69 produced not only a new political crisis for Mayor Lindsay but vehement denunciations when he ventured into the unplowed boroughs. The scars evidently persisted, for a year later a routine snowfall in New York brought Lindsay rushing back from a vacation in the West Indies. The tribulations of the

[6] See the interview with Naftalin, a former mayor of Minneapolis, in *The City* (Santa Barbara, Calif.: Center for the Study of Democratic Institutions, 1962).

[7] Wallace Sayre and Herbert Kaufman, *Governing New York City* (New York: Russell Sage Foundation, 1961), pp. 657, 717.

[8] Dahl, *Modern Political Analysis,* p. 86.

[9] Robert A. Dahl, *Democracy in the United States: Promise and Performance* (Chicago: Rand McNally & Co., 1972), p. 238.

mayor of New York are likely to be widely publicized, but this sort of heckling probably is commonplace in the mayoral experience. Stephen K. Bailey, former mayor of Middletown, Connecticut, describes being awakened early one morning by an irate constituent: "Why the hell don't you stop tryin' to build Radio City and come down here and collect my garbage. It stinks!"[10]

These conditions of mayoral life compare most unfavorably with the situation faced by state and national legislators. The low public visibility of most congressmen, combined with the diversity and relative weakness of most constituent demands, give individual members of Congress great latitude in how they spend their time and portray themselves to their publics: as advocates or bargainers, mavericks or team players, broad-spectrum philosophers or meticulous specialists, prophets for new causes or mediators between factions, leaders or followers, and so on. The committee system imposes specialization; few members expect to be expert in any but a narrow area of public policy or to spend much time outside that area. In addition to allowing members to find their own level of activity and most comfortable roles, legislative division of labor contributes to diffusion of responsibility, which makes it difficult for even the most interested and informed citizens to apportion blame and credit. These considerations make legislators' lives more pleasant and also result in greater job security. Probably the most secure elective careers are in Congress. Seventy-seven percent of senators in office in 1965 were still there in 1969. (This figure reflects the unusual losses suffered by the Democrats in the 1966 and 1968 elections.) The corresponding figure for the House of Representatives is 73 percent.[11]

Mayors do have different priorities and styles, but the demands of their office and the indivisibility of responsibility produce both shorter tenure and less freedom of action. For all these reasons, then, the life of the typical mayor tends to be nasty as well as short, a fact that diminishes both the appeal of the job to able politicians and the opportunities it offers for innovation. As Cavanagh remarked about the rewards of the mayoralty, "If you win, what have you won?"[12]

These consequences might be mitigated if the mayoralty led to a better

[10] Stephen K. Bailey, "A Structured Interaction Pattern for Harpsichord and Kazoo," *Public Administration Review,* 14 (Summer 1954), 204.

[11] For a succinct analysis of the congressman's freedom to choose how he will perform his duties, see Lewis Anthony Dexter, "The Job of the Congressman," in *Readings on Congress,* ed. Raymond E. Wolfinger (Englewood Cliffs, N.J.: Prentice-Hall, Inc., 1971), pp. 69–89. The low level of public knowledge of Congress is described in Donald E. Stokes and Warren E. Miller, "Party Government and the Saliency of Congress," in *ibid.,* pp. 5–20. For more data on turnover in Congress, see Raymond E. Wolfinger and Joan Heifetz Hollinger, "Safe Seats, Seniority, and Power in Congress," in *ibid.,* pp. 52–53, and the sources cited there.

[12] Quoted in James Q. Wilson and Harold R. Wilde, "The Urban Mood," *Commentary* (October 1969), 60.

job, for, as Joseph A. Schlesinger argues, "the ambitions of any politician flow from the expectations which are reasonable for a man in his position. . . . The more transitory the office, the more its holders must handle it primarily in terms of where it can lead. . . ."[13] One might think, therefore, that if the American mayoralty were a good steppingstone to higher (and more secure) offices, mayors would be more likely to follow Lee's strategy, and city hall would attract able politicians willing to endure temporary unpleasantness in hopes of future rewards. But in fact the mayoralty is a dead-end job.

One way to demonstrate this is with Schlesinger's data on the prior political careers of all governors elected from 1900 to 1958 and everyone elected to the Senate from 1914 to 1958. Schlesinger used four categories of prior experience: state legislative, law enforcement (district attorney, judge, sheriff), administrative, and local elective (including county officials and city council members as well as mayors). The first two types of experience, service in a state legislature and law enforcement, were by far the most common of the four in the backgrounds of the senators and governors. Local office was rarest. Only 19 percent of the governors and 15 percent of the senators had held local elective office earlier in their careers.[14] A similar study of the political background of all people elected to the United States House of Representatives between 1949 and 1967 produced almost identical results: only 15 percent had held any elective municipal office before reaching Congress; the two most common types of prior experience were in state legislatures and law enforcement.[15]

It appears, then, that municipal government is the least useful pathway to higher office. Schlesinger's conclusion from his findings:

> When we know that the local law enforcement offices, the offices of county and district attorney, are important bases from which to launch a political career and that the offices of mayor and city councillor are not we can reasonably ascribe progressive ambitions to local public attorneys while ascribing static or discrete ambitions to local executives and legislators.[16]

What happens to mayors after leaving office? While the mayoral post may not be the most promising route for a politician to follow in search of a secure career, what are the prospects for former mayors? A partial answer to this question is provided by Marilyn Gittell, who studied the subsequent

---

[13] Joseph A. Schlesinger, *Ambition and Politics* (Chicago: Rand McNally & Co., 1966), pp. 9, 48.

[14] I computed these percentages from the data in *ibid.*, pp. 91–92; see also p. 73.

[15] Michael L. Mezey, "Ambition Theory and the Office of Congressman," *Journal of Politics*, 32 (August 1970), 568.

[16] Schlesinger, *Ambition and Politics*, p. 199.

careers of the mayors of 24 large cities in the 1940–60 period.[17] She found that only 10 of the 96 mayors had been elected to a statewide office (a category which presumably includes such posts as lieutenant governor and secretary of state). These findings apply only to large cities and only to state office or the Senate.

If not destined for the heights, might mayors at least enjoy some further political rewards? A preliminary answer to this question can be provided by looking at the subsequent (as of the end of 1969) careers of all the ex-mayors in the 1961–65 and 1965–69 tabulations described above. In the earlier period, only 18 of 59 cities had the same mayor in 1965 as in 1961. The political fortunes of the forty-one ex-mayors are not impressive. One was later elected to the United States House of Representatives, one became a federal circuit court judge and another a state judge, two more were appointed collector of customs and ambassador to Costa Rica, respectively, and a sixth became a regional official of the Civil Service Commission. There was no indication that any of the remaining thirty-five former mayors held any recorded political office.[18] It is certain that none subsequently achieved any public position remotely comparable to the mayoralty. For what it is worth, almost all were dropped from the pertinent regional *Who's Who* after leaving city hall.

The 27 men who were mayors in 1965 but not in 1969 have had less time in which to attain other political positions, yet it is noteworthy that only two of them are still in public life, one as a United States Representative, the other as a judge in his state's superior court. The other 25 have vanished from the public record.

Why does the mayoralty so seldom lead to higher office?[19] One possible explanation may be the "insulation" of local politics from the parties by means of the nonpartisan ballot. About half of all cities which directly elect their mayors do so in nonpartisan elections.[20] In most of these cities the

17 Marilyn Gittell, "Metropolitan Mayor: Dead End," *Public Administration Review,* 23 (March 1963), 20–24.

18 The six offices reported in the text are the only public positions held by the ex-mayors that could be determined by examination of the following sources: *Congressional Directory,* 1963–69 (these list many presidential appointees); *Biography Index,* 1961–69; regional editions of *Who's Who, 1969–70* (1966–67 for *Who's Who in the East*); *New York Times Index,* 1961–69; *Martindale Hubbell Law Directory,* 1963–69; and *Who's Who in American Politics 1967–68.*

19 Mayors have a great comparative advantage in seeking other elective positions: their terms typically do not coincide with those of any other office, and thus they usually can have a "free shot" in other elections as they can run for another job without giving up the one they have.

20 In 1960 there were 308 cities with populations of more than 50,000, of which 126 used the council-mayor form of government. Only half of these had partisan municipal elections. See Raymond E. Wolfinger and John Osgood Field, "Political Ethos and the Structure of City Government," *American Political Science Review,* 60 (June 1966), 312–13.

parties do not play an important role in recruiting or electing candidates to municipal office, and often they are not a major factor in local government.[21] But the parties are, of course, the channel of access for higher elective positions. It seems reasonable that mayors in partisan cities are more likely to go on to higher office because local politics is more organizationally interdependent with the two parties. This is, of course, an eminently testable proposition. The only relevant data I know of are consistent with it: Gittell found that mayors in the Northeast were far more likely than those elsewhere to be elected to statewide office. Northeastern cities with mayors almost invariably elect them in partisan elections, while the overwhelming majority of mayors elsewhere are elected nonpartisanly.[22]

Another possibility is that urban electorates are so different from larger constituencies that politicians who appeal successfully to the former can do so only at considerable risk to their ability to attract support from the latter. This applies both to explicit positions on issues and to more general questions of "image." Many successful urban political personalities may raise the hackles of suburban and rural voters. Fiorello La Guardia is an obvious but hardly unique example. Disparities in urban and nonurban constituencies vary a good deal from region to region and from time to time, and the upward mobility rates of mayors might vary proportionately. There are places where a popular appeal to a city constituency precludes any further advancement. This is clear in the following remarks by Ivan Allen, who was elected and reelected mayor of Atlanta by a coalition of Negroes and liberal whites:

> There's no question that the tendency of the Board of Aldermen of Atlanta to enact fair legislation, and not to discriminate against the Negro community, and the conduct of the mayor's office, are protected by the strong voice of the Negro community here. You just don't go out and alienate 35 or 40 per cent of the vote by misusing your position.
>   ...If I had been ambitious to run for the Senate or for governor I would not have taken some of the positions I have.
>   If I ran for governor,... There would be just one issue, and that would be *nigger* and Martin Luther King. They would absolutely whip me to death every time I got up before a crowd in rural Georgia. I had to face this in the beginning and put aside any political ambitions I might have had at that time to do my job properly here.[23]

---

[21] Charles R. Adrian, "A Typology for Nonpartisan Elections," *Western Political Quarterly,* 12 (June 1959), 449–58. By the same token, men already active in the parties are reluctant to run for nonpartisan offices. See Adrian, "Some General Characteristics of Nonpartisan Elections," *American Political Science Review,* 46 (September 1952), 770.

[22] Wolfinger and Field, "Political Ethos," p. 320.

[23] Quoted in Powledge, "The Flight From City Hall," p. 82.

As more cities become blacker and poorer, the disparities between them and larger constituencies will grow, making the mayoralty even less a steppingstone than it is now.

Most mayors who have attracted attention for their innovative policies have tried to use local governmental performance as a means of appealing to broader constituencies and moving up to higher office. In his analysis of progressive urban leadership, Alexander L. George cited as models Lee, Richard Daley, and Joseph S. Clark and Richardson Dilworth of Philadelphia.[24] One interesting thing about George's list is that everyone on it has used the mayoralty in the service of ambitions transcending the city limits. Clark went from city hall to two terms in the Senate. His successor, Dilworth, failed in a campaign for governor and then retired from active pursuit of higher office. Daley is importantly constrained and motivated by his position as Democratic leader in Illinois and an elder of the national party. The same pattern of ambitions is found in other celebrated mayors. Cavanagh was an unsuccessful contender for the Democratic senatorial nomination in 1966. Mayor Lindsay's futile pursuit of the Democratic presidential nomination in 1972 is not likely to mark the end of his interest in leaving New York City for greener pastures.

Like Lee, these men deviate from the common run of mayors both in their ambitions and in the high level of governmental innovation they have introduced. Because the mayoralty typically is a brief, unrewarding, dead-end job, it is unlikely to attract the ablest men aspiring to political careers or to motivate incumbents to develop strategies of urban improvement that will help them on to higher office. Such strategies are unnecessary and unwise for most mayors.

Because able, innovative mayors have been not only scarce, but stirred by ambitions that are neither commonplace nor generally realistic, it becomes important to consider possible substitutes for mayoral leadership. Another argument for turning to less heroic models of urban leadership is the simple fact that most American cities do not have elected mayors. All five cities with more than 1,000,000 inhabitants use the mayor form, as do 73 percent of those with populations of 500,000 to 1,000,000; but below this point only about 40 percent elect their mayors.[25] For the other 60 percent, governed by commissions or by councils acting through an appointed city manager, the style of leadership displayed by popularly elected mayors is less relevant.

[24] Alexander L. George, "Political Leadership and Social Change in American Cities," *Daedalus* (Fall 1968), 1194–1217.

[25] Wolfinger and Field, "Political Ethos," p. 315.

Cosmopolitan Professionals as Urban Leaders

The most popular form of government for all cities above 50,000 population is the council-manager plan, used in 146 of the 309 cities.[26] Although originally conceived as the impartial executor of the council's decisions, the manager in fact seems to be the most important public official in the realm of policy formation.[27] For the same reasons that the manager can play this role, analogues to his leadership can be found in other appointed officials in both mayor and manager cities.

Professional municipal officials, ranging from city managers to city planners, are an increasingly important independent element in local political systems. Their impact will be felt in varying degrees in all localities, in the development and execution of innovative—if fragmentary—policies in a variety of areas. Because these officials are oriented toward goals, norms, and publics beyond their city of current employment, and because they have skills needed by other actors in local politics, they can bring to bear resources of power somewhat independent of the contending local interests that often stymie progress. It is unlikely that such officials will be able to build the political base and muster the autonomous political support necessary to execute massive, coordinated programs of the kind typical of New Haven.[28] But they can produce a number of substantial segmental innovations which add up to a considerable improvement over the status quo.

Evidence for this argument is rather scanty but consistently supportive. Such data are limited to city managers, although these findings apply with equal force to a number of other posts whose principal characteristics are the same: they are held increasingly by specialists, the specialists are recruited in a national market, and their frames of reference and standards of success come from their national professional community rather than the local environment in which they find themselves at a particular time.

The findings of Charles R. Adrian about the influence of city managers seem to be typical of research on their political role: "...the manager and

[26] *Ibid.*

[27] For example, see Charles R. Adrian, "Leadership and Decision-Making in Manager Cities," *Public Administration Review,* 18 (Summer 1958), 208–13; Karl Bosworth, "The Manager Is a Politician," *ibid.,* 216–22; Ronald O. Loveridge, "The City Manager in Legislative Politics: A Collision of Role Conceptions," *Polity,* 1 (1968), 214–36; and Oliver P. Williams and Charles R. Adrian, *Four Cities* (Philadelphia: University of Pennsylvania Press, 1963), pp. 292, 303–8.

[28] Harold Kaplan's account of the large urban renewal program in Newark suggests that a professional official can achieve much when both politicians and businessmen are inclined to passivity. Kaplan's study leaves unanswered some important questions about the development and maintenance of political support, however. See his *Urban Renewal Politics* (New York: Columbia University Press, 1963).

his administration are the principal sources of policy innovation and leadership in council-manager cities, even though the manager seeks to avoid a public posture of policy leadership."[29] Ronald O. Loveridge found on the basis of interviews with 58 city managers in the San Francisco Bay Area that the vast majority of his sample rejected the classic dichotomy between "politics" and "administration" and, instead, believed that they should be innovators and advocates, and even involve themselves in controversial issues. Indeed, 40 percent of the managers whom Loveridge interviewed said they believed that they should intervene in local politics to the extent of encouraging candidates to run for the city council. Some of Loveridge's respondents said they wrote speeches and planned campaign strategy for such candidates.[30]

This activist political role may seem incongruous. Its importance has been denied by some well-known scholars. Edward C. Banfield and James Q. Wilson say that "the typical manager's mentality is probably still a good deal closer to that of the engineer than that of the politician."[31] On the other hand, Banfield and Wilson then discuss various research findings indicating that city managers in fact do not take such a restrictive view of their jobs.[32]

If the first city managers were primarily engineers, the younger managers, who of course constitute an increasingly large proportion of the profession, have very different training. The most common single undergraduate major among city managers is political science; many others majored in the other social sciences; and most younger managers have had graduate work in public administration.[33] City managers typically are recruited from outside the city in which they serve and have had prior managerial experience. Those whom Loveridge interviewed had an average tenure in their city of less than five years.[34] Another study, based on interviews with 55 city managers in Michigan, also points out the nomadic quality of the profession: "The city managers' preoccupation with moving from place to place is apparent in the striving of individual managers to advance."[35]

Originally city managers may have been envisioned as executives with the values of businessmen, drawing on friendships from the local business community. Now the profession has become national and has developed a dis-

29 Adrian, "Leadership and Decision-Making in Manager Cities," p. 208.

30 Loveridge, "The City Manager in Legislative Politics," pp. 221–24.

31 Edward C. Banfield and James Q. Wilson, *City Politics* (Cambridge, Mass.: Harvard University Press and The M.I.T. Press, 1963), p. 174. They cite a finding that "of forty-eight managers hired from 1918 to 1937, thirty-nine had been to college and of these all but three were engineers" (p. 174n).

32 *Ibid.*, p. 175.

33 Loveridge, "The City Manager in Legislative Politics," p. 220.

34 *Ibid.*, pp. 220–21.

35 George K. Floro, "Continuity in City-Manager Careers," *American Journal of Sociology*, 61 (November 1955), 241.

tinctive value system produced through professional socialization in much the same way that other professions develop their characteristic norms. Similarly, the city manager profession has its own hierarchy, and again, the important thing is that it is a national hierarchy, not a local parochial one.

The principal professional organization, the International City Managers' Association, holds national conferences, publishes a monthly journal, and offers training courses, handbooks, and technical advice. State organizations perform similar functions, with their own conventions, conferences, and so on. The messages from these sources are a far cry from the antiseptic apolitical ideology of the old city manager movement. The professional journals exhibit "almost unanimous agreement that the city manager should be a policy innovator and leader."[36] The Code of Ethics of the International City Managers' Association, on the other hand, draws the hoary distinction between "politics" and "administration" and prescribes that the city manager stay on the latter side of the line.[37]

It appears that for most city managers success is defined as a function of their fellow-professionals' evaluation, and that such assessments in turn are an important stimulus to their conduct in office. Gladys Kammerer and her associates found that locally-recruited city managers were far less venturesome than those officials recruited outside the city in which they were serving.[38] Floro observes, "A manager may rise to prominence in one of two ways—either by moving to successively more prized manager cities as his reputation becomes established in the colleague group or by establishing his reputation among other managers while his city becomes known as especially well managed."[39]

Thus the short tenure that hobbles mayors has the opposite effect on managers, for mobility is the key to their careers. Successful managers go on to the same job in bigger cities. But mayors cannot advance to elective leadership of a larger city, and are not likely to be elected to any other important office.

While the manager is moved to activism by professional considerations, he is also prevented by local expectations from *too* unrestrained a role. Loveridge's interviews with city councilmen on their expectations of the manager's behavior provide a striking contradiction of the manager's beliefs about proper managerial conduct. The councilmen, of course, are far more devoted to the politics–administration dichotomy. While the managers apparently can get away with a good deal, they must observe the amenities of

36 Loveridge, "The City Manager in Legislative Politics," p. 221.

37 Banfield and Wilson, *City Politics,* p. 173.

38 Gladys M. Kammerer et al., *City Managers in Politics* (Gainesville: University of Florida Monographs, 1962), pp. 59–66.

39 Floro, "Continuity in City-Manager Careers," p. 242.

the role expectation by confining their political interventions to activity that is not widely observable.

Such aloofness from political involvement helps to give the manager—as doubtless it does other professional officials—an aura of "science" for his recommendations. Thus a carefully calculated blend of initiative and tact may let the manager exploit the information and expertise which no one else possesses, while at the same time he avoids being considered just another contender for power. It is also often the case that the expert's advice may be the most convenient compromise when various vested interests each have a favorite solution. In such circumstances the experts can often "persuade the party leaders that the adoption of objective, nonpartisan, professional standards in deciding questions of the kind at issue is the easiest way out for everybody concerned."[40]

The city council can always discharge its manager, but not too often, because "a city with a rapid turnover of managers, for example, is a 'bad' manager city or a 'hot spot.' "[41] Thus councilmen will not be quick to fire their manager for fear that they may find it difficult to hire an adequate successor. Skilled municipal professionals are not common and cities often compete for the ablest ones. A reputation as a bad place for an ambitious professional to work is not a municipal asset.

One consequence of this prototypical situation is that the city manager cannot use those political resources connected either with public advocacy and symbolic leadership or with open participation in the selection of elected officials. He is severely handicapped in his leadership efforts by being unable to mobilize public opinion overtly or to affect the careers of municipal legislators. Because he cannot exploit the advantages of embodying and personifying dramatic campaigns to rid a city of slums, for instance, a city manager is inevitably a drabber figure than an activist mayor. But he still is a force other than the traditional local bureaucracy, the political parties, or private social and economic interest groups. In cities without mayors the managers are likely to provide the nearest thing to civic leadership on a broad scale.

What has been said about city managers applies also to a variety of other occupations that are becoming established as professions and are increasingly important in city government. (The manager, of course, is likely to be the most influential of these officials.) There are, for example, national organizations of public health officials, traffic engineers, city planners, and redevelopment officials. Each of these has its journals, conventions, and training

---

[40] Sayre and Kaufman, *Governing New York City*, p. 471; see also pp. 472–73. When professional officials play the part of disinterested experts tendering scientific advice, there is an increased need for a middleman to adjust their proposals to political constraints and merchandise them to the politicians. Logue played this part skillfully in New Haven.

[41] Floro, "Continuity in City-Manager Careers," p. 241.

institutes. Some, such as city planning and public health, are reflected in university departments. Most important, each of these professions defines success within the profession rather than locally. Such officials have power bases somewhat independent of other local forces, and they can be sources of pressure on politicians and private interests alike. They are therefore a force to be reckoned with in local politics. The similarities between the new breed of municipal official and college professors are considerable: many people in both lines of work are oriented nationally, which in turn frees them considerably from subordination to local control.

The consequences of such cosmopolitan expertise will be innovation and the expansion of public programs. This is not to say that the relevant professionals are necessarily progressive or sympathetic to the real or attributed wishes of the poor. But the incentive structure in these professions emphasizes not jealous defense of routine but rather a venturesome ambition. As is usually the case, these officials have a vested interest in maximizing the programs for which they are responsible and therefore want to expand their own domains, if necessary by appealing to their specialized constituents in the local community. The likelihood is that such expansion will be in the direction of more services for the poor, improvement of the social and physical environment, and attempts to impose a greater degree of rationality and coordination on market processes.

Many of the newer professions are in policy areas where federal grants provide a substantial part of the budget and where skill and national connections are the most important factors in obtaining such aid. Local fiscal control generally is weaker in such situations.

The innovative impact of cosmopolitan experts was felt in New Haven, although Lee's receptivity to new ideas and his insistence on being the boss in his administration precluded attempts to appeal over his head to specialized constituencies. For example, his imposition of control on the Board of Zoning Appeals resulted from Logue's realization that the permissive granting of zoning variances was inconsistent with a rational renewal policy. New Haven's pioneering poverty program was the product of initiatives by cosmopolitan experts led by Howard Hallman, who played the principal role in developing the proposal approved by the Ford Foundation that led to the formation of Community Progress, Incorporated.[42]

One implication of the foregoing discussion is that evaluations of the influence of experts in municipal politics often employ excessively demanding

---

[42] Russell D. Murphy, *Political Entrepreneurs and Urban Poverty* (Lexington, Mass.: D. C. Heath and Company, 1971), Chap. 2. While antipoverty establishments include a diversity of functions and programs, the officials in these agencies are often independent and vocal actors in local politics. They may be on their way to creation of a new profession, fulfilling the implicit promise of a mid-1960s symposium at Howard University on "New Careers in Poverty."

tests. The most obvious example is the literature on city planners. It is easy enough to show that master plans are rarely if ever realized, that they are "civic New Year's resolutions."[43] This is not all there is to say about the political role of city planners, however, although it is often the burden of the discussion for many writers.[44] While land-use decisions seldom are pure reflections of technical planning criteria, they may still be shaped markedly by the contributions of planners. Thus to discover that master plans have had little or no effect on the character of a city is not to say that city planners have been irrelevant. By the same token, to discover that a traffic engineer's flow plan had been changed in response to political pressures would be a long way from showing that the engineer was without influence in devising city policy in his specialty. At the very least, experts' recommendations are an input that must be dealt with, both as "objective truth" and as a likely rallying point for particular private interests. More commonly, however, the experts will themselves become advocates and coalition builders for proposals to realize their visions and enhance their power and professional standing. The overtness with which they assume these latter roles will depend in part on individual personality factors and in part on the political culture of the city. It seems likely that such active and explicit participation by professionals in the political process will be greatest in larger cities, where the diversity of social, civic, and economic life spawns more complicated and open political action.[45]

The trend toward greater influence by cosmopolitan professionals is not a "solution to the urban crisis," but rather a contribution to the development of discrete programs for particular needs. It will be felt in limited but consequential ways, in programs for job training or neighborhood parks, for example; rather than in sweeping, root-and-branch attacks on urban decline. This is not to deny that experts are influential in the grander forms of urban policy, à la Lee, but only that these forms require such unusual accumulations of political power and talent that—impressive as they may be—they are not a model with very wide direct and total applicability.

[43] The phrase is Norton Long's. See Charles Press, ed., *The Polity* (Chicago: Rand McNally & Co., 1962), p. 192.

[44] For example, see Banfield and Wilson, *City Politics,* Chap. 14, which dwells at length on the frustrations likely to be encountered by city planners.

[45] A recent study of city planners in the San Francisco Bay Area confirms these propositions about the conditions of professional activism. See J. Vincent Buck, "City Planners: The Dilemma of Professionals in a Political Milieu" (unpublished doctoral dissertation, Stanford University, 1972).

index